Only in New Mexico

Only in New Mexico

An Architectural History of the
University of New Mexico

The First Century, 1889–1989

Van Dorn Hooker

with Melissa Howard
Foreword by V. B. Price

The University of New Mexico Press • Albuquerque, New Mexico

© 2000 by University of New Mexico Press
All rights reserved.
FIRST EDITION
Design by Emmy Ezzell

Library of Congress Cataloging-in-Publication Data:
Hooker, Van Dorn, 1921–
Only in New Mexico: an architectural history of the University of New Mexico: the first century, 1889–1989 / Van Dorn Hooker with Melissa Howard and V. B. Price.—1st ed.
  p.   cm.
Includes bibliographical references.
ISBN 0-8263-2135-6 (cloth: alk. paper)
1. University of New Mexico—Buildings—History.
I. Howard, Melissa.
II. Price, V. B. (Vincent Barrett)
III. Title
LD3781.N534 H66 2000
727'.3'0978961—dc21
99-006976

Contents

*Note: Building numbers in parentheses throughout the text refer to the maps on pages xx–xxv.

*This book is dedicated
to all those people who in their own ways
have had a part in the development
of the University of New Mexico campuses.*

Preface

Why is the University of New Mexico justifiably famous for its architecture? Why do its buildings elicit such strong responses, both aesthetic and emotional, from so many people?

The second question is easier to answer. For thousands of us, the campus is where we spent some of our most important years. The photographs in this book can trigger a myriad of memories. But the campus's appeal is more than nostalgia. The nineteen-year-old who first notices that the winter-afternoon sun turns the south face of Zimmerman Library the color of honey is not just storing up a memory; she is experiencing what Tony Hillerman called the spell of New Mexico.

UNM's architecture is famous because it embodies some of what makes our state special: the sky, high and blue above a roofline; the soft-edged planes of mountain and mesa; the palette based on colors from the earth; the sincere if clumsy homage to cultures we are displacing.

Defining, let alone maintaining, the spell of New Mexico has never been easy. But Van Dorn Hooker's history of UNM architecture allows us to imagine some of the defining moments:

> William Tight returning wide-eyed from a visit to a nearby pueblo and vowing that the territorial university should have the same air of belonging to a special place.
>
> David Ross Boyd engaging the winner of a prestigious international design competition because the small and dusty campus must have the best architect.
>
> Mrs. Reed Holloman and her fellow regents, perhaps fresh from lunch at the Alvarado Hotel or the new University Dining Hall, agreeing that the new campus buildings should be in the Spanish Colonial–Pueblo Style, even if they aren't sure exactly what that means.
>
> James Zimmerman staging his inauguration at the Estufa, foreshadowing his leadership during the creation of the Administration Building, the Library, and the President's Residence.

Congressman Jack Dempsey introducing the dean of Pueblo Revival designers, John Gaw Meem, to some of the regents and President Zimmerman during lunch at another famous New Mexico building, La Fonda.

Tom Popejoy persuading skeptics that a basketball arena could be dug out of the ground—and demonstrating that historical roots need not strangle innovation.

Sherman Smith, accepting yet another assignment because he is willing to exercise the authority to maintain an architectural vision in the face of competing demands.

Van Dorn Hooker was a key player in many of the defining moments of UNM architecture. He first saw the campus in 1947 while honeymooning with his wife, Peggy. Perhaps their chance meeting with John Tatschl, who was working on his now-iconic Lobo statue, first cast the spell. Van Dorn remembers thinking, "I've *got* to get this job" as he drove his yellow Studebaker convertible down La Bajada for an interview for the new position of University architect in 1963.

Between 1963 and 1987, when Van Dorn retired, some seventy-five major buildings, additions, and remodelings were completed. The Medical School, the North and South Campuses, and the branch campuses in Gallup, Los Alamos, and Valencia County were developed. Campus architecture was redefined to include landscaping, historic preservation, and facility planning, as well as parking, energy conservation, artwork, handicap access, capital funding, security, and interior design. The classic Pueblo Style was adapted to accommodate the modern idiom and the demands of size and technology.

How did it happen? The Office of the University Architect had no written guidelines about design; Van Dorn simply says he urged each contracted professional to do the best work possible and to work with the *context*. Key elements of the campus context include master plans and the organic relation of each building to its neighbors, expressed in wall shapes, materials, and colors. The University received more than thirty design awards for architecture and landscaping during Hooker's twenty-four years—and thousands more students fell under the spell of New Mexico.

Why is the University of New Mexico's architecture still so important, now that we have modified and modernized the Pueblo Style so much that the untrained eye may barely perceive its historical roots? Those roots are the answer. The key elements of the Pueblo Style, imaginatively interpreted under Van Dorn Hooker's leadership, have proved adaptable to gyms, dorms, laboratories, and classrooms. Buildings in their tenth decade stand comfortably next to buildings completed only months ago. They are united by their warm textures, their artful asymmetries, their humanity.

As New Mexico moves into the twenty-first century, time and technology move it closer to the American mainstream. Confronted with theme-park versions of our history elsewhere, we are in danger of forgetting what the spell of New Mexico really is. The UNM campus reminds us.

Melissa Howard

Foreword

Just as New Mexico and its culture can rightly be described as unique among America's fifty states, so can the architecture and planning of the University of New Mexico in Albuquerque be considered unique among America's colleges and universities.

UNM's blend of Pueblo and Spanish Style architecture with regionally sensitive modernist forms is a direct reflection of New Mexico's singular place in American culture. No other major college campus in this country is so deeply rooted in indigenous American and Hispanic history, nor so intimately tied to a long-existing regional outlook and aesthetic.

While other campus planners and designers around the nation traditionally looked to Europe and used classical, Collegiate Georgian, Collegiate Gothic, Mediterranean, and International Style models, among others, UNM's leadership, for the better part of a century, wanted the state's flagship university to be a distinctly New Mexican place, what one writer called "a pueblo on the mesa."

New Mexico can unequivocally claim to be the heartland of both Native American Pueblo culture and the first indigenous Hispanic culture in North America. The nineteen distinct Pueblo governments and cultural milieus in New Mexico that have survived European contact largely intact express what the late Tewa anthropologist Alfonso Ortiz called a "clearly unbroken cultural continuity" over more than two millennia. That unprecedented record of survival in the New World is mirrored by the tenacity of Hispanic culture that arrived in Pueblo territory 450 years ago. The isolation of New Mexican Hispanics from Spain and Mexico in the eighteenth and nineteenth centuries resulted in the evolution of a still-thriving local Catholic culture with a community ethos devoted to service, and complete with its history of creating stone and adobe mission churches, first built with Pueblo labor and employing both European and Pueblo engineering practices and aesthetics.

Historian Marc Simmons puts in perspective the interaction of these two cultures with what he calls "alien" Anglo-American society when he writes, "Through principles supplied by the Declaration of Independence … [Pueblos and Hispanics] have tried to win equality while remaining different and have sought liberty to pursue a time-honored way of life. That history also includes the long story of Anglo-America's adjustment to things that are uniquely and engagingly New Mexican."

The story of UNM's campus architecture and planning provides a perfect example of that mainstream American "adjustment" to Pueblo and Hispanic culture. As campus planning and design consultant Richard P. Dober has written, "Perhaps more than any other regional architecture in North America, the Pueblo Style gives clear clues as to its origins." UNM's sense of place is unmistakable.

The school's elegantly eccentric regional style campus was pioneered by a mainstream academic, UNM's third president, William George Tight, and an Anglo architect, E. B. Cristy, who both fell in love, as the expression goes, with New Mexico in the late nineteenth century. Their visionary appreciation of the social vitality and creative genius of Hispanic and Pueblo architects, artists, and craftsmen helped to solidify the burgeoning regional style. Tight hired Cristy at the turn of the century to remodel UNM's Main Building, the brick Richardson Romanesque Hodgin Hall, along patterns that both men had noticed in New Mexico mission churches, which they early considered blends of Pueblo and Hispanic building practices. Tight's advocacy of the Pueblo Style, as it's sometimes called, has been described as "an inspired act of image-making."

In 1927 the Spanish Pueblo Revival Style was approved for four new buildings, including Carlisle Gymnasium, thereby returning to the style advocated by President Tight. Between 1933 and 1962, Dober writes, "thirty-eight UNM buildings were constructed in the Pueblo Style, almost all of them influenced, where not actually designed, by the inspired vision of one man, John Gaw Meem." While Meem was not the creator of the style, known by numerous variations on the words Spanish and Pueblo, he was its greatest practitioner.

Meem was a transplanted New Mexican and modernist architect with a profound respect for indigenous cultures. He worked in the avant-garde tradition, drawing from so-called primitive and vernacular imagery, not unlike Picasso and others. Meem was adamant that the Spanish-Pueblo Style was not merely cosmetic, or what we might call today Disneyesque.

He wrote that "some old forms are so honest, so completely logical and native to the environment that one finds—to one's delight and surprise—that modern problems can be solved, and are best solved by use of forms based on tradition." He continued by saying that "the value of this use may be questioned by some; but to me, it seems to add a richness and actually to enhance a series of values. In a world tending more and more to inevitable standardization—welcomed from the practical point of view, but spiritually repugnant to us—it is truly refreshing to feel that in our contemporary architectural movement [there] is still an opportunity for the expression of ancient values."

One of New Mexico's premier architects, George Clayton Pearl, has written that UNM's "collection of buildings and grounds provides one of the most moving built environments in the country." Pearl, a designer of several contemporary UNM buildings, believes the school managed to emerge from the "cataclysmic expansion" the campus underwent from the 1960s to the 1980s with "its character not only intact but also enlivened and enriched" primarily because of the respectful sensitivity and management genius of University Architect Van Dorn Hooker, the author of this book.

"The essential values of the campus," Pearl wrote,

> the intense feeling of knowing exactly where you are in the world and where you are in continuum of time, the architectural unity with no sacrifice of vitality or individuality, the temporal texture—these are intuitively perceived. One need not be aware of that complete history of a regional style which is more visible here than anywhere else, from its earliest stirrings in the remodeled Hodgin Hall through its classical peak in the buildings of John Gaw Meem, to the post-internationalism of the past two decades, when archaeology is abandoned but context is celebrated.

Hooker managed to reconcile at UNM a regional style grounded in vernacular architecture with functionalist concerns by guiding the architects UNM commissioned in the 1960s and beyond to allow modernist geometric forms to reflect the New Mexico cultural milieu. This he achieved largely through the use of earth colors, modularization, and evocative shapes that did not confront or offend the functionalist abhorrence of decoration.

The result is a campus that not only alludes to the full cultural atmosphere and texture of New Mexico but also demonstrates how the building technology and philosophy of late twentieth-century American architecture can adapt themselves to local needs, conditions, and meanings.

Many American universities, UNM included, can pride themselves in having a coherent campus environment, enlightened by a singular architectural style. Aesthetically unified campuses such as the University of Washington, the University of Chicago, and Stanford are the most obvious examples. But no flagship university in the nation, other than UNM, has had an indigenous architectural tradition to draw from, even though California Mission style buildings have contributed to the regional flavor of many universities in the west.

The "exotic harmony" in New Mexico mission churches that architectural historian George Kubler described in his *Religious Architecture of New Mexico* was translated into the Spanish-Pueblo Style and given an extended life at UNM. The vigorous sensitivity of this style to its immediate surroundings brings to the campus an originality and grandeur that mirrors the New Mexico landscape itself. In an epigraph in his book, Kubler quotes Sheldon Cheney and Martha Candler's views on the unique place of New Mexican architecture in American life. They wrote in 1935, "It is not amiss to say . . . that we waited too long to acknowledge the unique and very great heritage we had in the early New Mexican missions. We now see them as one of the country's painfully few genuine creative achievements."

The cultural hybrid vigor of those buildings transported into an academic setting have made the University of New Mexico's central campus, in my judgment, an architectural homage to one of the few places in the New World that Europeans and indigenous people worked out a cultural symbiosis in which native and European worldviews interacted with each other but preserved their independence and integrity. That makes the "exotic harmony" of UNM's campus symbolic of the possibilities for not only cooperation between cultures but even empathetic and self-respecting collaboration.

V. B. Price

Introduction

In its first one hundred years the University of New Mexico grew from fewer than a hundred students in a mostly preparatory school to a 25,000-student institution with a reputation for quality undergraduate and graduate programs, a strong research effort, a growing library, a highly rated medical school, and a competitive intercollegiate athletic program. The annual operating budget, which was in the low five figures in the beginning, was moving toward a billion dollars as the decade of the 1980s ended, with little more than 25 percent of that coming from state appropriations.

This is a history of the first one hundred years of the development of the Albuquerque campuses of the University of New Mexico. It was an exciting time for building and planning the campuses and structures to house the various activities of the University but the complete story has never been told. That is why I decided to write this book about the rich architectural heritage of the University. This is an abridgment of a much longer, more detailed history that I first compiled. I'm sure the unabridged version has more information than anyone but a research scholar would be interested in. There is considerable information about the funding, or lack of funding, of University buildings and the politics involved. It also contains the history of planning and building the Gallup, Los Alamos, and Valencia Campuses, and the Taos properties: the Harwood Foundation and the D. H. Lawrence Ranch. A copy is in the University Archives if anyone wants to delve into it.

This book is mostly factual with little editorializing or architectural criticism: I leave that for the professionals. I felt I had the experience to chronicle this building-planning effort since I was the University architect for almost one-quarter of this hundred years and prior to that I had worked on University buildings while employed by the architectural firm of Meem, Zehner, and Holien. I began to think about this book before I retired in 1987 and collected material I thought would be useful references: newspaper articles, copies of archival items, photographs, and other documents.

Because I feel that introductions to books should be brief and to the point, I will only mention a few background items here. I have included stories about building, planning, and artwork that, for better or worse, did not come to fruition. Some basic information about major buildings such as dates, costs, architects, and contractors is contained in Appendix 3.

What is the name of the building? Almost every building at UNM has gone through name changes. There is the name used when the building is being planned and built, like the 400-Man Dormitory, now Mesa Vista Hall. But this is the second Mesa Vista Hall. The Co-Op Dormitory, now the Naval Science Building, was the first Mesa Vista. There are later formal names, such as Ortega Hall, which was in the old Dining Hall and later moved to its present building. Some names are descriptive: the Basic Sciences Building; the Basketball Arena, popularly called The Pit; Farris Engineering Center, combining the name of a person with the building's function.

The only sure way to identify buildings is to number them, and I have used the numbers developed by my office, the Office of the University Architect, in parentheses in this text. The building numbers are not in chronological order. When numbers were assigned in the 1960s, one to ninety-nine were given buildings inside the then-projected loop road, Redondo Drive. One hundred to 199 were assigned those buildings on the Central Campus outside the loop road. The 200 numbers went to the North Campus; the 300 numbers, to the South Campus. The building numbers, with a legend, that were in effect in 1989 are shown on the campus maps following this introduction.

Lately the Department of Facilities Planning has started reusing numbers of removed buildings for new ones. For example, the number assigned to the first boiler plant, 102, is now applied to the new bookstore. The bookstore is now in its fourth, maybe fifth, location—and its second separate building. The boiler plant, sometimes called the heating plant, the power plant, and now Ford Utility Center, is in its third location with other facilities on the Central and North Campuses.

When was a building built? This is a confusing question because large university buildings can take more than a year to build. Planning a complex structure and obtaining funding can add years to the process. It is best to use the date the building was sufficiently completed for the users to occupy it.

What did the building cost? There are references to bid figures, contract amounts, construction costs, and project costs. The figure the successful contractor put in his bid may be increased or decreased by negotiations or acceptance of alternates before the contract is signed. The contract amount changes during the course of construction as change orders are approved. The construction cost used in this book is the final cost of constructing the building, which may include several separate contracts. The project cost includes everything that went into the building: construction cost, professional fees, furniture and equipment, landscaping, and any other expenses.

How are buildings approved and financed? Other than providing funds for the first building in 1889, the state did not appropriate much money for buildings until the 1960s. The University borrowed money from local banks, and in some cases individual regents did the borrowing. Later, student fees were imposed for bond issues for all building construction. Now the University relies on appropriations from the legislature, state general obligation bonds, and some federal grants and loans for constructing academic buildings and sometimes nonacademic ones. Income from services such as dormitory rents, athletic events, and profits from food sales and the bookstore are added to the student fees to cover University bond issues for nonacademic facilities. The formal approval process begins with the president and his vice presidents who are convinced by deans and chairs that a building is needed. Architects are selected and the preliminary design is approved by the Campus Planning Committee. Then it goes to the Board of Regents for design and budget approval. The Commission on Higher Education (CHE) must approve the budget and method of funding. The CHE then makes a recommendation to the legislature on need and suggested budget. A legislator introduces a bill to fund the project, and it is referred to a committee or committees. If approved, it is placed in an appropriations bill for consideration. University-funded projects and bond issues follow a similar pattern of approvals but obviously do not have legislative appropriations. I have not written much in this abridged version about the politics involved in the process—but it is there. Once the money is in hand, bids are taken and the regents accept or reject them. Construction can begin when the board's approval is given and contracts are signed. The final approval is when the building is completed and ready for occupancy. The project architect then issues a certificate of substantial completion, the University moves in, and the contractor gets final payment and everyone is more or less happy.

How big is the building? Reference is made to gross square footage, which includes all the space measured from the outside of walls with allowances for portals and zaguans (spaces covered but not enclosed). Assignable square footage, usually the same as net square feet, is space that can be assigned to a function but not including circulation space, toilets, service areas, chases, and wall thicknesses.

What is the University's style of architecture? This hallmark style of the Southwest has been given various names: Spanish Colonial–Pueblo Revival Style, Pueblo Style, Modified Pueblo Style, Santa Fe Style, Spanish-Pueblo. Taoseños claim their own version. What we have on the University's central campus is what I would call Modified Pueblo Style except for the buildings designed in the true Pueblo Style by John Gaw Meem, Charles Gaastra, and Miles Brittelle in the late 1920s and 1930s. Before that time there were some attempts at imitating the architecture of nearby Indian pueblos by President William George Tight with architect Edward B. Cristy and other architects and designers. Their attempts were crude compared to the Meem buildings. Later architects trying to use the style produced some unattractive buildings such as

Johnson Gymnasium and the New Mexico Union, which are too large for the inherent small scale of the Pueblo Style.

Is the Pueblo Style the officially approved style for the Central Campus? In 1928 the Board of Regents approved the designs of four buildings in the style but, contrary to popular belief, did not mandate use of the style in future buildings. Not until January 1961 did the regents adopt the General Development Plan by John Carl Warnecke and Associates, which included this statement: "It is University policy that new buildings conform to the Spanish-Pueblo style of architecture. New buildings must, in many instances, be three and four stories high to avoid excessive land coverage, and the volume and mass of new buildings will be greater. Faithful interpretation of the style will require sensitivity in design." No such architectural restrictions were imposed for the North and South Campuses, but hope was expressed that new buildings would have regional character. The UNM Board of Regents policy manual states, "The consistent use of a single architectural style has become a unique feature of the University of New Mexico campus, and contributes to an aesthetically pleasing environment for all members of the University community."

It is my opinion that since the middle 1960s the spirit of the campus has been maintained without architects slavishly attempting to follow Pueblo Style detailing. Consistent use of a simple palette of materials, evocative forms, and a harmonious color scheme has produced a unified campus the likes of which is found at few other institutions. Richard Dober, an internationally recognized authority on campus planning, recently wrote: "I think there are some benchmarks that campus planners might study to their benefit. . . . For continuity of campus design: the University of Chicago, the University of Colorado, Harvard Yard, the University of Miami, the University of New Mexico, Stanford University, and the University of Virginia."

In order to maintain that continuity I required every architectural firm employed to design a major project to build a model of the proposed building and, in most cases, to include at least the facades of the neighboring buildings. I resisted developing a manual of style and told architects they must respect the campus and do the best job they had ever done. I learned to say "no" to designs that seemed inappropriate.

I would not say the style has been consistently interpreted as John Meem espoused it in his early buildings, and even his firm deviated from it after World War II. That the development of the style has met professional approval is evidenced by the many awards for design given the University and its architects and landscape architects over the last thirty-five years. Public approval is expressed in the many praiseworthy articles that have appeared. In 1982 John Meem was quoted as saying: "I get quite a bit of exhilaration when I visit the campus. Sure, yes, they have all departed from the Pueblo Style, but people have to experiment a little bit. They have to have a little freedom to keep the campus alive. When you forbid these things, it starts dying."

In writing this book I have been careful to be as accurate as possible and give credit where due. I know readers will find mistakes and omissions and I accept full responsibility for them. So many people have been helpful to me that I am sure I will overlook some in my acknowledgment of appreciation and to them I give my thanks. I would like to mention several who have been most involved in giving me support. Melissa Howard is the editor and has spent untold hours reading, correcting, and giving encouragement. The book would not have been possible without her help. My friend V. B. Price graciously consented to write the foreword. Terry Gugliotta, the University archivist, has searched for documents and photographs and fed me ideas and stories. Architect George Pearl read the manuscript and gave me his professional viewpoints. University Secretary Emeritus Anne Brown checked the final copy.

Jan Dodson Barnhart and Kathlene Ann Ferris, who worked with the John Gaw Meem Archive of Southwestern Architecture, have been most helpful. Janet Johnson, archivist with the Health Sciences Center Library, likewise. Floyd B. Williams, former director of the Physical Plant Department, made many helpful comments and corrections. Professor Max Bennett and Dean Leonard Napolitano reviewed and commented on those portions of the manuscript pertaining to the Medical School. Susan McColeman Elder, Edith Johnson, and Margaret Novitski in my office helped collect material through the years. Carolyn Tinker, associate director of the Development Office, has enthusiastically encouraged me and, with Elizabeth Hadas, director of the UNM Press, helped arrange the funding with Vice President David Mc Kinney. I also thank the staff in the Center for Southwest Research who located material for me and smiled often. And to my wife and fellow architect, Marjorie (Peggy), who named the book and was helpful and patient during the years I worked on it, my sincere love and appreciation.

My tenure as university architect would not have been as pleasant and rewarding as it was without the help of the many fine people who worked in that office. Some of them not mentioned in the text include: Lt. Col. (ret.) Robert J. Schmidt kept the office and the many projects running smoothly for over twenty years; job inspectors Charles D. Little, Antonio Sedillo, Earl D'Arcy, E. H. Blumenthal, Jr., Edward Ladley, and Pablo Abeyta; secretaries and administrative assistants Carol Holt, Anne Snider, Dorothy Moore, and Florence Chakarian; and Michael Jerome who ran the drafting room. Many students worked in the office including Richard Ruminski now with the Physical Plant Department and Roger Lujan the director of the Department of Facilities Planning. Thank you all and anyone I may have omitted.

Van Dorn Hooker

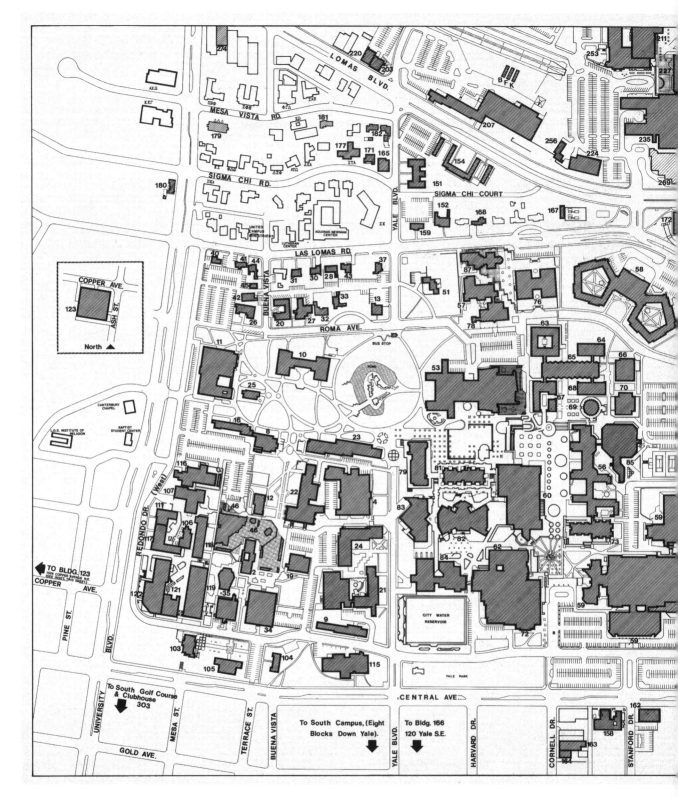

CENTRAL CAMPUS c. 1989

2. Classroom Annex
4. Carlisle Gym
8. Bandelier East
9. Marron Hall (office)
10. Administration (Scholes Hall)
11. Anthropology & Maxwell Museum

12. Anthropology Annex
13. 1821 Roma NE
16. Bandelier West (offices)
19. Biology Annex
20. Speech Communication
21. Biology (Castetter Hall)

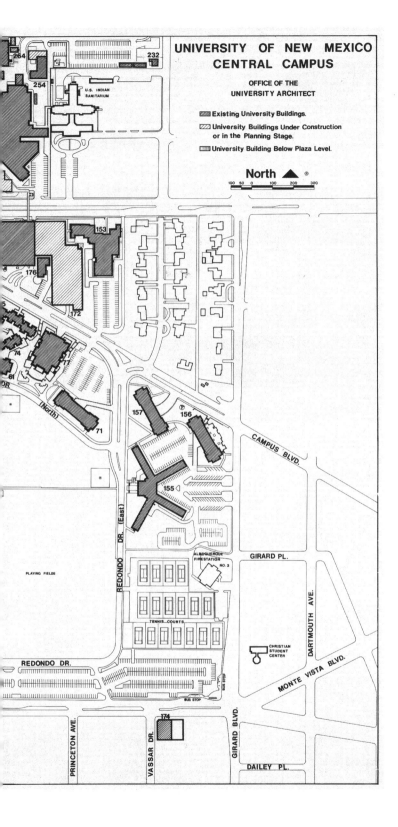

NORTH CAMPUS c. 1989

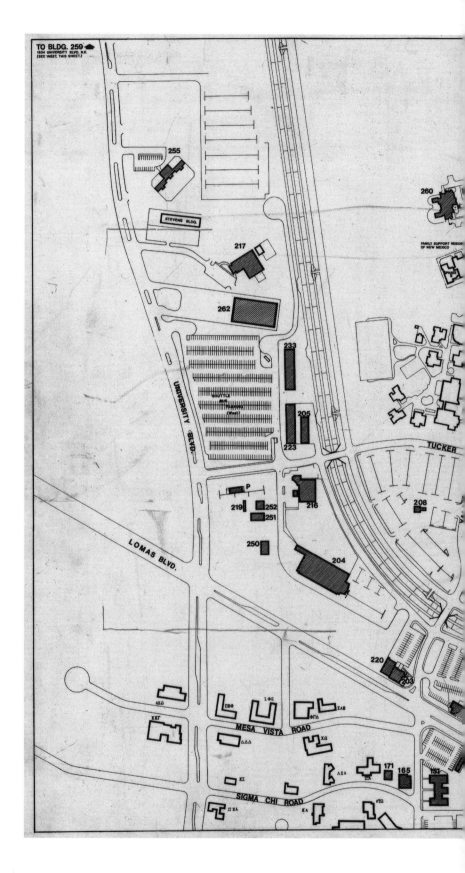

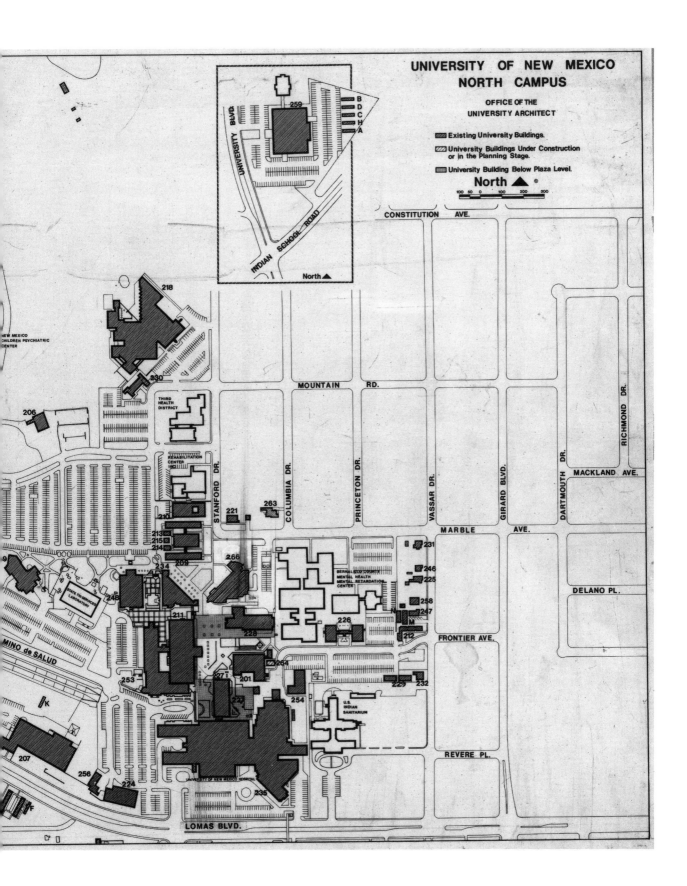

SOUTH CAMPUS c. 1989

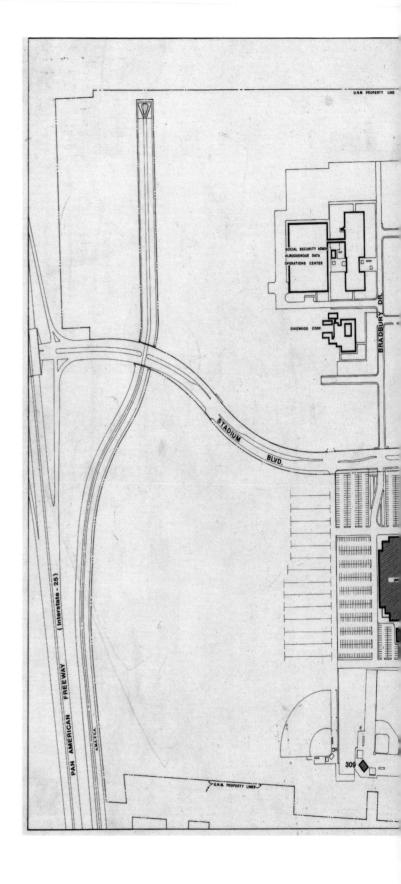

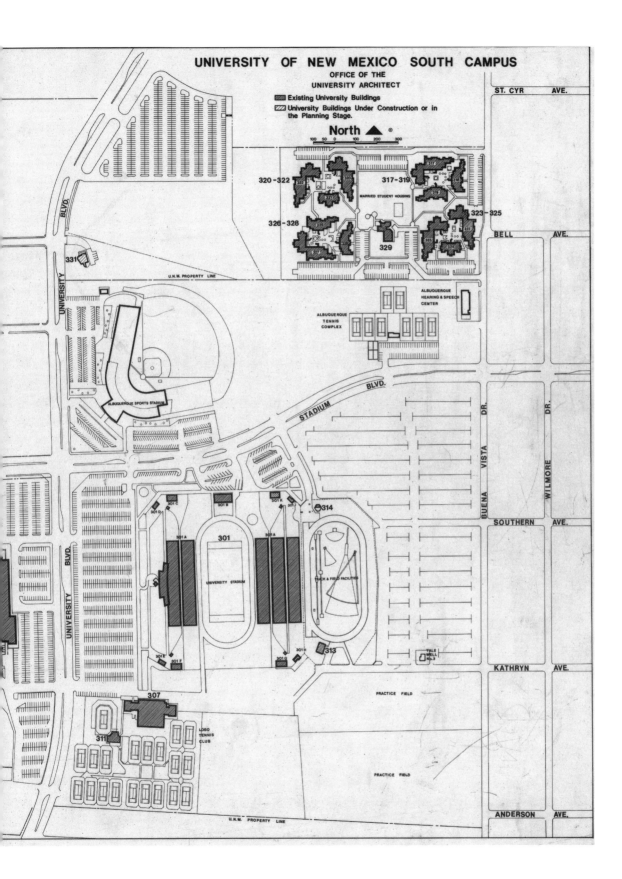

UNIVERSITY OF NEW MEXICO SOUTH CAMPUS

OFFICE OF THE
UNIVERSITY ARCHITECT

Existing University Buildings

University Buildings Under Construction or in
the Planning Stage.

North

100 50 0   100   200   300

ST. CYR   AVE.

320 -322   317 - 319

MARRIED STUDENT HOUSING

323 - 325

326 - 328   329

BELL   AVE.

331

U.N.M. PROPERTY LINE

ALBUQUERQUE
HEARING & SPEECH
CENTER

ALBUQUERQUE
TENNIS
COMPLEX

STADIUM   BLVD.

UNIVERSITY   BLVD.

BUENA   VISTA   DR.

WILMORE   DR.

ALBUQUERQUE SPORTS STADIUM

SOUTHERN   AVE.

301 C   301 B   301 K   301

314

301 D

301 A   301   301 A

UNIVERSITY STADIUM   TRACK & FIELD FACILITIES

301 E   301 H

301 F   301 G   313

FALSE
WELL
NO. 3

KATHRYN   AVE.

307

PRACTICE   FIELD

311   LOBO
TENNIS
CLUB

PRACTICE   FIELD

U.N.M. PROPERTY LINE

ANDERSON   AVE.

Only in New Mexico

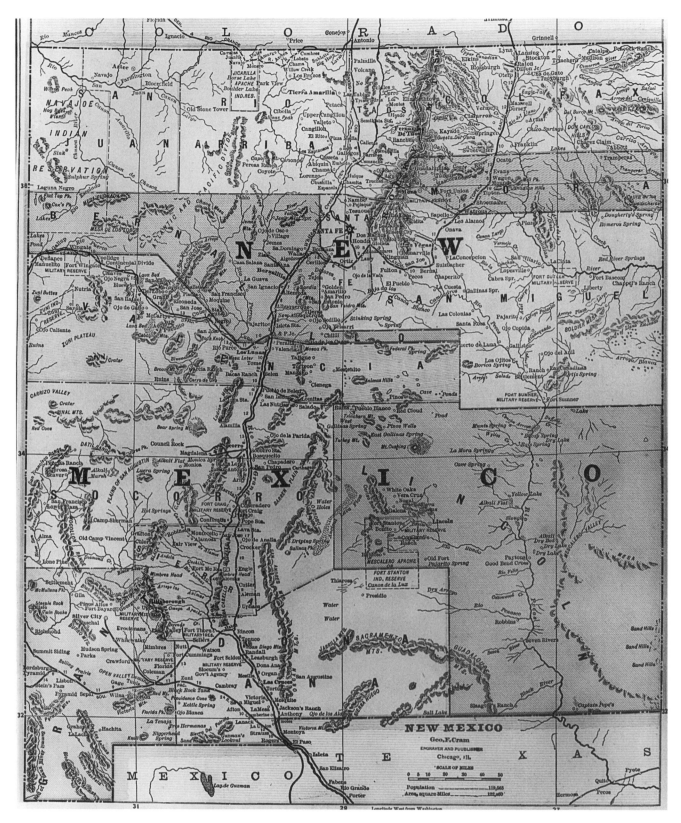

Map of New Mexico, circa 1880. Library of William E. Wylie.

There Were Pioneers
with Dreams

In order to fully appreciate the efforts of the founders of the University of New Mexico you must have a picture of the Territory of New Mexico in the 1880s. The population in 1870 was only 91,874; in 1880 it was 119,565; by 1890 it had increased to 160,262, 1.3 persons per square mile. In 1880 San Miguel was the most populous county, and Santa Fe, at 6,690, was the largest city followed by Las Vegas, Albuquerque, Taos, and Silver City in that order. Roswell, Artesia, and Hobbs did not exist.

The 1880s were a time of turmoil. The Lincoln County War lasted from 1878 to 1881; there was a ranchers' war in San Juan County; and there were gold and silver strikes, gunfights, Indian raids, hangings, many questionable land deals, and a contentious political atmosphere.

The territory was desperately poor. There was almost no industry, only some farming and ranching, mostly on a subsistence level, and logging in the northern counties. Mining towns sprang up when gold or silver was found and just as quickly disappeared when the veins ran out. There was short-term work for many men laying track for the railroads that entered the territory beginning in 1879. Governor Lew Wallace's wife, Susan, wrote her son, "My Dear—General Sherman was right. We should have another war with Mexico to make her take back New Mexico."

Not much thought was given to public education by the general population—children were needed for many tasks and could not be spared to the classroom. In 1856 a public education bill had been defeated 5,016 to 37. One source says that in 1874 there were only 128 public schools in the entire territory with an enrollment of 5,420 and 143 teachers, but no public high schools. For many the Catholic church took care of what education was needed. The church established Saint Michael's High School and College for boys and Loretto Academy for girls in Santa Fe. A Jesuit college opened in Las Vegas but soon moved to Denver, where it became Regis College. The Sisters of Charity founded Saint Vincent's Academy for girls in Albuquerque in 1885.

Bernard S. Rodey, the "Father of the University."

Colorado College was active in establishing private schools with a first grade through high school curriculum in western cities where public school systems had not been developed. With the college's assistance Albuquerque Academy opened in Old Town but soon moved to New Town. Enrollment increased so much that in 1890 the school rented Perkins Hall, a building owned by banker Joshua Raynolds and his wife, on the northwest corner of Edith and Railroad Avenue. The building was designed by Chicago architects Patten and Fisher. When the public school system was established in 1891 the academy was dissolved.

Hiram Hadley, an education pioneer from Indiana, arrived in the Mesilla Valley in July 1887. He had come to New Mexico to be near his son, Walter C. Hadley, who was in poor health. The elder Hadley joined a group of prominent citizens who were interested in taking advantage of the Morrill Act of 1862, which provided grants of public lands for agricultural schools. During the fall of 1888 mass meetings were held in Las Cruces and plans were made for the coming legislative session. Similar efforts were taking place in Albuquerque and Socorro.

Bernard Shandon Rodey, an Albuquerque attorney who had a dream of establishing a university in Albuquerque, went to Santa Fe in 1889 as Bernalillo County's senator. He favored the creation of a single territorial university that would include the land grant agricultural college and a school of mines. He faced a legislative agenda heavily weighted toward acquiring statehood and improving the poor economic condition of the territory. Rodey soon realized that as a first-term senator he had little hope of getting his bill passed without the help of influential politicians such as were found in Doña Ana, Socorro, and San Miguel Counties. Among these politicians was John R. McFie who was soon to be appointed to the New Mexico Supreme Court by President Benjamin Harrison.

After weeks of political maneuvering a compromise was reached three days before the end of the legislative session. Albuquerque would get the University of New Mexico, while the agricultural college would be located in Las Cruces, the school of mines in Socorro, and an insane asylum in Las Vegas.

The first University of New Mexico was founded in Santa Fe in 1881 by Congregational minister Horatio O. Ladd. The territory's supreme court justice, L. Bradford Prince, was made president of the first board of trustees and several faculty members were recruited including Ladd and his wife, Julia. Whitin Hall, an imposing three-story building, still stands at the corner of Garfield and Guadalupe Streets near the old Denver and Rio Grande Railroad station. The school was not well accepted by the public and closed its doors in 1888. For years the building was occupied by Saint Mary's convent; a few years ago it was remodeled into apartments called appropriately "University Apartments."

Rodey sent word to his lawyer friend Neil B. Field of Albuquerque to frame an outline for the bill and get it to Santa Fe as soon as possible. When the outline was received, Rodey, McFie, and Fred Simms, a black stenographer with the Rodey firm, shut themselves in a room in the Palace Hotel and worked nonstop for thirty-six hours. The bill was introduced in the waning hours of the session and passed just before adjournment on February 28, 1889. Rodey became known as the "Father of the University"; McFie received credit in the Mesilla Valley for acquiring the school of agriculture.

The passage of the Rodey Act was a personal triumph for Bernard Rodey. Perhaps his enthusiasm for education stemmed from his own lack of formal schooling—about three months altogether. The son of a farming family, he was born on March 1, 1856, in County Mayo, Ireland. He was brought to this country by way of Canada as a boy of seven. He was self-educated and worked as a court reporter and stenographer while reading law. He came to Albuquerque in 1881 and was admitted to the New Mexico Bar in 1884. As Rodey's reputation and practice grew, he became an authority on international law and founded what became one of the largest law firms in the state. He served two terms as territorial representative to Congress where he helped lay the foundation for New Mexico's admission to the Union. He was later appointed a federal judge in Puerto Rico and then U.S. attorney for Alaska. Rodey Hall, an assembly building and later a theater, located on the north side of Hodgin Hall, was named in his honor. After that building was demolished in 1971, Rodey Theater in the Fine Arts Center was given his name.

The first action required after the Rodey Act was passed was the acquisition of land for the campus. There had been much squabbling over the location of the new university: some factions wanted it in Barelas in the south valley; others wanted it near the river and downtown. Rodey settled the matter by writing into the act a provision requiring the school to be located not more than two miles north of Railroad Avenue (now Central Avenue) on high and dry land. G. W. Meylert, mayor of Albuquerque, was to receive the land and convey it to the territory. On August 6, 1889, twenty acres of barren east mesa land far from settled neighborhoods were donated by four couples.

The Rodey Act was signed by Governor Edmund G. Ross, but it was his successor, Governor L. Bradford Prince, who appointed the University's first Board of Regents on September 2, 1889: Elias S. Stover and G. W. Meylert of Albuquerque, Frank W. Clancy and Judge Henry S. Waldo of Santa Fe, and Mariano S. Otero of Bernalillo. The first meeting was held in the San Felipe Hotel at the corner of Gold and Fifth Street in Albuquerque on November 13 with Judge Waldo presiding. Otero was elected president and Meylert secretary-treasurer. A motion was made by Judge Waldo and seconded by Stover that bids be solicited for plans for the construction of a University building and that the secretary advertise in Denver, Kansas City, Santa Fe, and Albuquerque newspapers.

At the meeting on January 10, 1890, secretary Meylert reported that the adver-

The often-told story that the City of Santa Fe turned down an opportunity to acquire the University of New Mexico, choosing instead the state penitentiary, is not true. The 1884 territorial legislature passed a bill authorizing a prison in Santa Fe, and on August 9, 1884, the *Santa Fe Daily New Mexican* reported the letting of a contract for the project. The August 7, 1885, issue told of the gala housewarming in the completed penitentiary, referred to as "New Mexico's first public building." A dinner was served to the large crowd while the 13th U.S. Infantry Band played waltzes and quadrilles from a high platform at the end of the spacious chapel.

The original twenty acres superimposed on the 1979 campus map.

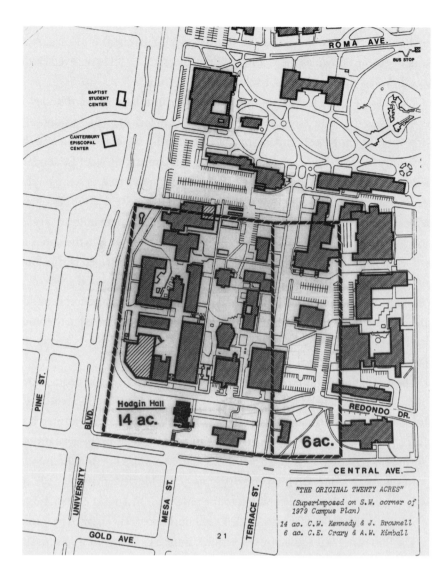

tisements had been printed. He submitted a letter he proposed to send to architects who would then ask for information. In the letter he said that within the next year the University would have about $25,000 from a territorial property tax for erecting and furnishing its first building. The board proposed that the building have three stories plus a basement, stone walls in the basement and brick above, a chemical laboratory and the furnace and coal bins in the basement, a recitation room on each of the three floors, and professors' offices on the first and second floors. The top floor would be an assembly room. There was no requirement for a library. The letter stated that the regents were to be the sole judges of the plans and no compensation would be made for any submittal except the one chosen. The regents stipulated that penitentiary brick (a soft, salmon-colored brick made at the Santa Fe prison) could not be used because it did not weather well.

The board met again on May 25, 1890, and the secretary reported that four architects had submitted plans and sketches. Two of those were Jesse M. Wheelock and a Mr. McKinney of Albuquerque. When the regents met on July 14 Wheelock was selected to be the architect, and the Ruttan heating and ventilating system was approved for the building. Wheelock presented final plans and specifications at a board meeting on August 16, and the bid opening was scheduled for September 15.

Jesse M. Wheelock was born December 13, 1859, in Booneville, Oneida County, New York. He briefly attended the State Normal College in Emporia, Kansas, and received his architectural training from his architect father, Charles W. Wheelock, who had a practice in Las Vegas, New Mexico, in the 1870s and 1880s. Jesse Wheelock moved to Albuquerque in 1885. Buildings he designed in Albuquerque included the Commercial Club, the Bernalillo County Jail, the Armijo Building, and the San Felipe Hotel.

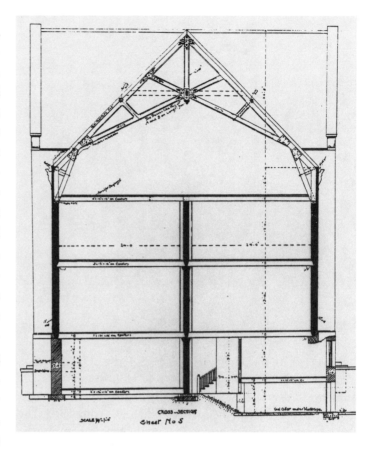

Cross section through the Main Building (Hodgin Hall) showing the roof construction.

When the bids were opened Palladino and Digneo of Santa Fe was the low bidder at $26,196 using Horne brick. The regents approved a contract for that amount and made a separate contract with the Ruttan Company of Chicago. The Ruttan heating system was a gravity circulating system that drew heated air from the coal-fired furnaces into the ducts supplying the building. Wheelock was sold on the idea that the Smead "dry closet" system could be incorporated into the Ruttan system and used in place of a cesspool or septic tank. Waste from the toilets, or sanitaries as they were called on the plans, was to be collected in a space underneath, and gases from the decomposing waste would be drawn off by the flue exhaust from the furnaces. A carbide-acetylene flue-heater would be used when the furnaces were not operating. Shortly after the building was occupied, complaints of foul odors led to abandonment of the Smead system and the building of two outdoor privies in 1894. The system itself was not removed until the summer of 1905 when the bricks in it were salvaged for use in remodeling the building.

Perkins Hall, on the northwest corner of Edith and Railroad (Central) Avenue, was leased by the first Albuquerque Academy in 1890 and by the University of New Mexico in 1892 for general classes until the Main Building was completed. The Department of Music continued to use the building until 1905. UNM Catalog 1903–4.

The first class of seventy-four students met in June 1892 in Perkins Hall, which had previously housed the Albuquerque Academy. In September the University moved into its new building but continued to rent space in Perkins Hall for music classes until 1905. The building later became the Albuquerque Public Library. The first graduating class of five members received their bachelor of pedagogy degrees in 1894. For many years the University was little more than a preparatory school, and not until 1919 was that program phased out.

It is possible that the design of Perkins Hall influenced Wheelock in the design of the University building. He had been construction superintendent for the Chicago architects who had designed the three-story red brick and sandstone building in the Richardsonian style popular at the time.

The University's Main Building (103) (later named the Administration Building and then Hodgin Hall) was red brick with light-colored stone trim, typical of midwestern school architecture. "The finest school building in the territory," it was symmetrically designed so that both east and west façades had inscription blocks above the arched entrance panels reading "University N.M. 1890." The main entrance was on the west side, and there was no back door as such for many years. The roof, a complex combination of hipped and gabled framing, added twenty-six feet to the already imposing structure.

The building was situated on the southwest corner of the campus, easily visible from the valley below. As Charles Hodgin, UNM vice president for many years and head of the Education Department, recalled later: "Visualize it if you can: without a tree, with no houses between it and the town, and none between it and the mountains, and no street leading to the mesa except the extension of Railroad Avenue, by the mere scratching of the gravel over the undulating and ungraded foothills. The only approaches for vehicles . . . were two sandy arroyos, one coming up at the north line of the campus, and one several blocks to the south."

The lonesome University building was unprotected from the strong west winds, which blew out several panes of glass until heavier glass was used as replacement. In

Main Building under construction.

Main Building from the southwest after completion.

View of campus looking toward the Manzano Mountains. In the beginning, the University was virtually alone on the East Mesa. Weinzirl Collection, 000–293–0011, CSWR.

Library in the Main Building, circa 1900. Cobb Collection, 988–012–0001, CSWR.

1901 storm doors were installed in the west entrance. The wind pressure on the roof structure was transmitted through the roof trusses to the exterior brick bearing walls, which because of the large number of closely spaced windows were not strong enough to resist the pressure. Bulges in the upper walls were noted as early as 1901. Architect Edward Buxton Cristy recommended five iron rods be run through the top floor of the building in both directions and the regents ordered it done. The roof structure continued to be a problem and in July 1904 the regents employed two men to repair the roof, gables, and chimneys with the possibility of completely rebuilding the gables.

Cristy graduated from Columbia College in 1891 and moved to Albuquerque the following year. He was employed for a time as drawing instructor at both the University and Albuquerque Academy. Cristy designed several buildings in New Albuquerque in the styles popular in the East including Central High School in 1900 and the City Hall in 1906.

Hiram Hadley, first president of the New Mexico Agricultural College, served from November 1889 until June 30, 1894, when he was fired for political reasons. In August he was appointed vice president of the faculty of the University of New Mexico, a position described as placing him "in charge of the University" at an annual salary of $2,000. He served under the first president, Elias S. Stover, a businessman with no experience as an education administrator. Hadley remained at UNM for three years and then returned to Las Cruces.

Things were not going well financially for the University in the 1890s. In the fall of 1893, Regent Otero was appointed a committee of one to try to arrange a loan of $1,000 to pay the salaries, but not until the following February were the arrears paid. Interest was frequently paid on overdrafts at the Bank of Commerce during 1894 and 1895. By 1896 enrollment had dropped to seventy-four.

The next building erected on the campus was a small wood-frame men's gymnasium designed by Cristy. On August 22, 1895, the regents approved a contract with John W. McQuade to build it from Cristy's plans. First located about one hundred feet northeast of the Main Building, it was moved more than once during its existence. The gymnasium was barely large enough for basketball games, with no room for spectators. Gymnastic equipment was added outside.

In 1892 the University employed a most unusual man to be the custodian, a Civil War veteran named Mathias Lambert Custers, known to everyone as M. Custers. He had come to New Mexico with his family for health reasons and worked for the *Albuquerque Journal* until he took the job on "the hill," as the University was called. Custers had a great knowledge of mathematics, surveying, and trigonometry and was soon offered a faculty position. He was the University's first librarian, when the library occupied a single room in the Main Building. There was a story in *Ripley's Believe It or Not* in 1968 about his rise from janitor to faculty member.

When the Board of Regents met on July 14, 1898, Custers, who had been provided living quarters for his family in the Main Building, proposed to advance money to

The men's gymnasium showing the outside gymnastic equipment. The building was moved several times before being demolished. Cobb Collection, 988–025–0013, CSWR.

construct a residence of his own design on the campus. The board accepted the offer, with the provision to pay him back if the University needed the house or land. The Custers family lived in what was called the Custodian's House only a short time before the regents relieved Custers of his custodial duties because they thought they could get the services he performed for less money and he was losing his eyesight. They paid off the balance of the note he held on his house on June 4, 1902. The first floor became the Dining Hall, and the second floor housed a few women. It was called the Ladies' Cottage. A limited number of rooms for men were made available on the second floor of the Main Building.

The second major building to be erected on the campus was largely the gift of friends of the University and Mrs. Walter C. Hadley whose father-in-law was Hiram Hadley. She offered the Board of Regents $10,000 to erect a science building not to cost more than $15,000 as a memorial to her deceased husband. The balance was raised from small donations. The student body contributed $300. Architect E. B. Cristy's plans were accepted by the regents in June 1899. He reported the receipt of bids to the board on July 20. In order to get the cost of the building within available funds, several changes were made in the specifications, including using Cerrillos sandstone in place of granite, installing roof tile instead of galvanized steel, omitting the concrete floors in the basement and the dumb waiter, and cheapening finishes throughout. Contractor John McQuade completed the building on February 1, 1900, on a site about where the Art Annex (105) is located today.

(Above) The home of Mathias Lambert Custers financed by him and built on the campus in 1898. He rose from the building and grounds custodian to professor and was the first librarian. UNM bought the house and turned it into a girls' dormitory and the Dining Hall.

(Left) The Hadley Climatological Laboratory Building from the southwest. The building burned in 1910 and was not rebuilt.

Dorothy Hughes described Hadley Hall in *Pueblo on the Mesa*:

> As designed by Mr. Cristy, the basement was of light colored sandstone five feet above ground surmounted by brick walls twenty-seven feet high, laid in colored mortar with tooled joints. The sills and lintels were of grey sandstone. The facade was accentuated by a central projection of seven feet in which was placed the main entrance. A broad flight of stone steps was flanked by a pilaster thirty feet high which supported the roof of the central bay. Several dormers intersected the main roof which had a deck surrounded by an iron casting. The interior woodwork was of Missouri pine. Hot water heat was provided. The laboratories were supplied with gas from the University plant and with water from the city system.

(Above) Tight's house on Central Avenue while being used by the Sigma Tau fraternity. Photograph by William R. Walton.

(Left) William George Tight, president of the University from 1901 to 1909.

When John Dustin Clark, professor of chemistry, first came to the campus in August 1907, he found President Tight dressed in overalls hammering away in the auditorium of the Main Building. Clark was soon doing the same thing. Another story is that a shabbily dressed Tight was working on the landscaping when a visitor arrived and asked to see the president. Tight promised to fetch him, went indoors, changed his clothes, then presented himself to the visitor.

View of the campus from the south around 1907. *Left to right:* Main Building, Hadley Hall, the Dining Hall. Weinzirl Collection, 000–293–0006, CSWR.

Dr. Clarence Luther Herrick was the second president of the University, serving from 1897 to 1901. A scholar and scientist, Herrick, at thirty-five, had been chosen to chair the geology department at the University of Chicago when his health failed. He came to New Mexico and the University had the good fortune to secure his services. He knew how to deal with students and was admired and respected by them. He could lecture with no preparation on almost any subject, including astronomy, psychology, philosophy, evolution, and stream erosion to name a few. When Herrick's health would no longer allow him to continue as president, he recommended a brilliant former student to take his place, William George Tight.

President Tight had just received his Ph.D. from the University of Chicago when he assumed his office on July 1, 1901. Tight, who was by profession a geologist, was dubbed "the human dynamo" by students and colleagues with good reason: he was a tireless worker. Tight was a well-built man, six feet, two inches tall; he was a good athlete and entered into games with the faculty and students. His exploits are too numerous to tell here; he is best remembered for the establishment of the Pueblo Style of architecture on the campus, which influenced the revival of the style in Santa Fe and throughout the state.

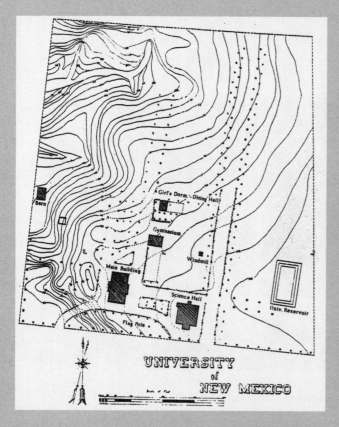

Topographic map of first twenty acres, circa 1905.

Early Campus Water Supplies

How much did an existing supply of water have to do with the location of the University of New Mexico campus? In 1886 Angus Grant, owner of the Albuquerque Water Works Company, received a franchise to develop a municipal water system that included building a reservoir on the east mesa where the present city reservoir is located at Yale and Central. In seeking donations of land for the campus the regents must have considered the availability of water from this source just east of the original twenty acres. The problem was the reservoir was only a few feet higher than the campus so water could only be supplied to the basement and first floor of the first buildings, leaving them with little fire-fighting capability.

When Tight became president one of his first thoughts was the improvement of the campus landscaping because he believed an attractive campus was essential for an educational environment. He dug the ground and planted trees himself. He sent men students into the mountains to bring back trees, and every Arbor Day was a holiday. Students and faculty worked on the grounds in the morning and there was a picnic followed by games and sports in the afternoon. Bringing plants from all over New Mexico and from afar was his idea. Gifts such as student memorials, the fish pond, and the sundial in the rockery were inspired by Tight.

In order to irrigate the new landscaping and fight fires, President Tight turned his attention to improving the water supply. At their meeting on November 19, 1903, the regents approved digging a well and installing a water system. This well was located a few hundred yards northeast of the Main Building. It was hand-dug by William and Ferdinand Wolking—with the help of a horse named Dick—to a depth of about two hundred feet and lined with brick. In 1904 a large Aeromotor pump was installed on top of the tower, which was painted cherry and silver, cherry for the Sandia Mountains at sunset and silver for the Rio Grande. The tower was seventy feet high and the wind-driven pump added another twenty feet. By 1907 electric lights had been installed on top. There was a storage tank on the tower that periodically overflowed.

Architect F. W. Spencer examined the corridor walls in Hadley Hall and reported they were capable of supporting four water tanks each holding seven thousand gallons in the attic above the corridors. When installed, this system gave the campus a gravity water supply.

Servicing the well fascinated the little boys of the University neighborhood. A. C. Frank, son of Harry Frank, superintendent of buildings and grounds, wrote that one of the things he enjoyed most was watching a man on a board seat being lowered into the well to clean it and service the pump. David B. Mitchell, the eldest son of Professor Lynn Mitchell, remembered the well cleaning in an article in 1979. He said the well was located in a small corrugated steel building.

During President Tight's administration two groves of trees were planted to the north and the east of the Main Building. A shipment of yucca from Silver City was received in February 1905. About thirty evergreen trees were set out west of the building in April, the start of Tight Grove, which is still in existence. Next came an "arbotheater" in a natural depression in the area just south of the Estufa. It had a stage and seating for one thousand. Grading was completed in March 1906, and on Arbor Day forty cottonwood trees were planted in two semicircular rows to shelter the audience. A poplar tree was set at each end of the stage.

In March 1908 the Campus Improvement League planted a variety of trees and ornamental shrubs. A tamarisk, or salt cedar, hedge lined both sides of Terrace Boulevard, the main street of the campus. Four or five of the tamarisk survived until the 1980s when they were removed for a new building. By the time the league had completed their work, about 5,000 trees and plants had been set out around the campus. Professor Hodgin said, "One of the trees was called the Hodgin Elm, but it was too much for the tree—it withered and wasted away."

The boiler plant, built in 1905–6, was the first UNM building designed in the Pueblo Style. Architect: E. B. Cristy.

On July 1, 1904, the regents leased the Solon Rose House situated just east of the campus for $100 per year and authorized $100 for putting it in good repair. The campus newspaper reported that "the boys' dorm has been removed from the Main Building to the neat little cottage just over the campus line, so that hereafter there need be no conflict between the recitation and sleeping rooms." The University later bought the house.

At the regents meeting on June 24, 1905, separate bids were approved for constructing and equipping a boiler plant. Wallace Hesselden was low bidder for construction and T. M. Jordan was awarded the contract to set the boilers. Another contract was let for plumbing. The president and the secretary were authorized to borrow $5,000 for the construction. The boiler, or power, plant, later called the heating plant designed by

E. B. Cristy, was the first campus building done in the Pueblo Style, a style Cristy had not employed before.

Since his arrival in the Southwest, President Tight had been interested in the architecture of the Indian pueblos, particularly the Hopi villages in Arizona. He visited the pueblos in New Mexico, photographed them as he traveled on University business, and passed his ideas to Cristy. Tight's dream was to have all new campus buildings designed in the Pueblo Style and to remodel some existing ones to conform.

Tight was probably influenced by the articles on Pueblo architecture published in 1897 by archaeologist Cosmos Mindeleff in the Boston-based journal *American Architect and Building News*. The first example of Pueblo Revival had occurred in California in 1894 when San Francisco architect A. C. Schweinfurth designed a "country hotel" that was more Pueblo Style than California Mission. He attempted to popularize the adobe walls, projecting beams, and terraced roofs of the Indian pueblos in other projects. Other architects became interested, including Charles F. Whittlesey, who mixed Pueblo Style with Beaux-Arts planning in his designs, and Mary Colter, who was literal in her 1905 Hopi House on the rim of the Grand Canyon. A 1907 article about the UNM campus in *World's Work* by E. Dana Johnson, who later became editor of the *Santa Fe New Mexican,* said,

> The model for this college pueblo is the prehistoric town of Sikyatki, perhaps the oldest of the communal towns in this part of the world. It is situated in northern Arizona, amid limitless deserts and frowning mesas, in that strange land of sunshine and silence.
>
> The shapeless ruins of Sikyatki, which was destroyed long before the Spanish invaders came, are about three miles from the little settlement of Isba. Dr. Jesse Walter Fewkes, of the Bureau of Ethnology, made in 1895 a thorough investigation of these ruins, and his report has been used as a basis in planning this new type of college architecture—a university pueblo.

The Smithsonian Institution, publisher of the Bureau of American Ethnology reports, donated fifteen volumes of Fewkes's early documents followed by annual reports to the University, which were available to Tight and Cristy.

Cristy, accompanied by architects Spencer and Wallingford, presented plans for a new dormitory in November 1905 but no action was taken by the regents probably because the funds were not yet available. The plans were resubmitted and approved in March 1906 and a call for bids was issued. The president and secretary were authorized to borrow construction money from the Bank of Commerce or some other source. The proposed dormitory, divided into connected wings for men and women, was shown on the 1907–8 campus plan.

Wallace Hesselden was awarded the building contract and Whitney and Company the plumbing and heating. These contracts were canceled two months later when Hesselden submitted a proposal to build two separate dormitories with his own funds

Kwataka Hall, the men's dormitory, was built in 1906. Architect: E. B. Cristy.

and rent them to the University for a dollar per year until they were paid for. The University agreed to purchase them within four years. The regents borrowed money from the Bank of Commerce to make the necessary payments and assigned the contract as security.

The dormitories were given "Indian" names—Kwataka, meaning "man-eagle," for the men's, and Hokona, signifying "butterfly-maiden," for the women's. They were Sikyatki or Tusavan names found in reports of Fewkes's expedition. Kwataka was said to be a powerful bird worshipped for its strength, alertness, and swiftness. Another interpretation said he was "a voracious monster who abode in the sky, and whose chief delight was to plague the children of men. Hokona was a beneficent deity whose good will was sought from planting to harvest time." *U.N.M. Weekly* reporter Allan F. Keller admonished the residents of Kwataka dormitory to forget the baser parts of the legend and think of the "virile conquering might of the Man-eagle" and not forget that "virility is an American's greatest attribute." To the Hokona ladies, "the butterfly in its grander sense, its signification of the spiritual, should carry naught but remembrance of that great principle of which Socrates dreamed as he sank neath the power of the hemlock."

Tight and Miss Ethel Hickey, an English teacher, painted symbols that depicted Kwataka and Hokona on the walls of the dormitories. Information in the Fewkes report also assisted them in designing the interior decor and furnishings.

Kwataka accommodated twenty-four men; Hokona, thirty women. The rooms were arranged in suites with two bedrooms and a study room. The interior walls were

Hokona Hall, the women's dormitory, was built at the same time as Kwataka. The two buildings were financed and built by Wallace Hesselden.

The first campus master plan appeared in the 1908 *Mirage*. It was probably prepared by E. B. Cristy.

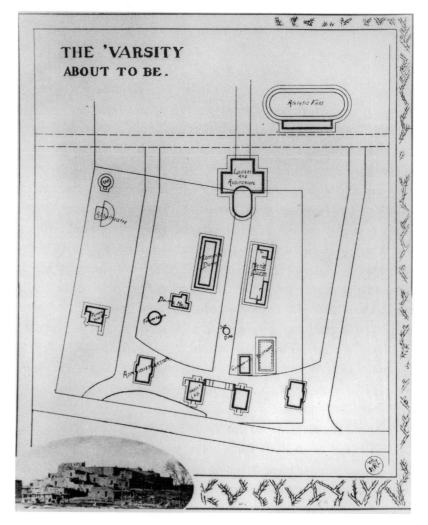

painted plaster with no decoration, and the furnishings were simple. Students decorated their rooms with Indian rugs and paintings. The curtains were emblazoned with Indian symbols. Light fixtures were made in the shape of Indian swastikas. O. W. Strong and Sons equipped the buildings except for desks and chairs, which were furnished by E. Gustafson.

The unique design of Hokona, Kwataka, and the heating plant received nationwide coverage in newspaper and magazine articles that had titles such as "Prehistoric Home for New University," "A University Pueblo," and "University Buildings of Adobe." A feature the writers all mentioned was the dormitories' solar water heating system with the tank and heater on the roof. The tank was concealed in a replica of an *horno*, an Indian oven. An article in the campus newspaper explained, "If the sun is not hot enough to heat the water, then, as steam [from the central heating plant] would be necessary to heat the rooms anyway under such conditions, it can be used to heat water also. This system easily solves our hot water problem and at the same time saves the University much expense and trouble." This may have been the first application of mechanical solar heating in New Mexico.

A 1909 article in *Technical World* magazine described the Tight-Cristy plan and the buildings:

> The buildings, as might be imagined from the generally square ground plan of this type of Indian architecture, are in the shape of irregular rectangles. Each of these, and there will be two, separated by a 50-foot tree-lined avenue, when the plans on the campus are completed, will consist of about six buildings, so connected and so built under one roof as to appear to be one building.
>
> Three and one-half stories will be the highest part of this communal house; from this the square rooms will slope down to one story. . . . Inside the entire structure will be a spacious patio or placita, which will be devoted to flowers and foliage plants indigenous to the desert in which the pueblo cities were built.

By 1908 it was clear that strong winds battering the roof structure of the Main Building were causing severe damage to the supporting walls. Engineers and architects had declared the situation dangerous, and one had advocated razing the whole building. This was President Tight's opportunity to bring the building into conformity with the Pueblo Style. The pitched roof would be removed and replaced with a viga-supported flat roof, the brick walls covered with stucco, the top of the arched window openings blocked off, and numerous changes made in the interior. E. B. Cristy presented his plans on May 18, 1908, and received bids on June 1. All bids were rejected as being over the budget and

Since the University owned a few horses and some students rode to the campus, a barn and corral were a necessity in the early days. The first barn, about three hundred feet northwest of the Main Building, was destroyed by fire in 1905. It was replaced immediately; a new corral was built in 1918.

The Main Building with Rodey Hall after the 1909 remodeling by President Tight and architect E. B. Cristy.

Cristy was told to revise his plans. When bids were received again on June 12, A. Y. Hayden was awarded the contract. A separate contract for the plumbing and heating went to J. H. Cox. The contractors were told payment would come from the future sale of territorial institutional bonds.

The many summer improvements prompted the following article in *U.N.M. Weekly*:

> The Administration Building, as we used to know it, is gone. In its place stands an immense three storied pueblo. It is easily larger than anything of similar style erected in modern times and seems more pleasing to the eyes than any specimen of pueblo architecture on campus. It is almost incredible that a building of such pronounced character, could be, in so short a time so completely changed. . . . Arches have been removed or straightened, doors cut through, walls torn out, porches made, a room built on the south side, the old top heavy third floor torn down and two new rooms built in the center, a flat roof built to replace the old one, a thousand and one changes made. North of the Main Building and seemingly a part of it is Rodey Hall, the new assembly building. . . . It is cross shaped, the platform occupying the shorter arm of the cross. The ceiling is quite high and a balcony is being constructed in the upper part of the longer arm of the cross. Large rough pine logs are used for rafters, joists, and pillars in both this and the Administration Building. The walls and corners are heavily buttressed and the general effect of this building is that of an old Pueblo church.

The interior of Rodey Hall. Ladd Collection, 000–003–0071, CSWR.

The UNM building at the 1908 Territorial Fair. Cobb Collection, CSWR.

Tight wanted to advertise to the citizens of the territory the adaptability of the Pueblo Style of architecture. He, the faculty, and students erected a wood-frame movie-set building for the Territorial Fair in 1908. It cost the University $138; the fair contributed $275. The fair was held while Tight was hosting the annual meeting of the National Irrigation Congress.

"Many articles have been published concerning the style of architecture of our University buildings," said a campus newspaper story.

Our local papers have been strong in their praise of the uniqueness of the Pueblo architecture, but none have given the actual material advantage of it. The uniqueness of the "University Pueblo" appeals to the people throughout the country, and we receive hundreds of letters of inquiry and comment upon it. Tourists on their way across the continent stop here to see the Pueblo University. These facts show the advantage it gives us in advertising.

Not everyone agreed with Tight's use of Pueblo Style architecture on the campus. Dorothy Hughes paraphrased the dissenters, "If you are going to be consistent, the president and the faculty should wear Indian blankets around their shoulders and feathered coverings on their heads." She wrote that Charles Hodgin "pointed out [that] people did not seem to think it odd to go back several thousand years to copy Greek architecture, but they could not tolerate what belonged in their own land."

Friction between Tight and the faculty began in 1908 when a new ranking of the faculty was made and only four retained the title of full professor. Tight initiated other sweeping changes in the policies of the University that were generally accepted by the faculty. But when he asked two professors to resign they appealed to the regents who censured Tight for exceeding his authority. In April 1909 the regents asked for Tight's resignation, which he gave. He received an excellent recommendation from the board. Nothing was said about his introduction of the Pueblo Style of architecture. The former president lived only a short time after leaving UNM, dying suddenly in January 1910. A memorial stone on Hodgin Hall reads, "His monument stands before you."

In spite of the water tanks in the attic and other fire protection measures, Hadley Hall was destroyed by fire on May 23, 1910, three days after the end of the spring semester. The city fire department was called when the fire was discovered but because of the difficulty of getting the trucks up sandy Railroad Avenue, they arrived much too late. Lost in the fire were the irreplaceable geological collection of Dr. Herrick, the botanical collection, and the ethnological museum with many ancient specimens. The entire mineralogy collection—gold and silver ores and specimens from mines throughout the territory that had been exhibited at the St. Louis World Fair—was destroyed. The burning chemicals and numerous explosions made it dangerous to go near the building. After the fire was over, Chemistry Professor John D. Clark raked through the ashes and recovered all but a small amount of platinum, but the gold, silver, and other precious metals had melted into the earth, making that site figuratively the most valuable on campus.

Hadley Hall was replaced within a year by an unattractive one-story masonry and concrete building with a pitched roof, and the campus's adherence to the Pueblo Style was abandoned. Originally called the College of Science and Engineering Building, it housed many other University departments including music, engineering labora-

HADLEY SCIENCE HALL. U.N.M

ERECTED 1889, BURNED 1910

The remains of Hadley Hall after it burned in 1910. It was built in 1899–1900. Hodgin Collection, 000–015–0004, CSWR.

The College of Science and Engineering Building was built to replace Hadley Hall in 1910. It was demolished in 1971 after housing various tenants from science to music. Photograph by Herter-Milner.

In 1956 Professor John Clark reminisced on his seventy-fourth birthday about the early days at UNM. He lived across Railroad Avenue from the campus and his children often played there. He said there was a large open cesspool (located about where the Civil Engineering Building is today), and all the sewage from the campus went into it. "It was covered with a heavy coating of oil and the water in it did not smell very badly, not much, and I remember very well that one time my younger daughter was up there and fell in and my older daughter pulled her out. . . . Mama didn't seem a bit pleased."

---

tories and offices, and some art studios. President E. Dundas McQueen Gray, who succeeded Tight, stated that it had "a good foundation and good walls but no architectural style." He added that he was planning as economically as possible so that when "a uniform architecture is decided upon the building can be remodeled without undue loss." It is said that he preferred a California Mission style with red tile roofs as was being used by the Santa Fe Railroad for its hotels and stations. The College of Science and Engineering Building was never remodeled and remained an eyesore until it was removed in 1971 to make way for Logan Hall, the Psychology Building (34).

President Gray, an Englishman, an Oxford graduate, a distinguished professor and clergyman, attempted to create an "Oxford on the Rio Grande." During his tenure there was little construction activity as he concentrated on improving the academic standards. Gray did not adapt well to the informal ways of the West and was soon asked to resign, to be succeeded by David Ross Boyd in 1912.

The early years of the century had been exciting times for the fledgling University mainly because of the dynamic president, William George Tight. He gave up all thought of research and devoted his heart and soul to building the University. The campus was expanded, new buildings in a unique style were built, and the students were made to feel the campus was their home. Unfortunately for higher education Tight was not allowed to pursue his vision and he did not live to see his dream of a pueblo on the mesa come to fruition—some said he died of a broken heart. Professor John Clark wrote in 1934 that two finer men never lived than President Tight and Professor Hodgin.

The Estufa

This strange looking little building called the Estufa sits between University Boulevard and Redondo Drive on the south side of the Martin Luther King Jr. Avenue (formerly Grand Avenue) entrance to the UNM campus. Most people passing by today have no idea what it is or its history. Spanish-English dictionaries define *estufa* as "stove, steam room, hothouse." Early Spanish settlers in northern New Mexico used the word as an appellation for the Pueblo Indians' kivas since they got so hot and smoke-filled during ceremonials. The UNM Estufa has no windows or other means of ventilation and must get terribly hot on warm days when filled with fraternity brothers.

The Estufa was built by students inspired by President Tight in 1906 or 1908. It is one of two adobe structures on campus, the other being the Naval Sciences Building (151) built as the Co-Op Dormitory in 1941.

President Tight encouraged the building of the Estufa in 1906 or 1908 as a meeting place for a local social fraternity known as the Yum Yum Boys. Several years later, the boys decided to change their title to Alpha Alpha Alpha and became a local Greek fraternity. On May 25, 1915, Alpha Alpha Alpha officially became Pi Kappa Alpha, the first national Greek organization on the UNM campus. Supposedly the Yum Yum Boys were given a ninety-nine-year lease when the Estufa was built, but a search several years ago by University administrators and the fraternity could not find a copy. The Estufa and Hodgin Hall are the oldest buildings on the campus still standing. The Estufa is still used by the Pi Kappa Alpha fraternity.

Former Judge R. F. "Deacon" Arledge, UNM 1930, recalled a fraternity prank during which a ladder from Isleta Pueblo mysteriously disappeared into the Estufa. Suspicious members of the pueblo kept a vigil at the Estufa for several days before giving up. The roof of the Estufa was a common meeting place, and the building was the most popular landmark on the campus before 1920. There was a great rivalry between Pi Kappa Alpha and Sigma Chi when they were the only fraternities on campus, and there were many break-ins at the Estufa by the Sigma Chis. By 1956 an estimated 1,000 men had been initiated in the Estufa.

In June 1958 an explosion occurred when someone lit a match and ignited natural gas that had seeped into the basement from an outside source. After the accident, the basement was filled with dirt. The exterior was painted bright yellow with red Greek letters with donations from local alumni, and a plaque was placed on it.

President Boyd and UNM's Australian Plan

David Ross Boyd, the first president of the University of Oklahoma and the fifth president of the University of New Mexico, was by dictionary definition a "dauntless" man. A native of Ohio (as was his predecessor at UNM, William George Tight), he obtained his undergraduate degree and Ph.D. from Wooster College. He began his career as a schoolteacher and administrator. He was superintendent of schools at Arkansas City, Kansas, when he was selected to become president of the University of Oklahoma. The beginnings of the school in Norman were not unlike those in Albuquerque a few years earlier. When Boyd assumed the presidency in 1892, the first building was under construction on forty acres of donated land.

Boyd took great interest in landscaping the Oklahoma campus. Just south of the university building a nursery of five acres was started and thousands of young trees were planted. The source of the trees was a bankrupt nursery in Kansas from which Boyd bought the entire stock. People did not believe trees could be made to grow in the hard-packed soil and asked for his resignation for wasting state money—until they found out he had used his own money for the purchase. Most of the trees lived.

In January 1903 Oklahoma's newly constructed main building burned down; a new structure replaced it and it too burned in 1907. The next year, in the first elections following statehood, a powerful group of religious conservatives demanded a housecleaning at the university. Boyd was not rehired, and many of the most qualified faculty members' contracts were not renewed for such reasons as smoking, drinking, playing cards, and dancing.

Boyd had long been active in the Presbyterian church and soon found work with the church's Board of Home Missions in New York. However his heart was still with higher education and when the position of president at UNM became vacant with the

David Ross Boyd, president of the University from 1912 to 1919.

The twenty-fifth anniversary of the founding of the University was celebrated on March 2, 1914, with an exercise featuring speeches by Charles E. Hodgin, Elias S. Stover, Bernard S. Rodey, David R. Boyd, and the Reverend A. Toothaker. The University was acknowledged for raising the standards of the elementary and secondary schools in the state.

dismissal of Edward Gray, he dauntlessly sought the job, was appointed, and assumed the presidency on July 1, 1912.

One of the things that interested him most was the architecture of the campus, the Pueblo Style started by Tight. Boyd wrote an interested architect that the regents were thinking about having a competition to select an architect if and when the legislature gave them some money. He also said they were thinking of looking for architects in southern California who they thought had done successful work.

One of Dr. Boyd's closest friends at the University of Oklahoma had been V. L. Parrington, professor of English literature, who was fired in 1908 ostensibly because he smoked too much. Just before the 1908 upheaval he had written a very thoughtful report to the board of regents titled, "On Recent Developments in American College Architecture." Parrington studied the use of Gothic and neoclassic styles and argued the pros and cons of each. He said most eastern schools were not paying much attention to adopting a clearly defined style of architecture. He noted Stanford University where "early Spanish architecture" was used and said he understood a somewhat similar style was being proposed for the University of the Territory of New Mexico. In his conclusion Parrington stated: "If we hope to educate cultivated men and women we shall do well to surround them with those things which will inspire a wish for culture. I hold that it is a social crime, graver still because committed against youth, for any state to educate its young men and women amidst surroundings that are ugly, shoddy, or pretentious."

After Parrington left Oklahoma, he went to the University of Washington where he became a respected teacher, won a Pulitzer prize, and had a building named for him, albeit he said it was the ugliest building on campus.

Boyd wrote Parrington on July 23, 1912, that he thought President Tight's idea of introducing Pueblo Style architecture on the campus was an excellent one but he felt the existing buildings suffered from faulty construction. He thought the style would lend itself to a variety of building types. Boyd wrote to a former University of Oklahoma student, Ralph "Inky" Campbell, then a newspaper reporter:

> The idea of adapting a style of architecture to be entirely different from the usual state university architecture, which has become very monotonous to those who have seen a great deal of it, was the idea of former President W. G. Tight. He was hampered by lack of funds, so that he could not carry out his ideas thoroughly, and as he was not an architect himself, he failed therefore to have the work adapted very well, but he did a splendid thing. The idea of having the grouping of the buildings, the style of architecture and position in the landscape surroundings to represent, as much as possible the historic background of the state, was most commendable, and in a very high degree, successful.

We expect to get an up-to-date landscape architect and town planner to make a plan for the grounds of the University and their surroundings.

Campbell wrote an article for the *Kansas City Star* titled "University Buildings of Adobe, The Oddest in the World Are Those in New Mexico." "New Mexico is rather proud of the uniqueness or originality of its University buildings. Artists, architects and educators arriving at Albuquerque rarely fail to visit the University and inspect the buildings. They are agreed that nothing like them may be found elsewhere in the whole world."

In 1912 the Chicago area was home to many famous and yet-to-become-famous architects, including Louis H. Sullivan, Frank Lloyd Wright, and Walter Burley Griffin. The professional lives of these men were intertwined, beginning in 1887 when Wright went to work for the firm of Adler and Sullivan. Sullivan was the acknowledged leader of the "Chicago school" of architecture at that time. Wright spent five years with Sullivan as a draftsman and then established his own practice in Oak Park, Illinois, in 1893. Sullivan had a great influence on Wright, so much so that Wright referred to him in his writings as "Lieber Meister."

Griffin met Sullivan in 1901, and throughout his life Griffin spoke, lectured, and wrote of Sullivan's teaching and of his debt to this man. While Griffin was a student, many of Sullivan's major works were under construction, including the first section of the famous Carson, Pirie, Scott Department Store.

Griffin attended the University of Illinois where he studied architecture and landscape gardening. Griffin joined Wright's office in Oak Park in 1900 and remained for five years. After he established his own office, besides doing residences and public buildings, he prepared several town plans mostly in the Midwest. He also designed parks and gardens and campus plans for both Eastern and Northern Illinois Normal Schools. When the international competition for the design of the proposed capital of Australia was announced in 1910 Griffin entered it. The announcement that he had won the competition was made on May 23, 1912, and immediately he received a tremendous amount of publicity both in the United States and abroad. This focused attention not only on his work but on the Chicago group as well. An article praising Griffin's work by William G. Purcell appeared in *Western Architect* and it may have been that or a similar article that caught the eye of President Boyd.

Apparently determined to hire the best architect he could find, Boyd visited with Griffin in Chicago and discussed the proposed campus development. Griffin was enthusiastic about the Pueblo Style of architecture and the possibilities of the arrangement of desert vegetation on the campus. He planned to adopt this style for the University work. "Nothing Greek, Roman, Gothic or German about this architecture: nothing but American," wrote a patriotic reporter in the campus newspaper.

In 1915 the regents complained about the extravagant use of coal to heat the buildings: the bill had risen from \$1,106 in 1913 to \$1,740 in 1915.

The University Campus Expands

George L. Brooks was elected president of the Board of Regents in 1913 following the death of G. W. D. Bryan. He operated a large food store, was invested in mining operations, and owned quite a bit of real estate. Brooks had been credited with bringing the Santa Fe Railroad shops to Albuquerque.

Few regents before or since have exhibited their enthusiasm for the position as Brooks did. His ambition was to beautify the campus according to the ideas of President Tight, but he also saw the need to expand the campus. Not only did he serve as regent, he voluntarily and without remuneration became the business manager of the University. Professor John D. Clark quoted Brooks, "I'll attend to the physical plant. Dr. Boyd will run the academic side." Clark said that more and more Brooks took over the operation of the University and Boyd resented it. Brooks gave his personal attention to the campus landscaping. He improved the irrigation system, restoring life to the neglected trees that Tight had planted and allowing for plantings of shrubs, flowers, and more trees. Regent William G. Hayden, paying tribute to Brooks, said that he had been depressed by the appearance of the campus when he first visited it but a few years later, "It looked to me as if a magic hand had touched the picture. The beautiful flowers, grass, trees, and vegetation, the fine buildings on the grounds which met my eye, form a greater monument to his memory than any tribute that can be written."

One of Brooks's first moves was to secure authorization of the board to purchase the land east of the city reservoir known as the Ghost Lands, or Ghost Ranch. When the matter came before the regents at the meeting on August 28, 1913, the faculty strongly opposed spending any money for an enlarged campus "which would never be needed." The eighty-acre ranch included

At the time there were just ninety-nine students enrolled in the University, of whom twenty-one were in the preparatory school and one was a graduate student. New Mexico had just achieved statehood and was spending less on higher education than any of the surrounding states. Legislative appropriation was $45,000 in 1913 plus $6,941 from land income.

Griffin wanted to keep the Chicago office open and maintain his client contracts while he was in Australia, so he asked Francis Barry Byrne, who had been an apprentice draftsman in Wright's studio when Griffin was there, to take over the office while he was away. He assured Boyd that his work in Australia would not interfere with his completing the plan for UNM.

Griffin was informed in March 1913 that construction had started on Canberra, the capital of Australia, but not to his design. A layout of the city had been prepared by a departmental board, which outraged Griffin. In order to keep the project on the right track, he had to spend more time in Australia than he had anticipated. Eventually he opened an office in Sydney.

land east of Girard Boulevard where residences and Jefferson Middle School now stand.

In 1914 Brooks negotiated the purchase of 277 acres just north of the campus, which included twenty-six lots bought from P. F. McCanna. Another forty acres were bought through a surrogate, Ed Ross, who immediately deeded it to the University. With this expansion the Methodist Sanitarium wound up surrounded by University land. After some negotiations, the University bought the sanitarium land.

Brooks also had heard a rumor that acreage in the vicinity of Louisiana Boulevard might soon be irrigated by water from a proposed Cochiti Dam project. Food could be raised there for University tables, Brooks said, so the property was purchased for $3 an acre at 4 percent interest with nothing down and more than thirty years to pay off the principal. Comptroller and later president Tom Popejoy once said that he often looked at the "big"

interest bill of $60 a year in the early 1940s and wondered what good the land would ever be. The answer: the University sold 160 acres to developer Ed Snow for $287,000. Then another 160 acres went to Dale Bellamah for $420,000. A third parcel of 160 acres was part of the Winrock Center lease arrangement.

Other University land purchases followed Brooks's example. The property at Eubank and I-40 was bought for around $10,000 in the 1940s and part of the land the Sigma Chi fraternity had bought from the Albuquerque Country Club was purchased. These early land acquisitions rounded out the campus as we know it today and gave Popejoy enough land to build his golf courses. Not only have the lands proved invaluable in meeting the expansion needs of the University, but the sale of land not contiguous to the campus for several times its purchase price has paid for many campus buildings.

Construction at this time included an addition to the Dining Hall and a girls' gymnasium. Five cottages, each housing four men, were built around Kwataka Hall in 1914, for less than $500 apiece. Nine more were added later, and they proved to be so popular that the regents adopted a policy that future housing needs would be met by building more cottages.

In January 1915, before the beginning of the legislative session, George Brooks, president of the UNM Board of Regents, wrote Governor William C. McDonald requesting funds for the coming year. He made an impassioned plea for $85,000 to replace the old science building, Hadley Hall I, which had burned down in 1910. He noted that other territorial institutions had received money to replace burned buildings but UNM had not. The University had struggled for the intervening years with inadequate teaching facilities for all the sciences. Professor of Chemistry John D. Clark was not at all hesitant in pushing the regents and the administration for a new building.

The next mention of planning activity is contained in letters Boyd wrote in 1915. In one to his friend Dr. Preston W. Search, he said, "We have increased our campus to 400 acres, and are preparing a landscape architecture scheme. We are also preparing to erect an $80,000 laboratory building or buildings. We hope to make something unique out of it. The work will probably be in charge of Walter Burley Griffin."

Then in a letter to James T. Brown of the Beta Theta Pi Club, Boyd stated that he was negotiating with Griffin for a landscape plan: "The plan we propose for our landscape architectural scheme is to be unique, as distinctive as Leland Stanford campus is but different in that it will be based on the lines of the Indian pueblo style combined with the features of the so called 'Mission Architecture.' We will also introduce features adapted from the history and development peculiar to the region."

President Boyd, in an undated letter to Francis Barry Byrne written while Griffin was in Australia, noted that the legislature had "made provision" for $80,000 for a science building. He wrote that it was very important to prepare a landscape architecture scheme before proceeding with planning the building. He told Byrne that Regent Brooks wanted Griffin to revisit the campus when next in this country. Brooks inserted himself more and more into the planning process and several letters passed among the three men.

In August 1915 Griffin submitted his "nucleus plan," which he prepared in his Sydney office. He described the plan: "You can see that . . . the general scheme is a compact, continuous pueblo, to afford a maximum of shelter, convenience and coziness. The whole group is low-lying (1 and 2 stories) with economical plain masses, even permitting use of adobe if necessary . . . and all dominated by a lofty pyramidal central structure and rendered attractive by a wide variation of correlated courts and axial vistas." Griffin drew two diagonal sections through the plan to explain it and show the style of architecture he was proposing.

The buildings were not in the Pueblo Style as Boyd had wished, but what might be a style influenced by both Mayan architecture and the Prairie School even though Griffin, in his correspondence, described his design of the Science Building as of the "pueblo type." The connecting loggias between the buildings are very reminiscent of some of Frank Lloyd Wright's designs. The tower atop the library gives the whole scheme a special feeling. There is no correspondence in the University Archives relating to this plan and there is nothing in the minutes of the regents meetings to indicate that it was ever presented to them for approval. It is possible Griffin sent the original drawing of his "nucleus plan" directly to Byrne to make prints and forward to Brooks. Since Byrne was working on his own plan, he may not have ever sent Griffin's plan to the University.

On November 17, 1915, Brooks again wrote Griffin saying he could not wait any longer for the plans of the science building and would contact Byrne. On the same day, he wrote Byrne asking for his ideas on the building. Griffin finished his design on December 14 and sent it to Byrne, who had already submitted his own design.

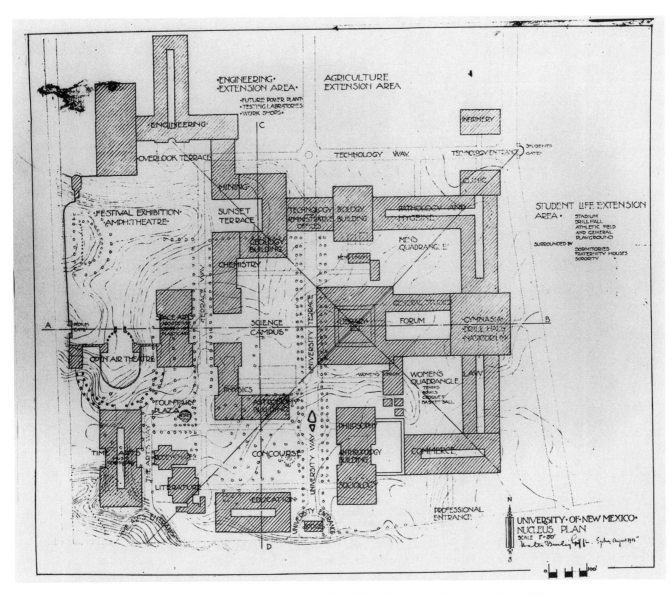

Walter Burley Griffin's "nucleus plan" was drawn in his office in Sydney, Australia. Avery Library, Columbia University in the City of New York.

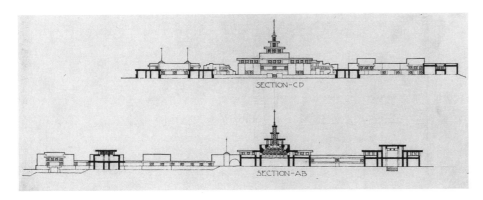

Section through the plan shows the Maya influence on Walter Burley Griffin's design. The library with the tower was the focal point of the plan. Avery Library, Columbia University in the City of New York.

Griffin's design for the science building prepared in his Sydney office. Avery Architectural and Fine Arts Library, Columbia University in the City of New York.

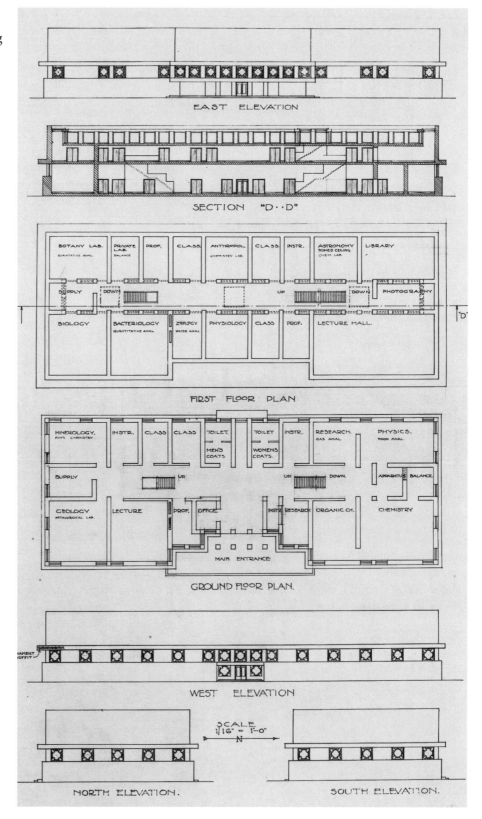

On December 20, 1915, Boyd submitted the proposal of the firm of Griffin and Byrne, prepared by Byrne, to prepare "plans for the laying out of the University grounds and campus," covering approximately 320 acres. They were also to do plans and specifications for a science building estimated to cost $80,000 and another building, the purpose of which was not designated, to cost not more than $80,000. The regents approved the contract, which was signed on January 5, 1916. Byrne signed as "attorney in fact" for Griffin.

When Griffin found out what had happened he was furious. In March he sent a copy of his design for the science building directly to Brooks. He tried to find someone else to take over the Chicago office from Byrne but was unsuccessful.

Byrne immediately began work on a Building Location Plan, which he mailed to G. L. Brooks on June 27, 1916. There is no known copy of this plan.

Byrne's plan went through several revisions before it was finally completed in February 1918. The main entrance to the campus was to be centered on Grand Avenue to the west. There is an entrance court with what may be a fountain in the center with a low physics building on the east interrupting the axis that is centered on the massive library-auditorium, which served as a dominant center with "an elastic arrangement of study groups in adjacent or continuous buildings." Colonnades provided covered connecting ways between the study groups.

There is a small building, noted as the School of Medicine, in the science area. The relationship of buildings shown on Griffin's plan is almost totally changed. The buildings are still grouped around quadrangles but, significantly, the existing buildings, Hodgin and Rodey Halls, are left outside the confines of the new campus. The football stadium is moved to the north part of the campus. Terraces on the west break the slope of the land down to Plum Street (University Boulevard). The reservoir is left in place and to the east of it Byrne showed student housing. He noted that the reservoir would soon be removed from the campus. There is a proposed lake surrounded by landscaping and, for the first time in University planning, spaces for parking.

There is some confusion as to what transpired immediately after the contract was signed. The working drawings that Byrne produced, dated April 15, 1916, were for a smaller chemistry building and a science building. A local architect, J. S. LaDriere, was appointed supervisor of the work. Bids were received on July 10 for the Chemistry Building only. The contract was awarded to the lowest bidder, Campbell Brothers. Not until the regents meeting on December 11, 1916, was LaDrier authorized to advertise for bids for the science building. Bids were received on March 12, 1917, and on March 21 all the bids were rejected. This was the last mention of the science building in the minutes of the board meetings, and it was not built.

In 1960 architectural historian H. Allen Brooks wrote in *New Mexico Architecture,* "We may regret that Griffin's project gave way to a less ambitious scheme for, in spite of a certain stiffness of composition, this admirable design would have been an impressive addition to the campus."

In 1936 Professor Clark wrote that in the early days of the University there was no place east of Broadway to buy anything, so in 1915 an enterprising student, Earl Gerhardt, received permission to establish a store in one of the cottages near Kwataka Hall. He named it Earl's Grotto, and it became the place where students could buy candy and soda pop, and play cards. Clark said tobacco, forbidden on campus, was bootlegged there. Eventually the store was taken over by the University and named Varsity Store.

The campus plan by Francis Barry Byrne. Byrne kept some of Walter Burley Griffin's ideas but he showed a domed auditorium with the library to make a more dominant building. Courtesy of Bart Prince.

One of the most important events of the era was the extension of street car service to the campus. M. P. Stamm and the University Heights Development Company offered a bonus to the City Electric Company, which owned the street car system, for such an extension. The University agreed to buy 2,500 special transportation tickets for $2,000 and to remove the "hump" in Central Avenue. The "hump," in front of Presbyterian Sanitarium, was several feet high, steeper than the cars could climb. Twelve-minute service was started on July 22, 1916, with Professor Charles Hodgin driving the first car to the campus from First Street and Central Avenue. Before that, the University had provided horse-drawn carriages from the railroad depot to the campus.

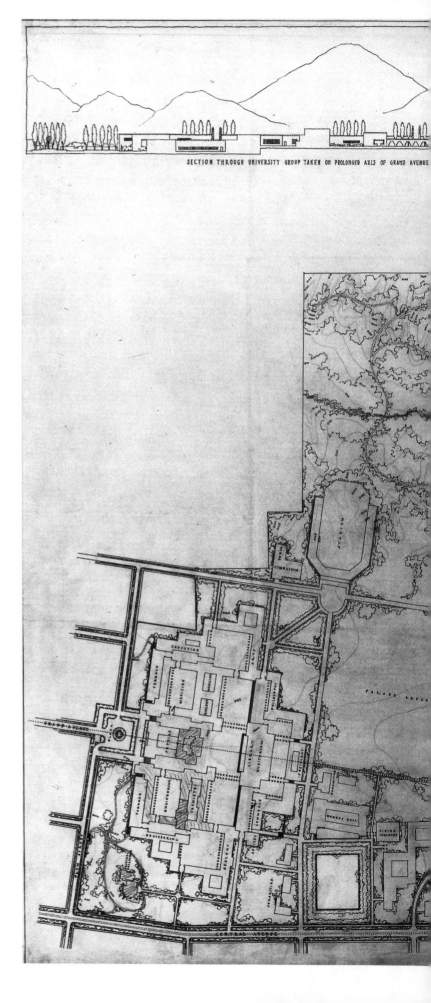

SECTION THROUGH UNIVERSITY GROUP TAKEN ON PROLONGED AXIS OF GRAND AVENUE

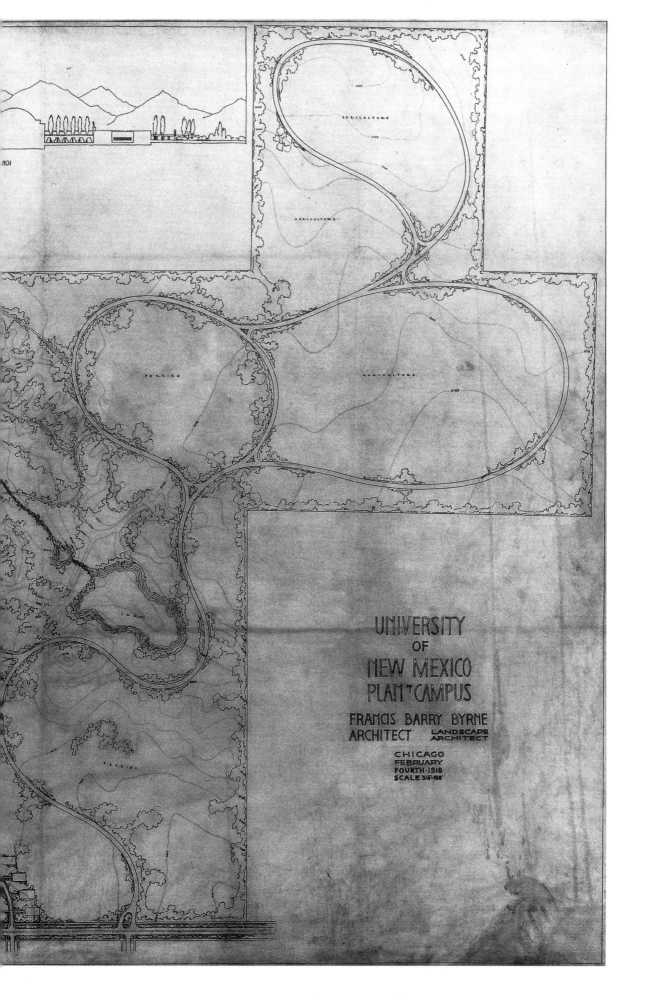

UNIVERSITY
OF
NEW MEXICO
PLAN of CAMPUS

FRANCIS BARRY BYRNE
ARCHITECT   LANDSCAPE
              ARCHITECT

CHICAGO
FEBRUARY
FOURTH·1918
SCALE 3/4·100'

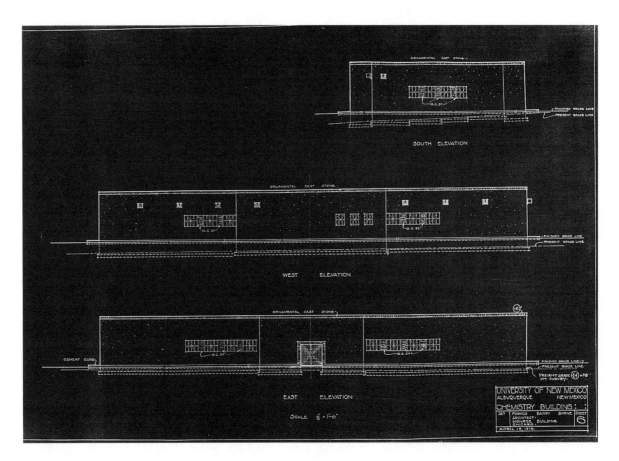

Drawings by
Francis Barry
Byrne for the
Chemistry
Building, which
was built in 1917.

The Chemistry Building (2), designed by Byrne, was a single-story structure with four windows on each side of the front entrance separated by spaces a few of which have terracotta reliefs depicting some of the sciences. These were added later by Professor Clark. An ornamental cast-stone coping at the top of the wall is shown on the drawings but for some reason, probably financial, was not done. There is an ornamental iron gate at the entrance. An open entry leads to a patio in the center into which open all the laboratories and classrooms. According to Dr. Clark, the patio was to be used for experiments that produced noxious fumes. The building is very simple in design and has been said to reflect the influence the southern California architect Irving Gill had on Byrne when he visited there before going back to Chicago in 1913–14.

Brooks said the Chemistry Building was "virtually a new conception." The feeling of pre-Columbian architecture is no longer preserved and except for a vague relationship to a pueblo, the design is free from historical precedent.

When the new Electrical and Computer Engineering–Centennial Library Building (46) was designed in the 1980s, I was determined that Byrne's Chemistry Building should be saved, so the new buildings were designed to fit around it and it was

It is not clear when the original round pool in front of the Main Building was built or when it was removed. It was a focal point of student activity for many years. Albuquerque Museum Photo Archives.

made into a classroom facility. As the remodeling work began, it was found to be a very poorly constructed building that required much stabilization to meet current building and seismic codes. The renovation cost much more than had been originally estimated. The building has been designated a Historic Landmark by the City of Albuquerque and has been placed on the State Register of Cultural Properties.

On April 6, 1917, Congress declared war on Germany and its allies. Most of the men on the campus enlisted immediately and University life was totally disrupted. That summer the Board of Regents leased land east of the reservoir for a mobilization training camp for the 1,500 members of Battery A of the New Mexico National Guard. It was named Camp Funston for General Frederick Funston, the controversial hero of the Philippine campaign of the Spanish-American War. Twelve frame buildings with pitched shingle roofs were built as barracks for the enlisted men; the site also included a Red Cross hospital, a mess hall, a YMCA building, and some horse stables. The officers lived in Kwataka Hall. After the National Guard was called up, the barracks housed men enlisted in the Student Army Training Corps (SATC). The camp was decommissioned in December 1918 after the war ended and the SATC was disbanded. UNM inherited the camp water system, which enabled the University to begin another extensive campus landscaping program.

When the war ended on November 11, 1918, and University life more or less returned to normal, the planning done during the war seems to have been abandoned. I have found nothing in the University records to indicate how the money appropri-

Soldiers from Camp Funston enrolled in the Student Army Training Corps stand in front of Hodgin Hall on a sunny morning in early September 1918. Bugler Herbert C. Stacher is the soldier standing on the left with his arm raised.

The Chemistry Building in 1920.

A laboratory in the
Chemistry
Building, circa
1920.

The first campus telephone system was installed in 1915, with an instrument in each dormitory, the Dining Hall, offices, public reception rooms, and the residence of the superintendent of buildings and grounds.

ated for the science building was used or if the University actually received it. In the 1920s, when some new buildings were located, no attention seems to have been paid to the Griffin-Byrne plans except for Hadley Hall II, which was positioned to form part of a future quadrangle. Professor Clark wrote President David Spence Hill that he had a copy of a plan hanging on the wall of his office, done by a Chicago architect, which showed an enlarged Chemistry Building and he wanted that addition.

President Boyd, deciding he had had enough of the unrelenting battle for funds for the school and interference from Brooks, resigned in 1919. Professor Clark in 1958 wrote that Boyd was well-to-do and over sixty. "One day he came to my office, pulled out two cigars and told me he was going to resign. He said, 'If I were younger I'd not put up with this (meaning Brooks's interference), but I don't need the job and I'll resign.'" He tendered his resignation to the Board of Regents on May 22, 1919, asking to be relieved of duty on July 1. Brooks resigned from the board about a week later. Both men, in their own way, had made invaluable contributions to the University through some very troubled times.

Dr. David Spence Hill was appointed president after Dr. Boyd resigned. Hill had taught at several universities and at the time of his appointment was a faculty member of the Department of Education at the University of Illinois.

Walter Burley Griffin remained in Australia and established himself as the best-known architect in the country. He received several commissions in southeast Asia and was killed when some scaffolding collapsed while he was inspecting one of his projects in India. Francis Barry Byrne carried on his practice of architecture in Chicago until he died in 1963.

In June 1919 bids were opened for construction of a mechanics arts building. The building contained space for the Civil Engineering and Practical Mechanics Departments, some elements of the electrical engineering program, the Department of Mathematics, a pattern shop, mechanical drawing room, and a machine shop. The library would move into space vacated by these functions. Arno K. Leupold, who was on the faculty, drew the plans, wrote the specifications, and supervised construction.

The building was sited due west of the Chemistry Building and due north of Rodey Hall. The location was determined by the Griffin-Byrne plans so that it would form the western annex to the engineering building shown on those plans.

The Not-So-Roaring Twenties

The 1920s were a period of fast enrollment growth but little building and planning, except for a new library, until 1927–28 when four major buildings were constructed. Enrollment in the fall semester 1920 was only 227, which quadrupled to almost 1,000 in the fall of 1929. President Hill, hampered by lack of funding, particularly in the early 1920s, managed to strengthen the faculty, emphasize the college program and graduate and research work, and greatly improve the library. In 1922 the University was accredited by the Commission on Higher Education of the North Central Association. However, much of the time Hill was at odds with the faculty, the public, and some of the regents.

The meeting of the Board of Regents, on January 26, 1920, began with an inspection of some campus facilities. Included were the Chemistry Building (2), biology laboratories, the state health laboratories, two rooms occupied by the Home Economics Department, and the new Practical Mechanics Building. The latter building had many other names: the Engineering Building, Mechanical Arts, Practical Mechanics, and finally Hadley Hall II. It is now part of the Civil Engineering Research Laboratory (106).

The Engineering Building, built in 1920, was named Hadley Hall, replacing the name of the first Hadley Hall that burned in 1910.

J. A. Reidy, secretary-treasurer of the board, reported that in order to pay $9,177 due the contractor, he and the president of the board, Nathan Jaffa, had secured a loan from the State National Bank at 8.0 percent interest. It was not uncommon in the early days of the University for the regents to borrow money personally to meet obligations of the school. In all cases they were eventually repaid.

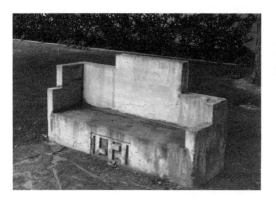

The very uncomfortable memorial concrete bench built by the senior class of 1921.

In 1920 an inventory of University property prepared for the Bureau of Education of the Department of the Interior for the fiscal year ending June 30, 1920, listed the following:

Value of library, scientific equipment, machinery, and furniture	$60,520.47
Value of grounds	$40,000.00
Value of buildings (including dormitories)	$283,879.58
Total value of buildings and grounds	$384,400.05

In 1919 President Hill had formed a committee composed of George A. Kaseman, A. B. McMillan, Frank Hubbell, Horace B. Hening, and M. L. Fox to consider an urgent need: the young women students were limited in the study of home economics by the lack of space and poor equipment in the basement of the Administration Building. The committee began to plan a building for home economics instruction. Their appeal to the Albuquerque Chamber of Commerce met with such approval that the fund-raising was placed in the hands of forty prominent men. They were given a tour of the campus, some seeing it for the first time, and served a turkey dinner with all the trimmings in the Dining Hall.

President Hill announced at the January 1920 regents meeting that more than $10,000 had been pledged. The executive committee of the board and the president were authorized to proceed with employment of an architect, preparation of plans, receipt of bids, and construction of the building. (From about 1912 until the early 1930s, most matters concerning building and planning were referred to an executive committee composed of the officers of the Board of Regents. Sometimes, as in this case, the committee was empowered to make final decisions of which the full board would be informed later.)

In February 1922, the building that housed the library at the New Mexico Normal School (later Highlands University) at Las Vegas burned to the ground. This prompted President Hill to declare the UNM library space in the Administration Building a firetrap and to prohibit smoking in it.

Arno K. Leupold, a member of the faculty who had some knowledge of drafting, was appointed to draw the plans and write the specifications. There was considerable delay in agreeing on a site, but finally Leupold was able to present his plans on April 24, 1920. Bids were opened on June 28 and the executive committee accepted the bid of E. J. Marchant. Leupold left the University at the end of June after receiving $400 for his drawings, and architect E. B. Cristy was given a contract to carry the project through to completion.

A dedication ceremony was held at the building on Mother's Day 1921 for all the 100 or so donors. A copper box containing their names and newspaper clippings was placed in a niche in the wall and covered with a bronze plaque. When the College of Education Complex was built in the early 1960s, the plaque was re-

Sara Raynolds Hall under construction. It is one of the few brick bearing wall buildings on the campus.

Sara Raynolds Hall a few years after completion. It was named for the mother of Joshua Raynolds, an Albuquerque banker who contributed funds for equipping the building. Photograph by L. J. Waterhouse.

This fearsome World War I artillery piece greeted campus visitors for several years.

moved and placed on the wall of a patio on the north side of the Home Economics Building (66).

At the dedication the Albuquerque Indian School band provided music and several people made speeches. Mrs. Robert F. Asplund, a member of the Board of Regents, officially accepted the building on behalf of the state. After the benediction, the building was opened to the visitors and refreshments were served by the home economics students. One account says a baseball game was played between teams of the Kiwanis and Rotary clubs.

The two main contributors to Sara Raynolds Hall were George A. Kaseman and Joshua Raynolds, who gave money for equipment in honor of his mother, Sara Raynolds. Frank Mindlin gave a silver tea service and two silver candlestick holders, and Arthur Prager gave a Hoover vacuum cleaner and an electric range.

A statement was presented to Governor Octaviano Larrazolo by the regents on December 1, 1920, that set forth needs for buildings and improvements and pointed out that the age of the buildings was contributing to the increased cost of maintenance and repair. The boiler house needed new equipment. The low-pressure boilers then in use were secondhand units that were serving three more buildings than intended. The statement continued: "The present dining hall is a temporary device which cannot last indefinitely. In accordance with practice of the best institutions, the students—men and women, need a suitable place for social life under controlled, supervised conditions—a Recreation Hall."

Librarian Wilma Shelton had fond memories of the old Dining Hall: "I became Counselor for University Women and lived in old Hokona Hall, the girls' dormitory, and ate at the students' dining hall, of which Elizabeth Simpson had supervision while also serving as chairman of the Home Economics Department. Separate tables were reserved for faculty. As we gathered around these tables where we felt the best and cheapest food in town was served, our hearty appetites were satisfied, and lots of social chitchat and banter indulged in."

Other requested projects included a men's dormitory with forty-two rooms and a women's residence hall of about the same size, a small women's gymnasium, and a larger men's gym. In addition, money was requested to purchase equipment for Hadley Hall II. An appeal was made for an added wing to the Chemistry Building (2) for more chemistry and biology laboratories. The final request was for a library to house the 39,000 bound volumes and 11,000 pamphlets, the most valuable collection in the state, then housed in the Administration Building, which was not a fire-resistant structure. The proposed building would have a war memorial hall containing mementos and trophies and an auditorium that would be used by students and citizens of the whole state. The total price tag for these projects came to $331,500. Certainly they were all needed and would have made a great difference in the physical plant of the

The regents authorized plans to be drawn for a men's dormitory but later changed their minds and told architects Trost and Trost to design another addition to Hokona Hall, the women's dormitory, instead. The contract was let to A. S. Hall and Son for $18,610 and was increased to $19,056.70 by a bonus allowed for early completion. The addition, opened in September 1923, was sometimes called Central Hall.

A large illuminated U was erected on top of the Administration Building at the request of President Hill. Note that parking was no problem.

University, but the chance of getting them funded by the state was almost nil. What was built during the decade was funded mostly by University bond issues.

Six thousand dollars was appropriated by the regents in July 1921 for an addition of sixteen rooms to Hokona Hall. The plans had been done by Trost and Trost, architects from El Paso with an Albuquerque office in the Commerce Building at Gold Avenue and Fourth Street. Bids were opened on August 26 and all bids were rejected. A meeting was called with E. J. Marchant, the low bidder, E. B. Cristy, and President Hill. They were able to make adjustments to the contract documents, which lowered the bid to an acceptable figure. What resulted was a much skinned-down building omitting exterior buttresses, between-floor insulation, plaster and other finishes, and the contractor's bond. The board's executive committee approved a contract immediately. The construction funds came from invested permanent fund income. The construction went smoothly and the addition was accepted as complete on January 10, 1922.

In the 1920s the firm of Trost and Trost was designing most of the major buildings in New Mexico. Adolphus Gustaphus Trost and his brother, Henry Charles Trost, began their practice in the early 1900s and became the largest firm in the Southwest. In Albuquerque they were architects for many buildings including the Franciscan Hotel, the Sunshine Building, the First National Bank, the Occidental Building, and a building for Albuquerque High School. They maintained an office in Albuquerque until around 1933 mostly for construction administration. Engineer George Williamson was an associate until he opened his own office in 1924. He later recruited William Miles Brittelle Sr. as architect-designer. Brittelle was associated with Trost and Trost in 1931–32 and then established a partnership with John Ginner. All these firms did projects for the University at different times.

The thirteen wood-frame cottages erected around Kwataka Hall between 1914 and 1916 were still in use in 1923. They each had a study room and two open-air sleeping porches. The cottages had steam heat and electricity and were furnished with beds, tables, and chairs. I presume the students used the plumbing in Kwataka. Only five cottages were being used for housing in 1923; the Varsity Shop (the student store), student publications, and a laundry occupied others. Many of the cottages were in poor condition and all of them were removed in the late 1920s.

When the board met on April 5, 1924, Regent A. A. Sedillo moved to build the first unit of a new library, as suggested by librarian Wilma Shelton. The matter was referred to the executive committee to select an architect and obtain plans and specifications. The regents were able to identify sufficient funds to authorize the construction; they also began an effort to raise $10,000 from private donations. They asked interested architects to submit free sketches in the "Indian Style," however that might be interpreted. The regents examined the submittals on July 26, 1924, by Trost and Trost, Gaastra and Gladding, and Elson H. Norris with Angelo Zucco as the structural engineer. They chose Norris and instructed him to prepare drawings and specifications and to ask for bids with alternates for complete construction or exterior completion only. Final plans were approved on August 30 and bids requested on September 15, 1924. The contractor was E.J. Marchant. A ground-breaking ceremony was held on September 27. Librarian Shelton, who had worked hard to obtain the building, turned the first shovel of earth.

Governor Arthur T. Hannett visited the University on January 13, 1925, and had lunch with the top administrators and some of the regents. He was buttonholed by Regent Charles Lembke who told him, "We have outgrown our accommodations. We should either close up or get accommodations sufficient to take care of the increased enrollment and wider scope of work done." He said the University wanted a gymnasium and more dormitories and would ask for an $833,000 bond issue to fund them. Lembke must not have impressed the governor because Hannett later said he did not favor erecting new buildings at any of the educational institutions.

The retirement of Charles E. Hodgin, dean of the College of Education and vice president of the University, was announced on June 6, 1925. He had been with UNM twenty-eight years.

Two antenna towers and the radio station buildings were in place when Carlisle Gymnasium was planned to go next to them. The towers were being removed when this picture was taken.

UNM on the Wireless Waves

Radio broadcasting began on the campus of the University of New Mexico shortly after the end of World War I when, with the help of a grant of $500 from Mrs. Jacob Korber and A. P. Korber and an anonymous gift of the same amount, surplus "wireless telegraph and telephone" equipment was bought from the U.S. Merchant Marine and the Westinghouse Corporation at large discounts. The station was named for Mrs. Korber's husband and for as many years as it remained on the campus it was referred to as the Korber Radio Station. Professor Charles E. Carey of the Engineering Department was in charge of buying the equipment and setting up the station. The newspaper article that told of this endeavor said the equipment he purchased was capable of

sending messages up to 1,000 miles and receiving signals from as far away as Washington, D.C.

By October 1921 the equipment was in hand and construction was started by students on two steel towers seventy-two feet high to carry a 200-foot antenna. The station began broadcasting on December 16, 1921, with weather reports from the weather station on the campus that had been established by the Albuquerque Chamber of Commerce in 1918. It was located in an office in the 1910 Science Building (1) until 1924. Curious people came from all over the city to listen to music from Denver and other places. There were concerts of music each Sunday in Rodey Hall from broadcasts received at the station. One listener was quoted as saying the music was clear and had lost nothing on its long journey on "wireless waves."

The station, with the call letters RYU, was being operated in 1923 by Wiley M. Price and Professor E. S. Donnell. The first broadcast of a Lobo football game was made in November of that year. A little later the call letters were changed to KFLR. In 1924 donations were received for the construction of two thirty-by-twenty-foot frame buildings, one to house the studio and the other the transmitting and receiving equipment. The buildings were designed by Professor Donnell. (Carlisle Gymnasium was built just south of these buildings in 1928–29 and they were incorporated into the gym on the northwest corner. The University printing plant and press occupied them for several years and later Veterans Affairs was housed there. A large decorative door was installed to allow pieces of printing equipment to be moved in and out; that door is now in the Department of Facilities Planning Building [224].)

Shortly after Carlisle Gymnasium was built, the station and the towers were moved to a location on Buena Vista Southeast, nine blocks south of the campus, on land leased from Albuquerque Public Schools. The University operated the station for a few years before it went off the air in the mid-1950s.

In 1959 a campus radio station began broadcasting from the basement of the New Mexico Union via telephone lines to very low-power transmitters in dormitories and fraternity and sorority houses. Later the regents approved the establishment of station KUNM, which used the studios in the Union basement until Oñate Hall was converted from a dormitory to offices and the studios moved there. When the transmitter and antenna were placed on Sandia Crest, signals were sent there from a large dish antenna.

The University teamed with Albuquerque Public Schools to apply for a license for an educational television station in 1951, but lack of funding prevented any progress. President Popejoy announced in February 1957 receipt of a grant from the Ford Foundation for television programming. In November 1957 negotiations were completed with KOB-TV to buy its old transmitter. The University applied for an educational station license and received the call letters KNME-TV, the acronym for New Mexico Educational Television.

The first KNME studio was in the Speech Communication Department at Roma and Buena Vista (20). In 1968 APS gave the University sixty-five acres on the South Campus, valued at $10,000 an acre, for its share of the cost of a new studio building and equipment. A site was selected on University Boulevard north of the Physical Plant Department. The building was set on the highest part of the site next to the flood control channel in order to get a clear line of sight to the transmitter on the crest. The architects, Neuner and Cabiness, were selected by APS; Bradbury and Stamm were the builders.

Not too long after completion of the KNME-TV transmitter facility on Sandia Crest, my office received a call saying male mountain sheep were butting the building. We found the sheep were able to walk along the narrow ledge on the west side and could see their reflection in the window in front of the receiving antenna focused on the studio relay transmitter on campus. The male sheep, thinking another ram was intruding on their domain, could not reach the glass so they butted their heads against the southwest corner of the building causing considerable damage to the steel siding. There was no reason to keep the glass window since the transmission could be received through a piece of plywood. Once the glass was replaced the butting stopped.

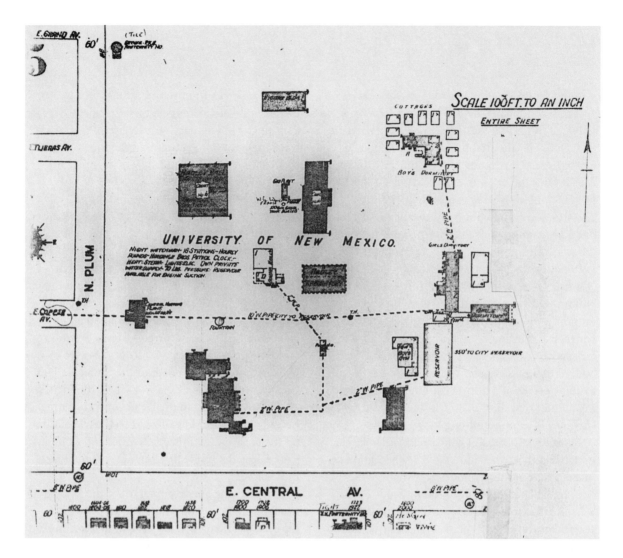

A 1924 insurance map.

A matter of considerable importance to the University was the discovery of oil on its trust lands in 1924, when Illinois Producers Oil Company brought in two wells fourteen miles east of Artesia. Other institutions were eager to share the royalties UNM was receiving. During the legislative sessions of 1924 and 1925 efforts were made to pool the trust lands of all the universities. Regents President Jaffa said, "This land was given the University by Congress and there is no justice in the state taking it away." The idea did not die easily. Congress was petitioned and permission was granted for the state to vote on a constitutional amendment that would divide the income from oil royalties among all the institutions. The University led a campaign against it. The amendment was defeated 23,528 to 18,334. After the vote the regents resumed planning and bidding on several projects, including the library furnishings, the radio station, a new dining hall, and the dormitories.

On January 31, 1928, the New Mexico Supreme Court ruled that the University must put the income from oil royalties into a permanent fund and use only the interest.

The first University library building (105) faced toward the campus. Architect: Elson Norris. Photograph by Milner Studio.

The main reading room was well lit with the large windows during the day, but the light fixtures were less than adequate. Ladd Collection, 000–003–0066, CSWR.

The successful bidder for construction of the library, contractor E. J. Marchant, and architect Norris were arguing about construction procedures and it must have reached a crisis when Marchant called President Hill at ten o'clock at night wanting to talk about it. Hill refused to talk and problems with the project continued. Hill began to take a personal interest in the library construction and stopped by the site almost daily. He worried about small cracks in the concrete floors and employed a civil engineer to investigate the structure. The engineer, J. F. Brozo, assured him there was no problem. Nevertheless Hill

Early Football Fields

Football began to be played at UNM sometime around the turn of the century. The first games were played mainly with high school teams and attracted few spectators to a field west of Old Town or the Barelas baseball field. Records of the earliest games were either not kept or were lost. John D. Clark said that in 1907 he was put on the athletic council and it was the custom to play a game on the spur of the moment when another school issued a challenge. He arranged the first regular schedule and the first game with the University of Arizona.

The 1908 campus plan, "The Varsity to Be," showed an athletic field about where Carlisle Gymnasium is today. In 1915 President Boyd was able to get a small wood-frame pitched-roof field house built near the city reservoir. It contained shower and locker rooms and served for all athletic events.

In 1918 a new athletic field was built northwest of the reservoir, which included a quarter-mile cinder running track and football and baseball fields. The field house was moved to a site nearer the field and was used until the football stadium was built in the 1930s. The field was pure sand and gravel, and it was the custom for people to drive their automobiles to the edge of the playing field to watch the game in comfort.

During the football season of 1921 a group of students decided to build some wooden bleachers at the field; they got contributions of money and material from local businesses and fans. By November they had enough lumber for the project and the approval of the administration. A holiday was declared on the fifteenth. All the male students began the construction work and women students prepared lunch. Two sections were finished the first day and all six sections were done in three days.

In 1926 the football field was resurfaced with "drift dirt" and silt from arroyo bottoms. (A mixture of sawdust and sand had been considered.) The ground was harrowed to replace the rocky surface, which took a heavy toll in injuries and ruined equipment.

Mr. and Mrs. Henry Long donated 100 poplar trees to border the streets and the football field to commemorate their four children who had graduated from UNM and the 1927 football team. Some of the trees lasted until the early 1950s.

In 1928 the Athletic Department had enough money to plow and plant a Russian rye grass turf. It was top irrigated until high enough for flooding. A new playing surface was installed with the building of the stadium in the early 1930s. There is a story that Clyde Tingley, who was a friend of Roy Johnson, arranged to have an unmetered water line run to the football field from a water main that was being laid in Central Avenue so Johnson could plant the grass. It was not discovered until years later when the University then had sufficient water for irrigation.

(Opposite, top) The sand and gravel football field was located north of the city reservoir in the early 1920s. A grass playing surface was planted in 1928.

(Opposite, bottom) Men students were let out of class to build wood seating at the football field while home economics students prepared lunch.

convinced the regents to approve adding more steel beams to the stack area floor. When I saw the beams, uncovered during the 1984–85 remodeling, the flanges were only inches apart. They could probably have held up a steam locomotive.

Norris approved final payment to the contractor in November 1925 but Hill objected because he felt the floors were still not all right. They agreed to withhold $2,000. After the floors were accepted Hill mailed Marchant a check for the amount due and

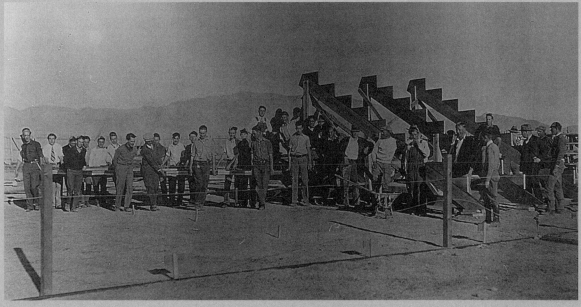

then a citizen complained that the window putty was not done properly. Hill stopped payment on the check and then held back $250. A year later he found bubbles in the linoleum floor covering and the window putty had not been redone to his liking so he kept the $250.

President Hill presented his capital outlay proposals to the regents on October 1, 1925. They included a combination auditorium and gymnasium, a dining hall, three

This is probably the first aerial photograph of the campus. When it was made in the early 1920s, only a few residences were on the south side of Central Avenue. The city reservoir is in the foreground with the tree-laden campus beyond. Hodgin Collection, 000–015–0002, CSWR.

The plan for Reservoir Park, later named Yale Park, from Yale to Cornell and north to the athletic fields was approved by the regents on April 13, 1928, and Hodgin Grove was located in it. The city was given permission to beautify the park at no cost to the University and use it as a public park until such time as the University had need of the land.

dormitory units, an addition to the Chemistry Building (2), and some "minor" buildings, all totaling $300,000. Other projects included building a retaining wall on Central Avenue, insulating steam lines, and purchasing equipment for the library and engineering laboratories. He proposed a University bond issue to fund the projects. Hill said the money for the library construction came from timber sales, land income, fees, and gifts, and the estimated value of the University physical plant was $847,000.

In early May the library was accepted. Wilma Shelton organized moving the material into the new building on the afternoon of May 17, 1926, and for the first time there was a real University library. Dorothy Hughes wrote, "With appropriate ceremony, the faculty, students, and campus force carried the books from the outgrown corner of the old Administration Building to the new building, the library being open for business as usual the next morning." They moved 57,000 volumes including 30,000 bound books and other items. Pine tables and chairs were used until the University could afford better.

The first meeting of the Board of Regents in 1927 was on January 18 with three new members. Mrs. Reed Holloman of Santa Fe was elected president, the first woman to serve in that position. She was elected president each of the four years she served on the board. She was the wife of Judge Reed Holloman of the First State Judicial District. Mrs. Laurence F. Lee was elected vice president and John F. Simms was made secretary-treasurer.

There was so much opposition to President Hill that several people had asked the governor to appoint a new president and Board of Regents. At a regents meeting Hill protested what he called the continuing unsatisfactory services of Professors Clark and Mitchell. Eventually an agreement was signed with Hill to not seek reappointment and to take a leave of absence until the end of his contract on September 1, 1927.

The open mesa east of the City Reservoir was used as a landing strip for airplanes in the early 1920s. Cobb Collection, 988–024–0001, CSWR.

Professor James Fulton Zimmerman was appointed acting president on February 15, 1927. In March he was offered the presidency beginning in September. When he became president the University seemed to take on a new life. Throughout his seventeen-year administration he paid much attention to the building program and the total development of the University.

On March 14 the board approved issuance of building and improvement bonds for a gymnasium, a lecture hall, an extension to Kwataka Hall, and biology and administration buildings. Architects were asked to present sketches for those projects. It was the practice in those days for the regents to request schematic drawings free of charge with only the chosen architect being compensated. Architects Gaastra, Gladding, and Johnson; Norris and Brozo; and George Williamson offered sketches for the projects at the meeting on April 1, 1927. Action was deferred, but the Gaastra firm was later selected to design the four buildings.

Gaastra, Gladding, and Johnson presented final plans for a gymnasium, lecture hall, men's dormitory, and biology building on August 2, 1927. They were all done in the Pueblo Style and were approved by the Board of Regents "to conform to the design of older buildings." There is no record of the board at that time making a formal statement establishing the style of architecture to be used on the campus, but the regents' actions reestablished, with no elaboration, the style initiated by President Tight. The dormitory, later named Yatoka Hall, and the Science Lecture Hall

In 1926 the regents offered the city land for an airstrip. Private planes often used what is now the playing fields, but in 1927 the regents denied a formal request from H. C. Baker and Jerry Phillips to use the area for an airstrip and canceled the earlier offer to the city. In 1928 they agreed to work with the Chamber of Commerce to find space for an airstrip for mail planes.

The Pi Kappa Alpha fraternity house sat just east of University Boulevard and south of Roma. It was bought by the University and demolished because it had fallen into disrepair.

were approved as presented, but the gymnasium and the biology building had to be revised to keep within the budget.

In November 1927 the regents entered into a contract with E. J. Marchant to construct a biology building and named it Parsons Hall (3) in honor of Josephine S. Parsons, who had served in many capacities, including head of the Commercial Department.

The first regents meeting in 1928 was on January 12. They approved, on the recommendation of Major Carrithers, executive assistant to the president, moving the sundial, the howitzer, and the drinking fountain to make way for a walkway leading to the Administration Building from Sara Raynolds Hall.

The board approved a proposal to make land available to lease to fraternities and sororities. Zimmerman was responsible for approving the sites. He approved the location for the Sigma Chi fraternity; the lot was to be leased for one dollar per year.

President James F. Zimmerman was inaugurated on June 4, 1928, at the spring semester commencement. The ceremony took place at the Estufa. Chiefs from five Indian pueblos shared a peace pipe with the new president. Governor R. C. Dillon and Albuquerque Mayor Clyde Tingley were in attendance.

Zimmerman delivered a lengthy address in which he gave great emphasis to the pressing need for additional buildings and general campus development. He did not forget to praise the architecture: "This architecture, so appropriate to our environment, will of itself give the University a distinct place in the educational life of America." He noted the construction of four new buildings and said:

The problem of parking on the campus was addressed for the first time by the regents in August 1927. The board told President Zimmerman to create some parking lots to relieve "driveways," and to establish and enforce parking regulations.

Yatoka Hall, a men's dormitory, was completed in 1928. Architect: Gaastra, Gladding, and Johnson.

The Science Lecture Hall, a favorite with some professors, was demolished in 1984 to make way for the Electrical and Computer Engineering–Centennial Library Building. Architect: Gaastra, Gladding, and Johnson. Cobb Collection, 988–010–0008, CSWR.

If we now take the position that since we have a few new buildings we should be content and wait a few more years for further construction, then the University will inevitably enter upon a period of stagnation. The fact is, youth demands progress and those who would serve youth must plan on an ever growing scale. If we fail to recognize this fact, and to act in accordance with it, we shall not only soon cease to grow, but shall also inevitably lose the gains that have been made.

Professor Charles F. Coan died on September 19, 1928. He was chairman of the Department of History and Political Science. Later, in a eulogy for Professor Coan, President Zimmerman said:

James Fulton Zimmerman was inaugurated president of UNM in a ceremony at the Estufa with several pueblo chiefs in attendance.

James F. Zimmerman, president of the University from 1927 to 1944.
Photograph by Warner Woods Studio.

He had an unusual interest in the revival of the Pueblo type of architecture on the campus of the University and was a pioneering spirit in seeking to adapt this type of architecture to homes in Albuquerque. His own home on Harvard was constructed when the interest in Pueblo architecture had waned. His architectural ideal is perhaps best remembered in the present Kappa Sigma house, which he designed. When it was known that new buildings were to be erected on the campus of the University, Dr. Coan urged a return to the Pueblo type. His influence in this field, I am sure, will never be forgotten.

The Charles Florus Coan Award was established February 4, 1930, for students in history and political science in honor of the professor who was the champion of Pueblo Style architecture for the campus in the 1920s.

After Mrs. Holloman was elected president of the Board of Regents for the third time, the board gave approval for President Zimmerman to borrow $8,000 from the First National Bank to buy trees and shrubs and install a sprinkler system and grass. In President Zimmerman's biennial report covering 1927 through 1928, he listed several improvements that had taken place on the campus. A total of 481 trees had

been planted in the two groves. The aspect of the campus along Central Avenue had been improved with the assistance of the city and private donors. The embankment was lowered and grass was planted on the slope. The athletic fields had also been improved.

President Zimmerman recommended a building program including a new dining hall and a girls' dormitory. A general campus plan was prepared that showed the location of future buildings, landscaping, and expansion of the campus. No copy of this plan has been found.

When the board met on July 30, 1929, plans for the Chi Omega house to be located at 1805 Roma were reviewed but final approval was left to the president. A campus subdivision named Sorority Row on Roma had been recently laid out by Ross Engineering and the Chi Omega sorority was assigned a lot.

The biology building was named Parsons Hall in honor of Josephine Parsons, a long-time University staff and faculty member.

The University Dining Hall, designed by George Williamson and Co. and constructed by Edward Lembke and Co. in 1929, has since housed many functions and was the first Ortega Hall. Photograph by Clarence E. Redman.

The executive committee met in the Santa Fe home of Mrs. Reed Holloman on November 21, 1929. The committee voted to have George Williamson and Company complete the final plans for the President's Residence (51) and to authorize preliminary plans for a women's dormitory and a classroom building.

The Board of Regents meeting on December 14, 1929, named the new gymnasium for Hugh Carlisle, one of four UNM students who died during World War I. The regents approved the preliminary plans by Williamson for a dormitory and classroom building and told him to complete the final bid documents.

The stock market crash in October 1929 marked the beginning of the Great Depression. Its effect on the University building program was not immediate but came gradually with a slowdown in construction caused by a lack of funds, cuts in the University budget, and little or no increase in enrollment.

In April 1927 the Board of Regents approved paying an assessment of $9,800 for paving 2,298 feet of Plum Street, now University Boulevard. Extending from Central Avenue to the north side of the athletic field, the street would be thirty-two feet wide curb to curb. Yale Boulevard was to be paved from Central Avenue to the north side of the athletic field. A new unpaved street (Roma Avenue) from the Country Club Addition on the west side of the campus to the Mesa Vista Addition on the east side was approved with the understanding that it was not a public street and the University could close it at any time. The State Highway Department agreed to open Yale north to intersect with Roma. The paving of Yale and Plum Streets was completed in 1928.

The Depression Years

Following the stock market crash in October 1929, in which some $30 billion to $50 billion were lost, banks began to fail, workers were laid off, and a general slowdown began in the nation's economy. But by 1933 the University found a silver lining in the cloud of the depression as federal make-work programs financed many construction and landscape projects including several large buildings befitting a major university campus. Some of architect John Gaw Meem's finest buildings, including Scholes Hall (10) and Zimmerman Library (53), established a standard of design for all future buildings.

Some projects on the campus that had prior funding continued to completion. Bids were received on February 2, 1930, for the construction of the President's Residence (51). Miles Brittelle Sr. designed the house while he was with George Williamson and Company and Joseph Gagner was the builder. About a year later, President James F. Zimmerman was called before the Senate Finance Committee to explain why he bought a rug that cost $25,000 for the house with University funds. He had furnished a large part of the house with his own money. A rumor had been heard about the extravagant rug; he had to prove he had spent only $250 of the $750 authorized for purchase of rugs.

The just-completed President's Residence sat all alone on the north edge of the campus.

The Kappa Kappa Gamma house, located at 221 North University Boulevard, was demolished for the relocation of the street in 1967–68.

The Stadium Building was completed in 1934. This photograph was made around 1950.

At the regents meeting in September 1930 plans for a large administration building, a science building, an auditorium, a civil engineering building, and a field house and stadium were discussed.

The regents also considered adding a law college, a college of commerce and business administration, and a college of fine arts. No conclusions were reached. At this time, the Art Department was housed in the Solon Rose Cottage. A petition for the creation of a law school, signed by forty-nine lawyers and prelaw students, had been presented to the Board of Regents in June 1930.

In December 1930 plans were approved for an addition to Hadley Hall II (now part of 106) for engineering. A wing was added to the north side of the square building that contained a large room for a steam and internal combustion engine laboratory, three classrooms, a drafting room, and an instrument room. Bids were received on January 26, 1931, and the contract was awarded to Anderson Brothers of El Paso. There must have been quite a problem in getting agreement on the design of the addition since George Williamson asked for and received additional compensation for having prepared two sets of plans before getting final approval on the third set.

Mrs. Reed Holloman and Judge John F. Simms left the Board of Regents in 1931 and Frances Halloran (Mrs. O. N.) Marron and Dr. William Randolph Lovelace were appointed. Henry G. Coors was elected president; the other members were Glenn Emmons and Ralph Brown.

In July 1931 the first of several contracts for a football stadium building was awarded. The field at that time was on the land where the Humanities Building (81), Woodward Hall (82), and the Art Building (84) now stand. Brittelle and Wilson were architects for the project, which included offices, classrooms, and space for the Athletic Department beneath the seat banks. The project was designed to be built in phases. After the steel frame and the bleacher seats were built, walls could be built to form the exterior and some time later, as funds became available, the floors supporting the offices and classrooms could be installed and the various rooms partitioned off. The stadium was described as being 187 feet long and eighty-seven feet deep. It had thirty sideline boxes of six seats each. In September bids were to be taken on completing the stadium with exterior walls, stairs, toilets, and a press box. However the work was postponed for lack of funds.

In early 1932 Professor J. H. Dorroh was authorized to prepare plans for a 5,000-seat concrete bleacher addition with an alternate for steel construction. Brown voted against using Dorroh saying architects skilled in remodeling should be hired. Dorroh was paid $150 for the work. When the bids came in, steel was cheaper and was approved; Brown again

1932 aerial view of campus from the southwest. Photograph by the Three Hawks.

voted against it saying using concrete would provide more jobs for New Mexicans. Separate bids were taken on other elements of the project. In some instances the University bought material then bid for installation. It would take a thorough audit to determine the final cost.

Architect Miles Brittelle was told in August 1933 to complete the plans for adding the offices, classrooms, and locker and shower facilities to the Stadium Building. A federal grant for the construction was received in April 1934 and bids were taken in June. When the work was completed later in the year, the contractors had to wait on their final payment until the University received the grant money.

In 1932 the economy was in a deep depression with a bleak outlook for any recovery. The State Labor and Industrial Commission had told the architects to add a requirement to specifications that contractors must use New Mexico products wherever possible. The construction industry in Albuquerque was particularly hard hit because several major buildings, including the Veterans Administration hospital, the post office, Monte Vista school, and the addition to UNM's Hadley Hall II, had just been completed and there was no money to build more.

In 1928 an agreement with the School of American Research in Santa Fe to buy the ruins in Chaco Canyon had been approved. In March 1938, the WPA approved several projects at Chaco Canyon, including an administration unit, hogans for UNM students doing archaeological work, and a reservoir.

During March 1933 Professor W. C. Wagner prepared plans for reworking the playing fields, and Professor Dorroh drafted plans for a vault in the Administration Building. Springer Transfer Company was the low bidder on the athletic fields, but when the regents voted to accept the bid, Regent Ralph Brown voted against acceptance saying Springer was not paying the state wage rate of thirty-five cents an hour but instead was paying a flat two dollars per day. He was also opposed to faculty members competing with private engineering firms in preparing plans and specifications.

Governor Arthur Seligman said in December there would be no state money for buildings in 1933, therefore the institutions should make no requests. This was followed in January 1933 with an announcement that faculty salaries would have to be cut. The University budget had dropped from $376,027 in 1929–30 to $308,772 in 1932–33.

When Franklin D. Roosevelt assumed office in March 1933 plans were put into effect immediately to jump-start the economy. The National Industrial Recovery Act was passed, which led to the creation of the National Recovery Administration, the Federal Emergency Relief Administration (FERA), the Emergency Public Works Administration (PWA), the Civilian Conservation Corps (CCC), and other federally funded relief programs that had long-lasting effects on New Mexico.

As early as April 1933, the State of New Mexico had begun to recruit its quota of 750 CCC men. Most of the men who worked in the Albuquerque area came from Sandia Park Camp F-8-N. During its existence the CCC crews did some general landscape work on the campus.

The PWA was designed to provide substantial loans and grants-in-aid to state and local government agencies, including state universities, for major, long-term, labor-intensive, capital projects. PWA improvements initially operated on a 45 percent federal–55 percent state match. Because there was difficulty in obtaining the state matching funds quickly from bond issues or legislative appropriations and because the large projects required lengthy planning and federal monitoring, clearly the PWA projects would not provide immediate jobs.

To overcome this problem President Roosevelt issued an executive order creating the Civil Works Administration (CWA), a totally federally funded temporary work relief program. The CWA had $800 million to spend. The University administration saw this as an opportunity to get many long-awaited improvements to the campus at little or no expense to the school. During the winter of 1933–34 the CWA construction crews built small additions to the first power plant (102) and some tennis courts, remodeled

Open-air swimming pool located on the west side of Carlisle Gymnasium.

the Press Building, and built an open-air swimming pool to the west of Carlisle Gymnasium. The old wooden gymnasium, which had later been used for art studios, was demolished and the salvaged material used in the addition to the power plant.

In the spring of 1934 the FERA and CWA had more than one hundred men on campus waterproofing and painting the pool, constructing curbs on Terrace Boulevard and around the athletic field, installing sprinkler systems, and planting shrubs and trees and five acres of lawn. They also repaired storm and sanitary sewer lines and repaired, reroofed, and painted the exterior and interior of older campus buildings.

President Zimmerman and Comptroller Tom Popejoy jumped at the opportunity to use the federal assistance programs to get major buildings for the University. Zimmerman had strong feelings about what kind of buildings were preferable, and he told the governor and the legislature what he thought:

> For four years, the plan of erecting small and absolutely necessary structures to take care of immediately pressing needs has been followed. Such a policy is short-sighted, costly in the long run, and can be justified only on the grounds that funds for an adequate, economical, and long term building program have not been available.
>
> We are in the process of filling up the campus with small, ordinary, and unimposing buildings, inadequate for the future, and making exceedingly difficult adequate building plans for the future. If circumstances would permit, I would favor postponement of other buildings until funds for a building program of some proportions could be secured. . . . The immediate demands for space and additional facilities will not permit delay in some new construction.

In those early depression years there were not sufficient funds for even a meager building program, much less one "of some proportions." On October 28, 1933, the Board of Regents approved applying for federal funds. The administration asked for grants and loans for a major expansion: an office-laboratory-classroom building now known as Scholes Hall (10); a new library, later named for President Zimmerman (53); a heating plant that now houses College of Engineering functions (107); a student union that today is home to the Department of Anthropology (11); and other smaller projects, all totaling about $600,000. The application was turned down in January 1934, because all the PWA funds had been appropriated.

President Zimmerman thought there was the possibility of obtaining a grant and a low-interest PWA loan from the next allocation of funds for the University's highest priority project, the office-classroom-laboratory building, so another application was made. It was approved in August 1934. A program analysis indicated the need for much more square footage than the funds would allow, so severe cuts had to be made in both space and quality of materials.

Architect John Gaw Meem of Santa Fe, who had become well known regionally for his refinement of the Pueblo Style of architecture, was given his first commission for a building for the University of New Mexico in 1933. In an interview with Meem in 1979, I asked him how this came about and he explained it was through his friendship with John (Jack) Dempsey, University regents president and congressman. Meem had designed a house for Dempsey (which was not built) and helped with a development north of Santa Fe. Dempsey asked Meem why he didn't seek work at the University and Meem replied that he had no contacts there. Dempsey arranged a luncheon in mid-September at La Fonda with Meem, President Zimmerman, and Regent Lovelace. The group wanted the best architect available and decided Meem was the one.

The 1934 legislature passed a bill authorizing the state institutions to use student fees and income from land and the permanent fund to obtain matching funds for PWA grants.

The firm of John Gaw Meem and Associates had done a great deal of work on the plans before they received a signed contract on August 27, 1934, to design the Administration-Laboratory Building (10) at 5 percent of construction cost. The associates in the firm were Hugo Zehner and Paul Hoover. For many years afterward the Meem firm was given all the architectural commissions at the University much to the displeasure of other in-state architects. Not until 1956 was another architectural firm employed to design a University building.

Terrace Street was the main street of the University at this time. The site se-

The National Forest Service cooperated with UNM to landscape the area around Hadley Hall II and the power plant. Twenty men from the Sandia Park Civilian Conservation Corps camp did the work. Seven tents were erected north of the campus to house them. The project, which included grading, cleanup, a sprinkler system, lawns, shrubs, flowers, and a few shade trees, was completed in the fall of 1935. In early 1935 the University received federal funding for several small projects including the completion of the football stadium.

lected for the Administration Building was north of the intersection with Ash Street and close to Roma. The monumental building was to be the focal point of the growing campus. Terrace Street was closed and the building was centered on the street creating an axis all the way to Central Avenue, along which other buildings would be built. A circular drive in front with a rose garden in the center lasted until Ash Street was removed as part of the landscaping of the south side of the Administration Building in 1972. A new rose garden has been planted at the northern terminus of the Terrace Street Mall.

The building was one of the largest projects Meem had had in his office since he began practice in 1924 and one he hoped would influence future buildings on the campus with good design and careful detailing. The exterior design is based on early mission church architecture and particularly on San Esteban del Rey Church at Acoma. The shape of the two towers and their relation to the front wall between them are much like the Acoma church. The building is H-shaped with the longer legs of the H, the front, facing south. The south facades of the two wings are treated differently, with a balcony on the second floor west side and a bank of three windows on the east wing. The large laboratories, classrooms, and the Anthropology Museum demanded large windows, so for the first time Meem placed the double-hung windows in groups of three, four, and five on all faces of the building except the south and used precast concrete spandrels between floors. The two wings are two stories while the center portion is three stories plus a partial basement. The panels have an art deco appearance with abstract Indian symbols: mountain, rain, clouds. Later, precast concrete panels were used on the library stack tower and many other buildings. Color on the Administration Building panels was applied, while those at the library used colored concrete.

In order to stay within a spartan budget, the interior finishes were kept simple: plaster walls, asphalt tile floors, some exposed concrete ceilings in corridors, and acoustical tile in other places. An elevator shaft was in the plans, but the equipment was omitted. Like all Meem's buildings, the exterior bearing walls, on continuous concrete footings and stem walls, were structural clay tile and brick with the batter achieved with the brick. The exterior stucco had integral color. The interior corridor walls were poured-in-place concrete, which made cutting openings in them during remodeling very difficult.

Things moved rapidly after the funds were approved. The Board of Regents approved Meem's final plans on November 1, 1934, and bids were received on the twenty-second. All the contractors bidding the job were from out of state. Thomas Bate of Denver was the lowest bidder and within the estimate. The regents then authorized Meem to prepare plans for a basement and get costs. The state PWA engineer gave his approval on December 8 and said work could begin on the nineteenth.

Construction photograph of the Administration-Laboratory Building (10).

The completed Administration-Laboratory Building.

It is interesting today to see the wage scale for the 1934 project. John R. McMaster had been hired by Meem earlier as the clerk of the works. His salary of $150 per month was changed to $30 per week with 75¢ per hour for overtime work. Laborers received 40¢ per hour; truck drivers, 50¢; plumbers, painters, electricians, and most other trades, $1.00. The highest paid trades were stone cutters and glaziers at $1.25. The construction cost of the building including equipment was $5.84 a square foot, which was high at that time.

When the building was completed the president, bursar, registrar, and the deans moved into the west wing of the first floor. The Anthropology Department took the east wing, and the museum was located in the center portion of the same floor. The Geology and Physics Departments moved into the second floor and the Psychology Department was on the third floor. The post office was moved from Rodey Hall. A telephone switchboard was installed in the bursar's office and for the first time all departments in the University were reached through one number.

A big shifting of space took place when the old Administration Building was partially vacated. The College of Education was already in the building and Dean S. P. Nanninga took the former president's office. The departments of English and Languages were given additional space. The departments of Classics, Sociology, Philosophy, and Government were placed in the old Science Building.

In June 1935 the University was planning to ask for $1 million in PWA funds for buildings. PWA low-interest thirty-year loans would cover 55 percent of the cost and grants would cover the balance. Included were a student union building (since there was not one on the campus), twenty faculty houses, a new library, a power plant with new boilers, a fine arts center, a women's gymnasium, another dormitory, and several smaller building and utility projects. President Zimmerman and Regent Hugh B. Woodward appeared before the State Board of Finance in July with a total cost estimate of $1.25 million, which they said would take care of building needs for twenty-five years, to 1960. The board approved the matching-fund bond issue in August, but limited the amount they thought the University could afford to $712,000. The regents agreed to include funds in the bond issue for a state public health laboratory to be located on the campus since the State Bureau of Public Health could not borrow money.

At their first meeting in 1936, the regents accepted the Administration Building, which was to open on February 3, the beginning of the spring semester. At that same meeting the board renamed the old Administration Building Hodgin Hall (103) for Charles E. Hodgin, former vice president of the University, who had died on August 27, 1934. The regents also approved the sites for the new library and heating plant and, at the prodding of Dean M. E. Farris, authorized houses for faculty

The shortage of campus housing for men was so severe before the start of the 1936 fall semester that the University advertised for prospective landlords. Anyone with a room to rent was asked to call the University.

The Alpha Delta Pi house on University Boulevard at Ash Street opened for the 1935 spring semester. Photograph by Bill Winnie Photographers.

members to be built on Roma and Las Lomas west of the President's Residence with Federal Housing Administration loans and 20 percent down payment by the owner. The University leased the land to them for ninety-nine years. Almost all the residences in this area have since been acquired by the University and removed or remodeled. Even though the homes offered a soft edge to the north part of the campus, this area was always looked at as space for future academic buildings, which would make Zimmerman Library the center of the campus.

The building for the State Health Laboratory (12) was bid in March 1936 and the contract went to K. L. House Construction Company. The Student Union Building (11) contract also was let to House in July. It had a ballroom ninety feet long by sixty feet wide, club rooms, offices for student organizations and publications, two lounges, a bookstore, a cafeteria–lunch room that could seat 110, a barber shop, two meeting rooms, and a basement for recreation and storage. Tables for table tennis, Ping-Pong in those days, were put in the basement, and the soda fountain from downtown Arrow Drug was bought and installed.

The State Health Laboratory Building (12) was designed by John Gaw Meem and dedicated on November 11, 1937. Myrtle Greenfield was the director.

(*Opposite*) The second University heating plant (107) was designed by John Gaw Meem in 1936.

(*Below*) The Student Union was completed in 1937. The building has been remodeled and added to several times since it was built.

The State Health Laboratory Building (12) consisted of laboratories, support spaces, and offices. It was a very simple split-level Pueblo Style structure, with the entrance on the upper level facing east toward Terrace Boulevard. The scale was residential and the long portal on the front reinforced that feeling. Service access was on the west side lower floor. After the new facilities for the Health Department were completed on the North Campus in the 1970s, the building was renovated and remodeled by architect Patrick McClernon for use by the Department of Anthropology and Contract Archaeology. Great respect was paid to the exterior and it looks almost exactly as it did when finished in 1937.

Drama Professor Edwin Snapp returned from studies at Yale University and immediately began making some improvements to Rodey Hall. When the Department of English Drama Club gained control of the hall in 1933, the flat floor severely restricted the view of the stage. On one occasion, students sitting on chair-backs fell into some archaeological display cases along the wall when the chairs collapsed, doing considerable damage to the cases. Snapp enlisted the help of students to install new seating and more efficient stage lighting.

Bids for the heating plant (107) were received on May 14, 1936, and after analyzing an extremely complicated bid the administration recommended the contract be given to Bate Construction Company. Work on the project was held up later because of a shortage of carpenters. One reason was the limitation on hours of work permitted per month by the WPA.

On September 25 the Student Union Building was dedicated after a football victory with more than a thousand people at the ceremony. That was followed by an open house and a dance.

When dandelions became a problem on the athletic fields in the spring of 1938, sheep were brought in to graze.

The annual report on building needs was presented to the regents in early January 1938 and included the following: a sixteen-bed infirmary; an addition to Sara Raynolds Hall for a nursery school; a dining room and a home demonstration unit; four tennis courts; a dormitory; remodeling the old library (105) for art; and an enclosure for the swimming pool. It was also noted that all the lots designated for faculty houses had been leased and more land should be allocated. Zimmerman recommended that lots be set aside on the east fringe of the campus along Girard.

In December 1937 the Athletic Council sought approval for lighting for the football field after rejecting the proposed lighting of the tennis courts. The regents approved the project, which had to be finished before the fall football season when three night games were already scheduled. After the steel towers had been erected and the fixtures installed, the lights were turned on for football practice on Friday, September 23, 1938, and the "blaze of light" could be seen all over town, attracting huge crowds. One man said it was so bright you could read a newspaper in the stands.

Senator Carl Hatch notified Joseph L. Dailey, president of the Board of Regents, on March 4 that President Roosevelt had approved an allocation of $34,345 toward construction of a men's dormitory. This was called the Co-Op Dormitory and is now the Naval Science Building (151). The WPA approved a project to remodel the old library (105) for the Art Department.

For some reason a decision was made to rename all the campus streets. Meem was asked for his suggestions following a meeting with Zimmerman in October 1938. He wrote, "[it] was my thought in submitting this list that it should consist of names associated with the early Spanish colonization period of New Mexico. . . . The names should not be confined exclusively to soldiers, but should include also men who achieved prominence through cultural efforts." When the names were finally approved by the regents Terrace became Quivira, Yale became Villagra, Cornell was renamed Cibola, and Ash, the only east-west cross street, Coronado. The city approved the changes, but they did not stick and campus maps a few years later were using the old names.

The University celebrated its fiftieth anniversary in June 1939 with great ceremony. The main speaker was Harold L. Ickes, secretary of the interior. Ickes pointed out the several buildings on campus that had been financed totally or in part by federal funds. As part of the celebration UNM Press published *Pueblo on the Mesa* by Dorothy Hughes, a history of the University's first half century.

In order to house the growing student body the University administration planned to build two dormitories. Planned occupancy had to be reduced because of budgetary restraints so the revised plans cut the number of residents to seventy in each dormitory. The men's dorm was built on the west side of the Dining Hall (8) and is now named Bandelier Hall West (16). The women's unit (9) was built on the east side of old Hokona Hall and named for Frances Halloran Marron, UNM Class of 1901 and a regent from 1931 to 1933. What had been called the "new men's dormitory" would no longer be the newest when the new dormitories opened, so the regents decided the former needed an official name and selected Yatoka, pronounced with a long *o*, which was said to be an Indian name meaning "sun." Another source says it was a Kiowa word meaning "thunderbird."

The three major structures of the 1930s—the Administration Building, now Scholes Hall (10); the Library, later named for President Zimmerman (53); and the Student Union, now the Anthropology Building (11)—firmly established the mark of John Gaw Meem on the campus. He refined the Pueblo Style, which became the pattern for future architects to follow. Other buildings he designed during that period—the Co-Op Dormitory (151), the heating plant (107), the State Health Laboratory (12), and other smaller projects—followed the same design and all are still standing today. Their functions have been changed and all have been remodeled, some several times, but the exteriors are essentially unchanged.

During this decade the University of New Mexico grew from a small school with small buildings into a major institution with buildings befitting its stature.

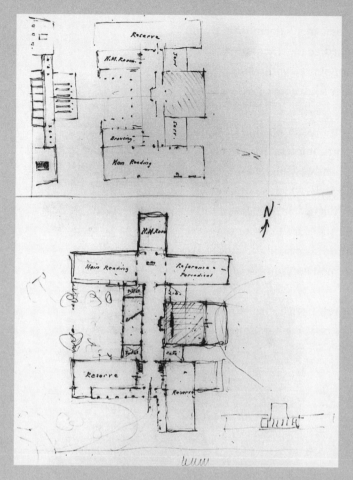

John Meem expressed his ideas about the design of the library in these early sketches.

John Gaw Meem's Library

The biggest and most important building built during the 1930s was the new library. Even though there were no funds for paying Meem to plan the library, he had given it much thought and had written President Zimmerman in late 1933 outlining his approach to the design. There were five goals: maximum accessibility with a minimum of corridors, ease of supervision with a minimum staff, flexibility of plan to allow for expansion, correct exposures depending on the site, and the use of the Pueblo Style.

Construction bids were received on October 31, 1936, and the low bidder, in keeping with previous WPA projects, was an out-of-state contractor, this time Platt-Rogers from Pueblo, Colorado. A ground-breaking was held on December 2, 1936, with Librarian Wilma Shelton digging the first shovelful of dirt at her second such ceremony.

Meem envisioned a tall stack tower that would provide a focal point for the campus and be large enough to hold 70 percent of the collection. The rest would be shelved in the reserve reading rooms on the south side and in bookcases along the walls under the windows in the main reading rooms. The front entrance would be to the west under a portal with another entrance to the south also covered by a portal. They opened into a long, high-ceilinged lobby with the circulation desk and card files opposite a reading room. There were three reading rooms at the north end that are certainly the most magnificent interior spaces on the campus, with their large size and high, decorated beams unobscured by light fixtures. The scheme shown in early sketches was carried out in concept as plans were developed. Offices and work spaces were clustered around the tower with some space on the second floor.

The exterior walls are all load-bearing structural clay tile and brick with a space between the inner structural wall and the outside battered wall. Great attention was paid to the batter of the walls, which simulate the effect of erosion on adobe walls. There were forty-one profiles on the working drawings showing every possible situation and the distance of the batter from a base line: the outside of the inner structural wall. Meem had had to order some of the walls on the Administration Building redone so he wanted to be more exact in describing what he wanted on the library.

The bearing walls support the reinforced concrete floors and roof. In the reading rooms and elsewhere in the building the concrete beams are encased with one-inch-thick wood boards that were hand-carved. The wood lintels over openings are also carved boards on wood furring. The beautifully

---

The library had 149,000 books and unbound magazines when the 1935 fall semester began. Student enrollment was 1,352.

Perspective drawing of the proposed library. CSWR.

Scaffolding around the library tower during construction. Photograph made June 24, 1937. 1980–061–038, Albuquerque Museum.

carved corbels are wood timbers, but they support nothing. The carvings throughout the library were done by Faustin Talachi from San Juan Pueblo, Justin Yassie, a Navajo, and Daniel Mirabel from Taos.

Tin fixtures throughout the library were made in the shop of Walter B. Gilbert in Albuquerque. The fixture that still hangs over the desk in the crossing between the reading rooms was described by a writer of the day as being the largest tin chandelier ever built, measuring five feet in diameter and seven feet high. Mirrors were built into most of the interior fixtures. Specially designed fixtures were used on the portals also.

The nine-story stack tower is concrete frame construction with precast concrete spandrel panels at each floor. It was designed to have self-supporting steel-frame stacks with one open internal stair and a shaft for a small service elevator. The stacks were not installed until after World War II for lack of funds. When remodeling

was done in 1965, bringing the tower up to building code requirements was very difficult because of the small size and the requirements for enclosed fire stairs and a passenger elevator.

A large skylight in the lobby opposite the circulation desk was removed not too long after the building was finished because it leaked badly and no repairs could fix it. When the last remodeling was done in the 1990s a skylight manufactured with modern techniques was installed. It does not leak.

During construction of the library, cracks were noted in the concrete beams at the crossings between the reading rooms. Professor Dorroh studied the design of the beams and reported to Meem that the dead and live loads exceeded the allowable for the reinforcing steel and the concrete by quite a bit. The problem was corrected by installing steel angles at the bottom of the beams and bolting them together through the beam. The beams were encased in wood so the repairs did not show.

On March 5, 1938, students and faculty, led by Mrs. J. F. Zimmerman, moved some of the books to the new library. The University band led the procession. Trucks were later brought in to move the bulk of the material. In March 1938 Kenneth Adams was commissioned to paint a series of four murals in panels behind the circulation desk in the new library. The cost of the paintings was covered by a grant from the Carnegie Foundation.

By 1942 the exterior stucco began to crack and pop off the masonry because improperly slaked lime was used in the mixture. Finally Earl Bowdich, the superintendent of the Buildings and Grounds Department, removed all the stucco and replaced it. Then he and Hugo Zehner began a search for an exterior paint they considered capable of long-term protection. This was during World War II when material was in short supply, but they finally found a suitable paint tinted to nearly match the original stucco color. What remained had to be sandblasted off in 1982 when the library was covered with a cementitious coating.

Repairs to the building through the years were not done with great respect, and maintenance was not performed as promptly as it should have been. The light level in the library was too low for comfortable reading even though the fixtures were beautiful, so when fluorescent lamps were developed, unattractive fixtures were hung from the beams and ceilings with little thought to aesthetics. Damage was done to the wood fascias then and later when smoke detectors and fire alarms had to be installed. Most of the damage was repaired when the library was last remodeled.

A few years before John Meem died, I asked him and his wife, Faith, to visit the campus. I showed them the new landscaping and some of the recent buildings and then took them into the original part of the library. As we stood in front of the old circulation desk, John said he thought it was the finest building he ever designed in the Pueblo Style and I agree. It was made possible by a rather generous budget for its time and the low cost of labor and material. Later buildings designed by his firm were faced with austere budgets and mounting inflation. Meem designed the library stack tower to be the dominant element on the campus, and it was until it was challenged by large, tall structures such as Popejoy Hall and the Humanities Building. The strength of the library's careful design have nevertheless made it the symbol of the University, as it should be.

The exterior of the original building and the interiors of the main rooms have remained virtually intact. Zimmerman Library is recognized as a historic landmark by the City of Albuquerque but was denied listing by the State Cultural Properties Review Committee because some members objected to the additions made to the building even though the architect planned in the original design for them to happen. It should be on the National Register of Historic Places.

(*Opposite*) The completed library from the southwest. Photograph by Wyatt Davis. Ladd Collection, 000–003–0079, CSWR.

The main lobby of the library. 988–014–0010, CSWR.

1941 aerial view of the campus looking west.

CHAPTER FIVE

World War II and the GI Bill

The war in Europe was being won by the Germans and their allies in 1940. On September 8 President Franklin D. Roosevelt declared a state of emergency and created an Office of Production Management to coordinate defense output and speed aid to Britain in every way "short of war." In October 1940 the new Selective Service Law, the draft, went into effect, and by the war's end 15 million Americans had served in the armed forces. UNM felt the effects of the defense and later the war effort as enrollment declined, federal funds for construction were cut off, and training programs for the navy were established on campus.

Even though the United States was not at war in 1940, many students enrolled in a pilot training program sponsored by the Civil Aeronautics Administration. Engineering Dean Marshall E. Farris sent a memorandum to President James F. Zimmerman saying Governor John Miles had suggested the University create a school of aviation. The Board of Regents approved the addition of a wing to the Engineering Building (107) for an aeronautical engineering program and the pilot training program.

In order to cut down on cost, Comptroller Tom Popejoy cut architect John Gaw Meem's fee from 6 percent to three-fifths of 6 percent on two dormitories, Marron Hall (9) and Bandelier Hall (16), and from 5 percent to three-fifths of 5 percent on the Co-Op Dormitory (151). Earl Bowdich, the superintendent of buildings and grounds, did the inspection during construction instead of Meem's office. The University bought material for the Co-Op Dormitory through the Government Procurement Office at a large discount. Ground was broken for the dormitory in September 1940.

In late 1940 the University was notified it would receive a prefabricated steel building to house the National Youth Administration (NYA) program. This caused much concern because the prefab was not compatible with the established architectural design of the campus buildings. The site selected for the building was on the east side

1940 women's dormitory, an addition to Hokona Dormitory, later named Marron Hall (9) in honor of Frances Halloran Marron, an alumna and regent. Photograph made August 23, 1941. 1980–061–372, Albuquerque Museum.

(Right) The Co-Op Dormitory (151), now the Naval Science Building, just completed. Photograph made August 23, 1941. 1980–061–370, Albuquerque Museum.

of Cornell about where Johnson Center is now located. Dean Farris argued to have it located in the engineering area and finally won. It was placed just south of the present Civil Engineering Building (117) and was demolished when the Mechanical Engineering Building (122) was erected in 1979–80. The NYA agreed to add $6,100 to the project to cover the cost of making the exterior conform to the Pueblo Style. Meem added a portal at the front with stuccoed corner walls, wood columns, corbels, and beams and gave it his blessing.

A list of sixteen proposed projects totaling almost $3 million was prepared for submittal to the Public Works Administration. The buildings would provide 253,800 new square feet. The package included two more dormitories, classrooms, a science building, an auditorium, a women's gymnasium, a natural history

A woman student from New York who had been assigned to Mesa Vista Hall I (the Men's Co-Op Dormitory) for the summer session of 1946 wrote the State Department of Public Health seeking advice on how to avoid carrying bedbugs back home in clothing and bags. Though the dormitory had been sprayed, she said, the bugs were still around. She was advised to use more DDT on her mattress.

museum, and an addition to the new library, as well as the re-modeling of four buildings. It was a very imaginative long-range plan, but along came Pearl Harbor.

A grant for a new wing on Hokona Dormitory was approved by the Works Progress Administration, but it was stated that construction might have to wait until the war ended. The Co-Op Dormitory (151) was completed and named Mesa Vista Hall. Kwataka Hall was closed for remodeling into offices for Inter-American Affairs.

There was a drop in enrollment of 12 to 15 percent in the spring 1942 semester. The Co-Op Dormitory opened in late January. Gordon Herkenhoff, state director of WPA operations, announced approval of projects to improve buildings and grounds, build an adobe clubhouse for the golf course, add new water lines, and remodel Kwataka Hall.

By 1943 World War II had caused the suspension of all construction not related to the war effort, but by the end of 1944 there was hope that both the European conflict and the war in the Pacific would be over soon so the University began to plan for the future. President Zimmerman died on October 20, 1944, and Comptroller Thomas Popejoy chaired a board of deans that served in place of the president until a new appointment could be made. A building committee appointed by the board of deans was charged with surveying the existing buildings, equipment, and resources, and listing the needs for the next ten to fifteen years by priority. In December the Board of Regents approved plans for a new building for the College of Pharmacy and asked the administration to look into the possibility of constructing an armory for the Navy ROTC.

President James Fulton Zimmerman's administration extended over seventeen years through the depression and almost to the end of World War II. President Zimmerman was very interested in the building program and argued successfully that the University should concentrate its resources on larger buildings for the future. From the 1928 buildings to the library he supported the return to the Pueblo Style of architecture that had been initiated by President Tight and disregarded afterward. The University had matured during those seventeen years to the point that when World War II ended it was able to meet the educational demands of the returning servicemen and the expanding postwar economy.

After the war UNM, like all colleges and universities in the country, was faced with the overwhelming problem of providing for the veterans enrolled under the GI Bill. By the end of the decade a building program was in place that would see many major buildings constructed and would put the University on the way to becoming a large institution.

Jesus Guerrero Galvan, a professor from the National University of Mexico in residence at UNM, was commissioned to paint a fresco at the east end of the first-floor east-west corridor in the Administration Building. "The Union of the Americas," a true fresco, was unveiled on February 13, 1943, at a conference on postwar planning.

Two of the many surplus buildings from the military training camps in the state and Bruns Hospital in Santa Fe arrive on the campus in 1950.

The years following the end of World War II saw a surge in college enrollment like never before in history. In his "fireside chat" to the nation on July 28, 1943, President Franklin D. Roosevelt advocated government-financed education and training as one part of veterans' benefits. Congress jumped at the idea and had Public Law 346, the Servicemen's Readjustment Act of 1944, the GI Bill, ready for his signature on June 22, 1944, not long after the Normandy invasion.

Before the war ended, studies and polls indicated only about 7 or 8 percent of those eligible would take advantage of the benefits. Educators believed the veterans were too old and too changed by their war experiences to return to the classrooms, or if they did they would not make good students. The fact was no one knew what to expect, so most universities, including UNM, were totally unprepared for the flood of veterans that began in 1944 and peaked in 1946 when total enrollment in the colleges and universities in the country reached more than 2 million, almost 50 percent of whom were veterans attending under the GI Bill, including 60,000 women and 70,000 African Americans many of whom had never expected to be there. Enrollment at UNM in the fall semester 1943 was 1,078. It rose to 1,812 in 1945, increased dramatically in 1946 to 3,649, and by 1949 it was 4,795.

John P. Wernette was appointed president of the University in 1945. In May 1946 the building committee was preparing a list of priorities that included a new science building or separate buildings for chemistry and biology, engineering laboratories, and a home economics facility. When Dean John Robb of the College of Fine Arts heard about it he wrote a strong memorandum to the committee stating the serious space needs of his college. The committee, chaired by Professor A. D. Ford, added fine arts to its list. In the final presentation the committee said the laboratory and class-room buildings should be grouped along Terrace Boulevard running south from the Administration Building with a maximum walking time of seven minutes between buildings. They also recommended a new men's dormitory, a press and printing plant, and the remodeling of the Student Union Building. When the University Building Committee sent its recommendations to President Wernette in June 1946, the committee underestimated the space needs. There was little money to construct new buildings and no time to wait to plan, find funding, and build them. So like almost every other university in the country, UNM began to acquire surplus military buildings being released by the government.

Housing was the biggest problem facing the University. Negotiations were started with Kirtland Air Force Base for the use of bachelor officers' quarters as dormitories. As many as 600 men were eventually housed in seven buildings on the base. A small library, a dining room, and lounge were located in an officers' club.

In the summer of 1947 the University contracted for concrete foundations, plumbing, heating, and power for seven barracks to be moved to the campus from Bruns Hospital in Santa Fe. These buildings were remodeled into eighty-three one- and two-bedroom apartments that formed Varsity Village on Stanford Boulevard Northeast about where the Basic Medical Sciences Building (211) is now located. The buildings were made as habitable as possible, which was difficult with uninsulated wood-frame buildings that had already seen hard use.

Other buildings came from as far away as Carlsbad, until there were thirty-four on the North and Central Campuses. There was a public outcry when a large rock, a landmark, overhanging the highway in Tijeras Canyon was removed to make way for the buildings. "Sometimes well-planned architectural programs do go astray. At the University of New Mexico there is an intrusion of surplus army barracks into a unified plan of Pueblo architecture," commented one writer.

All the permanent dormitories on the Central Campus, except Yatoka, were turned over to women students. Double-deck beds were used to increase the capacity to 391. Yatoka was converted to offices and classrooms. Barracks used for women's dormitories were erected east of Zimmerman Library on Cornell facing the golf course and the mountains. The lounge was three buildings tied together with a sunroom along the east side. A double fireplace was located in the center of the room and round wood columns, false beams, knotty-pine paneling and furniture, and tin and wrought iron light fixtures gave the place a New Mexico feeling.

In September 1952 the University began to dispose of the World War II barracks by giving three to the Albuquerque Public Schools with three more to follow. But in the fall of 1954 twenty-four "temporary" barracks were still in use.

The first new building constructed after the war was a small building on University Boulevard for the Department of Chemical Engineering (111). The firm of John Gaw Meem–Hugo Zehner and Associates was the architect. Work was started on

Lobo by sculptor
John Tatschl was
first located in
front of the
Stadium Building.
Photograph by
Tyler Dingee.

October 8, 1946, by K. L. House Construction Company. It was one story with a mezzanine in a high-ceilinged area and there were offices, classrooms, and laboratories. It was not finished until September 3, 1947, probably because material was in short supply.

In the fall of 1947, the statue of the UNM Lobo by Art Professor John Tatschl was placed on the west side of the Stadium Building. The statue was commissioned by the Inter-Fraternity Council of the University. The plaque on the side reads, "Dedicated to those students of the University of New Mexico who gave their lives in World War I and World War II."

The first time I visited the campus was in June 1947 when my wife and I were on our honeymoon and rode the bus up the hill from downtown. We started walking north on Terrace Boulevard when we saw John Tatschl working on the statue of the Lobo in his studio on the lower floor of the Art Building (105). The campus was almost deserted so we went in and asked directions and John told us about the sculpture. We had coffee at the old Student Union and decided it was a beautiful small campus. It was a very pleasant introduction to UNM. We tried to find work in architects' offices in Albuquerque to no avail and did not get back to New Mexico for three years.

On February 2, 1948, K. L. House Construction Company received a contract to build the Pharmacy Building, the first major building to be constructed after World War II. The firm's bid of $115,848 was negotiated down to $68,095 with University employees doing some of the work. Separate bids were taken on the laboratory equipment. After all the fooling around with award of the contract, it ended up costing about $90,000. John Gaw Meem–Hugo Zehner and Associates was the architectural firm.

Thomas Lafayette Popejoy was appointed to the presidency of UNM effective July 1, 1948. An editorial noted that the regents had selected as president a man with administrative ability rather than high academic ranking and said, "Popejoy knows more about University affairs in general, particularly as to the physical plant and its future needs, than any man in New Mexico."

A 400-man dormitory had been on the University's list of needed projects for some time. However, a project of that size had to be financed with University revenue bonds because the legislature would not appropriate money for any campus buildings in those days. The firm of John Gaw Meem and Hugo Zehner had been working on the drawings for some time when the regents decided to sell bonds supported by student fees to pay for the dormitory.

Bids were taken by the state purchasing agent in August 1948 and O. G. Bradbury received the contract for UNM's first million-dollar–plus building. Construction was delayed several times because of material shortages and occupancy was postponed, creating housing problems.

The "new men's dormitory" (56) was so called until months later President Popejoy decided it needed a better name. It was then named Mesa Vista Hall since the earlier dormitory (151) had been converted to other uses. It was built with fire-resistant materials except for wood balconies and portals with wood columns and vigas. There

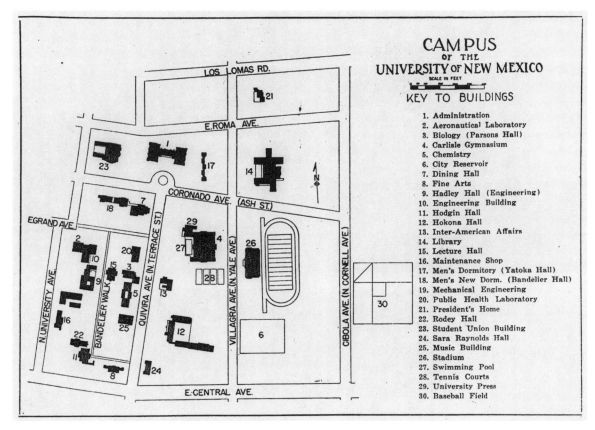

Plan of the campus around 1946.

The Pharmacy Building (19) was one of the first buildings built on the campus after World War II. Photograph by Richard P. Meleski, UNM Photo Service.

The east facade of the 400-man dormitory, later named Mesa Vista (56). Photograph by Clarence E. Redman.

The dining room in Mesa Vista Dormitory. Photograph by Tyler Dingee.

was a large dining room for students, a small private dining room, and one for the employees, all served from an ample kitchen and food storage space. There were quarters for the director, a dietician, the housekeeper, and a building engineer. In the basement were walk-in refrigerators and repair shops. Every floor had lounges and study rooms, and there was a game room on the fourth floor. The penthouse opened onto a sun deck. Altogether twenty balconies adorned the exterior and the various wings of the dormitory enclosed five patios. The *Albuquerque Journal* noted that "Bobby" Stamm, later to become a partner in the company, was assistant to the superintendent of construction for Bradbury Construction Company. Stamm says he was only the carpenter foreman.

The Totem Pole

In the fall of 1947 a woodpecker, or flicker, was drilling holes in the figure on the totem pole that then sat on the north side of the Administration Building. John (Jack) Martin Campbell, now a UNM professor emeritus, was a student of anthropology at the time and was known to have a shotgun. He was asked by Anthropology Professor W. W. "Nibs" Hill to go over to the pole just when it got light enough to see and shoot the bird before any of the sorority girls across the street woke up. Jack got the bird but he woke up the young ladies.

How the totem pole came to the UNM campus is an interesting story. It began in 1941 when Frank Hibben, now professor emeritus, was in British Columbia on the trail of ancient man and a totem pole for UNM. The University had agreed to pay the freight.

Hibben found a well-preserved forty-six-foot totem pole that belonged to the sole survivor of the Seaweed clan, Jim Seaweed. Hibben bought the pole for two cases of whiskey, one for Jim and one for his wife who, according to tribal custom, actually was the owner. Hibben towed the four-ton totem pole behind his boat 600 miles to Ketchikan, Alaska, where it was hauled aboard a freighter to Seattle. From there, because of its length, it went by rail to Albuquerque on special flat cars over a carefully worked-out route. Hibben wanted to erect the pole in the center of the rose garden on the south side of the Administration Building, but there were objections to that location and the pole was placed in storage in the stables on the east side of the campus where it gathered dust for five years.

The debate over the pole's permanent location was renewed after the war and the Campus Improvement Committee, then chaired by Biology Professor Howard Dittmer, could not reach a conclusion so the problem was referred to the Faculty Senate. Suggested locations included the rose bed, the football field, and just east of the Administration Building. After much debate a decision was made to erect it on the north side of the building. It was repainted in 1951 with twelve colors and the woodpecker damage was repaired

The totem pole, now in the patio of the Anthropology Building (11), was first erected on the north side of the Administration Building (10).

with the help of an Albuquerque Fire Department hook-and-ladder truck. In 1972 the totem pole was moved to its present location in the patio next to Maxwell Museum. As Jess Price, director of public information, wrote: "While the suitability of a totem pole in New Mexico may be questioned by cultural purists, the fact is that the transplanted totem pole is one of the relatively few outstanding examples extant of a North American art form now dead. High, dry New Mexico has helped preserve the totem pole for future generations, just as it has been a treasure chest for other vestiges of primitive culture."

The New Mexico State Highway Department operated a materials testing laboratory in part of Hadley Hall II (part of 106) that blew up at 7 A.M., February 12, 1949. Fortunately the laboratory was empty and students had not yet arrived in the rest of the building. A fire followed the explosion, which caused damage estimated to be between $50,000 and $100,000. An unlit Bunsen burner was blamed for the accumulation of gas.

Twenty small faculty apartments were authorized by the Board of Regents in early 1949 to be designed by John Gaw Meem–Hugo Zehner and Associates. They were to be located on the south side of New York Avenue, now Lomas Boulevard Northeast, east of Yale. There were five separate units. The three in the middle formed a U, with a portal connecting them around a central patio. The other two were free-standing units on either side of the center buildings. Like all the buildings being designed for the UNM campus by the Meem firm, they were done in the Pueblo Style, built with clay tile and stuccoed. Ten of the apartments were furnished. The apartments (154) were occupied beginning October 24, 1949. They were later used as married student housing and more recently as offices.

Three buildings were bid and the contracts signed on November 12, 1948: a building for the Physical Plant Department (204) on the North Campus west of Yale with administrative offices, shops, and warehouse space; a printing plant with space for the Journalism Department (115); and a new heating plant that formed the nucleus of what is now Ford Utility Center (116). The mechanical design for the plant was done

Hadley Hall II was badly damaged by an explosion and fire on February 12, 1949.

(Above) The Faculty Apartments (154) on Lomas Boulevard were converted to offices many years ago. Photograph made in April 1950. 1980–186–038, Albuquerque Museum.

The Journalism Building by John Gaw Meem–Hugo Zehner and Associates. Photograph by Tyler Dingee.

The third University heating plant (116), now part of Ford Utility Center. Architect: Meem, Zehner, Holien, and Associates. Photograph by Tyler Dingee.

by Professors Marshall E. Farris and A. D. Ford. The boilers were installed by the Physical Plant Department.

Jonson Gallery (152), the first art gallery on the campus, was designed to provide living and studio space for artist Raymond Jonson and exhibition space for his paintings. The building was financed by Jonson and his wife, Mr. and Mrs. Frank Rand Jr., and Miss Amelia White of Santa Fe with the understanding it would become University property when Jonson and his wife died. Work was completed in November 1949.

Jonson Gallery (152) by the Meem firm was the first building built on the campus with private donations. Photograph by Tyler Dingee.

Finally the men's dormitory opened on April 3, 1949, although the kitchen and dining room were not functional until April 28. The architects did not declare the dormitory totally complete until July 6, 1950. It was certainly the most imposing building on the campus, and with 111,870 gross square feet it was by far the largest building at UNM at that time.

The Board of Regents met on September 9, 1949, and authorized preliminary planning for a classroom building, a law school, a science building for two departments, a nine-hole golf course, and a clubhouse. The plans for the classroom building, later named Mitchell Hall (23), were presented to the regents on December 12, 1949, and approved.

In 1949 Hugh B. and Helen Woodward established the Sandia Foundation to receive the bulk of their estates, administer them, and distribute the net income to UNM; Dickinson College in Carlisle, Pennsylvania, their alma mater; and various charitable organizations. The estates included land from south of Lomas Boulevard to Indian School Road, from University west to Interstate 25, and some parcels east of University. Hugh Woodward died in 1968; his wife died in 1974. Income from these properties has been substantial. Woodward Hall (82) is named for the couple.

Other housing problems were causing concern. A fire inspector recommended removing the Varsity Village buildings as soon as possible and in the meantime installing more fire protection devices. The administration announced that no more married students would be assigned to the apartments. Dormitory space for women was in short supply so President Popejoy announced on April 15 he would seek federal funds for a new Hokona Dormitory.

In January 1950 Jonson Gallery had its first show, a retrospective of Raymond Jonson's work over the past eighteen years.

In March 1949 the regents authorized the construction of a Civil Engineering Building. They were told at the same meeting that the damaged part of Hadley Hall II could not be repaired. The Civil Engineering Building (117) was started on June 6,

1949, by Clough and King Construction Company and completed in record time on December 8. The building was attached to the Chemical Engineering Building (111) on the south side and faced University Boulevard. It contained classrooms, laboratories, and faculty and administrative offices.

John Meem told me several years ago that during the final inspection of the Civil Engineering Building he noticed disturbing cracks in some exposed concrete beams over the materials laboratory. He went back to the office and upon checking the drawings and calculations found there was insufficient reinforcing steel in the beams. He told President Popejoy that occupation of the building would have to be postponed. He said Popejoy told him he was not worried for he knew Meem would take care of it. The structural engineers made a truss of the beams with steel cables extending through the supporting walls and covered them with furred lath and plaster.

As the 1940s came to a close, several buildings were under construction on the campus and more were in the planning stage, including science buildings, a classroom building, a law school building, and dormitories. The University under Popejoy's guidance was meeting the space crunch head-on and, taking President Zimmerman's advice, building significant structures.

The Civil Engineering Building (117), Wagner Hall, facing University Boulevard. Photograph by Tyler Dingee.

The Sigma Phi Epsilon fraternity house at the northeast corner of Yale and Las Lomas, now the Aerospace Studies Building, was completed in 1941. The Kappa Alpha fraternity bought the Kenneth Balcomb house at 1635 Roma in 1948. It was described as being "Spanish Colonial."

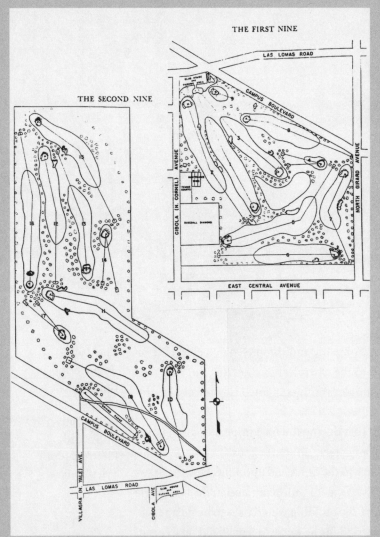

The plan of the golf course in the 1940s.

(Opposite) The North Campus Golf Course Clubhouse by Meem, Zehner, and Associates. Drawing by John W. McHugh.

(Opposite) President Popejoy, William Tucker, and Charles Lanier discuss planning the North Campus Golf Course.

(Below) The Albuquerque Country Club Clubhouse that was bought by the Sigma Chi fraternity is said to now be part of the Newman Center on Las Lomas Road.

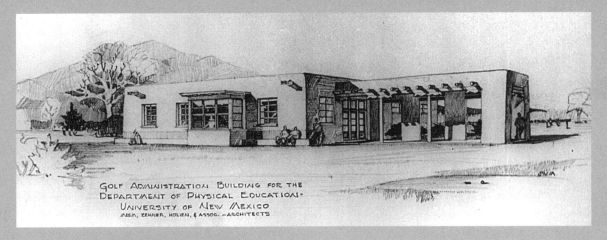

GOLF ADMINISTRATION BUILDING FOR THE
DEPARTMENT OF PHYSICAL EDUCATION·
UNIVERSITY OF NEW MEXICO
MEEM, ZEHNER, HOLIEN, & ASSOC.—ARCHITECTS

Central and North Campus Golf Courses

Campus planners have long said that golf courses are a good way to use land constructively while saving it for future development. The UNM Central and North Campus courses certainly proved the truth of this.

Lynn Boal Mitchell came to the University in 1912 as associate professor of Latin and Greek. As time went by he became known to his students and friends as "the Old Roman" and, unofficially, was the ranking assistant to President Boyd. He served the school in various administrative positions including dean of the College of Arts and Sciences. Mitchell was an advocate for the expansion of the University and is quoted as saying, "You can't expect customers to come to your hotel unless you first build the hotel." He was one of the builders of the "hotel."

Mitchell and a young biology professor, Asa Weese, decided they would like to play some golf and, since there was no golf course in the city, they cleared and leveled land just north of the "University Fence" and created a nine- or five-hole course (depending on the source). The University Fence enclosed the campus, and on the north side it was about where the south facade of Zimmerman Library is today. Mitchell and Weese used what tools and material they had to build the course: shovels, old gas pipe, and "tin" cans for the holes. They used arroyo sand for the greens and gravel on the fairways. They did not plant grass since it was

impossible to irrigate. Keeping the weeds under control was a major problem. The only place they could buy clubs and balls was a mail-order house in Chicago. As soon as they began play, a group of townspeople asked to use the course, which led to the founding of the Albuquerque Country Club. Twenty-two men incorporated the club in April 1914 and a small clubhouse was built. The club had a hard time surviving during World War I, but was able to build a new clubhouse in 1920.

A history of the Albuquerque Country Club says, "The view was magnificent in those days and although golfers fought dust storms and rattlesnakes, the game was just as enjoyable (and as frustrating) in 1914 as it is now."

During the 1920s the club sold the grounds and clubhouse to the Sigma Chi fraternity and a new course was established in the valley south of Old Town and east of the river. The clubhouse became the Sigma Chi fraternity house and now is said to be part of the Newman Center. When a street was put in, the address became 1735 Las Lomas Road. The present Sigma Chi house was built after World War II.

The first request for funds for a golf course on campus came in April 1938 from George White, head of the Division of Physical Education. He said a large number of students in golf classes and the faculty were interested in the sport. The regents approved constructing a public course on land west of Girard Boulevard and north of Central Avenue contingent on city cooperation.

President Tom Popejoy thought it would be possible to obtain a WPA grant to build a small course so he made an agreement in May with William C. Wagner, who later became chairman of the Civil Engineering Department, and William Hume II, who became a professor at New Mexico Institute of Mining and Technology, to survey the land, prepare drawings and specifications for a sprinkler system, and design a pedestrian overpass at Campus and Las Lomas.

In 1940, Popejoy began a long, futile effort to get the City of Albuquerque to help the University by underwriting the cost of the water over and above what income from the use of the course would cover. Correspondence continued for several months without a commitment even though Mayor Clyde Tingley indicated his support. Finally, in October, Tingley wrote Popejoy that the city would have to add pumping facilities if it were to furnish 600,000 gallons per day, the estimated amount of water required to irrigate the entire campus and the golf course.

Popejoy gave up and instructed Hume to estimate what it would cost the University to install its own water system. On December 12, 1941, Popejoy got the regents' approval to build a water plant for the campus including two wells, pumps, and a pressure storage tank. He applied to the WPA for a grant to build a "Recreational Center" since that type of facility qualified for WPA funds. The project was described as comprising an eighteen-hole golf course, a small clubhouse, and some tennis courts all circled by 12,000 feet of three-foot-high adobe wall. The wall was never built. The grant was approved in March 1942, but in April the War Production Board shut the projects down. The board later allowed the University to complete the projects.

John Gaw Meem—Hugo Zehner Associated Architects had been commissioned to design the clubhouse to be located west of the intersection of Las Lomas Road and Campus Boulevard. It would face south toward the first tee. Zehner presented the preliminary design to Popejoy in November 1941. After reviewing the drawings Popejoy wrote Meem that the elevations appeared to "reflect a departure from the pueblo architecture which you have recommended for all University buildings." Meem had not used parapets above the roof level of the porch. Meem replied that he had understood Popejoy to say he wanted to use adobe and he had extended the roof over the walls to protect them. He cited the problems with the new library's parapets where small cracks were occurring. Meem wrote, "This sounds as if I were trying pretty hard to sell you on a departure from orthodox Pueblo architecture. But if we could find a sound compromise, I really believe we could avoid a lot of future trouble." Meem made the design changes Popejoy requested but because of the war production demands the clubhouse was not built. Instead a small temporary wood-frame clubhouse was erected on the site.

William H. Tucker, an internationally recognized golf course architect, first contacted Tom Popejoy in 1940 offering his services in designing the course. He was subsequently hired to lay out the course and supervise the construction. When the first nine holes were opened for play he was appointed greenskeeper and he continued with work on the next nine and eventually, in 1946, the last nine holes on the North Campus to replace the loss of the first nine to construction of Mesa Vista Hall.

Tucker was born in England in 1871 and came to this country in 1895. When Saint Andrews Golf Club in New York had to move, he was asked to design the new course. In the 1920s he formed a partnership with his son William H. Tucker Jr. as golf course architects. During his professional life Tucker designed or remodeled more than 120 courses including courses in Portales and Carlsbad.

In early 1942 Popejoy wrote to all the people living near the University asking for donations of trees and shrubs to be transplanted to the new golf course. The response was probably better than he had hoped for because more than 1,000 trees and shrubs were planted on the first and second nines.

Lewis Martin, a recent graduate of UNM and an outstanding golfer, was hired as golf pro, and J. C. McGregor was employed as the business manager. McGregor had been news editor at radio station KOB for eight years. He immediately started making plans for a tournament to open the course with Bing Crosby and Bob Hope participating, but the U.S. Golf Association said it was too late in the season to schedule it.

Even before the war ended in October 1945, it was apparent there would be a large increase in enrollment and a demand for more buildings. Some land would have to be taken from the course to accommodate dormitories and academic buildings and to meet the need for playing fields for intramurals and physical education. The city had plans to improve the streets on the north side of the campus, such as New York Avenue (now Lomas Boulevard) and Las Lomas Road, which would be a formidable barrier to expansion.

Mesa Vista Hall (56) took some of the land on the west side of the course in the late 1940s, and Hokona Hall II (58), a dormitory for women, took more in the early 1950s.

The office of Meem, Zehner, Holien, and Associates was contacted in 1950 to design a permanent clubhouse (206) on the North Campus where Tucker had located it near the fourteenth hole of the course. The small building, designed in the Pueblo Style, contained administrative offices, locker rooms, and a club room. It was finished in early 1952 and during the 1950s the North Course was a flourishing operation.

The first serious encroachment on the North Golf Course occurred shortly after World War II when several buildings were moved onto a site on the west side of Stanford Boulevard. They were converted into apartments for married students and dubbed Varsity Village.

When the General Development Plan for the campus, prepared by John Carl Warnecke and Associates, was approved by the regents and made public in 1960, it showed the North Campus taken over by the School of Medicine, married and single student housing, and an expanded Physical Plant Department. The golf course was obliterated. With the exception of the student housing the plan has been followed in a general sense with resulting contraction of the golf course.

The plan mentioned the proposed Albuquerque Metropolitan Arroyo Flood Control Authority channel, which was in the planning stage, and stated that it should be placed underground, otherwise it would require a wide easement of very valuable land, would have to be bridged at street crossings, and would be very unsightly. Since the University could not pay to have it put underground, all the predictions came true. When the ditch was constructed and a site for the Basic Medical Sciences Building selected, the golf course had to move farther north and operate with thirteen holes. Yale Boulevard was paved from Lomas to the intersection with Tucker, and Tucker was paved from University Boulevard to Stanford.

The new dean of the Law School, Thomas W. Christopher, was pushing hard for additional space and did not believe there was enough room around old Bratton Hall (57) on the main campus to accommodate what he had in mind, particularly since the College of Business Administration next door would also want to expand some day. In late 1966 President Popejoy asked me to recommend a new site. I spent some time thinking about it and finally suggested the Law School be placed on the west side of Stanford just north of the intersection with Marble Avenue—another bite out of the golf course. That site would put the two fully graduate schools, law and medicine, together where they could someday share facilities such as a bookstore and a student union.

The golf course administration abandoned the greens and fairways on the west side next to the embankment and stopped irrigating. The trees died and native grasses and weeds took over the area. Almost. There was a leak in the irrigation line that went unchecked for several years. It was not much but there was enough water to keep a small area, maybe a quarter-acre, constantly wet. Tall grass, and even cattails, grew and many birds and small animals lived in and around it. A flock of Gambel's quail were permanent residents. This all disappeared when the leak was finally fixed and the area became known as the "barren fairways."

In order to provide an adequate water supply for irrigation, in 1983 a large plastic-lined reservoir was built in the northern part of the golf course to hold 1 million gallons. A dirt trail around the golf course is popular with walkers and joggers.

A great deal of concern was voiced in the neighborhood surrounding the golf course in the early 1980s that the University was going to do away with the course and develop the land. I do not know how the rumor got started, but it may have been because of the buildings being erected on the west side of the extended Yale Boulevard. The plan for the North Campus, done in 1977, stated: "The golf course at the northerly end of the site contains the only mature trees and vegetation on campus, and it is clear that continued irrigation and sensitive planning efforts should be applied to maintain this environmental amenity. The golf course should be kept operational as long as possible since the income from it maintains the landscaping of the area." There was no thought on the part of the University administration to do anything other than follow the plan.

Nevertheless, open meetings were held by the neighborhood group, which took the name "Friends of the North Golf Course," to gain support for keeping the area undeveloped. One of the meetings was attended by the state legislators representing the district, one of whom said there was a total lack of planning by the University. A pair of burrowing owls was found on the west side and protecting their habitat became a *cause célèbre*. The issue gained representation for the neighborhood groups of both the North and Central Campuses on the Campus Planning Committee.

Today the golfers still golf and the joggers jog and the course is fairly attractive. It provides a fine view from the north courtyard and library of the Law School. It now contains about ninety-three acres. Someday the golf course will have to go as the University grows and space is needed for new buildings, but it will take a tough administrator to make that decision and stick by it.

Patio south of Zimmerman Library.

All color photographs courtesy of Robert Reck.

"It takes more than the profile or outward appearance of its buildings to make a university, but if aesthetics mean anything in the intellectual development of students, and I feel certain that it does, then the University of New Mexico has an asset which gives it a unique position among the institutions of the nation."

Thomas L. Popejoy

View of Scholes Hall across the Duck Pond.

I hope that this campus can demonstrate some of the values of architecture and planning that those students who experience it will remember later. Most of all, I hope this campus gives them a rich memory to keep as long as they live.

Van Dorn Hooker

Walkway to Alumni Memorial Chapel.

Steps at Smith Plaza.

Clark Hall area in the spring.

Humanities–Woodward Hall.

Walkway between Woodward Hall and
the Art Building.

When you visit UNM for the first time, you know one thing right away—that you've never seen
any campus like it before. There is only one place you could be—New Mexico. The architecture,
the overall planning of the campus, is as unique as the state itself. It's a conscious reflection of
the land, its history and its cultures.

V. B. Price

Southwest entrance to Scholes Hall.

The Duck Pond, with
Ortega Hall in the
background.

Walk on southwest
corner of
Zimmerman
Library.

Seating area on the northeast corner of Mitchell Hall.

Anderson Schools
of Management
breezeway.

Anderson Schools of Management–
Social Sciences Building.

The architecture of the central campus demonstrates that the old and the new can harmoniously co-exist, enlivening and deepening each other's value . . . that a place can remain true to itself through a process of respectful change.

V. B. Price

Mesa Vista Hall–Student Services Building Patio.

Intramural fields east of Johnson Center.

Student Union–Fine Arts Center fountain.

Hodgin Hall (facing page, bottom).

A university doesn't just happen. There must be men before there are buildings; there must be dreams and well-wrought ideas before the grass is planted where student feet will move; there must be ideals and practical plans before the door of learning may be thrown wide. That the University of New Mexico has been singularly blessed with men of vision and of will throughout its years, we know.

Dorothy Hughes   1938

Farris Engineering Center, seen through Tight Grove.

Health Sciences and Services Building.

Dreams and Nightmares: Journey on a Broken Weave (facing page, top).

Family Practice Center Courtyard (facing page, bottom).

Health Sciences Center Library.

Bratton Hall north patio, with High Ground sculpture in background.

CHAPTER SIX

Coping with Postwar Enrollment

The decade of the 1950s began on a note of high hope and frantic development. Buildings were being planned and constructed as fast as President Popejoy and his associates could find funds and architects Meem, Zehner, and Holien could design them. There was no help from the state legislature so all the buildings were financed with added student fees and income from revenue-producing facilities such as housing, dining, and athletics. Enrollment was skyrocketing and student housing was still in short supply. Academic buildings planned and funded in the late 1940s were completed and attention turned to a fine arts center, a city-University auditorium, physical education and Athletic Department needs, a larger student union, and general campus development. Serious talk started about establishing a medical school.

The State Highway Department made an agreement with the University in 1948 to build a testing laboratory on the campus to replace the one lost in the Hadley Hall II explosion. Land was made available in the far northeast corner of the Central Campus. The building (153), designed by Meem, Zehner, and Holien, took advantage of the sloping site with the main entrance facing north toward Las Lomas (now Lomas) Boulevard, and the lower level, which housed heavy equipment, opening to the west. A construction contract was signed in 1950.

The Sigma Chi fraternity house at the southwest corner of Sigma Chi Road and Yale was designed by architect William Ellison as a two-story building to house forty members. Phi Delta Theta fraternity announced plans to build a house, estimated to cost $60,000, in the 1700 block of Mesa Vista. Bradley P. Kidder of Santa Fe was selected to be the architect.

In mid-1950 President Popejoy stated that 160 acres of the 480 acres of University-owned land northeast of the State Fairgrounds would be put on the market. The State National Guard had announced in 1937 that it would salvage material from two of the cavalry stables and use it to build new quarters on the State Fairgrounds. Stables had been located in the area now occupied by the College of Education Complex and Mesa Vista Hall.

Around 1949 Edward Holien designed an auditorium attached to a law school to be located at the north-west corner of Roma and Cornell (Cibola). It contained several features he later designed into Popejoy Hall. Photograph of rendering by Clarence E. Redman.

UNM and the Civic Auditorium–Performing Arts Center

As I researched the history of the University's fine arts facilities, I was intrigued to learn how long the City of Albuquerque has been trying to get a performing arts center and how deeply involved the University once was.

Some sources say the effort to build a civic auditorium began in the 1920s but one thing after another happened to thwart the plans. In 1935, when 25,000 people attended conventions in the city and spent an estimated $500,000, the Chamber of Commerce pushed the city to obtain funds for an auditorium. The city tried twice for a WPA grant and was turned down.

As soon as World War II ended, the auditorium was again high on the city's priority list and in 1946 a bond issue for $500,000 was approved. It was at this time a movement began, headed by the Community Concert Association and the Albuquerque Civic Symphony, to get the auditorium built. It was determined that more money was needed for a facility large enough for the growing population, but there was no consensus on a site. The organizations asked the City Commission for a $400,000 bond issue to add to the existing approved funds.

In April 1950 UNM President Tom Popejoy said the city wanted to build an auditorium on part of the campus golf course and the University needed an auditorium. City planner Ed Engel identified the site as west of Girard Boulevard between Central Avenue and Las Lomas, which at that time was designated to become part of a main arterial street, Lomas Boulevard. Later the site was more closely defined as west of the State Highway Testing Laboratory, then under construction, and south of Las Lomas. Ferguson and Stevens were appointed architects and directed to prepare a preliminary design.

The City Commission appointed an Auditorium Committee headed by S. Y. Jackson, president of the Albuquerque Board of Education. Popejoy appointed a UNM Auditorium Study Committee, chaired by himself, that included Director of Student Affairs Sherman Smith, Academic Vice President France Scholes, and Professors Howard Dittmer and A. D. Ford.

The two committees agreed on the campus site, and the University pledged to provide enough dirt to fill the arroyo that ran through it and bring it up to street level. A gravel parking lot for 1,000 cars would be provided south of the auditorium. The University would assist with the maintenance, provide janitorial service, and share the cost of utilities.

Just when it appeared the auditorium was going ahead, another roadblock loomed: the Korean conflict. Federal restrictions were placed on construction of certain types of buildings, including amusement and recreational facilities. Senator Clinton P. Anderson helped get the restrictions on the auditorium lifted, citing its cultural and educational benefits.

By early autumn 1950 concern about the size and purpose of the auditorium was being expressed by many individuals and organizations led, more or less, by Clyde Tingley, city commissioner and former mayor. The commission approved a 3,500 theater-type auditorium in October over Tingley's opposition. He said it was so small it could not even seat the student body of the University and it should seat 7,000. He described the campus site as a hole nobody could find.

An editorial in the *Albuquerque Tribune* agreed that it was too small and said, "Spending almost a million dollars for a cracker box is like pounding sand down a rat hole." A later editorial in the *Albuquerque Journal* blamed the University for dominating the planning and said the City Commission paid no attention to the needs of the city that must pay the bill. More and more user groups were criticizing the auditorium as being too small, but the Chamber of Commerce supported it. Just before Thanksgiving, Tingley was saying he wanted a sports arena rather than a theater.

Bids for the construction of the auditorium were received on February 6, 1951, and O. G. Bradbury's bid was low, but it was over the budget by quite a bit. Finally in October 1953 the city formally requested a three-acre site at Central and Cornell for an auditorium to be built with the funds on hand. The regents agreed, and architect Gordon Ferguson said he could adapt the 1950 plans to fit the new site.

At their January 1954 meeting, the regents asked the City Commission either to unanimously support the existing contract with the University or to release them from it. President Popejoy wrote the City Commission that the University did not consider three years of wrangling within the definition of "diligence." He also wrote, "As soon as funds are available, the University expects to

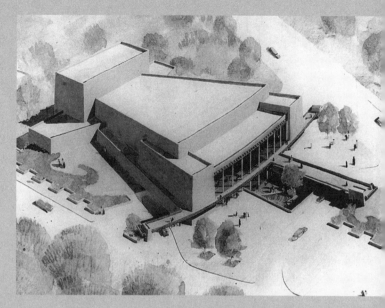

In 1950 George C. Pearl, the designer with architects Ferguson and Stevens, produced this drawing of a civic auditorium to be built in the northeast corner of the Central Campus. Courtesy of George C. Pearl.

construct a theater-type auditorium that will seat 2,000."

The city gave up the idea of building on the campus and after several months found a site on the west side of proposed Interstate 25 north of Saint Joseph Hospital. The community was divided in support of the location but by this time was getting bored with the whole controversy. Architects Ferguson and Stevens were then commissioned by the city to design a facility that could seat 3,500 in permanent balcony seats overlooking an arena floor where portable seating for several thousand could be placed. The building would house some sports events as well as concerts and large meetings. Eventually named Civic Auditorium, it was a round, concrete-domed structure, quite unusual in design. The city sold it to the hospital in the 1980s. It was demolished to make way for an out-patient clinic.

Mitchell Hall (23) north facade. Photograph by Tyler Dingee.

After considerable discussion, the southwest corner of Ash and Cornell was chosen as the site for the proposed student union building, later named the New Mexico Union (60) but often called the SUB. The building would be funded by a bond issue backed by student fees. The Meem firm was told to proceed with preliminary design by the regents at their meeting on April 4, 1950. At the same meeting, Popejoy was authorized to seek a federal loan for the construction of the new women's dormitory. The regents agreed to vacate Varsity Village as soon as possible and remove the buildings.

In May 1950 the Board of Regents approved the plans and specifications for the Classroom Building (23). The building had two floors plus a partial basement and forty classrooms ranging in size from 20 to 150 seats. Bids were taken at the State Purchasing Office in Santa Fe on June 12, 1950. K. L. House Construction Company was awarded the contract and work began on June 19. The building has a reinforced concrete frame, masonry walls, concrete floors, stucco finish, and a flat built-up roof. There was no air conditioning in the original building, which was finished in June 1951.

The Korean conflict began when North Korea invaded South Korea on June 25, 1950, and the United States was immediately involved. This set off a series of actions by the federal government, including establishment of the National Production Authority (NPA), to control the use of construction materials needed to support the military buildup. The Meem office had completed preliminary plans for the new Student Union Building (60) by November 1950, but they were not presented to the regents for approval since there was concern that the building would not be approved by the NPA.

Fund-raising began in 1950 for construction of a memorial chapel on the Central Campus honoring alumni who died in the two world wars.

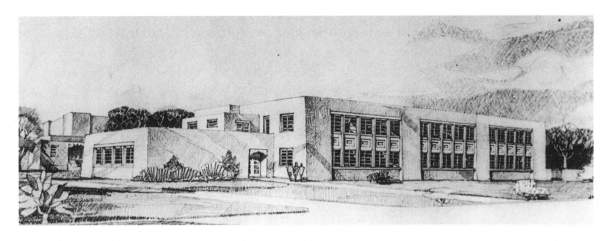

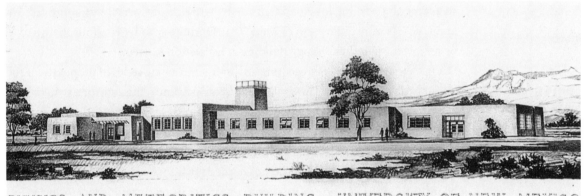

When the UNM Board of Regents met on April 2, 1951, finished plans for new Biology (21) and Chemistry (22) Buildings were approved and the architects were told to complete working drawings and specifications for the Physics and Meteoritics (207) and Law (57) Buildings, but not the women's dormitory. The regents imposed a $10 "building fee" on the students to pay for a bond issue for construction of these buildings.

The NPA approved construction of the Biology, Chemistry, Law, Geology, and Physics and Meteoritics Buildings to begin within sixty days, but with no guarantee of allotment of material. Stainless steel, copper, aluminum, and structural steel were in particularly short supply. At the meeting on July 6, 1951, the Board of Regents approved bidding the excavation for the basement of the Geology Building in order to get the project under way within NPA's allotted time. The Meem firm was authorized to complete the final drawings on the Geology Building at this same meeting. I began work in the office of Meem, Zehner, and Holien on July 5, 1951, having been hired by Hugo Zehner, and this was my first project and the beginning of a four-year-plus term of employment with the firm.

Bids were received at the State Purchasing Office in Santa Fe on July 31, 1951, for the Law, Chemistry, Physics and Meteoritics, and Biology Buildings. All the bids were over

(Above) Perspective drawing of the Chemistry Building (22) by John W. McHugh. Architect: Meem, Zehner, Holien, and Associates. Photograph by Parkhurst Studio.

(Below) Rendering by Jay Andrews of the proposed Physics and Meteoritics Building (207) designed by Edward O. Holien.

In September 1951 Earl Bowdich retired. Myron F. Fifield, a UNM alumnus, was appointed director of the Physical Plant Department; Richard A. Kendrick was made assistant in charge of buildings, grounds, and utilities.

the architects' estimates. The architects were authorized by the regents to negotiate with the low bidders to get the projects within budget. The bids were cut and the project contracts awarded. It was decided not to fund the Geology Building at that time and to issue more bonds when it was bid.

At the August meeting of the Board of Regents, the new Chemistry Building (22) was named Clark Hall for John D. Clark, professor emeritus of chemistry and former chairman of the department. The just-completed Classroom Building (23) was named for Lynn Boal Mitchell, professor emeritus of classical languages, former dean of the College of Arts and Sciences, and former academic vice president. The building was dedicated on September 9, 1951.

With all the construction on campus, parking was becoming a problem so construction of a parking lot along Central Avenue east of Cornell was approved. Six tennis courts were built south of Mesa Vista Dormitory to replace four that were to be removed when the Geology Building construction started.

The 1951 Studebaker dates the construction of the Chemistry Building, (22).

On October 27, 1951, the regents heard another in a long series of proposals for the sale or lease of University-owned land on Central Avenue, this one for a strip of land 2,000 feet long and 150 feet deep between Cornell and Girard. The land was appraised at $1.6 million and was said to be the most valuable vacant land in the city. A faculty committee appointed earlier to make a recommendation on the matter had made the brilliant decision that the land was not needed for future campus development. The board authorized Popejoy to appoint a committee of real estate agents to advise "on

The Biology Building (21) was designed by Edward O. Holien to fit between barracks, which had laboratories that had to remain in use until the building was completed.

The completed Biology Building was later named Castetter Hall.

the use and disposition of the strip." Fortunately, President Popejoy did not seem to favor the sale and made no effort to dispose of the land, although Senator Reginaldo Espinosa stated he would introduce a bill to establish a UNM branch campus in Santa Fe with funds from the sale of UNM land on Central Avenue.

The Geology Building was bid in October and contractors Maxey and Leftwich were low bidders. They agreed to hold their bid for thirty days, but by late December no steel had been allocated for the project by the NPA and the bonds had not been sold, so the contract was not awarded until the January 11, 1952, regents meeting when it went to the third lowest base bidder, Lembke, Clough, and King, for $833,994 after accepting three of the alternates both additive and deductive.

In 1950 the campus was composed of 440 acres with seventy-three buildings valued at $10 million. Even though the state was not appropriating money for University buildings, Governor Ed Mechem opposed any new University construction because of high costs and material shortages.

Bratton Hall, the Law School (57), by the Meem firm, later housed the Department of Economics. Photograph by Tyler Dingee.

Just before Christmas 1951 President Popejoy said he wanted $6 million in the next five years to build six buildings: a women's dormitory; a $2 million field house; and facilities for engineering, business administration, fine arts, and the social sciences. These would replace all the barracks, he said. Popejoy noted that enrollment doubled during the 1940s, that UNM granted 53 percent of all the degrees awarded by New Mexico state universities and had 47.9 percent of total enrollment, but received only 43.6 percent of the state funds. Popejoy's argument that UNM was not receiving its fair share of state funds was carried on throughout his administration in presentations to the Board of Educational Finance (BEF), the Legislative Finance Committee, and the House Appropriations Committee.

The Physics and Meteoritics Building (207) was completed in July and plans were being made for the dedication to coincide with the meeting of the American Physical Society at the University. The dedication of the Meteoritics Wing was to be held during the meeting of the Meteoritics Society.

The Law Building (57) was completed in October and the school moved in with 150 students. The dedication exercise was held on October 4, 1952, with U.S. Supreme Court Justice Hugo L. Black giving the main address. President of the UNM Board of Regents Paul Larrazolo was the master of ceremonies. Other speakers included Dean A. L. Gausewitz, President Popejoy, and Judge Sam G. Bratton of the U.S. Court of Appeals for the tenth circuit, who introduced Justice Black. The building was later named for Judge Bratton.

Popejoy announced in November that the sale of the 160 acres near the fairgrounds for Snow Heights had netted almost $300,000 that could be used for an auditorium,

but the regents said they wanted it used for the Department of Electrical Engineering. The site and the preliminary plans by Meem, Zehner, and Holien for the Electrical Engineering Building (118) were approved at the regents meeting on June 3, 1953. The building was designed to complete a quadrangle with the Civil Engineering Building (117) and the Chemical Engineering Building (111) to the west. This site arrangement can be traced back to the plans done by Griffin and Byrne around 1916. The architects were told to have the working drawings and specifications ready for bidding when the funding was approved. The regents also passed a motion saying the land along Central Avenue, eagerly sought by developers, should be kept for future University use.

The final plans for the Electrical Engineering Building were approved at the meeting on September 4, 1953, and the University purchasing officer was ordered to request bids. With the establish-

The Geology Building being constructed was to be named for Professor Stuart A. Northrop.

The Geology Building (24) by Meem, Zehner, Holien, and Associates. Photograph by Lowell Johnson.

The Electrical Engineering Building (118), Tapy Hall, in 1955. The campus was crisscrossed by power lines until a utility tunnel system was built. Photograph by Richard P. Meleski, UNM Photo Service.

NEW WOMEN'S DORMITORY
· UNIVERSITY of NEW MEXICO ·
· ALBUQUERQUE, NEW MEXICO ·
· MEEM, ZEHNER, HOLIEN, AND ASSOCIATES ·
ARCHITECTS
SANTA FE

Preliminary design of Hokona Dormitory (58), then called the New Women's Dormitory, by Edward Holien. Photograph of drawing by Kafan.

ment of the University Purchasing Office, bids could now be opened on the campus instead of at the state office in Santa Fe. The results were reported to the regents on October 17.

There was an interesting tabulation of building costs and sources of funding made in 1954 for distribution to members of the Board of Educational Finance who were to make a tour of the campus. It showed that to date only $102,628 of state-appropriated funds and $750,000 from a state bond issue had been applied to construction of UNM buildings. University bonds totaling $4.6 million, paid for in large part by student fees, were used after 1948. The University also applied land income and sales, plant fund reserves, and gifts and bequests toward the cost of buildings. Federal funds totaled about $600,000 mostly from PWA/WPA grants and loans in the 1930s.

The alumni chapel fund reached $44,000 in April. The Meem firm said drawings and specifications would be finished by May 1. The plan was to go to bid when $80,000 had been raised. In July the Physics Department broke ground for a small astronomical observatory (208) on the North Campus. Bernalillo County–Indian (BC-I) Hospital, adjacent to University land on the north side of Lomas Boulevard, was completed in August and plans were made to open it to the public on October 15, 1954.

In October 1954, Popejoy stated that the University had a crisis in housing: enrollment was increasing very rapidly—12.7 percent in 1953 and an expected 12 percent over each of the next three years. Enrollment, now at 4,692, would reach 6,000 by 1960. (It actually reached 7,595 in the fall of 1960.) Dean of Students Sherman E. Smith said because enrollment creates demand for housing, "the handwriting is on the wall." John Perovich, the comptroller, said any money for dormitory construction must come from state appropriations or University revenue bonds. There were 488 men and 283 women in dormitories in 1954. One of the old army barracks was put into use to house men, and two were renovated for women.

Popejoy said the University was planning a dormitory shaped in two pentagons connected by a commons area to house 600 women at an estimated cost of $2 million. One pentagon and the commons would be built first.

A state general obligation bond issue of $4.5 million was on the November 1954 ballot and was receiving editorial support across the state. The New Mexico Taxpayers Association opposed it on the grounds that it did not specify how much money each school would get. Popejoy made a presentation to the BEF in early December 1954 concerning building priorities, saying the top needs were a gymnasium and a women's dormitory. Later he had to explain to the legislature why the estimated cost of the gymnasium was so high when Highlands University had just completed a gym for between $10 and $12 per square foot: UNM's was a larger, multistory facility with more functions, more expensive materials, and higher labor costs. It wound up costing just a little more than $13 a square foot.

In anticipation of the predicted growth to 10,000 students, a campus plan was developed by Edward Holien incorporating projects in the planning stage and concepts for future buildings. The plan was developed under the direction of the Campus Improvement Committee headed by Biology Professor Howard J. Dittmer. The plan was shown to the regents on December 18 and there was a long discussion about what it proposed. The student union would be located at the north end of the practice fields, at the southwest corner of Ash and Cornell; the auditorium would be south of the union; and the gymnasium south of Mesa Vista Hall. Dormitories would be sited on the east side of the campus from Central Avenue northward. The plan showed streets running through the campus and parking concentrated around the gymnasium. It kept the earlier idea of placing related buildings in zones such as engineering in the

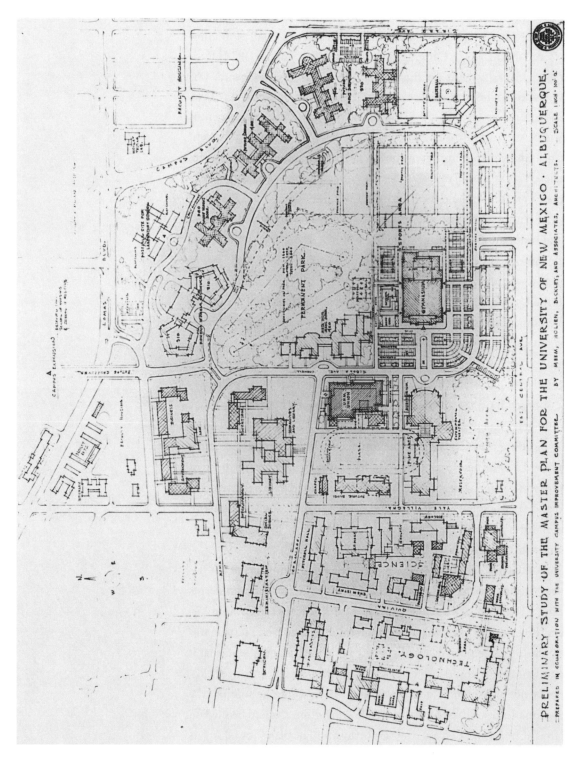

PRELIMINARY STUDY OF THE MASTER PLAN FOR THE UNIVERSITY OF NEW MEXICO · ALBUQUERQUE.
PREPARED IN COLLABORATION WITH THE UNIVERSITY CAMPUS IMPROVEMENT COMMITTEE   BY MEEM, HOLIEN, BUCKLEY, AND ASSOCIATES, ARCHITECTS.   SCALE 1 INCH = 100'-0"

Edward O. Holien produced this plan of the campus in 1954. The crossover connection to the North Campus was to be an extension of Cornell. Holien's plan shows existing buildings in white with black outline and proposed buildings and additions with cross-hatching. In the engineering and Law School areas, the placement of the buildings shows the influence of Walter Burley Griffin's concept of quadrangles enclosing interior patios. This plan had a great influence on future campus planning.

Aerial photograph of the campus made after a light snowfall, circa 1954.

southwest part of the campus and arts and sciences in the center near the library. One interesting proposal on the plan was the removal of the President's Residence from the campus; an academic building was shown on that site. The Alumni Memorial Chapel was to be on the southeast corner of Yale and Ash, and the football field was to be moved to the North Campus. The first building for the proposed medical school was shown on about the same site as the Basic Medical Sciences Building was eventually placed.

Cornell was to be the main connecting street to the North Campus with an overpass at Lomas Boulevard. Yale was closed between Roma and Ash. There was a hint of what might be a loop road on the perimeter of the campus, but it was not carried through between Cornell and Yale, probably because of the city-owned water reservoir and pumping station. The area north and east of Mesa Vista Hall was designated as a permanent park with playing fields, but there were no dedicated open spaces in

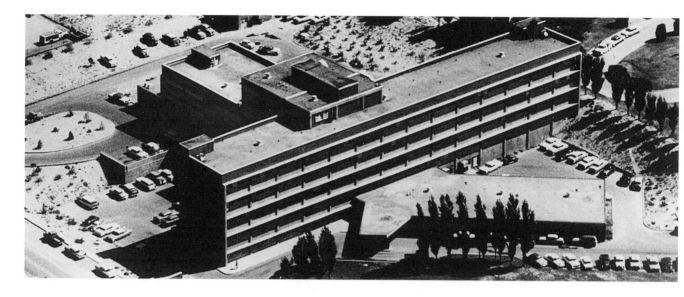

The original portion of Bernalillo County–Indian Hospital was completed in the early 1950s and is now part of the University of New Mexico Hospital. Architect: Ferguson and Stevens. Designer: George C. Pearl.

the central part of the campus except a "plaza" west of the Student Union.

There was no central focus to the Holien campus plan, no easy circulation pattern, and a vastly underestimated space need. There were no space studies, enrollment projections, or other supporting data with the plan. It was drawn with pencil on tracing paper and revised several times until it was superseded by the development plan done by John Carl Warnecke and Associates in 1959–60.

At the meeting of the Board of Regents on December 18, 1954, the plans for the first phase of the women's dormitory were presented by John Meem, Edward Holien, Frank Bridgers, Dean of Women Lena Clauve, and Dean of Students Sherman Smith. The plans were approved and a bid opening was set for March 1, 1955. Popejoy was told to arrange the financing using revenue and land income bonds. With the sites for several major new buildings set, it was possible to lay out a utility tunnel system connecting them to the main power plant. The tunnel would run east under the football stadium, around the proposed student union, and back to the plant along Roma. The tunnel project was approved to be bid at the same time as the dormitory.

The voters of the state had approved a $4.5 million general obligation bond issue for higher education on November 2, 1954, from which the University had requested $35 million. The State Board of Finance met on January 26, 1955, to divide the funds and after much discussion and compromise UNM received $1.65 million to be used for construction of the gymnasium. The board recommended the University be given an additional $325,000 from the general fund surplus.

On January 27, 1955, President Popejoy said a College of Education committee was working on space requirements for the gymnasium, which would be built south of Mesa Vista Dormitory on the golf course. Dean of Education C. R. Spain said the new

In December 1950 Representative Albert Amador Jr. from Rio Arriba County announced he had an education package for the legislature that included a junior college at El Rito and a medical college at UNM.

This construction photograph of phase two of Hokona Dormitory was made from the top of a hoisting tower. It shows the pentagonal plan of the wings of the building.

Left to right: Job inspector "Pat" Patterson, architect Edward O. Holien, and George McMahon study the plans of the new gymnasium. The photograph of the campus was made around 1950.

gym would have adequate, comfortable facilities for intercollegiate athletics and a complete physical education component.

The Board of Regents met on March 14, 1955, with two new members appointed by Governor John Simms. Finlay MacGillivray of Albuquerque and Dr. Ralph Lopez of Santa Fe replaced Paul Larrazolo and Jack Walton, both of Albuquerque. Remaining members were Wesley Quinn of Clovis and Jack Korber and Ethel Bond from Albuquerque. Korber was elected president. The board received a report on the bids for the first phase of the new Women's Dormitory (58) from John Meem and Edward Holien. Robert E. McKee was low bidder. The architects were told to prepare a contract and proceed with bidding the second phase. Popejoy was authorized to negotiate the sale of a University bond issue to pay for constructing and furnishing the dormitory.

Robert E. McKee Construction Company, already building phase one of the dormitory, was low bidder on the second phase and the contract was awarded at the May 16 board meeting. The two contracts were combined to simplify administration for a total of $2,411,400. Completion was scheduled for the fall semester 1956. During construction the Albuquerque Fire Department questioned the installation of locked gates at the entrance to the patios because access was needed for fire trucks. The dean of women wanted gates with an alarm to prevent entrances and exits after the 10 P.M. curfew. Of course there was opposition to the curfew from the coeds. In the end, the fire department won and electric eyes were installed to open the gates. After the dorm was occupied, students called it "the prison" and "the rock" after Alcatraz. They also named it "the brassiere" because of the shape of the two-wing plan. The construction superintendent called it "the maze." Upon recommendation of Dean of Women Lena Clauve, the new dorm took the name of the first women's dormitory on campus, Hokona. The east wing was named Hokona-Zia and the west wing was called Hokona-Zuni.

The regents met with their newly appointed real estate advisory board to form a policy on the sale of University land. About the same time, a realtor announced that a chain store wanted a fifty-year lease on the north side of Central Avenue between Girard and Cornell and would pay $500,000 a year for it. He said, "The University property kills this section of Central" and proper business development would make Central Avenue comparable to Wilshire Boulevard in Los Angeles. The administration objected to a lease because of fear the legislature would cut University appropriations by the amount of the lease income. Popejoy said the University had no plans to sell or lease the property since the Board of Regents voted in June 1953 to hold the land in perpetuity. He concluded that in light of recent plans for new buildings, it was "all the more vital to UNM programs that the land . . . be kept for UNM expansion."

After the preliminary plans for the gymnasium were presented to the regents, John Meem and Edward O. Holien were told to prepare final drawings and specifications so bids could be taken in September or October. The plan for what came to be Johnson Gymnasium called for 8,200 seats in the basketball arena, including 3,000 roll-away bleacher seats. The main arena would have a full-size basketball court lengthwise of the space and two courts across it to be used by physical education classes. A regulation-size swimming pool was planned, as were an auxiliary gymnasium, lockers for more than 2,400 students, offices for the Departments of Athletics and Physical Education, four handball courts, and a wrestling room. There were to be locker and shower facilities on the ground floor for coaching and physical education staffs, and training and equipment rooms. The south side of the building was devoted to intercollegiate athletics, with separate shower and locker rooms and a training room. The gymnasium was planned to be a state-of-the-art facility cloaked in a Pueblo Style exterior that did not come off very well, mostly because it was far too large for the small-scale style. This was the largest building Edward Holien had designed for the campus. At the regents meeting on September 26, 1955, final plans for the gymnasium were approved and November 10 was set as the bid date.

When the regents met on November 19, 1955, they accepted the low bid of Lembke, Clough, and King for construction of the gymnasium. The bid exceeded the funds authorized for the building, so the board accepted the bid with the provision that the proposal be reduced. John Meem listed several things that could be deleted, but President Popejoy recommended that every effort should be made build the project as planned and it was.

Meem biographer Bainbridge Bunting saw Johnson Gym as an example of the weakness of the Meem firm's post–World War II buildings:

> To accommodate this enormous [postwar enrollment] surge, a large number of new structures were required when time and money were both short. The fact that the standard for design was kept as high as it was is a tribute to Meem and his associates, and one is grateful that the Spanish-Pueblo style was retained for the campus even though the style was modified. Nevertheless, no one would contend that the remaining work by the firm or later by Holien and Buckley comes close to equaling the beauty of the two masterpieces [Scholes Hall and Zimmerman Library]. . . .
>
> Even more important in differentiating the late work is the basically formal approach to design. The postwar designs are tighter and harder; bilateral symmetry is not avoided. There is little of the old give-and-take between the parts, the lively equilibrium that gives an early Meem design such enduring vitality. One misses those charming irregularities such as . . . the subtle variations between the almost balancing wings of the Administration Building. The new structures are monumental and static, window spacing is mechanical, and the geometry of forms is unyielding. . . .

Sigma Alpha Epsilon fraternity took bids in 1950 on a house to be erected on Mesa Vista Road. George A. Rutherford was low bidder at $48,881, and the fraternity started a fund-raising drive. Alpha Epsilon Pi also planned to build a house. In 1951 architect William Ellison was designing an addition to the Pi Beta Phi sorority house on the northeast corner of Mesa Vista and University Boulevard. A dining room, kitchen, and dormitory space were to be added to bring the capacity to thirty residents and fifty for dining.

The Newman Center revealed plans early in 1954 to build a chapel estimated to cost about $100,000 and later a dormitory for one hundred residents. James S. Liberty was named the architect. The 1955 legislature authorized a $540,000 appropriation to be used to furnish Hokona, the gymnasium, and existing buildings.

Garnish the basic form of a latter-day building such as the Fine Arts Center with a few colonnades of Classical columns, a judicious sprinkling of aedicular forms, and an assortment of statues, and it could pass as a Beaux-Arts design in the grand style. Johnson Gymnasium, with its regimented hierarchy of forms that build to a heavy climax at the center of each facade, is pure Beaux-Arts—gone adobe.

These comments reflect the difference in design philosophy between John Meem and Edward Holien. Meem had little formal architectural training and he let his plans follow the functions of the internal spaces. In contrast Holien was an advocate of the Beaux-Arts concepts of formalism in planning. Another difference in their planning was Holien's use of varying floor levels to achieve space and volume while Meem's buildings were generally level.

When the gymnasium was remodeled in the 1980s and additions were made to it, all the facades were covered except for the north. Because of functional requirements the additions on the south side present a high blank wall to the public. Another problem with the gymnasium is its location at a main entrance to the campus. I felt the University's front door should not be toward an athletic facility but on a library or academic building. The Stanford entrance has become less important as other access points around the campus have developed, but today the visitors' impression of the campus is not improved when after parking they have to thread their way through the flea market of off-campus vendors in the mall by the Fine Arts Center and Student Union.

The regents met on April 30, 1955, to discuss the proposed campus plan drawn by Holien. Tom Popejoy said, "We are not rushing into any radical changes, but we would like to have a master plan toward which we can work and let any modifications that are necessary come about." He noted that three features of the plan had already been approved by the regents: relocation of the intersection of Campus Boulevard and Lomas to improve the overloaded Lomas-Stanford-Campus intersection; the site for the new women's dormitory; and the location of the proposed gymnasium on part of the old "front nine" of the golf course. The course had already been cut to six holes on the Central Campus.

Approval was given at the May 1955 Board of Regents meeting for the sale of a $1 million University revenue bond issue at 3.15 percent interest to finance the second phase of the women's dormitory. During May flash flooding occurred in the north Fourth Street–Edith Boulevard area of the city. The University opened Mesa Vista Dormitory to 200 displaced people whose homes were flooded. Center Hall, that portion of the old women's dormitory complex between Marron Hall and old Hokona, was demolished in October 1955. It had not been used for some time after a fire revealed unsafe wiring and structural problems.

A plan to remodel the President's Residence (51) included adding about 1,000 square feet to the living room, enlarging the kitchen and garage, installing new kitchen equipment, completely rewiring the house, and installing an air conditioning system. The project was approved on motion of Mrs. Franklin Bond.

In September 1955 President Popejoy said that within the next three to five years a new 400-man dormitory, a lecture hall, a student union, and an auditorium would be built on the campus. He said there was a "strong possibility" for including buildings for the proposed colleges of nursing and medicine. Also the golf course would be expanded on the North Campus and a new football stadium would be built. A classroom building estimated to cost half a million dollars would be located west of Marron Hall. He also said a million-dollar fine arts center would be erected in the parking lot on Cornell.

In October the State Highway Department, after only eight years in the laboratory building on the northeast corner of the campus, decided to move the operation to Santa Fe. The Board of Regents agreed to buy it for a home for government-sponsored research. It later became the Computer and Information Resources and Technology (CIRT) Building (153).

Popejoy, upon recommendation of Director of Student Affairs Sherman E. Smith, asked and received permission to start planning for a 330-man residence hall. It was later named Coronado Hall. He also said the removal of the center portion of the old Women's Dormitory was to make way for a new lecture hall. Old Hokona Hall would be remodeled for classrooms and offices.

John Meem, accompanied by Bess Popejoy, inspected the remodeled President's Residence and proclaimed it ready for occupancy. Mrs. Popejoy was particularly pleased with the new kitchen, which she said would be a great help with entertaining large groups.

At the February 1956 meeting of the Board of Regents, State Senator Calvin Horn, Paul W. Robinson, and Dr. Lewis Overton, representing the New Mexico Society for Crippled Children, requested land for a rehabilitation center near BC-I Hospital. The request was referred to the academic departments interested in rehabilitation projects. A similar request from the Young Women's Christian Association for a building site on the campus was referred to a faculty committee. Eventually the lease of a site for the rehabilitation center was approved and the YWCA request denied. Professor of Biology E. F. Castetter, who was active on University planning committees at the time, said, "A policy should be adopted of leasing land only to an organization that can demonstrate that its presence on the campus would make a substantial contribution to the enrichment of the academic program of the University." This was a very sound suggestion and was generally followed through the years.

Regent Quinn from Clovis asked Popejoy and Korber to look into the possibility of using architects other than Meem, Zehner, and Holien. He said Meem would still have overall supervisory responsibilities. After the war, many architects felt strongly that it was not fair to give all the architectural commissions at the largest state university to one firm.

John Gaw Meem; His Partners and Associates

John Gaw Meem's professional career, which began in 1924, can be divided into the following parts: the partnership with Cassius McCormick, which lasted until 1928; the middle years, 1929–41, when the office was small and the most distinctive work was done; the war years, 1942–45, which were devoted solely to engineering and planning for the military; and the late years, 1946 to 1959 when Meem retired.

Hugo Zehner came to work for Meem as his chief draftsman in 1930, was made an associate in 1934 and a partner in 1940. Meem said of Zehner, "He was a talented man if there ever was one. He was one of the most practical minded men, from the point of view of construction. . . . His judgment was always sound." Zehner handled projects from bidding through construction and assumed responsibility for structural problems, cost estimates, and most of the routine paperwork. This required much traveling to construction projects around the state, leaving Meem to direct the office in Santa Fe.

During the 1930s, while the country was in the depression and many architects and draftsmen were out of work, Meem had plenty of commissions. The numerous projects the office did for UNM from 1934 through 1941 were a large part of the work load. From 1932 until the beginning of World War II, several very capable draftsmen were employed in the office including Eugene Evans, Gordon Street, Paul Hoover, Leicester Hyde, Truman Matthews, and Bradley P. Kidder. Only Kidder returned to the office after the war. When he gave his drawings to the University Meem said, "I think that this group of drawings I'm turning over to the University don't represent me particularly, they represent a group of extraordinarily talented architects. I believe that few offices have had a more distinguished group of men—talented group of men, working together for so long a period of time."

The office did several projects for the military during the war including designing an air force academy to be built in Roswell. By 1944, only Meem, Zehner, and Ruth Heflin, who was both secretary and an associate, were left in the office, but Meem knew there would be a postwar building boom and began to prepare for it.

During the last period, 1946 to 1959, the office became much larger and most of the designing was done by Edward Holien who was made a partner in 1949. He had been trained in the Beaux-Arts tradition, taught architectural design at the University of Minnesota and New York University, and was a finalist in the 1926 Paris Prize competition. He worked on many large projects for major eastern firms. He came to Meem's office by way of Burnam Hoyt's office in Denver. In the

Planning for the new student union proceeded through the spring of 1956 and in April the students voted to increase their activities fee by $5.00, with $3.50 used to help finance a bond issue for construction of the building.

President Popejoy said on June 7, 1956, that the establishment of a medical school was close, maybe five years away. He said UNM was having trouble placing medical students in out-of-state schools (through the Western Interstate Commission on Higher Education) because of local demand. He said the State of New Mexico would sooner or later have to take care of its own students by establishing a medical school at the University. He argued that if it could use the local hospitals as training sites it would not be an extremely expensive matter.

letter offering Holien the partnership, Meem made it clear that he planned to take a less active role in matters of design, leaving that to Holien while he focused on overseeing the office and on public relations, by which he meant bringing in commissions and performing public service. Holien was assisted in the designing by John W. McHugh and Martin Beck who left to become a professor of architecture at Princeton University. Holien designed almost all the buildings, including those at UNM, produced by the firm after 1945. Holien acquired the nickname "Bung" because of his small stature: someone said he could fit in the bunghole of a barrel.

When I interviewed Meem on November 22, 1974, he said this about Holien: "I wish somehow I could have brought Bung more into the limelight in relation to the University plans. Because Bung certainly, more and more, became the designer of those buildings; certainly of the later ones. . . . He was a very great architect. He was a great man, yet so modest, so talented, a wonderful person."

Meem brought in much work after the war including many buildings for UNM, hospitals (Bataan, Presbyterian, St. Vincent, Espanola), public schools, buildings for Highlands and Western New Mexico Universities, and numerous churches and residences. When I came to the office in July 1951, there was still a great deal of work but the office had been trimmed to about thirteen people.

During the time I was in the office I did working drawings for the UNM Geology and Electrical Engineering Buildings and the remodeling of the President's Residence. I left the firm of Meem, Zehner, and Holien with John McHugh to open our own architectural practice in Santa Fe in 1955.

Hugo Zehner retired in 1955. William R. Buckley, who had been chief draftsman for several years, was made a partner and the firm became Meem, Holien, and Buckley. Meem served as a consultant in the completion of commissions and in guidance on some new work until he retired in April 1959, just short of his sixty-fifth birthday. The firm was then Holien and Buckley until Edward "Bung" Holien died in 1967, after which time Buckley continued in the old office on Camino del Monte Sol for several years. John Meem maintained his office on the north side of the building for consulting work with the assistance of Ruth Heflin, with whom he worked for almost forty years. When Meem decided to retire completely he gave the office to the Santa Fe Preparatory School, whose campus abutted his property.

Popejoy asked the 1957 legislature for funds for a preclinical building for the first two years of the medical school. John Dale Russell, executive director of the state Board of Educational Finance, saw the handwriting on the wall and said all two-year medical schools want to expand. He estimated a full four-year school with a teaching hospital would cost $20 million. The requested funds were not forthcoming.

At the meeting of the Board of Regents on September 8, 1956, approval was given for the purchase of the Kappa Alpha Theta house at 1801 Roma. The board looked at schematic plans for a 400-man dormitory and discussed the possibility of building fifty married student apartments. A proposal for the dormitory was submitted by architects Shaefer, Merrell, and Associates of Clovis. The dormitory would not have

Aerial view of Hokona Dormitory. Photograph by Richard P. Meleski, UNM Photo Service.

dining facilities since there was sufficient cafeteria space at Hokona Hall. The regents referred the plans to the deans of men and women for study and recommendations before the architects prepared preliminary drawings.

The request for capital funds from the 1957 and 1958 legislatures announced in September included money for a lecture hall, a fine arts center, a classroom building, a building for social sciences–anthropology, and a home economics facility.

An open house for the public was held at the new Hokona Hall on Sunday, November 11, 1956, and more than 7,000 visitors toured the facility. Until well after the scheduled closing time visitors were being escorted through the dormitory. President Popejoy, Vice President E. F. Castetter, several of the regents, John Gaw Meem, and many faculty members were on hand to greet people and answer questions.

When the regents met on November 16, 1956, Popejoy presented a plan to purchase the campus power distribution system from Public Service Company of New Mexico. This would allow the University to qualify for the "large power rate" and to put the lines in the utility tunnel system thereby getting rid of many unsightly overhead power lines and poles. He was authorized to begin negotiations.

In 1956 President Popejoy predicted a total enrollment of 7,500 by 1960 and 15,000 by 1970. He was low by only 95 in 1960, but enrollment on the main campus in the fall semester of 1970 was 17,364.

Frank Lloyd Wright Visits the Campus

In the 1950s Don Schlegel, a new faculty member in the Department of Architecture, was inviting world-renowned architects and engineers to give lectures on campus. After appearances by Buckminster Fuller, creator of the geodesic dome, and Felix Candela, Mexican architect and engineer, Schlegel arranged for Frank Lloyd Wright to speak.

The lecture was set for Wednesday, December 12, 1956. Wright wanted to interact only with students, so Schlegel arranged for Morris Rippel, Hildreth "Yumpy" Barker, and Robert Campbell to meet him at the airport and accompany him while he was in the city. Rippel remembers him wearing his famous "pork pie" hat and his dark cape and flashing a bright red scarf as he walked down the steps from the airplane. At this time Wright was eighty-nine years old, still very active, alert, and traveling by himself.

The lecture was held in the main ballroom of the old Student Union Building and it was packed. The crowd was estimated at 2,000. Schlegel described it as "chaos." Wright spoke without notes, as he always did, for about an hour and then answered a few questions.

The report of the talk was on the front page of the Thursday morning newspaper with the headline, "America Lacks Its Own Culture, Wright Declares." He reiterated his personal philosophy of architecture, politics, life, and culture and then accepted questions in a hectic session. Many questions were about Wright's recently published scheme for a 528-story, mile-high skyscraper. The last question was whether he approved of the work of any other architect, to which he replied, "I am not familiar with the work of other architects. I've never joined the profession."

Before the talk, a reporter asked Wright what he thought about the University's Pueblo Style of architecture. He answered, "Anything that is an imitation is base. It is especially sad to find this in an institution of education." He said he supposed this style was the best the school could do at the time it was begun, and the school had had to follow through with it. "I congratulate the University on its persistence."

Wright had been shown Zimmerman Library and other buildings in the Pueblo Style. He said they were artificial, borrowed from the past, and should remain in the past. He said John Meem was creating pseudo-Pueblo architecture out of steel and concrete.

Meem was asked by the Associated Press for a comment on Wright's statements. Meem made a gracious response: "He, Wright, is entitled to his opinion, and I'm entitled to mine. We do not try to imitate. We use those forms to recall the past in a symbolic, rather than an imitative, way."

The completed gymnasium named for Roy W. Johnson. This facade is now hidden by an addition. Architect: Meem, Holien, and Buckley. Photograph by Tyler Dingee.

A basketball game in the gymnasium. Photograph by Dick Kent, UNM Photo Service.

CHAPTER SEVEN

New Architects on Campus

Robert E. Merrell and Warren F. Pendleton, representing the architectural firm of Shaefer, Merrell, and Associates from Clovis, presented preliminary plans for the proposed men's dormitory (155) to the Board of Regents on February 1, 1957. There would be 379 beds in mostly double rooms. President Tom Popejoy suggested cutting the room size to 200 square feet. The plans were approved and the architects authorized to proceed with final drawings and specifications. The selection of Shaefer and Merrell opened the door to other New Mexico architects to receive University commissions. The fact that board member Wesley Quinn was from Clovis might have helped.

When Popejoy went to Santa Fe the following week, he was grilled by the legislators about the higher than anticipated cost of the planned gymnasium and its usefulness in relation to other needed buildings. He replied that more than 3,000 students would use the facility and that physical education was very important to student life. Popejoy said construction costs at all the state institutions were running 20 percent over estimates because of inflation. He also found the opportunity to point out that student fees rather than state funds had financed most of the construction on the UNM campus.

The Board of Regents, meeting on May 6, 1957, named the new gymnasium, still under construction, for Roy W. Johnson, not yet retired, recognizing his long service to UNM in athletics and physical education. The first basketball game in Johnson Gymnasium was played on Friday, December 6, 1957, before a crowd of 3,186. The Lobos beat Western New Mexico University 68 to 52. There was an open house on Sunday afternoon with faculty and students leading tours of the facility. A dedication tournament was held on December 27–28 with Wyoming, Michigan, Wisconsin, and the Lobos participating.

Sherman Smith, John Meem, and Edward Holien appeared before the Board of Regents at the March 11, 1957, meeting to explain plans for the Student Union Build-

In late March 1957 the Newman Center announced a fund-raising effort to build a $150,000 addition to its chapel, including a two-story chaplain's residence and a student lounge to seat 200 to 300. The old building housing the student center was to be removed.

ing (60). Meem pointed out that his firm had been working on the plans for almost four years and the preliminary sketches had changed many times. He said that through the Associated Students Organization a specialist in student union planning, Frank Noffke, had been brought to the campus and had helped the architects a great deal. Later, Roy A. Hilliard and Associates were employed to design the interiors and select the furnishings. The building was described as having three floors, extensive cafeteria facilities, student offices, guest bedrooms, bowling alleys, meeting rooms, administrative offices, and a large ballroom. Quinn expressed the opinion that the plans were as beautiful a job as he had ever seen.

The 143,000-square-foot building was estimated to cost about $3 million plus furnishings and architects' and consultants' fees. Student fees and income from the operation of the union would be used to pay for the forty-year bonds bought by the Housing and Home Finance Administration (HHFA). The regents authorized the architects to proceed with the final plans but noted the possibility of not receiving the loan. They agreed to pay the architects and consultants their fees from other University funds if the work stopped.

In the mid-1950s President Popejoy suggested to George M. Reynolds, president of Winrock Enterprises and former general manager of the *Santa Fe New Mexican,* that 160 acres of UNM land in the northeast heights had a potential for commercial development. Impressed by projected growth of the area, Winrock Enterprises checked out the location and became interested in the idea of building a shopping center—a $7-million project, the largest shopping center ever planned in New Mexico to that time. The University would receive a minimum rental of 5 percent of the appraised value of the land per year and would share in the profit of the venture with no liability and, after a determined time, would own the facility. Construction began in 1959 and the center opened on March 1, 1961, with forty retail outlets and room for expansion. It was the first regional shopping center within 400 miles of Albuquerque.

Winrock Center, as I write in 1998, has gone through various lease-holders and many additions and remodelings, but UNM still owns the land and buildings. Through the years millions of dollars have flowed to the University from its share of gross receipts and rentals. The leasing of University land to Winrock Enterprises is a great example of a cooperative venture between a private developer and a state university in which both profited.

Popejoy was put on the defensive again when the State Board of Finance told him to cut plush features in the new men's dormitory and use space more efficiently. The board noted that UNM would pay $1.3 million in interest over the life of the construction loan and pointed to the $4,500 cost per student whereas Highlands had built a dormitory recently for $2,000 per student—$13 per square foot versus $18 at UNM.

State Director of Finance Edward Hartman said, "UNM should look for more utility in new housing than any special refinements." The board deferred action and Popejoy said he would resubmit the project.

In August 1957 the regents approved revised plans for the new dormitory with cuts in the lobby and recreational areas. The air conditioning was eliminated—a costly mistake. The building was so hot in the early fall and late spring it was almost unbearable, and it could only be used sparingly in the summer. This brought the cost per student down to $3,640, but when air conditioning was installed in 1981 the project cost was over $300,000.

Comptroller John Perovich said in August that eight more World War II barracks would be turned over to the Albuquerque Public Schools, making fifteen donated for use as classrooms. He said the remaining twelve would be removed from the campus as soon as permanent buildings took their place. Departments and organizations that would continue to use barracks were the post office, placement bureau, Physical Plant Department storage, art education, architecture, home economics, Air Force ROTC, and one section of music.

There was considerable unhappiness in the Department of Architecture and elsewhere in the College of Fine Arts over the Holien and Buckley design of the Fine Arts Center. Some of the faculty, led by Don Schlegel, came up with an alternative design. It was in the International Style, which dominated worldwide architecture from the 1920s through the 1950s emphasizing function above all. The forms that resulted showed little distinction between public structures and office buildings. There was not a hint of Pueblo Style in the design developed by the faculty. The center had a flat roof and glass panel walls on the exterior. The square plan had a patio in the middle; an auditorium; classrooms for music, art, and drama; three theaters, one of which

Rendering of Fine Arts Center by Foster Hyatt shows the proposed art wing, which was not built. Architect: Holien and Buckley.

Aerial view of
campus, circa 1958.

would seat 2,500 people; an outdoor arena; and an art gallery. Once it was presented,
nothing more came of the idea. President Popejoy later presented a sketch by renderer
Foster Hyatt of the Fine Arts Center by architects Holien and Buckley and received
approval to proceed with the study of the building requirements.

In July 1958 Albuquerque Fire Department chief Art Westerfield said the barracks
used for student housing in Varsity Village were "dangerous firetraps." His report
brought on a spate of newspaper stories recounting the problems with the units. One
student's wife said, "It's horrible!" Another person said, "We can't get insurance on our
private property." Students said the only reason they lived there was that the rent was
so low. Physical Plant Department Director Myron Fifield said only four of the original barracks were left in Varsity Village. Academic Vice President E. F. Castetter said

Aerial view of Coronado Dormitory (155). Photograph by Richard P. Meleski, UNM Photo Service.

the regents and the administration had been considering the matter for some time. Chief Westerfield's report was not refuted.

The Board of Regents had approved building fifty apartments in September 1956, but for one reason or another, the project was not moving ahead. The regents also approved applying for funds from HHFA for the construction of one hundred married student apartments estimated to cost between $7,000 and $8,000 each. At that time, 25 percent of the student body was married. A survey found no apartments available near the University except at exorbitant rents. Ed Minteer, the *Albuquerque Journal* columnist, had a ready comment: "The university has been a trifle backward in providing housing for married students. Other state institutions, particularly A. and M. at Las Cruces, are far ahead of the university in providing such housing." W. C. Kruger and Associates' preliminary plans for one hundred married student apartments to be located on the South Campus were later approved, but the project was never built.

Popejoy said the University needed to erect eight new buildings in the next ten years to meet the needs of an enrollment of 15,000 by 1965. These included the Fine Arts Center, an addition to Zimmerman Library, a home economics building, classrooms near Bandelier, two dormitories for men, and one more for women.

The Lobo football team had a winning season in 1958 with total attendance at five home games of 51,293, second only to the University of Utah in the conference, so Athletic Director Pete McDavid was talking about more temporary seating at Zimmerman Field and plans for a new stadium north of the golf course that would seat 20,000 to 25,000. McDavid said, "We had an overflow crowd of 15,178 at the Air Force game which was beyond the maximum capacity of our facilities. If we'd had seats for 20,000 we would have filled them." The need for the land in the center of the

The Board of Regents, meeting on May 6, 1957, approved the purchase of the campus power distribution system from Public Service Company of New Mexico for $69,876.69.

campus occupied by Zimmerman Field was becoming pressing at the same time that pressure developed for a new stadium.

The University administration soon abandoned the idea of building the stadium on the North Campus since it was being considered as the site of a medical school. The regents met on May 9, 1959, and approved proceeding with planning a medical school.

A letter from Mr. and Mrs. Donald W. Herberholz, published in the *UNM Alumnus* issue of January–February 1959, asked the question, "When is the University going to break away from copying Indian dwellings and build buildings that speak for a progressing twentieth century institution?" This prompted a reply, published in a succeeding edition, from architect John Gaw Meem who stated that each new building on the campus fulfilled all technical requirements of a modern university and was functional and contemporary. He said the basic building forms were adapted from the rectangular terraced masses so characteristic of the landscape and evocative of the ancient Pueblos. Meem continued:

> This was done on the theory that good architecture, like all human experience, looks not only to its present and future but also to its artistic and historical heritage. With this in mind, certain features of Spanish-Pueblo architecture are used symbolically to further emphasize this point of view, such as the use of soft earth colors, the rounding of parapets and the battering of walls.
>
> It is objected that this conscious manipulation of materials to give them shapes and colors that they do not naturally possess is wrong. And yet, the history of architecture is full of instances where noble and beautiful structures have resulted from man's desire to express more than the materials have suggested. It is one form of spiritual functioning, just as important as material functioning. . . .
>
> There are other and vast areas in contemporary man's experience, including the use of forms with no other purpose than to give joy and to evoke pride in one's heritage. It is this spirit that I think is reflected in the unique campus of the University of New Mexico.

Myron Fifield, director of the Physical Plant Department, sent a memorandum to Comptroller John Perovich in mid-1957 estimating it would cost $18,968 to remodel the "Old Girls'" Dining Hall. It might more accurately have been called the Girls'—or better yet the Women's—Old Dining Hall, but no one seemed to object, not even the old girls. Named Joaquin Ortega Hall in honor of the professor of Spanish, director of the School of Inter-American Affairs, and editor of the *New Mexico Quarterly*, the building later housed the bookstore and the Department of Modern Languages.

Campus Improvement Committee Chairman Howard J. Dittmer sent a list of proposed projects to President Popejoy on May 28, 1959. The committee said the appearance of the campus had been deteriorating for the past several years, chiefly due to new construction, and little had been done to improve the grounds. The committee also felt it was working in the dark in locating sites for new buildings. Among the recommendations were paving and curbing the street being built between Coronado and

The New Mexico
Union (60).

Hokona dormitories, putting lawns around the new buildings, installing more benches and trash containers, planting more trees and shrubs, replacing the billboard at Girard and Central with a smaller one advertising the University and campus events, erecting signs in front of all buildings, paving and lighting parking lots, and using chain barricades to keep cars off walkways. These were good ideas, but it took many years to put them all into effect.

On June 9, 1959, the Albuquerque Board of Education agreed to an acre-for-acre swap of land with UNM that would give the University enough land for a football stadium, married student housing, and research facilities on UNM's South Campus. The swap involved about forty acres immediately, an additional thirty-six acres in the near future, and another fifty-three acres later, for a total of 129 acres. In exchange the public schools obtained forty acres of land east of Eubank and south of Lomas. The University Board of Regents approved the swap the next day and authorized Popejoy to negotiate the final deal.

The Board of Regents met for the first time in the new New Mexico Union on September 19, 1959, and the building was dedicated in an elaborate ceremony on November 14, 1959. The chairman of the union board, Frank Andrews, presided. The University symphony and choir performed and talks about what the union meant to them were made by Richard P. Howell, vice president of the student body, Ray A. Rodey of the Alumni Association, and Director of Student Affairs Sherman E. Smith. A $2 buffet luncheon was held in the Desert Room following the ceremony.

At the September meeting, the board rejected the two bids received for another part of the Eubank property feeling that they were too low.

The Desert Room in the southwest corner of the main floor of the union was an elegant dining room where staff and faculty and many people from off campus lunched. Photograph by Joel V. Barrett, Krome Studio.

The board authorized President Popejoy to submit the 30,000-seat football stadium and phase one of the Fine Arts Center, comprising a concert hall, an art gallery, space for the Music Department, and offices for the dean of the College of Fine Arts, to the BEF meeting on September 30, 1959. Popejoy announced a fund drive to raise $500,000 to supplement funds the regents had already approved for the Fine Arts Center.

Mrs. Winifred Reiter, managing director of the UNM Alumni Association, and Robert W. Hopewell, chairman of the association's building committee, asked the regents to call for bids on the Alumni Memorial Chapel. They pointed out that building costs had almost doubled since their fund-raising drive began and they were fearful they would never see the project completed unless construction began soon. They also hoped contributions would increase once construction started. General agreement was expressed on the proposed site between the old Student Union Building and the Administration Building (10), about where it is now located. The regents agreed to call for construction bids subject to the condition that no contract be made beyond the actual funds available.

John Meem objected to the location and stated that he hoped that area could be preserved as a park. He talked with Lawrence Lackey, the planning consultant, and suggested a site north of Mesa Vista Hall where the College of Education was placed. Another suggested site was north of Zimmerman Library opposite the President's Residence. Lackey later recommended the present site for the chapel saying the area in front of the Administration Building (10) could be kept as the park. The committee was persuaded to go along, which was a very wise decision.

A report on the planning of an addition to Zimmerman Library was given to the board by Regent Dorothy Woodward and Librarian David Otis Kelley. Dr. Woodward

The New Mexico
Union cafeteria.

pointed out the inadequacies of the present library and the need for adding research facilities, stack space, and more reader stations. President Popejoy said the planning had been going on for some time and that now Kelley and the other members of the faculty library committee wished to have an architect appointed so preliminary plans could be prepared. He said present plans were that the next two campus structures, other than the stadium and the Fine Arts Center, would be a building for the College of Education and an addition to the library. Financing would come, he hoped, from a proposed state general obligation bond issue.

The regents asked that a definite plan of procedure with respect to the library addition be worked out by the president, the librarian, and the library committee and brought to the board at the next meeting. Since Zimmerman Field would no longer be used for football after the new stadium was completed, the regents decided to name the library for former President James F. Zimmerman.

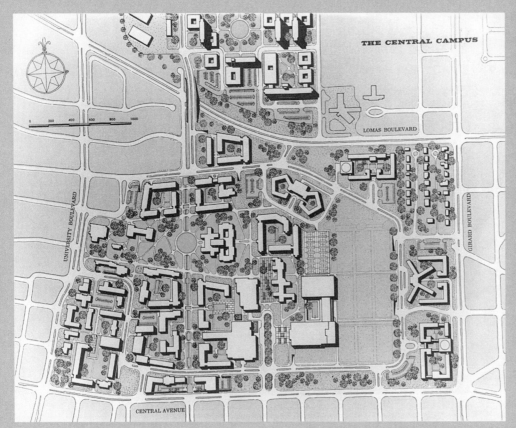

THE CENTRAL CAMPUS

LOMAS BOULEVARD

UNIVERSITY BOULEVARD

GIRARD BOULEVARD

CENTRAL AVENUE

(Left) The Warnecke Development Plan of the Central Campus.

(Opposite) The Warnecke Development Plan of the North Campus.

The General Development Plan

Board of Regents President Jack Korber indicated that the main purpose of the meeting on November 22, 1958, was to discuss a plan for the employment of an architectural firm that specialized in campus planning and development. A memorandum and proposal from John Carl Warnecke and Associates of San Francisco had been mailed to the board members several weeks earlier. After a lengthy discussion led by President Popejoy, a motion was passed to hire the firm to develop "a preliminary analysis of enrollment, student distribution, plant capacity—projection of needs," which would be part one of an overall program for a long-range general development plan. Lawrence B. Lackey was employed by the Warnecke firm as an urban design consultant; Alfred W. Baxter Jr. served as a University planning consultant. Lackey was born in Santa Fe and attended

UNM in the 1930s before getting his architectural degree from the University of Michigan.

Lackey and Baxter spent the next several months on the campus interviewing staff and faculty, analyzing existing space, and projecting future needs. Since there was no academic plan they had to rely on forecasts that were most often too conservative.

At the regents meeting on May 9, 1959, Lackey and Baxter reviewed their "preliminary analysis of growth and building needs" and explained that the next step would be a preliminary long-range development plan. This would include a land use plan, a summary of new facilities required, a development plan to 1970, and advice on immediate problems. The consultants said the result of the program would be a working document, flexible in character, which would serve as a handbook to

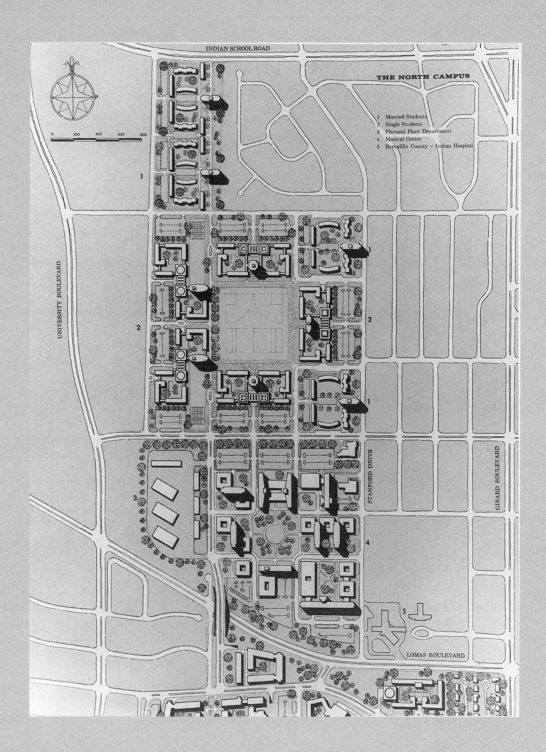

1 Married Students
2 Single Students
3 Physical Plant Department
4 Medical Center
5 Bernalillo County — Indian Hospital

guide the University in the development of any particular projects. The regents approved the consultants' suggestion for how to proceed with the work. President Popejoy said the administration, the University Building Committee, the Campus Improvement Committee, and the University Policy Committee would review the studies and make recommendations to the regents.

The planners made periodic reports on the progress of their work until March 1960 when the regents gave approval to proceed with the final document. It was dated August 1960 and titled the "General Development Plan."

The planners' philosophy is indicated in this introductory statement:

Individual response and capacity not-withstanding, it can be argued in the light of experience that the man or woman who experiences daily association with good architecture, sculpture, landscaping, and consciously ordered environmental design, must inevitably carry these associations into later life. These amenities should be an integral part of the educational plant.

Today eighty percent of all people in this nation live in urban areas. If future generations are insensitive to form, order, and delight in physical environment, the consequences will be devastating to our culture. The General Development Plan contemplates the creation of a campus which will arouse this sensitivity in the generations of students to come.

After extensive analysis and discussion with President Popejoy, Dean of Students Sherman Smith, and others, projections were based on an ultimate enrollment of 25,000, which represented a full-time equivalent of approximately 17,500, 3.4 times the 1959–60 figure. A space increase on the Central Campus of 1.6 million square feet of usable (assignable) space was predicted.

The document included a statement by President Popejoy that as enrollment increased there would be a shortage of qualified faculty, budgets would tighten, admission would become more selective, several two-year colleges would be created, graduate enrollment would increase rapidly, new instructional programs such as a school of medicine would be instituted, national policies would affect curricula, and research would become more related to New Mexico's needs.

Since only the football stadium had been built on the South Campus and the medical school on the North Campus was only a dream, plans for those campuses were only suggestive. The medical school was shown as covering the area from Yale to Stanford and from Lomas on the south to Marble on the north. Marble would be extended as a four-lane divided street to University Boulevard. Student housing was shown north of Marble. The golf course was eliminated as was the Physics and Meteoritics Building and the commercial strip on the north side of Lomas.

The plan set forth the following principles:

a. The Central Campus should be used primarily for academic purposes with Zimmerman Library as the focal point and all classrooms within a ten-minute walk of each other. Non-academic functions should be moved to peripheral locations.
b. Related subject fields should be grouped together as had been recommended by the Griffin-Byrne and Meem plans.
c. The North Campus should be used for the future medical school, student housing, and the Physical Plant Department.
d. The South Campus should be used for intercollegiate athletics, student housing, and research units.
e. Land coverage by buildings should be limited to 20 percent of gross land area.

f. The average story height aboveground of all buildings on the Central Campus should not exceed 2.5 stories.

These precepts were generally followed in the succeeding years, but it was impossible to meet the increased demand for space beyond the planners' projections while also keeping the height and land coverage within their recommendations. Nor was the recommended removal of several older, smaller buildings including Hodgin and Sara Raynolds adopted.

The core of the Central Campus would become a pedestrian preserve with a large green parklike area on the west side of the library. There would be a reflecting pool with water jets and narrow formal waterways linking small pools interspersed along the Yale Boulevard alignment leading to an overpass across Lomas Boulevard to the North Campus.

The plan stated that it was University policy that new buildings conform to the Spanish-Pueblo style of architecture and noted that faithful interpretations of the style would require sensitivity in design. In the appendix was a statement from John Gaw Meem written in May 1960 describing the characteristics of the Spanish-Pueblo style of architecture and its use on the UNM campus and adding, "the University has been under pressure to abandon its established style of architecture. It has realized, however, that in doing so, it would inevitably merge into a general stream of conformity, whereas by keeping its regional character, it possesses an individuality of appearance which belongs to it alone, a very great asset."

Baxter and Lackey estimated it would take fifty acres of surface parking to meet the demand of the developed campus—land not likely to be available.

They suggested placing parking lots near entrances to the campus and near activities that generated large parking requirements. However, the plan of the Central Campus as drawn showed only a few surface lots and an underground structure beneath the playing fields east of Johnson Gymnasium, the cost of which was far more than UNM could afford. The proposed parking solution is one of the shortcomings of the plan.

One of most important elements of the plan was the recommendation to build an internal loop road surrounding the academic core that would provide easy access to all parts of the Central Campus. Implementing this proposal for Redondo Drive has created the automobile-free pedestrian enclave the planners envisioned and made the Central Campus the haven it is today.

The final plan was given to the University in October 1959 and distributed to the regents, administrators, and various committees. At the January 31, 1960, meeting of the Board of Regents, President Popejoy recommended approval of the plan by the board. The Board of Regents would have to approve any major deviations in implementing the plan. The regents agreed to follow his recommendations.

Popejoy appointed the Committee for the Implementation of the Master Plan which later became the Committee on the Master Plan and was the foundation for the Campus Planning Committee. The chairman was Director of Student Affairs Sherman E. Smith who accepted the appointment in a memorandum to Popejoy saying, "As you know I enjoy this kind of work very much."

The Warnecke General Development Plan was a good plan and flexible enough to bend as physical demands changed. It remained the guide to campus development for more than twenty-five years.

Drawing of proposed Alumni Memorial Chapel by Edward
O. Holien. Architect: Holien and Buckley.

(Opposite) Physical Plant Department
personnel are shown with a model of
the proposed Alumni Memorial Chapel
they built to be used in the fund-
raising effort. Photograph by George A.
Kew. Alumni Association Collection,
CSWR.

CHAPTER EIGHT

Building for Athletics and Academics

The 1960s dawned with the University administration trying to find funding for several major projects: an addition to the library, the Fine Arts Center, and buildings for the College of Education. Land swaps on the South Campus between the University, the city, and Albuquerque Public Schools had cleared the site for the football stadium, and the architects, W. C. Kruger and Associates, were preparing the construction documents.

In January 1960 four trees were moved to clear the site for the Alumni Memorial Chapel (25). Bids were received in early February, and Bradbury and Stamm were low at $106,752, which was over the estimate and the budget. The furniture and some interior work were eliminated and a contract was let for $84,865. The Alumni Association had raised $76,300 and President Popejoy said the University could loan the association the balance.

There was a dedication ceremony for the chapel during the celebration of the seventy-third anniversary of the founding of UNM on February 28, 1962. The dedication sermon was delivered by the Reverend James R. Bruening, a Lobo football star from the class of 1955.

At the September 1959 meeting of the Board of Regents President Popejoy said that two architectural firms, Louis C. Hesselden and W. C. Kruger and Associates, had expressed interest in designing the football stadium. Regent Ralph Lopez pointed out that the Kruger firm was the

The chapel is of concrete block bearing wall construction as shown here.

Drawing of the interior of the chapel by Edward O. Holien. Courtesy of Robert Stamm.

The Atchison, Topeka, and Santa Fe Railroad Company donated two locomotive bells to the University to be used in the Alumni Memorial Chapel.

architect for the married student housing project in the same area. He made a motion, seconded by Regent Lawrence Wilkinson, authorizing the president to negotiate a contract with Kruger subject to approval of the project by the state boards.

When the Board of Regents met on October 30, 1959, W. C. Kruger, Robert H. Krueger, and R. O. Ruble presented schematic plans for a 30,000-seat football stadium with a provision to increase capacity to 40,000. The University would prepare the playing field and install the running track, grass, sprinklers, fencing, access roads, lighting, and movable bleachers. They were authorized to proceed with the planning.

On December 7 architect Robert Krueger, accompanied by structural engineer Fred Fricke, presented preliminary plans for the stadium to be built within the walls of a natural arroyo south and west of the Heights Community Center. This plan, however, was entirely above grade and did not take much advantage of the terrain. After much discussion about the steel shortage and the schedule for getting the project completed in time for the 1960 football season, the design was approved and the architects were authorized to proceed with the final drawings and specifications. The grading was to be bid on January 12, 1960, and the architectural work on February 5. Completion was set for September 1, 1960. Popejoy said the funding for the stadium would come from the sale of fifty acres in the northeast heights to the State Highway Department for right-of-way for the Coronado Freeway (I-40) plus money from other recent land sales.

On January 19, 1960, a ground-breaking ceremony was held, somewhat prematurely, for the football stadium (301). Bids were not taken until February 12 and they came in well over the architect's estimate. Popejoy then figured out a way to reduce the cost to an affordable figure. The fan-shaped seating design had already been sacrificed for a linear layout, which resulted in much poorer sight lines for everyone not seated near the 50-yard line. The president suggested doing away with the super-structure and making the stadium an all-on-grade facility in an excavated bowl-shaped depression. Popejoy said to lower the field ten feet and add fifteen rows in the below-grade portion, eliminate the running track (relocating track and field events to the area east of Johnson Gymnasium), and move the facilities planned to go under the stands (such as locker rooms, offices, concession stands, and public restrooms) to small ancillary buildings. Finally he said to cut the press box by half.

After bids for construction of the football stadium were rejected, the architects pared the project based on Popejoy's suggestions so that he was able to tell the regents the cost had been reduced to an acceptable figure. The bid package was broken into several parts: earth moving, building the seat banks, and bases for the lights. The press box, the concession stands, locker and rest rooms, underground utilities, and fencing was another package. George A. Rutherford Inc. did most of the work. The Physi-

The first game in the new South Campus football stadium was held on September 17, 1960. Photograph by Jerry Goffe.

cal Plant Department installed the playing field turf and the light towers. The opening game with the National University of Mexico was scheduled for September 17.

For the stadium seats the architects had specified a very dense tropical wood, greenheart, that had to be brought from British Guyana. It arrived in Albuquerque just three days before the opening game but was installed in time.

Early in the 1960 legislative session Popejoy presented the University's ten-year building program, as required by the BEF, with the highest priority going to buildings for the College of Education at an estimated cost of $1.5 million to $2 million. Buildings for the College of Business Administration, social sciences, and a medical college, if the two-year school was approved, were also listed. On February 15–16, 1960, President Popejoy presented plans for a two-year medical school to the regents and the Interim Committee on Medical Education of the state legislature. He estimated it would cost $2 million to build an adequate teaching facility for one hundred students. Their clinical work would be done at the Bernalillo County–Indian (BC-I) Hospital. He said the school would become a four-year institution in ten years. Popejoy said he would ask the 1961 legislature for money to hire a dean and staff to begin planning.

Popejoy persuaded Harold Enarson, an alumnus of the University and executive director of the Western Interstate Commission on Higher Education, to become academic vice president of UNM. One of his main duties was to foster the development of a medical school. Enarson put together an application for a planning grant from the W. K. Kellogg Foundation. In May the foundation announced a five-year grant of a million dollars for planning, salaries, and part of a basic sciences building. A jubilant Popejoy said he hoped classes could begin in two to three years and in ten years graduates would be practicing in New Mexico. At the next Board of Regents meeting, he asked for and received permission to employ a consultant to begin planning the school.

The legislature had not formally approved the medical school and Popejoy felt that approval had to be accompanied by an appropriation of funds to add to the Kellogg grant. With the support of Jack Campbell, speaker of the House and future governor, he asked for $100,000 but that was cut to $25,000 by the legislators.

With the Kellogg Foundation grant approved in May, planning for the School of Medicine could really get started. Dr. Reginald Fitz was appointed dean in July 1961 and assigned a small office in a corner of the Administration Building. Mrs. Kenneth Adams, wife of the famous painter and former secretary to Tom Popejoy, was made his secretary. Lester Gorsline, a medical school planning consultant, was employed to develop a program for facilities, and W. C. Kruger and Associates was selected as the architectural firm.

The regents gave the president authorization to condemn the private property north of BC-I Hospital for the Medical School since they felt it could not be bought for a reasonable price. During this same period, the administration was trying to purchase or trade for thirty acres of land on University Boulevard north of Lomas that was owned by the First Baptist Church.

At the June 8, 1960, commencement exercises, John Gaw Meem was awarded a doctor of fine arts degree by the University of New Mexico. The citation read:

> Nationally honored architect and recently retired founder and head of the firm which since 1933 has designed nearly forty buildings for the University, he has been the guiding influence in the creation of a homogeneous complex of campus structures which has been termed

President Popejoy reported to the regents on August 23, 1960, that names suggested for the new football stadium included University Stadium, Lobo Stadium, Varsity Stadium, and New Mexico Stadium. Regent MacGillivray said the New Mexico Boosters Club had suggested Popejoy Stadium. Popejoy said he appreciated the gesture but felt that no structure should be named after a person actively on the University staff. The board agreed to tentatively call it University Stadium and await a suggestion from the Building Committee—which has never come. It is still called simply University Stadium.

one of the outstanding examples of regional architectural style in the United States. By capturing the soft earth colors and characteristic shapes of the landscape, and through a sensitive use of symbolic design, he has been able to recall both form and spirit of the ancient and rich heritage of the Southwest while meeting the contemporary functional requirements of a growing University.

On the Central Campus, Professor Marvin May, a member of the Campus Improvement Committee, had worked with the Highway Department in getting the loop road paved from the dormitory area to Cornell Boulevard and a paved entrance from Central Avenue at Stanford Boulevard. The campus plan at that time showed the loop road, now Redondo, continuing west through the engineering area to join University Boulevard at Ash Street and Cornell extending through the campus and intersecting Lomas Boulevard to form a major entrance on the north.

The Lobo statue was moved by Physical Plant workers, in the teeth of a cold forty-mile-per-hour gale, from the front of the old stadium to the west side of Johnson Gymnasium. Professor John Tatschl, the sculptor, said, "You know quite often after looking at something for ten years, you want to disown authorship. But on the contrary, I look back on my work ten years later and I'm still proud I made him."

At the regents meeting on April 25, 1960, architects Holien and Buckley, successors to the firm of Meem, Holien, and Buckley, presented the final plans and specifications for the Fine Arts Center (62 and 72). No action was taken since no funds were available. The president said if the legislature would approve the sale of land in the northeast heights the proceeds could be used for the project.

When the regents met on June 8, 1961, more than a year later, Edward O. Holien reviewed the plans for the Fine Arts Center, which contained facilities for the Music Department (including a 325-seat recital hall later named Keller Hall), an art museum, a fine arts library, and a 2,000-seat concert hall. The project was divided into two phases, one the Department of Music space, the library, and the art museum; phase two, the concert hall.

Clinton Adams came to UNM in August 1961 to assume the deanship of the College of Fine Arts succeeding Edwin E. Stein. The program for the new building had been developed by Stein working with architect Holien. Adams was immediately involved with the project and found the plan would not meet the requirements of the college. It was very heavy on the space for the Department of Music, had insufficient space for a library, and no work or storage space for the art museum. He also noted that enrollment was falling in music and rising in art, and said the proposed art space was inadequate. Adams brought his concerns to Dean Sherman Smith, who feared delay in bidding would mean funding would go to other needed projects but allowed time for changes to be made. Dean Adams called in Mitchell Wilder, director of the Amon Carter Museum in Fort Worth, who had worked with John Meem on the design of the Colorado Springs Fine Arts Center, to advise on the modifications. The

A dental hygiene program was established in the College of Pharmacy with the help of a $113,000 Kellogg Foundation grant.

art museum and the fine arts library were included in the final drawings—over the stated University policy of no branch libraries. There was no great delay in completing the bid documents.

Professor Don Schlegel had been asked by President Popejoy to look into the problems that had arisen during the programming and planning of the Fine Arts Center. He found that the administration had exerted little or no control over the budget, the stated space needs, and University policies. Schlegel and architect George Wright, who was an adjunct professor of architecture, told the president that a University staff architect was needed to exercise the required control. This led to the establishment of the Office of the University Architect in 1963 as had been recommended in the Warnecke Development Plan.

In November there was some excitement on campus when 125 pounds of TNT was uncovered by Springer Construction Company, excavating for new construction northeast of what is now the site of the College of Education. The explosives were buried about twelve feet deep. General Russell C. Charlton, former captain of Headquarters Troop, 111th Cavalry, which had been using the campus for training, told a reporter the government had shipped the explosives to him in 1930 for use by the demolition team. There was no place to store it so it was buried in one of the horse stables. As time went by, everyone forgot about it. The explosive material was removed from the campus and destroyed.

At the November 11, 1961, meeting of the Board of Regents, several actions were taken affecting building projects. The board approved remodeling the old Student Union Building (11) for the Department of Anthropology and adding a museum. The board also authorized bidding for construction of the College of Education complex and phase one of the Fine Arts Center. Since the University's share of the state bond issue would not cover both projects, it was decided to leave off the concert hall and build it later when the Eubank land could be sold.

Sherman Smith reported that Coryell Berry, a nationally recognized consultant on University housing, had been contracted to prepare a long-range plan for dormitory construction and to establish design criteria. He recommended building dormitories for 153 women and 357 men, then adding more in three-year increments. It was assumed that Mesa Vista Hall would not be used for housing much longer as it was needed for office space. William W. Ellison was appointed architect for the proposed dormitories.

Architect Ellison developed plans for a three-story air-conditioned dormitory for 153 women east of Hokona dormitory.

Tony Hillerman, administrative assistant to President Popejoy, heard the Sandoval County sheriff needed mattresses following a fire in the jail. Hillerman knew some mattresses were stored on the campus by the Peace Corps and arranged for thirteen of them to be shipped to the sheriff. During lobbying for approval of the Medical School in the 1961 legislative session, a senator from Sandoval County expressed his appreciation to Hillerman for the mattresses and Tony asked for his help with the legislation. The senator said a committee member was in his debt and he would see he voted for the school. Hillerman says the story is true, so maybe the thirteen mattresses assured the founding of the Medical School. The vote was six to five according to one source and eight to seven according to another.

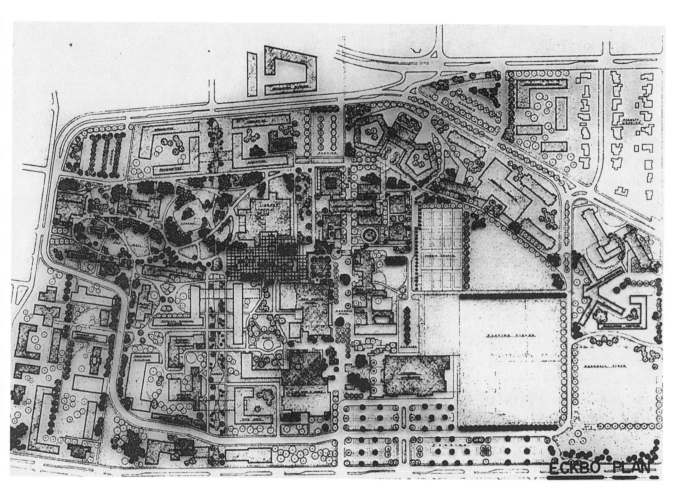

Garrett Eckbo, of the firm of Eckbo, Dean, and Williams, prepared a landscape plan for the Central Campus to implement the Warnecke Development Plan.

A men's dormitory for 175, but without air conditioning, was proposed northeast of Coronado dormitory. These dormitories were later named Santa Clara (61) and Oñate (157) Halls. Ellison's long-range plan called for six dormitories for women housing 1,058 and two service buildings, as well as another men's unit north of Coronado on Redondo Drive. A low-interest loan from the Housing and Home Finance Administration had been approved.

During 1962 the University bought, sold, and swapped many parcels of land. Negotiations were proceeding with C. R. Davis for the purchase of about a hundred acres on the west side of University Boulevard north of Stadium Boulevard. Davis was asking $13,500 per acre for land he had bought three years earlier at $2,500 an acre. The Board of Realtors said $6,000 to $8,000 was more reasonable. At the same time they asked UNM to change its land policy because they charged the University was using its tax-exempt status to compete with private enterprise and making land deals in secret. Popejoy pointed out that all recent actions concerning real estate, including the Winrock lease, were taken in open meetings. He also noted that some realtors had approached the University with proposals.

Addressing the regents on September 14, 1962, a committee of realtors expressed "grave concern" over what they termed unfair competition to private enterprise by the University in the sale, purchase, and leasing of land. The committee said the University should not seek income from real estate investments, such as Winrock, should divest itself of any land that had no future educational use, should not buy any more land not to be used for educational purposes, and should cease leasing and subdividing land. The charge that UNM was negotiating real estate deals in private was reiterated. President Popejoy rebutted the committee's recommendations item by item. He was supported by Regents Lawrence H. Wilkinson, Bryan G. Johnson, and Howard C. Bratton. Because two members were absent, action was deferred.

Plans for the development of a University-owned research park were presented to the regents on November 17, 1962, by Robert Nordhaus, president of the Albuquerque Industrial Development Corporation, and John Daly, the executive secretary. This time the Board of Realtors gave enthusiastic approval since it was not competing with private enterprise. The site would be either on the South Campus or on land north of Lomas Boulevard that could be leased from Southwest Construction Company.

A perspective of the area between the library and the New Mexico Union as originally designed by Garrett Eckbo.

Ash Street looking west from the just-completed mall in front of the New Mexico Union. Photograph by Richard P. Meleski, UNM Photo Service.

In early January 1963 President Popejoy announced that the research park would be located on the South Campus on land bounded by University Boulevard, Saint Cyr, and Coal, which had been acquired from C. R. Davis. The University proposed to sell part of the 2,000 acres owned near the airport to pay for the Davis property.

The city had acquired right-of-way for the widening of Central Avenue from Yale Boulevard east to Jefferson, but to extend the project west the University had to give twenty feet on the north side of Central from University to Buena Vista. The project widened the street sufficiently to provide two lanes of traffic each way, a fourteen-foot median for protected turns, and a parking lane on each side. It was done in phases, but the street was torn up for a long time.

This headline appeared in the March 15 *Daily Lobo*: "When They Build Those New Buildings—How in the Hell Will We Get to Them?" The writer, David Rogoff, complained that while Central Avenue was blocked because of the widening, the city closed Lomas for two weeks. The only ways to get on campus were by a dirt street off Girard to the Johnson Gymnasium parking lot and from University Boulevard on the west. To make matters worse, the night he tried to reach the New Mexico Union the police had closed Redondo on the east side of the campus to control traffic to and from the state basketball tournament being held in Johnson Gymnasium.

Garrett Eckbo's landscape architectural firm, Eckbo, Dean, and Williams from South Pasadena, California, had been commissioned in 1962 to prepare a landscape plan of the central part of the main campus. He worked for several months with Sherman Smith and the Committee on the Master Plan. The Eckbo plan took the Warnecke plan as a base. Both plans had a water element between Zimmerman Library and the Administration Building. Eckbo replaced the round pond in the Warnecke plan with an irregular pond with soft edges and a pedestrian bridge and omitted the lagoon projected down Yale. He planned a parklike area around the pond that extended on the west to the Alumni Chapel and to Roma Avenue on the north.

The park gave way to a more urban space on the south side of Zimmerman Library extending up massive steps to Mesa Vista Hall on the east and down what was Cornell Boulevard to the south side of the New Mexico Union. The area of the College of Education complex was designed as a separate unit using hard and soft (caliche and gravel) paving with limited grass areas.

The Committee on the Master Plan met on October 15, 1962, to review the Eckbo landscape plan with additional members present: Vice President Harold Enarson, Professor of Biology Howard J. Dittmer, and Professor of Mathematics James V. Lewis. Myron Fifield protested the inclusion of a pond, citing high maintenance costs, but the committee disagreed, saying the pond was a "must."

In December the University leased 8.5 acres behind Frontier Ford from Southwest Construction Company to be subleased for fraternity and sorority housing. The zoning was later changed to "special use." The street down the center of the property, Mesa Vista Road, terminates on the west in a cul-de-sac. The plot plan allowed lots for several houses, but to date only two sororities have built there, Alpha Chi Omega on the north side of the road and Kappa Kappa Gamma on the south side.

There was bad news from Washington in December when Congress did not approve a bill to finance medical schools. The Basic Sciences Building, designed by W. C. Kruger and Associates, would have to be cut back to three stories at 90,000 square feet. The reduced building plus movable equipment and utilities was estimated to cost $3 million. The plan was to complete the building when more funds were available.

The 7-Up Bottling Plant on Stanford Drive north of the BC-I Hospital was the first home of the School of Medicine. Photograph by Jim Squires, UNM Photo Service.

Within months Senator Clinton P. Anderson announced a National Institutes of Health grant toward construction. Dean Fitz and architect Robert Krueger presented the preliminary plans to the Board of Regents at their meeting on April 8, 1963. The estimate for construction was $3.74 million to be covered by the grant and Kellogg Foundation funds, some University funds, and the remainder from other smaller grants. This would be two-thirds of the building as originally planned. In June 1964 Senator Anderson and Representatives Joseph Montoya and Thomas G. Morris announced the award of an additional grant toward the construction of research space, so the building could be its original design of four floors and a basement.

A five-year lease-purchase agreement was finally reached for the old 7-Up bottling plant (201) on the east side of Stanford Boulevard north of the hospital. Medical School Dean Reginald Fitz and his secretaries occupied the upper level; the beginning of a medical library was on the ground floor. Physical Plant personnel added some research laboratories on the east and south sides of the building. Negotiations continued for the purchase of the Exeter-Tonella Mortuary just north of the 7-Up plant.

At the December 1963 regents meeting Popejoy predicted large enrollment increases in future years and announced a record-breaking building program that included a major addition to Zimmerman Library, additions to the Biology and Physics Buildings, new dormitories, $5 million to start the Medical School, and possibly $2 million to build the concert hall if the Eubank land could be sold. The Board of Regents had put 82.5 acres of the land on the market at $2.5 million.

A short time later the president's annual report came out. It added an addition to the Fine Arts Center for the drama department, an engineering building, more dormitories, and facilities for the College of Business Administration and the social sciences programs to the list of urgently needed buildings. The report said UNM would need $6.45 million in 1963–64 and $5 million in 1964–65. Other projects were a student health facility, utility extensions, an addition to the Chemistry Building, and equipment for the new year-round Peace Corps training center. The Peace Corps had moved into an unused part of Hodgin Hall while Don Schlegel was completing plans for their buildings later erected at the D. H. Lawrence ranch north of Taos.

Other 1963 projects were the first phase of the Fine Arts Center nearing completion, the addition to the Journalism Building for the University Press and the post office, and a 1.25 million-gallon underground reservoir north of Johnson Gymnasium with tennis courts on top designed by structural engineer Fred Fricke.

(*Opposite*) A plan of the campuses made from aerial photographs in 1964 by Limbaugh Engineering.

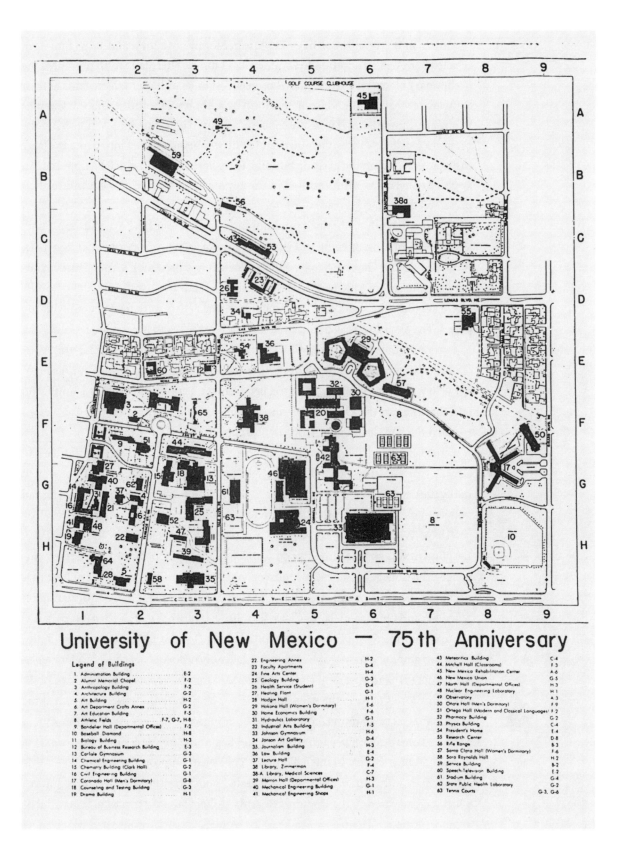

University of New Mexico — 75th Anniversary

Earlier in the year, the firm of Ferguson, Stevens, Mallory, and Pearl had been selected to design an addition to Zimmerman Library. Sherman Smith presented the preliminary plans with an estimated project cost of $2 million to the regents at their September meeting. It had been approved by a library committee and the Campus Planning Committee and was subsequently approved by the regents. While doing the program for the addition, George Pearl felt he was being pushed into using the large east reading room in the existing building for other purposes, which he opposed. An appeal to Sherman Smith resulted in the appointment of a review committee that preserved the beautiful reading room.

Clinton Adams had obtained funds for hiring a director of the Art Museum, Frank Van Deren Coke. An opening show, *Taos and Santa Fe Artists' Environment 1882–1942*, was scheduled for October 9, 1963. Mitchell Wilder had the Amon Carter Museum underwrite the cost of putting the show together, including a handsome catalog, while UNM supplied the space and the labor. Sixty-one artists were represented with 109 pieces. The exhibit was also displayed in Fort Worth, Texas, and La Jolla, California.

I was a partner in the firm of McHugh and Hooker, Bradley P. Kidder and Associates in Santa Fe when I heard the University was going to appoint a campus planner who would also have architectural involvement. I applied to Sherman Smith who was chairman of the Campus Planning Committee and after several interviews I received the appointment as University architect.

Some years later, Sherman Smith told me that when I applied, the committee had already made a somewhat reluctant selection and had asked President Popejoy to notify the person. Popejoy was in Santa Fe when Smith called him and learned he had not yet made the call. Smith asked him to wait until they interviewed me.

"UNM Will Not Soon Forget 1963" proclaimed the headline in the *Daily Lobo*. Enrollment was approaching 10,000 and several building projects were being completed. The College of Education and various components of the College of Fine Arts occupied their new facilities. The School of Medicine plans were proceeding on schedule, and Oñate and Santa Clara dormitories were opened. A research park was approved for the South Campus. By January 1964 Dean of Students Sherman Smith proposed going ahead with the next two smaller dormitories, which were later named Santa Ana (71) and Alvarado (157). Schlegel said the University had to look to high-rise dormitories to meet the need and conserve land. Action was deferred, but at the next board meeting Smith recommended building a 170-bed women's dormitory and a 230-bed men's dormitory immediately and beginning to plan a high-rise dormitory that would be occupied in the fall of 1966. The regents approved this plan.

Sherman Smith and I prepared a suggested policy for the selection of architects, which he presented to the Board of Regents at their January meeting. It stated that architects who wished to be considered for University work would ask the University

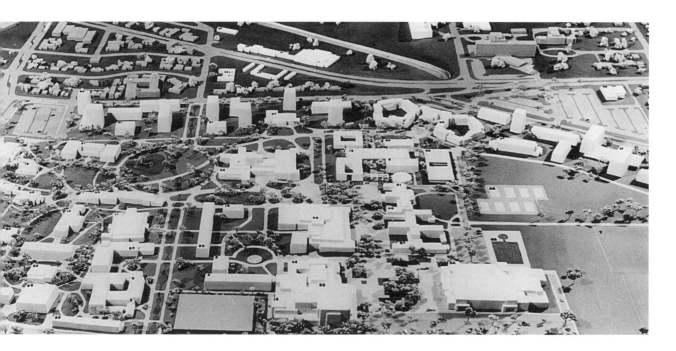

architect to keep their names on file. The Campus Planning Committee would review the applications, interview the architects, and recommend two or three firms in order of preference to the president, who would then make his recommendation to the Board of Regents for final approval. This procedure worked well for as long as I was University architect. Professor of English Hoyt Trowbridge reported to the regents that the Campus Planning Committee had followed this procedure in the selection of architects for two new projects. The committee recommended Ferguson, Stevens, Mallory, and Pearl for the addition to the Physics Building and Flatow, Moore, Bryan, and Fairburn for the Biology Building addition. The regents approved both appointments.

The seventy-fifth anniversary celebration was getting close. Don Schlegel and some of his architecture students had been working for months on a model of the campus. The model was made in a room in Schlegel's house at 1712 Ridgecrest Southeast, and when it was finished it was too big to get out of the house without tearing out an outside wall, which they did. Schlegel said they intended to remodel the house anyhow.

Myron Fifield, director of the Physical Plant Department, ordered 300 red flags with the University logo in white to be flown from fifteen-foot flagpoles set along Central Avenue from Girard to University and up the Stanford entrance to Johnson Gymnasium. Max Flatow designed some entrance structures to be built at Stanford and Central as his gift to UNM.

A large model of the campus prepared by Professor of Architecture Donald Schlegel and his students for the seventy-fifth anniversary of UNM.

The recital hall in the Fine Arts Center named for Professor of Music Walter Keller. Photograph by Richard P. Meleski, UNM Photo Service.

(Right) The organ in Keller Hall; Professor of Music Wesley Selby, organist. Photograph by Richard P. Meleski, UNM Photo Service.

Also part of the seventy-fifth birthday observance was an exhibit titled *Art Since 1889* in the Art Museum. It presented the major movements and styles in modern European and American art. More than eighty leading figures were represented beginning with a landscape painting by Paul Gauguin. Dean Clinton Adams described the show as the greatest in scope and quality ever exhibited in New Mexico to that time.

During the celebration, the College of Education Buildings were dedicated. A time capsule was buried on the east side of the walk leading to the south entrance of the administration unit. A University of New Mexico medal, designed by Art Professor Ralph Douglas, was presented to Senator Clinton P. Anderson for his efforts in behalf of the University. More than 600 people, clad in academic robes and representing many universities and national and international learned and professional societies, marched through the campus to Johnson Gymnasium for the convocation. Senator Anderson was the main speaker.

On March 16, 1964, the regents approved construction of an eighteen-hole golf course on the South Campus with Robert F. Lawrence of Tucson, Arizona, as the golf

The Art Museum in the Fine Arts Center. The sculpture in the center, *Torso,* by Gaston Lachaise and a piece by José de Rivera were purchased from an art allowance in the project budget of the Concert Hall. Photograph by Richard P. Meleski, UNM Photo Service.

The bell from the USS *New Mexico* was moved from the tower of the Administration Building to a bell tower designed by architect Max Flatow as a gift to UNM.

course architect. The Campus Planning Committee, meeting on March 24, approved a site at the head of the stairs on the new plaza north of the New Mexico Union for a tower to hold the bell of the USS *New Mexico* then mounted in one of the towers of the Administration Building. Max Flatow designed the fifteen-foot steel-framed structure, and Alpha Phi Omega fraternity financed it. It was dedicated in a ceremony on Armistice Day, 1964.

The UNM property at Eubank and I-40 was put up for sale in the first part of 1964 to obtain money for construction projects, including the concert hall. The asking price on the 82.59 acres north of the freeway was $1.2 million; for the 153.2 acres south of the freeway the University wanted $1.5 million.

Wylie Brothers Construction Company was given a contract to extend the loop road from Cornell to Terrace and had started grading in early 1964 when the *Daily Lobo* took the "Master Planner" to task for running a road through Yale Park and building what the writer termed a lizard–prairie dog reserve. A reporter wrote beneath the headline "Campus Goes into Chaos; Master Planner Hits Again":

> It seems that our campus is in the hands of a madman, hiding behind the title of Master planner. One of the many such solutions is the Redondo Drive project, a project which will make it impossible to get off campus once one gets in. . . . The sixty-foot right of way required through the city park was obtained by some sort of deal with the City of Albuquerque and enables the Master planners to continue the Drive on to the west and wipe out all the *Lobo* staff parking.

In an editorial, the editor, Carroll Cagle, complained about the tons of rocks that had been dumped near the College of Education complex. They were rocks brought in from the Sandia Mountains to be used in landscaping the college patios. He also wrote, "the campus is just plain ugly in certain parts—and is growing worse in others." This was certainly true. And it got worse as the campus literally became a construction yard for several years as more and more streets, buildings, and utility extensions disrupted campus life.

A commitment had been made to start the Medical School academic program in September 1964, and it was apparent the Basic Sciences Building would not be completed by then. A decision was made to erect temporary metal buildings (209, also called Med 4, 5, and 6) for laboratories and classrooms. In August 1964 Hesselden Construction Company was given the contract to erect the first one and a laboratory casework contract was let. An addition to the former 7-Up plant for the medical library was later added to the contract. Unfortunately, the "temporary" buildings have become very permanent.

The first unit of the Fine Arts Center had been occupied for more than a year when it was dedicated on October 20, 1964, with ceremonies in the recital hall. Regent

Howard Bratton and President Popejoy made the dedicatory statements. William Howard Schuman, director of the Lincoln Center for the Performing Arts, was the main speaker. Schuman and Rene d'Harnoncourt, director of the Museum of Modern Art in New York, received honorary doctor of fine arts degrees.

When the regents met on November 27, 1964, they approved the award of a contract to George A. Rutherford for the construction of a major addition of research space to the Physics and Meteoritics Building (207). The addition was funded in part by a grant from the National Science Foundation (NSF). Planning and programming had been done under the direction of the chairman of the Physics Department, Victor H. Regener, who also arranged for the NSF grant.

Rendering of proposed addition to the Department of Physics and Astronomy Building by George C. Pearl of the firm of Ferguson, Stevens, Mallory, and Pearl.

The College of Education Complex

When Chester Travelstead became dean of the College of Education in 1956, one of his main objectives was to obtain a new building. He was appalled at the poor physical condition of the several buildings in which the faculty, staff, and students worked and learned. He told President Popejoy that rats and pigeons had taken over the top floor of Hodgin Hall, closed off years before by the State Fire Marshal for code violations. The interior finishes in the lower floors were the same as when Hodgin was remodeled during Tight's administration and the original exterior stucco was now cracked and spalling. In 1958 the faculty rose in protest of their poor facilities. There was no indication the administration would do anything about the situation until Popejoy invited Travelstead and Professor Wilson Ivins to a Rotary Club meeting where the president gave a talk about the University. Much to their pleased astonishment he said a new building for the College of Education was at the top of the University's priority list.

After Popejoy had added a building for the College of Education to his priority list, a building committee was formed to select an architect and assist in the planning. This was the first UNM

Freshly poured concrete slabs at the College of Education collapsed the shoring underneath on May 21, 1962, causing considerable damage. Photograph by Richard P. Meleski, UNM Photo Service.

Aerial view of completed College of Education Complex. Photograph by Jerry Goffe.

project for which a detailed written program of requirements was prepared. A committee consisting of Professor Alexander Masley as chairman, faculty members Wilson Ivins, Grace Elser, and William Runge, and Dean Travelstead was to determine space needs and recommend an architect. Popejoy appointed Donald P. Schlegel of the Department of Architecture to be a consultant to the college, prepare a preliminary program, and be a liaison between the committee and the architect. The committee interviewed several architectural firms, visited their offices, and looked at their completed buildings. They finally chose the firm of Flatow, Moore, Bryan, and Fairburn. The president and the regents agreed and Flatow became the partner in charge of the project.

What was called a pre-preliminary plan was presented to the regents in February 1961 by Dean Chester Travelstead and Max Flatow. It was approved after Flatow said it would follow the Pueblo Style. The full preliminary plans were presented to the regents in April by Flatow and William Jette of the firm and Professors Don Schlegel and Frank Angel, who was chairman of the college building committee. The plans were approved and the architects were authorized to prepare the working drawings and specifications.

No other complex of buildings since Meem's 1930s work has had as much impact in shaping campus buildings that followed. Certainly none

created as much discussion about its design appropriateness as did this creation of Max Flatow and his architectural firm.

In selecting a site Flatow and the committee worked with Lawrence Lackey and Alfred Baxter Jr., who were doing preliminary work on the Warnecke General Development Plan. The planners were recommending creating a loop road and closing through-campus streets. The site chosen required closing Cornell, which met with widespread disapproval by the campus population, but it was done.

Flatow's concept was to build several separate buildings with different functions and locate them inside a semienclosed complex. Massive, sloping, windowless walls formed the exterior so that when viewed from the outside the complex had a fortress-like appearance. The metal curtain walls either faced into courtyards or were protected by end walls set in a few feet. Flatow compared the plan to the pueblo ruins at Coronado State Monument on the banks of the Rio Grande. He wrote: "In this design the architects were influenced by the Indians' mastery of using walls and buildings to create outside usable spaces within a controlled situation. The so-called 'mesa wall' theme is repeated but is of secondary importance to the spaces that these walls enclose."

The Education Administration Building (65) houses administrative functions in the west end

Interior of the Kiva, a large round classroom building. Photograph by Lowell Johnson.

and library-teaching functions in the east end separated by a through passageway that created many problems of noise, security, and cold drafts. The working areas were placed on a raised floor over a basement housing mechanical equipment and storage. Double-T precast concrete panels supported by round concrete columns form the roof framing system.

The Kiva (69) is a round classroom-auditorium that seats some 200 people depending on the configuration of the movable seating and tables. It is almost completely enclosed by glass curtain walls. The dome roof is built of sixteen-inch-deep by ten-inch-wide ribs that support a three-and-a half-inch concrete roof slab. The ribs are held in place by a concrete tension ring on the perimeter reinforced with prestressed steel wire and supported by round concrete columns. There is a concrete compression ring at the apex.

In addition to these buildings the complex includes the Faculty Office Building (63); the Industrial Arts Building (64); Simpson Hall (66), named for Elizabeth P. Simpson, former chair of the Home Economics Department, now called Counseling and Family Studies; the Classroom

Building (67); Masley Hall, art education, named for Alexander S. Masley, former chair of the department; and Manzanita Center, an education laboratory (70).

Bids on the College of Education complex and the Fine Arts Center taken on January 3, 1962, were both over budget. Negotiations during the next few days reduced both bids, and when the regents met on January 20 the board authorized the president to use all the University's resources to seek funds for the projects, including increasing student fees and getting approval from the Board of Finance for a bond issue. Lembke Construction Company was awarded the contract for the Fine Arts Center; Underwood and Testman received the College of Education project.

The worst construction disaster ever to hit the University occurred on May 21, 1962, at the College of Education construction site, when a concrete floor slab that had just been poured collapsed the shoring below and crashed to the ground. Fortunately no one was killed or injured. The slab, which damaged or destroyed eighteen columns as it went down, was 55 feet wide, 132 feet long, and 8½ inches thick; it weighed an estimated 370 tons.

The contractor had used a manufactured shoring system and the question was whether the patented system failed or had been installed incorrectly. It was a costly loss to the contractor, Underwood and Testman.

In the other buildings round concrete columns supported flat, two-way concrete slabs, 8½ inches thick and poured in place. These were all new construction techniques for the University. Deflection of the two-way concrete slabs has caused problems.

The Physical Plant's Myron Fifield was insistent that the precast concrete wall panels have a uniform color. It became apparent during their manufacture that color variances were occurring and he pointed this out to Flatow, who blamed the curing process and the small piece of sandpaper he was given to match. He wrote to Fifield, "This whole matter resolves itself down into an aesthetic one which we, as the architects, consider most important. In this regard we hope that responsible authorities at the University will evaluate closely the danger in monotony that would occur at the University if all of the buildings were exactly the same color and texture."

Many panels were rejected. Suggestions included putting panels of similar shading together or coating them with one of the newly developed epoxy products. The problem was not easily resolved and there was voluminous correspondence between Fifield, Flatow, and various companies that manufactured epoxy coatings for exterior walls. Flatow recalls that the contractor applied an epoxy coating to the panels to even out the color.

The low walls around the patios and plazas were of concrete block with no reinforcing, held together by a thin-set epoxy joint compound and stuccoed. They developed cracks immediately and some were blown over by high winds. Many of them have since been replaced.

During the summer of 1963 the College of Education moved out of Hodgin Hall and other scattered buildings into their new facility, which was immediately hailed by professionals as an "architectural milestone." Others on campus were not so pleased with the design, thinking it departed too much from the traditional Pueblo Style developed and refined by John Gaw Meem.

Tremendous heat gain in the Kiva from the sun shining through the glass walls prompted a professor to cover the glass with wrapping paper. The trapped heat caused many of the panels to shatter, so curtains were quickly installed several inches away from the glass. It helped, but the air-conditioning was always a problem. The noise of the circulating fans was very distracting.

Other than the structural problems, one of the most difficult issues to solve was the expanding space needs of the college. The one- and two-story buildings used all the existing area and made additions impossible. Therefore the college has moved into adjacent Mesa Vista and Hokona Halls.

For the first time since PWA-WPA days a significant amount of artwork was included in a new campus project. Art Professor John Tatschl designed and built the faceted glass wall on the west side of the Administration Building; Herman Goldman designed and built the fountain on the south side; and Art Professor Carl Paak created ceramic catch basins for the patios and a ceramic mural in the Classroom Building (67). All the basins and the mural have disappeared.

Landscaping was one of the first items to be eliminated when the construction bids exceeded the budget. Popejoy said it could be done later. For some time the complex sat in a sea of sand and gravel enduring mud when it rained and sandblasting on windy days. Landscaping was done incrementally over several years beginning around 1964.

In an article in *New Mexico Architecture*, Bainbridge Bunting wrote:

The heart of the design problem and the crux of the controversy that the buildings have raised is an old one: tradition vs. the modern—or at least what momentarily passes for modern. The distinction of Mr. Flatow's design, in the opinion of this reviewer, is that while it respects and draws inspiration from traditional architecture of this region, it also accepts modern technology without apologies. And in drawing from both the old and the new, the design avoids crippling compromise and rises, instead, to a new and creative plane which is uniquely appropriate to the particular problems at hand.

Bunting pointed out that the architect had omitted the usual clichés: viga ends and zapatas (corbels) and forced batter of the walls. Instead he respected the more basic roots of New Mexico tradition and drew ideas from them. He also said the critics who were looking for recognizable clichés were seeing the new buildings as "something Egyptian or equally absurd." He closed the article saying: "A significant chapter has just been written in the history of the University of New Mexico's campus development. A bold yet eminently logical and well-considered approach to the problem of a modern architectural expression for this region has been indicated."

The Education Complex received several design awards including, in 1964, a First Award from the New Mexico Chapter of the American Institute of Architects: "The jury found this group of buildings to be an unusually interesting group of traditional elements of the New Mexican culture … and it felt that the particular significance of this group of buildings is in the way it has caught the spirit of the place, and has broken with a tradition in a way which can set the sights of other architects toward carrying on in a similar spirit."

Tony Hillerman wrote in *New Mexico School Review*: "Flatow took a quick look at the design of the Indian pueblo itself. The result is a complex which suggests its pueblo heritage through massive, sloping exterior walls, through use of buildings surrounding and protecting interior patios, and through use of exterior colors matching the warm earth tones of the 'Pueblo on the Mesa' campus." The complex was chosen as the "Building of the Month" for April 1967 by *College and University Business,* a national publication, which featured another article by Bunting.

An award came in 1990 when the New Mexico Society of Architects honored the complex with a 25 Year Award for its influence on state architects and architecture. Some College of Education administrators wanted to know how this could be, considering the many problems with the buildings. These awards have increased acceptance of the design of the College of Education buildings and thus eased my task of gaining approval for other architects' innovative concepts that respected the traditional Pueblo Style, without attempting to copy it.

A wall of colored glass designed by Art Professor John Tatschl, shown here, and erected by him and two of his students.

A Symphony Hall and a Pit

In early January 1965 the Board of Finance refused to accept the Board of Educational Finance (BEF) recommendations for apportioning the $8 million general obligation bond issue approved by the electorate in November 1964. Several representatives of the public colleges and universities also protested the BEF's proposed allocations. Ben Hernandez, a UNM alumnus and a member of the Board of Finance, said New Mexico could not support six major institutions of higher education and should concentrate on UNM and New Mexico State. He said UNM should get $3.77 million, instead of the recommended $3.25 million, based on a table he presented showing that, on a pure enrollment factor, UNM had not received its proportionate share of the last two state bond issues. Hernandez said he felt UNM was penalized because it would probably be able to get federal funding for construction. He made a motion that the board postpone action and ask the BEF to review its decision. The unprecedented motion passed but not before Governor Jack M. Campbell, who was in attendance, made several suggestions to arbitrate the situation including improving communication between the BEF and the schools.

Governor Campbell called a meeting of the Board of Finance in his office on February 9 to hear a report from the BEF chairman, William Gilbert. Gilbert said the board had reviewed its allocation recommendation and found no reason to change it. The Board of Finance then voted 3 to 2 to approve the BEF's recommendation.

At the January 10, 1965, meeting the regents considered bids taken in December for construction of two major buildings. Lembke Construction Company was low bidder on both the Concert Hall (72) phase of the Fine Arts Center and the addition to Zimmerman Library (53). Regent Thomas Roberts asked whether the firm was able to do both projects simultaneously and I assured him it could since it was one of the largest construction companies in the state. The award of both contracts was approved.

Rendering of the proposed addition to Zimmerman Library by George C. Pearl of the firm of Ferguson, Stevens, Mallory, and Pearl. Photograph by Jerry Goffe.

The design of Zimmerman Library by John Gaw Meem in 1936–37 provided for an addition to the east behind the stack tower. Architect George Pearl wrapped the new building, which consisted of three floors and a basement of stack space, around the tower and created a new entrance on the south opening toward the future Smith Plaza. The addition totaled 97,160 square feet and was designed to accommodate 600,000 volumes. A large entrance lobby connected with the existing building, and space was allocated for administrative offices and technical services as well as a loading dock on the north side. Temporary faculty offices were located on the east side of the second and third floors. The east facade was a curtain wall with structural connections at each floor for a future addition. Other than the passageway to the new addition and the creation of the Anderson Room to house the collection of southwestern materials given UNM by Senator Clinton P. Anderson, the interior of the existing building was left virtually untouched. A new elevator shaft was erected on the east side of the existing stack tower, which was not too attractive but seemed to be the only way to provide access for the handicapped to the nine-level tower and to meet building code requirements.

During the planning of the addition President Tom Popejoy's attention was called to the proposal to remove the lower third of one of Kenneth Adams's murals to accommodate a connecting corridor. He wrote Dean of Students Smith that this should not be allowed, so the corridor was moved.

Construction of the first library addition was completed in the summer of 1966. The equipment had been bid earlier and was installed in time for the fall semester.

The Concert Hall (72) was named for Thomas Lafayette Popejoy, president of the University of New Mexico from 1948 to 1968. Sherman Smith had asked him if he would like to have the

In 1966 Mr. and Mrs. Gilbert Maxwell presented the University with $20,000 worth of oil stocks to start a fund-raising drive to build an addition to the Anthropology Museum.

football stadium named for him and he replied he would rather have the Concert Hall as his memorial.

The South Campus Golf Course budget included $120,000 for a clubhouse. I had been requested by many architectural firms to recommend them for University work, and it seemed to me this would be a perfect project for an architectural competition. I persuaded the administration and the regents to allow me to put the competition together. I followed the rules established by the American Institute of Architects, which provided for fair, unbiased judging. Only in-state architects who had never done work for the University were allowed to enter. Monetary prizes were awarded for the second- and third-place designs, and the first-place winner was given the contract to design the clubhouse. Judges were O'Neil Ford, FAIA, of San Antonio, Texas; Donald P. Stevens, AIA, of Albuquerque; and Tom Popejoy. I served as the professional advisor.

The competition was a great success. There were twenty-two entries from all over the state. The judging took place during the annual state convention of the three New Mexico chapters of the American Institute of Architects. The winners

(*Above*) The new south entrance to Zimmerman Library.

The Anderson Room was designed to house the collection of southwestern literature donated to UNM by Senator Clinton P. Anderson.

The South Campus Golf Course Clubhouse designed by architect John Reed, who won a statewide competition. Photograph by Jerry Goffe.

were announced at the annual banquet on May 29 at the Alvarado Hotel. John Reed's design was awarded first place. McHugh, Kidder, and Plettenberg of Santa Fe won second place, and John Peter Varsa was third.

In March, House Bill 243, introduced by Representative Bobby Mayfield of Doña Ana County, would place a $42.5 million bond issue on the ballot of the next general election on November 8, 1966. The money from this bond issue would be the state's match for federal funds from the Higher Education Facilities Act (HEFA). Included in the bill was the formula for distribution of the funds, which had been prepared by the BEF staff. The bill passed the House by 61 to 1 and the Senate by 26 to 3 and was signed by the governor.

President Popejoy announced on March 26, 1965, that UNM would soon have a unique all-weather Olympic-size swimming pool. He said the pool would cost about $400,000 but he did not know where the money would come from other than it would not be from state bond funds. He noted that New Mexico State University had built a pool recently using bonds backed by student fees. Popejoy said the pool would be fifty meters long and have eight racing lanes. There would be a separate diving pool with a ten-meter board. The facility would meet all competitive pool requirements established by the NCAA.

An infrared heated Olympic-size pool designed by Milton Costello was rejected because of cost. Photograph by Richard P. Meleski, UNM Photo Service.

The design by Milton Costello, a swimming pool consultant, consisted of curved steel ribs that supported transparent plastic bubble-shaped wall panels. The space above the pool was open to the sky. Electric radiant heat would keep the deck and the swimmers warm. The water would be heated to eighty degrees in winter. In the summer, the lower panels would be removed and the sides opened. Unfortunately the estimates for construction and operation, especially the cost of electricity for heating the deck, indicated it was more than the University could afford.

There were many projects in the works in 1965, including the addition to Zimmerman Library (53) and the Concert Hall addition (72) to the Fine Arts Center (62). The tunnel extensions had parts of the campus torn up. Planning was proceeding on the addition to the Biology Building (21) and the Basic Sciences Building (211). A deep storm sewer was laid from the northwest corner of the New Mexico Union around Mesa Vista Hall to join an existing line south of Hokona Hall. That project really messed up that part of the campus for the whole summer and some of the fall semester. This drainage line had to be in place before any of the planned landscape malls could be constructed over it.

In 1965 James Webb Young, long-time director and senior partner of the J. Walter Thompson Advertising Agency, deeded his land holdings in the Jemez Mountains to the University. The 9,550-acre Jim Young Ranch borders the Rio Grande and Cochiti Lake, the Santa Fe National Forest, Bandelier National Monument, and the Cochiti Indian Reservation. An orchard on the land raises and sells Old Jim Young Apples locally and by mail order.

A rendering of the proposed basketball arena. Architect: Joe Boehning.

The Pit

In the spring of 1965 I received a call from President Popejoy asking me to select an architect and bring him to a meeting in his office to discuss a new athletic facility. Joe Boehning had been by to see me recently about doing some work for the University. Knowing he had been active in athletics while a student at UNM, I called Boehning and we met at Popejoy's office with Bob King, basketball coach, and Pete McDavid, director of athletics. Popejoy said he wanted to build a basketball arena that would seat 15,000 or more. He suggested it be built across University Boulevard west of the football stadium using the same type of construction that made the stadium so economical to build: excavate a bowl for the seating area. King wanted the seating to come as close to the playing court as possible. Popejoy said there should be no columns to interfere with any spectator's view. Suggestions were made to make the playing area

large enough for tennis competition and to put an ice hockey rink underneath a removable basketball floor. These ideas were turned down—it would be designed for basketball only. Above all, the arena had to be built as inexpensively as possible, preferably for less than $1 million, and it had to be ready for the first game of the 1966–67 season.

The Board of Regents approved the appointment of Joe Boehning as the architect in June. He came up with a preliminary design of a round building using suspended steel cables supporting a catenary configured roof. When a uniformly thick cable is suspended between two points, the curve it forms is called a catenary curve. There were to be forty-eight concrete columns thirty-one feet high supporting the cables. Precast concrete panels would be attached to the cables and the roofing material applied over them. With this inverted domelike roof structure,

170

After the roof was erected, the area for the floor and seating banks was excavated. Photograph by A. W. Boehning Jr.

A view of the arena showing the roof trusses before the siding was applied. Photograph by Bob Dauner, UNM Photo Service.

it is no wonder the *Albuquerque Tribune* printed a section drawn through the center of the arena upside down. Estimates showed this scheme to be too expensive.

The next design Boehning presented had a more conventional roof framing system and a grade-level concourse with about one-third of the seats above it. Popejoy turned it down saying he did not want people on the concourse interfering with the view of people behind it. Boehning then placed the entire seating bank below grade.

I suggested we look at a long-span roof system manufactured by the Behlen Company in Columbus, Nebraska. This system was an expansion of their construction methods used to build steel-framed farm buildings. Behlen had never built a roof with flat top trusses of the span we were talking about, but their engineers had no doubt they could do it.

The Behlen system consisted of fifteen-foot-high light-weight steel trusses spaced forty-one inches on center. The corrugated steel roof deck

A full house in the basketball arena. Photograph by Jerry Goffe.

and ceiling were bolted to the trusses to form the top and bottom chords of the truss. It has been referred to as a stressed skin system. The roof had a 7½-inch camber built in which reduced to five inches when the scaffolding was removed. The ceiling panels allowed workmen to move about freely in the truss space to install mechanical, electrical, and sound systems. Because of the depth of the trusses mechanical equipment rooms could

be placed in the four corners containing evaporative coolers that distributed cooled air through the ceiling space formed by the trusses into the seating space below.

Boehning squared the circle, so to speak, into a 294-foot-by-338-foot rectangle that covered approximately 2.3 acres. The top of the roof parapet was set at thirty-five feet above grade. The clear span over the playing floor and seating area was 252 feet. The arena floor was thirty-seven feet below the concourse level. There were thirty-one rows of chair-back seats and forty-three rows of bench seating. Below grade were dressing and locker rooms, a mechanical equipment room, and other support spaces all reached by a ramp from the arena floor with access to the outside for service vehicles. Ticket booths were located in the northeast and southwest corners of the building. Concession stands and restrooms were located off the concourse.

Frank Bridgers, the mechanical engineer on the project and a partner in the firm of Bridgers and Paxton, had a difficult time explaining to Popejoy why so much cooling would be required if the temperature outside was near freezing, but lights and 14,000-plus excited fans generate a lot of heat, which he estimated to be about 4 million BTUs per hour when there was a full house.

A concrete frame supported the Behlen system and the roof over the concourse. The exterior walls were concrete block and the floors were all

I had always opposed the idea of building a high-rise dormitory at UNM although demand and limited space made it seem practical. It would be the tallest building on campus and would certainly be an undesirable landmark. In my opinion the tower on Zimmerman Library was the University's symbolic structure, and if a taller building had to be built it should be in the academic area. In late June 1965, at a meeting of the Association of University Architects at Stanford University, I met Ernest J. Kump, who was designing some buildings for Stanford and receiving wide acclaim for the recently completed Foothills College campus. Kump and his work impressed me, and I thought he might come up with a design to make better use of the land available and provide the capacity with three- or four-story dormitories rather than the eight or nine stories planned in the high-rise.

concrete except the playing court, which was hardwood. King wanted a firm floor just like the one in Johnson Gymnasium so wood sleepers, or nailing strips, were specified under the subfloor.

The acoustical system was designed by Dr. C. R. Boner, a professor at the University of Texas at Austin, who specialized in sound systems for large auditoriums and sport facilities. He used the truss space to locate speakers throughout the arena and special circuiting to eliminate echo.

Bids were taken for construction of the Basketball Arena (302) on December 16, 1965. K. L. House Construction Company was the low bidder. The construction plan called for building the concrete frame that would support the roof first, then erecting the roof and spraying the acoustical treatment to the underside, and finally excavating for the arena floor and seating banks. This saved an enormous cost in scaffolding, which only had to be about 15 feet high. In order to protect the acoustical coating, all exhausts from excavating equipment and trucks had to be turned toward the floor. But even with this precaution the coating suffered some discoloration.

The final seat count was 14,850 and the cost per seat was $116 to make it one of the least expensive arenas ever built. In the years following completion, architects, coaches, and administrators from many universities across the country, and one group from Mexico, came to see how it had been done.

The building was completed in time for the December 1, 1966, game with Abilene Christian College, which the Lobos won 62–53. When the arena celebrated its thirtieth anniversary in 1996, it welcomed its eight-millionth fan. Sportswriter Richard Stevens had no kind words to say about the design other than it had become a legend. He wrote, "Heck, let's just come out and say it: It's ugly."

I never thought of the Basketball Arena as being ugly; I saw it as an economical, functional answer to a very difficult architectural problem. Many architects agreed with me because it received an honor award in 1966 from the Albuquerque chapter of the American Institute of Architects (AIA). The later expansion of the arena received awards from the New Mexico Society of Architects and the Western Mountain Region of the AIA. The arena was never designed to be an architectural gem, but the University certainly got its money's worth many times over. Joe Boehning did a good job. Imagine, if you can, what it would have looked like in the Pueblo Style! In 1999 *Sports Illustrated* ranked the Pit as thirteenth among the top twenty "favorite places in the world to view sports." It was second among college facilities, behind Duke University's Cameron Indoor Stadium at number four. Rick Wright of the *Albuquerque Journal* wrote, "the Pit, after all, is more than a building. . . . It truly is a showcase of college basketball."

I explained the problem to Kump and he was interested. He came to the campus in August 1965, the same time I had O'Neil Ford, another nationally recognized architect, here to try to formulate a plan for old Zimmerman Field, which was to be developed for academic buildings. After meeting with Sherman Smith and other administrators, Kump was given a contract as design architect for the dormitories and William Ellison was appointed project architect. Planning began in March 1966. Kump and his chief designer, Arthur B. Sweetzer, were into an Italian hill-town mode at that time. They envisioned several dormitory units wrapping around each other with landscaped walks, changing elevations, clustered around a central dining hall. Flights of stairs led up from Redondo Drive into this cluster of dormitories. Unfortunately, only half the project was ever built so the total effect is somewhat lost.

The completed Basic Sciences Building west side. Architect: W. C. Kruger and Associates. Photograph by Jerry Goffe.

The Basic Sciences Building is supported by a concrete raft slab about three feet thick. After the steel reinforcing was placed, an uninterrupted concrete pour lasted approximately seventy-two hours. This photograph shows the steel in place and the concrete pump being readied for the pour.

Even though Ford and his firm had wide experience in planning several campuses, he did not make a favorable impression on the Campus Planning Committee and was not employed to plan the Zimmerman Field area. When Robert E. Riley joined my office a few months later as campus planner, he was given the task.

The Board of Educational Finance approved a University revenue bond issue at their meeting in October 1965, to finance the Basketball Arena (302), the Olympic pool, the Kump-designed dormitories and dining hall (74, 75, 77), new KNME-TV studios (262), a utility package, and landscaping. The board approved the purchase of houses belonging to Sigma Phi Epsilon (159); Alpha Chi Omega (26); Chi Omega (27); Kappa Kappa Gamma, 221 University; and Alpha Delta Pi, 423 University. The houses would be used for staff and faculty offices and administrative functions.

Action at the October 9 regents meeting included the approval of a contract with Lembke Construction Company for the Basic Sciences Building (211; later named the Basic Medical Sciences Building).

In 1965 the University administration was beginning to realize that serious actions had to be taken to control the ever-growing parking problem but had put off establishing a fee system with controlled lots. Faculty and staff could still park free in all off-street lots and on some streets. Students could park in all open lots east of Yale. Modest fines of a few dollars were imposed for violations.

The agenda for the regents meeting on March 19, 1966, was full of items related to planning, financing, and construction contracts. There was a long discussion about the proposal by Ernest Kump and Associates to design three- and four-story dormitories. Kump said a high-rise would not be compatible with the University's architecture. Popejoy said several smaller units would allow flexibility in phasing the construction and would give much better utilization of space. They would also have a more homelike atmosphere. Dean Sherman Smith said the buildings would cover about 50 percent of the site and that was all right since the Warnecke Plan had been criticized for not recommending denser land utilization. The board approved the design concept.

The regents also approved a lease-purchase agreement for a furniture store on the southwest corner of Central and Stanford owned by O. G. Bradbury, which would be remodeled and enlarged for the Department of Architecture, part of the College of Fine Arts. George Wright and Associates, architects employed by Bradbury, exhibited a model. In addition to remodeling the existing building, a second floor and a shop wing on the southeast corner would be added.

Another major building approved at this meeting was the Student Health Center–University College Building (73) by Holien and Buckley. This building was sited over the recently completed deep storm sewer, so the lowest level, housing the University College, was surrounded by a sunken patio rather than being a basement space. The upper two levels, which housed both in-patient and out-patient facilities, were tied into Mesa Vista Hall on the north side and to the landscaped mall on the west side. Hesselden Construction Company's bid for the construction of the mall between the New Mexico Union (60) and Mesa Vista Hall (56) was accepted, as well as Weaver Construction Company's bid for the Golf Course Clubhouse on the South Campus.

Model of proposed men's dormitories (74 and 75) and dining hall (77) shows only what was built. The design architect was Ernest J. Kump and Associates and the project architect was William W. Ellison. Photograph by Jerry Goffe.

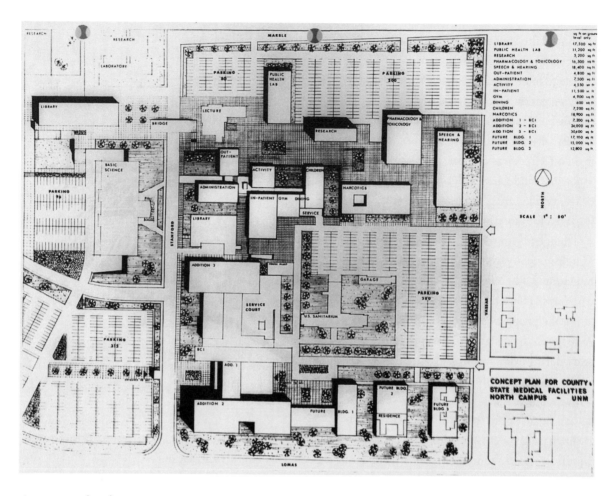

A concept plan for the North Campus was developed by Professor Don Schlegel in 1965.

Budgets were set for the biology addition, the Student Health–University College Building (73), and the College of Business Administration Building (76). Funds were to come from the state bond issue, HEFA, and some University sources.

The original design of the Albuquerque Metropolitan Arroyo Flood Control Authority (AMAFCA) flood control channel through the North Campus called for it to be open all the way from the intersection of Stanford Boulevard and Lomas Boulevard to the northern end. It seemed to me it would be wise to cover as much of the ditch at the south end as possible to provide parking for the hospital. After discussions with the administration and Regent Lawrence Wilkinson, a proposal was made to AMAFCA that resulted in their building a double box culvert 700 feet long from Stanford northwestward. The cost was to be paid for out of the money due the University for land taken for the ditch.

The faculty of the Medical School and the hospital had been developing plans for a mental health facility to be built by Bernalillo County on University land east of Stanford. W. C. Kruger and Associates was selected to do the architectural work in collaboration with Kaplan and McLaughlin of San Francisco, specialists in planning mental health facilities. A grant toward construction was made by the National Institute of Mental Health with funds from the Mental Health Centers Construction Act of 1963, and the county put in $800,000 from a bond issue.

At a Rotary Club meeting in April 1966, President Popejoy unveiled plans by Professor Don Schlegel for a vastly expanded Medical School with an estimated $150 million of future buildings including a Veterans Administration hospital. Until this time there had been little or no planning done beyond the siting of the Basic Medical Sciences Building. I was very concerned about this and with the cooperation of Dean Reginald Fitz had engaged Schlegel to prepare a plan that looked as far into the future as we could.

In describing the plan Schlegel said that building connections—the utility and circulation systems—were just as important as the buildings themselves. He planned a pedestrian-utility tunnel system going north from the hospital as far as necessary. Buildings would plug into it as they came into being and at ground level there would be a pedestrian mall connecting all the structures. He said the building forms were the most unpredictable aspect of the study and any statement of their location, size,

A section through Schlegel's plan showing how development could occur along the pedestrian-utility spine. Drawing by Don Schlegel.

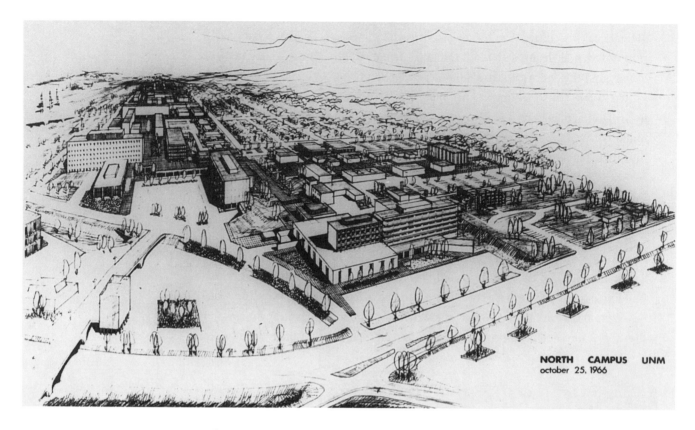

NORTH CAMPUS UNM
october 25, 1966

A perspective view showing potential North Campus development. Drawing by Don Schlegel.

More metal buildings were purchased in 1966 for the Medical School and erected on the east side of Stanford across the street from the Basic Medical Sciences Building. They were later moved to the northwest corner of Frontier and Vassar.

or shape would only be an educated guess and could well produce more problems than it would solve. The concept of the plan was well received and was followed to the extent that as buildings were built the tunnel system was extended. The heavily used tunnel extends from the hospital through the Cancer Research and Treatment Center (227) to the Family Practice Center (248) and the New Mexico Scientific Laboratory Building. The long uninterrupted pedestrian spine never materialized.

One of the pressing needs for the development of the plan was the possibility the Veterans Administration would build a hospital in the far north end of the North Campus Golf Course. One day Dean Fitz brought some VA representatives to my office to look at the plans. They indicated they would want the University to deed forty acres to the VA on which they would build a fully self-sufficient plant. Constitution Avenue would have to be extended through the golf course to connect with University Boulevard on the west. An agreement between the University and the VA was never reached and eventually buildings were added on their site in the southeast part of Albuquerque.

With strong backing from Governor Jack Campbell and in spite of some opposition from the medical community, the 1966 legislature approved UNM's request to add the third and fourth years to the School of Medicine.

An Arizona firm made an offer to purchase 82.59 acres of the University's Eubank-Coronado Freeway (I-40) property for $1.2 million. The plan was to develop a hotel–

The addition to the Biology Building, Castetter Hall (21). Architect: Flatow, Moore, Bryan, and Fairburn. Photograph by Jerry Goffe.

(*Left*) The Biology Building greenhouse. Photograph by Jerry Goffe.

tourist center on the north side of the freeway. The regents accepted the offer and this money paid for a large part of the construction of Popejoy Hall (72).

Architect Max Flatow and his staff at Flatow, Moore, Bryan, and Fairburn designed a unique addition to the Biology Building (21). The program had called for a large greenhouse; instead of making it a typical one-story adjunct to the building, they placed it at the main entrance. The existing building was L-shaped so the addition tied onto the short leg of the L leaving space for a sunken patio between. The greenhouse was two stories high, covered with tinted plexiglass domes set into the exposed structure. The department developed the main public area into a tropical botanical display with a water element, fish, birds, and flowering plants. The patio was planted with native New Mexico plants and the round pond was stocked with fish, frogs, and turtles. The pond is used in experiments by the students and faculty. This is a popular stop on all campus tours.

The other sides of the building were more of a problem. The lack of windows may have had some benefits in the laboratories but in reviewing the first presentation drawings, Sherman Smith said, "Max, you have given us the College of Education [again], can't you do something different?" All that resulted from that comment were a few small windows punched in the west wall.

The Business and Administrative Sciences Building. Architect: John Reed. Photograph by Jerry Goffe.

The infrastructure was in place in the South Campus Research Park and two buildings had been built when it was dedicated on June 6, 1966, by Governor Jack Campbell.

The design of the building for the College of Business Administration was "not strictly traditional, but regional" as Popejoy described it. Dean Thomas W. Christopher of the Law School said it looked like a lady's hat. Architect John Reed considered Kwataka Hall and territorial buildings in Santa Fe like Sena Plaza in designing the structure. By creating an open courtyard between the two elements he was able to provide windows into all the offices and work areas. There were four general-use classrooms in the south end of the ground floor with horseshoe-shaped seating banks. The Parish Library, named for former Dean William J. Parish, was located on the ground floor of the east section. The Bureau of Business Research was on the second floor; the west section was mostly classrooms and faculty offices. The regents approved the final plans at the meeting on September 21, 1966.

It was at this time President Popejoy decided it would be a good idea to remind committee members and architects involved in planning buildings of the "Regents' Policy" regarding architectural style. In a memorandum to Sherman Smith he quoted directly from the Warnecke Development Plan: "It is University policy that new buildings conform to the Spanish-Pueblo style of architecture."

The open passageway between the two segments of the Business and Administrative Sciences Building. Photograph by Jerry Goffe.

At the September 1966 meeting the regents approved the final plans for the Engineering Center (119) and the new dormitory complex later named Laguna (74), DeVargas (75), and La Posada (77), the dining hall. The Engineering Center was named by the regents the Marshall E. Farris Engineering Center. Farris had been with the University thirty-two years, twenty-nine as dean of the College of Engineering. The center was designed by Flatow, Moore, Bryan, and Fairburn to house laboratories on the lower floor and classrooms and administrative and faculty offices on the next three floors. A nuclear engineering laboratory with heavily shielded rooms was placed in a separate building on the southwest corner of the center.

October began on a gala note when Popejoy Hall (72) opened with a concert by the Utah Symphony Orchestra directed by Maurice Abravonel. Critics praised the hall's beauty and acoustical qualities. Howard Taubman of the *New York Times* wrote, "The sound is vivid, indeed too brilliant for complete comfort. Downstairs on the orchestra floor it is not only mellower, but also reasonably well balanced." Taubman said, "The hall is worthy of the finest metropolitan ensembles." He added, "The hall will certainly do for other events, but it is too big for straight drama." He was quite right in that statement.

On display in the foyer were pieces of art acquired with funds from the art allowance included in the construction project budget on direction of President Popejoy.

An orchestra on the stage of Popejoy Hall. Photograph by John Whiteside.

They included *Torso, 1927*, also known as *Elevation*, by Gaston Lachaise (1882–1935); *Construction Number 72*, a graceful, revolving, stainless steel sculpture by José de Rivera (1904–85); and several lithographic posters, including some by Henri de Toulouse-Lautrec (1864–1901), some of which were later stolen.

The University purchased ten acres on University Boulevard north of Lomas from the First Baptist Church. The City Commission finally approved the closing of Stanford from Marble to Lomas to clear the way for the addition to BC-I Hospital. The architects for the project were Flatow, Moore, Bryan, and Fairburn.

President Tom Popejoy officially opened the South Campus Golf Course on December 9, 1966, with a long drive down the center of the fairway. About 200 people attended the dedication and many of them played the new course. Playing in the first foursome with Popejoy were the architect for the club house, John Reed, Regent Lawrence Wilkinson, and Judge Howard Bratton. Popejoy told the crowd that the University had something going for it since the Fine Arts Center was completed, and

Aerial view of the campus, circa 1967.

"if things aren't going too well in sports we just tell the people that we're specializing in culture this year."

It was not long after this that *Golf Digest* ranked the course as one of the top five collegiate courses in the country, along with those at Yale, Stanford, Colgate, and Ohio State. It was also named one of "America's greatest tests of golf with eighteen long holes . . . home to roadrunners, ducks, jackrabbits, and cottontails plus some trout in the ponds."

CHAPTER TEN

Endings and Beginnings

The regents began 1967 by appointing Ferguson, Stevens, Mallory, and Pearl to design an addition to Clark Hall, the Chemistry Building (22); George Wright Associates to design a new building for the Law School (218); and Gathman and Long to plan the Automotive Maintenance Building (216) for the Physical Plant Department. Bids were taken on the Student Health Center–University College (73) project. George A. Rutherford's bid was below the architects' estimate and was approved.

The Board of Regents agreed in July 1967 to buy the Chi Omega house (27) at 1805 Roma and loan the sorority money to help finance a new house at 1810 Mesa Vista. It was designed by architect Dale Crawford; K. L. House Construction Company was selected to be the general contractor.

There was a land swap on the South Campus: the University got eight acres north and south of the football stadium from Albuquerque Public Schools. The City of Albuquerque leased land on the northeast corner of University and Stadium Boulevards for the proposed baseball stadium.

The city's long-range transportation plan called for University Boulevard to become a major north-south artery. Since the city owned the right-of-way of the existing street (which is now part of Redondo Drive) the city planners wanted to use it as the east portion of the new street. That would have put several University buildings too close to traffic. The UNM Development Plan called for Redondo to turn northward on Terrace to Ash then west to University. University was shown on the plan as a divided street, which would have taken a very wide strip of land. It seemed to me and my staff to be much more reasonable to try to get the city to move University Boulevard to the west and let the University have the old street as part of Redondo Drive with a buffer strip between it and the new right-of-way. This required several things to happen: the city would have to acquire right-of-way on the west side of University Boulevard, which meant condemning several pieces of property; the Kappa Sigma and Alpha Delta Pi houses on the campus would have to be taken; Redondo

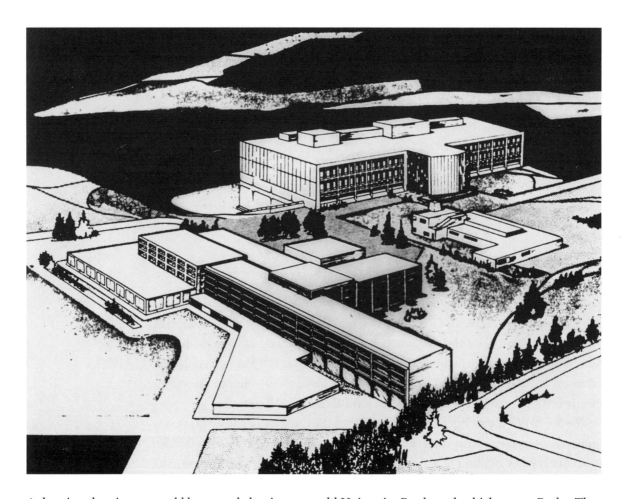

A drawing showing the addition to the west end of BC-I and completed Basic Sciences Building in the background. Architect: Flatow, Moore, Bryan, and Fairburn.

would be extended to intersect old University Boulevard, which meant Rodey Theater would be demolished; and UNM would have to pay the city for the cost of obtaining the additional right-of-way. The former Kappa Kappa Gamma and Kappa Alpha houses, which the University had previously bought, were also demolished. The Estufa would survive, however. After much negotiating and planning, the proposal was approved by the Campus Planning Committee and finally by the regents, who agreed to pay the city for the additional right-of-way.

The University had closed Yale Boulevard through the campus in 1954 between the summer and fall sessions as a test, and the reaction was very negative. Nevertheless, in September 1967 Yale was again closed as a through-campus street but left open to the parking lots. Professor Marvin May, who did much of the street and traffic planning for the University, said in a newspaper interview, "It is a traffic hazard to pedestrians and the confusion and noise has been building up until it has reached an intolerable level." The closing was done with the cooperation of the City Planning Commission and the City Commission, which transferred ownership to the University.

In March the Bernalillo County–Indian Hospital received a federal grant of almost $4 million for an addition to the west of the original building. These funds were added to revenue from the 1966 county bond issue and another federal grant. The addition, in the planning stage, was to be about 140,000 square feet, more than double the size of the existing hospital, which was being used for teaching by the Medical School. Plans included 110 new beds in medical, surgical, and pediatric wards including intensive care facilities. Also there would be new out-patient facilities, a cardiopulmonary laboratory, a new surgical suite, a new emergency area, diagnostic radiology, clinical laboratories, and research space.

Sherman Smith, who had been appointed administrative vice president, presented the revised plans for Laguna (74) and DeVargas (75) dormitories to the regents on November 4, 1967. The room capacity had been increased to 378 from 312 when several single rooms were converted to doubles by adding bunk beds. In La Posada, the proposed dining hall, capacity was increased to 1,525 by enclosing the center patio.

Laguna-De Vargas Dormitories courtyard. Photograph by the author.

In November the State Board of Finance gave its approval to build the new dormitories and the dining hall. Total estimated project cost was $4.3 million after the revisions had been made. Again the question was asked why the cost of these dormitories was higher than at other state universities. Smith replied, "Generally they are higher than others throughout the state. They are substantially higher than at New Mexico State. In that climate they are able to build dormitories with no inside corridors, motel style. This is the least expensive project in per student cost we've had." He produced documentation to show that if earlier dormitories were built in 1967 they would cost more per student than the proposed ones. The board approved the UNM project. When bids were received they were over budget and changes had to be made in construction methods and materials. After rebidding, the project was in the budget and the contract was awarded to Lembke Construction Company.

In other action the regents approved the final design for the Law School Building (218) to be funded from the 1967 state bond issue and the Higher Education Facilities Act (HEFA) Title II, for graduate facilities. Antoine Predock prepared the preliminary design while he was with George Wright and Associates. The board also approved the addition to the Research Center (153), which included space for math department computer instruction and the Office of the University Architect.

Interior of La Posada, the dining hall.

The recently completed addition to the Biology Building (21) was dedicated on November 10, 1967. Martin Fleck, professor of biology, was chairman of the ceremonies held in the sunken patio. I formally presented the building to Loren D. Potter, the chairman of the department, who had directed the programming and planning. The addition was later named the Loren D. Potter Wing.

The Basic Medical Sciences Building was dedicated on November 18, 1967, with short speeches by President Popejoy, Dean Fitz, and Regent Lawrence Wilkinson. Nobel Prize winner Dr. Fred Sanger of Cambridge University was guest lecturer during the weekend. The *Albuquerque Journal* ran a sixteen-page special section titled "UNM Medical School Begins a New Era," which described in detail the development of the school and plans for the future.

On December 14, 1967, the Board of Regents announced that Dr. Ferrel Heady had been selected to be the next president of the University of New Mexico, succeeding Thomas L. Popejoy who was retiring. Heady took office on July 1, 1968.

After failing to solve the problems with the original Olympic pool design and finding the estimated project cost to be too high, the University changed to a more conventional design. William R. Buckley, the architect for the project, entered into a joint venture with architects Albert Merker and Ted Luna. They proposed using precast concrete panels for the side walls and a Behlen roof system. The main pool and an adjacent therapy pool were to be made of heavy sheet aluminum by the Chester Pool Company. The board approved the design and the method of funding.

Interior of the Olympic-size pool. Architect: Buckley, Luna, and Merker, a joint venture. Photograph by Jerry Goffe.

Thomas R. Roberts, the president of the Board of Regents, took his own life on February 24, 1968. He had been a very effective member of the board and was sorely missed. Later in the year, Walter F. Wolfe Jr., an attorney from Gallup, was nominated by the governor to fill the term.

At the June 1968 meeting of the Board of Regents, the Biology Building (21) was named Castetter Hall for Edward F. Castetter, professor emeritus of biology, chairman of the department, and academic vice president.

The Student Health Center–University College Building (73) was completed in June 1968 and the University College moved from the old Stadium Building and Student Health from the building on Yale that had been the Co-Op Dormitory (151). Programming and planning the new facility had been done with Kenneth Young, director of the Student Health Center, and William Huber, dean of the University College. The building was designed by Edward Holien and the plans and specifications were finished by his partner William Buckley after Holien's death.

The Campus Planning Committee's recommendations of architects for several upcoming projects were presented to the Board of Regents at the August 1968 meeting by Sherman Smith. McHugh and Kidder from Santa Fe were recommended for the faculty office and museum additions to the Anthropology Building (11); Flatow, Moore, Bryan, and Fairburn for the proposed Psychology Building (34) and the remodeling of the vacated data processing space in the College of Education; Ferguson, Stevens, Mallory, and Pearl to design a Faculty Office–Classroom Building (79); and William R. Buckley for a third-floor addition to the Geology Building (24). All were approved.

In 1968 the Board of Regents named the College of Education Learning Materials Center for Loyd Spencer Tireman, professor of elementary education, and conference room 107 for Simon Peter Nanninga, former dean of the college.

UNM Building and Planning Committees

Until late 1944 all building and planning decisions had been made by the University presidents with counsel of their administrative staffs. After the death of President Zimmerman, the Board of Deans, which was acting as the chief administrative functionary, established the Building Committee as a regular committee responsible to the board. The members were A.D. Ford, professor of civil engineering; John Heimerich, professor of architecture; Veon Kiech, professor of chemistry; Vernon G. Sorrell, head of the Department of Business Administration; Everett H. Fixley, professor of school administration; William M. Dunbar, professor of business administration; and Lena Clauve, dean of women. The purpose was to inventory existing equipment, resources, and buildings and list by priority the needs anticipated over the next ten to fifteen years. Faculty opinion was to be sought on those matters.

On February 6, 1947, Chairman Ford sent a memorandum to President J. P. Wernette suggesting building procedures and recommending new buildings. The committee would deal with the appointed architect from the earliest planning to the completed building and approve all plans. The Building Committee would coordinate the work between the departments and the architect. Wernette replied that administrative responsibility for planning and executing University buildings was a proper function of the comptroller. He said he understood the function of the Building Committee was to check plans and specifications to prevent architectural mistakes.

The Building Committee continued to function under President Popejoy more or less as Ford had suggested and in 1951, with Ford still chairman, the members were Heimerich, Sorrell, Clauve, Eugene Zwoyer, professor of civil engineering; France Scholes, dean of the graduate school; William B. Runge, instructor in physics; and John D. Robb, dean of fine arts. Ford continued as chairman until 1959 when Heimerich succeeded him. The committee's duties, as stated in 1957, now included recommending building priorities and sites and working with the Campus Improvement Committee on the development of a campus master plan.

The Campus Improvement Committee, chaired by Biology Professor Howard J. Dittmer, was established in the 1950s to oversee the landscaping and general campus development. The minutes of a 1960 meeting included location of signs, plant material, utility poles, parking lot paving, street layouts, and traffic control. This committee had worked closely with Edward Holien, of the firm of Meem, Zehner, and Holien, in developing the 1955 master plan of the Central Campus and with Lawrence Lackey and Alfred W. Baxter from John Carl Warnecke and Associates in the preparation of the 1960 General Development Plan.

There was interest in having a new, more in-depth master plan developed, so President Popejoy appointed the Committee on the Master Plan consisting of himself as chairman, Dean of Students Sherman Smith, Comptroller John Perovich, Director of the Physical Plant Department Myron F. Fifield, Professor of

Architecture Don P. Schlegel, Professor of Civil Engineering Marvin May, and others. This committee reviewed and approved the Development Plan and eventually became the Campus Planning Committee. For a short time it was called the Committee for the Implementation of the Master Plan.

Sherman Smith became chairman of the Campus Planning Committee and in 1964 established the membership and functions of the committee, which were adopted by the regents. The members were to be the chairman of the regents' Campus Planning and Building Committee, the academic vice president, the comptroller, the dean of students, the University secretary, the University architect, and the director of the Physical Plant Department. In addition there would be one or two faculty members appointed annually by the president as was the chairman. The University architect was to be the secretary. The committee was to serve in an advisory capacity to the University architect. Committee duties included recommending architects and reviewing and approving changes to the master plan, building sites, building design, landscape plans, parking and parking lots, and street and walkway designs. Smith stated that the Planning Committee was an administrative advisory committee and that faculty members were included because of competence rather than as representatives of the faculty.

In June 1964 President Popejoy appointed an ad hoc committee to establish new building priorities. Sherman Smith was made chairman and the members were University Secretary John Durrie,

Vice President Harold Enarson, Director of Institutional Development Morris Hendrickson, John Perovich, Professor of English Hoyt Trowbridge, and me. The committee was to make its recommendations to the president who would carry them to the Board of Regents.

In 1970 Smith and President Heady established the Building Committee composed of the then six vice presidents and the University architect. Its duties as outlined by Smith included approving building projections, building programs, and budgets and advising the president on such matters. The committee also had to approve space reassignments. The committee functioned well until Smith's death; it was dropped during President William E. Davis's administration.

Following Smith's death the Campus Planning Committee became a faculty committee and more faculty members were added as were student representatives and, later, neighborhood representatives; a faculty member always served as chairman. The University architect continued to be the secretary. The committee has functioned in this manner since that time. Despite its name, the committee does not do planning. Campus planning is the function of the Department of Facilities Planning, formerly the Office of the University Architect. The Campus Planning Committee reviews and approves, or disapproves, the work of that office, the design of buildings and landscape projects; interviews and recommends architects; and recommends action to the president. Building priorities, budgets, and sources of funding are established by the president and the vice presidents.

Left to right: Van Dorn Hooker, George A. Rutherford, the general contractor, and President Tom Popejoy inspect the Student Health Center–University College Building. Photograph by Richard P. Meleski, UNM Photo Service.

Upon recommendation of the Campus Planning Committee, the regents at the meeting on October 19, 1968, approved George Wright Associates as architects for the remodeling of old Bratton Hall (57) for the Departments of Economics and Political Science and Pacheco and Graham for the Physics Laboratories and Lecture Hall project (35). A contract was approved with Bradbury and Stamm to build the addition to Clark Hall (22).

The regents and the administration were studying a proposal for the University to take over the operation of the former Bernalillo County–Indian Hospital, now Bernalillo County Medical Center (BCMC). Under the agreement, the county would own the physical plant, maintain fiscal control, and approve budgets, which the University would submit. All capital improvements would require joint approval. The University would provide staff and administration. There would be an advisory board composed of four county residents and one Indian. All hospital employees would be UNM employees. About this time, Robert Stone was appointed dean of the Medical School replacing D. Reginald Fitz who had resigned.

The Campus Planning Committee had reviewed plans for several projects including the Anthropology Building addition, the Athletic Department Building (307), and the addition to the Fine Arts Center (62) for the Art Department. The regents approved the projects at the meeting on May 10, 1969. Vice President Smith told the board the HEFA funds and National Science Foundation funds for construction were going to be cut back severely. In fact they were totally wiped out soon thereafter.

The athletic Booster Club, under the direction of Lee Galles, undertook a landscaping and beautification project at University Stadium. They hired Kenneth Larsen, a landscape architect, to do the overall planning, which included grass and trees on the slopes with irrigation systems. Larsen also designed a forty-foot-diameter concrete disk with raised block letters *NM* in the center, which was installed on the northeast

The Student Health Center–University College Building (73).

The Maxwell Museum of Anthropology addition to the original Student Union (11). Architect: McHugh and Kidder. Photograph by the author.

Farris Engineering Center (119). Architect: Flatow, Moore, Bryan, and Fairburn. Photograph by Jerry Goffe.

bank, and a similar disk depicting a football player at the southeast corner of University and Stadium Boulevards. At the same time the Physical Plant Department put in curbs and paved walks. The interior landscaping material was a mixture of pine and cottonwood trees with chamisa. It grew well and improved the appearance but was criticized by some writers as being too much like the desert. Plantings on the west exterior slope did not fare as well because the steepness of the grade made irrigation almost impossible.

Farris Engineering Center was completed in November 1968 after a year and a half construction time. Architects Flatow, Moore, Bryan, and Fairburn designed the structure of three floors plus a basement to accommodate laboratories on the ground level, administrative and faculty offices on the first floor, and offices, research laboratories, and graphics and design laboratories on the two upper floors. A separate building on the southwest corner houses nuclear engineering laboratories. K. L. House Construction Company was the general contractor.

A roadblock in the path to construction of the Law School Building was the "Love Lust" poem squabble. The allegedly obscene poem was given to a class in freshman English by a graduate-student instructor, Lionel Williams. Some people thought the poem objectionable and others, according to Governor David F. Cargo, had sent thousands of copies all over the state.

The Law School construction had been approved by the State Board of Finance in December 1968 but revisions were needed in the approval because the federal grant

The completed Bratton Hall II, the Law School. Photograph by Bob Dauner, UNM Photo Service.

was less than originally estimated and construction costs had escalated. When the new budget was presented to the board in June, former Governor Tom Bolack, a member of the board, moved to reject it and brought the poem into the discussion. Governor Cargo said, "I don't think we can convey the sins of someone who is paid $600 a month and transfer them over to the Law School. I think you've got to have some balance." Thomas W. Christopher, dean of the Law School, urged the board to consider the matter in perspective: "Don't tar us with the other thing—we're not guilty." He also said there was no more stable, solid state-supported school than the UNM School of Law.

Bolack said, "Some students and faculty have brought shame to this great institution." He said he believed a majority of the citizens of New Mexico agreed with him. However, he withdrew his original motion and moved to defer action until the next meeting of the board. The motion passed much to the dismay of the University representatives. Approval was given at a later meeting and the project was put out to bid.

Bids were received on September 30, 1969, for the Law School Building (218) and Bradbury and Stamm Construction Company was the low bidder. In order to start construction immediately, the regents agreed informally to accept the bid and they confirmed the award of the contract at the November 8, 1969, meeting. They also ratified the agreement for the University to operate BCMC.

A proposed building on the south end of the football stadium for the Department of Athletics (307) was presented to the regents at their June 1969 meeting by Vice President Smith. Approval was given for the design and a project budget. The architect was Joe Boehning.

The Faculty Office–Classroom Building (79) had been in the design stage for some time. George Pearl, the designer for Ferguson, Stevens, Mallory, and Pearl, came to me with his first design for the building and I was astonished to see that he proposed

A drawing of the original design of the Faculty Office–Classroom Building by George C. Pearl. Architect: Ferguson, Stevens, Mallory, and Pearl. Courtesy of George C. Pearl.

The Faculty Office–Classroom Building, later named Ortega Hall (79), as built with the added concrete panels around the first level. Photograph by Jerry Goffe.

using brick on the facade. I told him I could not approve the introduction of another strong material such as brick into the palette of the campus. Pearl accepted the objection gracefully and later agreed it was the right decision. But that was not the only problem with the design. He had planned a second-level deck for circulation to the many classrooms at that level and it overhung the first floor creating a covered portal, so to speak, around the building. Regent Lawrence Wilkinson saw the architect's rendering when it was presented to the Campus Planning Committee and voiced his objection that the building was sort of floating and should be tied more to the ground like all other University buildings. The committee approved the design over his objection. He came to see me a few days later and said if the design was not changed he, with the backing of Regent Cyrene Mapel, would see that the board rejected it.

The project was behind schedule and had to be completed by the fall semester 1970 so there was no time to lose arguing the design question. I asked Pearl to see what he could do to tie the building to the ground and he proposed setting some precast concrete panels in some of the openings. Regent Wilkinson moved to approve the design and Regent Mapel seconded it. The panels created a dark unpleasant walkway and destroyed the design concept. When the Humanities Building (81) was being built, I requested a price from the contractor to saw-cut the panels and remove the

"University Landmark Falls before Progress"

The headline above appeared over a story in the *Santa Fe New Mexican* on August 28, 1969. It covered the demolition of the Stadium Building, which was part of the Zimmerman Field complex. The writer pointed out that plans called for several buildings to be erected on the site including Ortega Hall (79). He wrote, "When the stadium first opened, the south end was designed for two handball courts but because of size they became classrooms. 'The north end was the art department with the music department upstairs,' said UNM athletic business manager, Bob DoBell. He should know, he was a student janitor in the building at the time and earned six bits an hour as a model in the art department."

The athletic offices remained in Carlisle Gymnasium until after World War II. During the war years the navy's V-5 program used the Stadium Building as a dormitory and later it became the offices of the Navy ROTC program and thus a site of anti–Vietnam War protests in the late 1960s. The School of Law, too, first saw the light of day in Zimmerman Stadium in 1947.

"I remember the first football training room was set up in 1936. I set up some tables and a couple of heat lamps in the boiler room, which served as the training room," said John Dolzadelli, UNM assistant athletic director.

The seating capacity in the original stadium was 5,000 but with the addition of temporary bleachers the capacity was increased to around 16,500. By the mid-1950s it was obvious that the University had outgrown the facility. The Lobo–New Mexico State game in 1959 attracted 16,445 fans—the largest crowd ever at Zimmerman Field. The following year the 30,000-seat University Stadium was opened on the South Campus.

Football historians agree on which game was probably the finest played at Zimmerman Field. In 1940 the Lobos under head coach Ted Shipkey played host to Texas Tech. New Mexico had a 4–3 record going into the contest while Tech, undefeated and once tied, was ranked eighteenth in the nation by one wire service poll and second in the nation in offense. Rumor had it the Raiders had been offered a Sugar Bowl bid to be announced at the UNM game.

Before an estimated 10,000 fans, the Lobos scored two touchdowns in the first quarter and held a 19–0 advantage going into the fourth quarter. Tech scored twice in the last quarter but it wasn't enough, as the Lobos won 19–14. A member of the Tech coaching staff was very upset: "It's disheartening to lose to a prep team—the Lobos are the poorest team we've played against."

I remember the old building being used for other things. One day in 1968 around noon I sat in the bleachers and listened to Robert Kennedy deliver a campaign speech shortly before his assassination in California.

lower portion, but the price was more than I could justify. Since then some of the panels have been cut, as I had proposed.

George Pearl designed the building so that all the corners are angled at forty-five degrees. He says he did it for two reasons: it eliminates the problem of people running into each other as they round the corner and he always disliked having to turn corners at ninety degrees when he marched in the army in World War II.

The Board of Regents, at the September 27, 1969, meeting approved several building names. The name Ortega Hall was transferred from the old Dining Hall, later the

South facade of Riebsomer Wing addition to Clark Hall (52). Architect: Ferguson, Stevens, Mallory, and Pearl. Photograph by Jerry Goffe.

Modern Language Building (8), to the new Faculty Office–Classroom Building (79); Ford Utility Center (116) was named for Professor A. D. Ford, chairman of the Department of Mechanical Engineering for many years and of the Campus Improvement Committee in the 1940s; the Administration Building (10) was named for France V. Scholes who came to UNM in 1925 as a professor of history and served as academic vice president and dean of the graduate school; Stuart A. Northrop, chairman of the Department of Geology for thirty-three years, was the honoree for the Geology Building (24); and the Civil Engineering Building (117) was named for William C. Wagner, who was with the department for thirty-three years, seventeen years as chairman.

The addition to Clark Hall, the Chemistry Building (22), was completed in December 1969. The designer, George Pearl, was faced with the problem of locating exit stairs so he placed them on the south wall and made a design feature of them. This building used the first post-tensioned concrete floor slabs on the campus. High-tensile-strength steel cables were placed in tubes in the slabs so they would not bind with the concrete and were then tightened and welded in place after the concrete was poured and partially set. The 43,000-square-foot wing, consisting primarily of advanced chemistry laboratories, was later named for Chemistry Professor Jesse L. Riebsomer.

The Campus Is One Big Construction Yard

Student unrest, which was occurring on almost all university campuses across the country, continued at UNM in 1970. Peaceful demonstrations were held against the Vietnam War and the expansion into Cambodia; the Administration Building was the scene of sit-ins; and there were marches, rallies, and speeches. President Heady and the regents were under constant, widespread attack from the legislature, from organizations like the American Legion, and from individuals who felt they were not exercising enough control over the University community.

The unrest reached a boiling point on May 6, 1970, when the student organizers called for a strike against the University and occupied the Student Union. This led to a week of demonstrations and the unnecessary calling out of the National Guard, bayoneting, rock throwing, arrests and accusations, and general disruption of University functions. Then an uneasy calm settled over the campus.

The planning and building programs were little affected during these chaotic times. Construction projects continued without interruption; the regents and the Campus Planning Committee continued to meet; and new contracts and projects were approved. But there were serious concerns that capital funding would be curtailed by an upset legislature and that, if the public image of the University were tarnished, future state appropriations and bond issues could be in jeopardy.

On March 14, 1970, the regents and the Board of Educational Finance approved the purchase of the IBM Building (162) on the southeast corner of Central and Stanford to house the Technology Application Center (TAC). It was an International Style two-story building of about 14,000 square feet, which could meet TAC's requirements without too much remodeling. In other action, the regents approved a contract with R. M. Swain and Son for an

On January 25, 1974, green paint was thrown on the southernmost of the Kenneth Adams murals in Zimmerman Library. Black paint had been splattered on the mural in 1970; repairs cost $3,000. The paint in both incidents was directed at the central figure depicting an Anglo man.

addition to the Computing Center (formerly the Research Center [153]) for data processing and accepted a bid from Nation-Payne for construction of a building for the Department of Athletics (307). This building was built at the south end of the football stadium on the South Campus. It is a split-level building with offices and locker, dressing, and training rooms.

At the May 1970 meeting the regents approved a contract with K. L. House Construction Company to build the office-classroom building (79), appointed Lawrence Garcia as architect for remodeling the central portion of Mesa Vista Hall for faculty offices, and gave approval to remodel the building at 108 Cornell Southeast for the Tamarind Institute (163). The institute, whose mission is to train lithographers, moved to the campus from Los Angeles primarily through the efforts of Art Professor Garo Antreasian and Clinton Adams, dean of the College of Fine Arts. Long and Waters were the architects for the remodeling.

Negotiations had been going on for some time with the City of Albuquerque concerning ownership of some of the campus streets. Vice President Sherman Smith reported to the president that the City Commission passed an ordinance vacating these streets on campus: Terrace and Ash, Roma between University and Cornell, and the alley between Roma and Las Lomas west of Yale. The city retained all existing utility easements. This action gave the University complete control over all the campus streets from Girard on the east to University Boulevard on the west and Central Avenue on the south to Lomas Boulevard on the north.

On August 14, 1970, the regents filed a counterclaim in a long-standing condemnation suit against the Albuquerque Metropolitan Arroyo Flood Control Authority. The authority had offered one dollar for easement rights for the North Diversion Channel constructed on the North Campus between Stanford and Lomas and Indian School Road. Condemnation proceedings began in October 1966 and on July 14, 1970, AMAFCA filed an amended petition claiming it had legislative authority and was "not required to pay monetary compensation for any of the defendant's lands or estates therein taken, damaged or occupied by it."

In the counterclaim the University said the ditch was a barrier separating the campus into two parts causing damages and creating visual blight. In order to help prove the point, I asked Garrett Eckbo, who was doing landscape design for the University, to prepare a plan showing what would be required to overcome the problems created by the ditch, which included the need for additional bridges, restrictions on the ability to extend utility lines, and many planning problems. The University was represented by attorneys Jackson G. Akin and John P. Salazar of the firm of Rodey, Dickason, Sloan, Akin, and Robb. The case eventually went to court and the judge said UNM should receive compensation for the land taken based on value of surrounding land. He did not allow compensation for aesthetic damages.

In January 1971 budgets of the projects that had counted on federal funds had to be increased because inflation was driving up costs while bidding was being delayed and other funding sources were sought. The Anthropology Building addition budget was increased to include 6,000 square feet to be leased to the National Park Service for the Chaco Canyon Project.

Governor Bruce King appointed Calvin Horn of Albuquerque and Austin Roberts of Farmington to the Board of Regents on February 5, 1971, and at the organization meeting in March, Horn was elected president of the board, a position he held for six years. King insisted that Horn be the president so there would be a close relationship between board and governor.

Sometime in 1969, Albuquerque Fire Chief Ray Kuhn had explored with me the possibility of locating a new fire station on University land along Girard. Old Fire Station Number 3, also known as the Monte Vista Station, on Central Avenue east of Girard was too small for the new equipment and traffic was getting too heavy for safe exiting by the fire trucks. It seemed to me like a good idea to have a fire station on campus so I broached the idea to the administration, which agreed. The site selected was the southwest corner of Girard and Girard Place. John Reed was the architect selected by the city and his design was approved by the Campus Planning Committee and the regents at the April meeting.

The new Bratton Hall (218), the Law School Building, was dedicated on April 17, 1971, with Byron (Whizzer) White, associate justice of the U.S. Supreme Court, as the honored guest and speaker. There was a Navajo ceremony blessing the building followed by a symposium, "Identity for Modern Man," chaired by Dean Thomas W. Christopher.

At a rare Sunday meeting on June 6, 1971, the regents appointed architects and engineers for several projects: Ferguson, Stevens, Mallory, and Pearl for the plaza south of Zimmerman Library designed by Garrett Eckbo; Bridgers and Paxton, mechanical engineers, to design an addition to Ford Utility Center to house two 1,200-ton chillers; and William Ellison to plan a warehouse on the North Campus for storage of library material and Department of Physics and Astronomy equipment. Another agenda item was the request of K. L. House Construction Company to withdraw their low bid on the Geology Building addition because of an error made in compiling the bid. I felt their request was legitimate and recommended the regents approve it, which they did. The contract was awarded to Bill Stuckman, the next lowest bidder.

With the demolition of old Rodey Hall the Department of Theater Arts was left with the old Comedia Theater in a portion of the original boiler plant. They held performances in the recital hall in the Fine Arts Center but it was not well adapted to stage shows. When it appeared funds might be available from the 1971 state bond issue, the drama wing was given a high priority.

Smith Plaza soon after completion in 1972.

The Design of Smith Plaza

The Warnecke General Development Plan of 1960 did not show the area south of Zimmerman Library as a hard-surfaced plaza. Instead it was a grassed area with diagonal paved walks with a major walk in the Ash Street alignment. The library's main entrance, which faced west, was to remain as additions were made to the east. However, as soon as planning and programming began for the first addition it became apparent that the major entrance would have to be created on the south side and this was indicated to Garrett Eckbo when he designed his landscape plan in 1962–63.

Eckbo continued the idea of a lawn south of the library with winding walks through it. Later it became clear that this plaza would be the most heavily used pedestrian space on campus. Sherman

Smith and I concluded that the only solution was to create a large paved area.

Smith sent a memorandum to members of the Campus Planning Committee outlining his thoughts on the plaza. The committee met on May 2, 1968, and discussed his ideas, which included making the plaza an important focal point of campus activity. It could be made exciting by having the scale different from adjacent spaces. He wrote that the design of the plaza was as important as the design of buildings that surround it. Smith described it later as "the main central plaza of the ultimate campus."

Robert Riley, the campus planner at that time, made several studies comparing the space to well-known European plazas such as Saint Mark's in

Venice. He found the space almost too large in comparison to the scale of the surrounding buildings that were being planned. In order to confine the space a bit, Eckbo introduced rows of sycamore trees around the periphery. The design of the Humanities Building (81) reflected the need for a massive structure on the south side to oppose the scale of the library of the future on the north and Ortega Hall on the west.

A small semienclosed patio was created on the south side of the original library building. Some time previously Sherman Smith had purchased a stone fountain, thought to have come from a house in Mexico City, and it was made a feature of the patio.

Lighting Smith Plaza has been a problem from the beginning. Eckbo's idea was to have fixtures at ground level that would spread light over the plaza without shining in a person's eyes. The special fixtures were quickly vandalized and never replaced. The lighting problem has not yet been resolved. Floodlights on top of parapets are not the solution.

Dense brick pavers set on sand were used for the lower part of the plaza, but asphalt was used to pave the upper levels and it has cracked and sunken with time. There was not enough money to put in an automatic irrigation system for the trees and they have not done well. The whole plaza, as I write this, is in need of total refurbishing.

Vice President for Regional and Community Affairs Alex Mercure wanted to have murals painted on some of the walls of buildings around Smith Plaza as part of UNM's participation in the bicentennial celebration in 1976 of this country's independence. I opposed the idea on the grounds that the walls were not designed for murals, that murals did not play much of a part in Pueblo architecture's development, and that they can become outdated quickly. Instead, I suggested a sculpture competition for a major piece to be placed in the plaza. The matter was eventually dropped.

After Smith Plaza was constructed, the annual spring fiesta was held there. As the fiesta grew in size more booths selling food were brought in along with cars and trucks, which were doing a great deal of damage to the walks and brick paving. Oil dripping from the vehicles and grease splattering from the cooking were staining the brick. Cleaning up the debris afterward was a major job for the Physical Plant Department. Because of these problems, the fiesta was moved to the north end of Johnson Field.

The patio on the south side of Zimmerman Library.

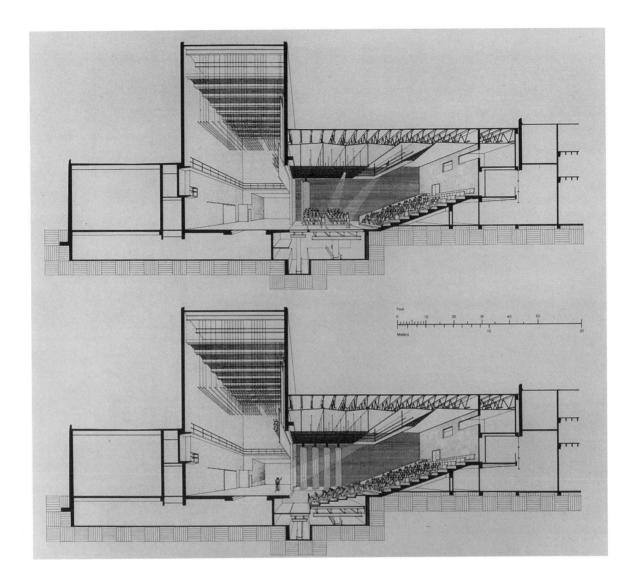

Section through
Rodey Theater
showing the thrust
stage in position
and retracted.
Courtesy of George
Izenour and
Pennsylvania State
University.

When the Fine Arts Center was being planned, a complete set of working drawings
was done, which included the wing for theater arts and Rodey Theater. After the funding for the project was found it was decided to have William R. Buckley, the successor
to Holien and Buckley, make necessary changes. He worked with Chairman of Theater Arts Robert Hartung and Professors Gene Yell and Nadene Blackburn. George
Izenour, the theater design consultant, revised the interior of the theater including the
mechanized thrust stage and movable seating banks. An experimental theater called
the "Black Box" was created, but the top floor of the wing had to be eliminated in order to keep within the budget. This included a dance studio, which was relocated to the
basement under the theater that had been planned as rehearsal space.

Bids for the construction of the drama addition to the Fine Arts Center were received
on April 19, 1972. In March the BEF had approved money from the state bond issue to

Landscape area on south side of Woodward Hall. Photograph by Jerry Goffe.

replace federal funds that were not received. The University added some of its own funds to cover the estimated project cost.

The Psychology Building (34) was in the design stage when Pacheco and Graham were commissioned to design the Physics Laboratories and Lecture Hall (35). The site was between Farris Engineering Center (119) and the Psychology Building (34), both large structures. Jesse Pacheco decided to design a "nonbuilding" with only the lecture hall above grade and undergraduate laboratories under a plaza deck. The deck is covered with pavers on top of a two-way post-tensioned concrete slab designed to be watertight.

Planning for the Physics and Psychology Buildings was proceeding simultaneously even though they were being done by different firms. The projects were bid at the same time and a contractor could bid on either or both buildings.

The *Campus News* reported in February 1974 that a new but old-fashioned pipe organ would be installed in the Alumni Chapel choir loft after Professor Wesley T. Selby, who designed it, trucked the parts from Illinois and assembled them. Selby described it as a nine-stop baroque pipe organ, the only one of its kind in the state. The only electrical part is the blower that provides wind for the pipes. The valves are operated by the organist. It joined an electric organ already in the choir loft. Professor Selby and former UNM Director of Development Bill Weeks planned the organ as a memorial to Walter Keller, former chairman of the Department of Music, who died in 1970 while on sabbatical in Portugal.

The Physics
Laboratories and
Lecture Hall (35).
Architect: Pacheco
and Graham.
Photograph by Jerry
Goffe.

Bradbury and Stamm submitted a low combined bid that was accepted by the regents at their July 1971 meeting. At the same meeting, they rejected a bid from the same firm for construction of the addition to the Anthropology Building (11). Only $900,000 was available for construction. Their instructions were for my office and the project architects to negotiate with the contractor, search for more funds, do a little of both, and if not successful, revise the drawings and rebid.

At the same meeting, Bert Hanson, president of the Graduate Students Association, made a plea to the board to consider building housing for married students. He said there were only twenty units available on campus while there were 1,600 accommodations for single students. Vice President Smith noted it would be difficult for the University to build apartments that would be cost competitive with similar units erected by private builders. The board asked the administration to consider the matter and the Campus Planning Committee to look at sites on both the North and South Campuses.

There was a long-standing need for space for the School of Medicine and associated agencies to house funded programs and research projects that existed for only a limited time. Medical schools around the country had built these types of structures and called them "surge" buildings: the tenants "surge in and surge out." To meet this need on the UNM campus, a site was located on the north side of Frontier Street north of the hospital, and Barker-Bol was recommended as the architectural firm by the planning committee. The regents approved the architects and a budget at their meeting on October 23, 1971. It was to be financed with rental income from grant-supported research and School of Medicine overhead. At the same meeting the regents set budgets for a bookstore to be built between Johnson Gymnasium and Popejoy Hall; a building for the dental program, then housed in the last of the World War II barracks; a building for the Colleges of Nursing and Pharmacy; and a chilled water plant on the North Campus.

Paid parking was the hot topic at the meeting. A parking study had been done by Harold Thompson, a vice chancellor at the University of California at Los Angeles, and Robert Crommelin, a parking and traffic consultant, which concluded the only way UNM could have a workable parking program was for fees to be charged to everyone parking on campus. The consultants said the money generated would help pay for enforcement and construction of new lots and, eventually, parking structures. The Campus Planning Committee, chaired by Sherman Smith, approved the concept, but the regents wanted to provide free spaces for students or anyone who could not afford to pay. The board discussed how to provide free parking on the South Campus lots with shuttle buses to the Central Campus and fee parking in zoned lots. The Faculty Compensation Committee opposed paid parking saying it eroded fringe benefits.

After listening to all arguments, the regents approved paid parking, accepting a suggestion for a graduated fee for faculty and staff, ranging from $27 to $78 per year based on salary, and reducing the proposed student fee. The plan was to be put into operation for the fall semester 1972. Opposition to the plan and questions about specific concerns, such as patient parking on the medical campus, were so strong that the board postponed the matter until the May 1972 meeting.

The Electrical Engineering Building (118) was named for Ralph W. Tapy, long-time professor and chairman of the Department of Electrical Engineering. A park west of Johnson Gymnasium was named for Lawrence R. Klausen, a student who was a cancer victim.

At the meeting in March 1972 the regents authorized application to the Department of Housing and Urban Development (HUD) for a long-term, low-interest loan through the College Housing Program to fund a married student housing project. An attorney for the Albuquerque Board of Realtors protested, saying it was a turnaround position against private enterprise, and asked for a postponement. I told the board that responses to our request for proposals (RFP) for construction of housing by four private developers had been received and none offered rents specified in the RFP and at the same time had a feasible plan of finance.

The attorney for the realtors called the University's approach "socialistic." Regent Arturo Ortega replied, "If it is socialism for the University to provide housing for married students, isn't it just as much socialism to provide housing for single students as the University has traditionally done?" The reply was that married students had more money. Horn said if the private sector could come up with a proposal with lower rents the University would withdraw the application.

An editorial in the *Albuquerque Journal,* "The Realtors and UNM," about a resolution from the Board of Realtors concerning UNM's acquisition of land not needed for educational purposes appeared late the next year. The writer harked back to the 1972 action and wrote: "As for student housing, UNM is moving tardily to fill a void that the

Realtors and the land developers they represent have been, for too many years, neglecting, niggardly. Admittedly the private sector in recent years has erected quality student-type residential quarters within walking distance of the campus—but with rental fees at such a level as to compound the rising cost of higher education and to push that cost beyond the reach of the deserving many." Eventually the regents authorized the HUD loan application and it was approved.

The regents approved preliminary plans for the Humanities–Lecture Hall project at a meeting in Gallup on May 6, 1972. The design called for an overhead concourse to connect Ortega Hall and these buildings to the Student Union and later extend all the way to the Fine Arts Center. Unfortunately, the connection has never been made to the union so it does not work as well as it might.

Contracts with George A. Rutherford were approved at the Gallup meeting for construction of the drama addition to the Fine Arts Center and the North Campus chilled water plant (224). Antoine Predock was appointed the architect for the Art Building (84), and Robert C. Walters was named to design a building for the New Mexico Bar Association (230).

In June 1972 the Physics Laboratories and Lecture Hall project was completed, but the rest of the campus was one huge construction yard. The area in front of Scholes Hall and the Alumni Chapel over to the future duck pond was torn up for a large landscaping project. The swimming pool addition to Johnson Gymnasium, the Psychology Building, the North Campus Chilled Water Plant (224), and the addition to the Anthropology Building were all under construction on the Central Campus, while on the North Campus a big parking lot, the Surge Building, and the chilled water plant were being built. To make matters worse, before all these projects could be completed, work was to begin on the Humanities–Lecture Hall (81, 82) project followed by the bookstore (83) and the Cancer Research and Treatment Center (CRTC) (227). At no time in the history of the University, before or since, has the campus been in such disarray. However, the plan was beginning to come together. Major buildings in the center of the campus were being built; the landscaping was following along; Redondo, the loop road, was completed; and you could see the form of the campus taking shape.

Nature did not help when we had a near-record three inches of rain in the month of October. A hole large enough to hold a pickup truck appeared alongside a utility tunnel east of the College of Education. Many sinkholes appeared, and the earth collapsed in front of Scholes Hall over a newly installed fire line and sewer. The construction yards were turned to deep mud, which made access to the work very difficult. There were the usual roof leaks, which kept the Physical Plant Department busy, but there was no serious damage.

Programming and planning for the CRTC had been under way for some time following the March 1972 appointment of Dr. Morton Kligerman as director, a post he held until 1980. There had been some confusion about the appointment of the architects since the firm of Flatow, Moore, Bryan, and Fairburn was being seriously considered for the Humanities–Lecture Hall complex when the word came down from Santa Fe that the governor would like for W. C. Kruger and Associates to have a major architectural commission on the main campus. So the administration switched and gave Flatow, Moore, Bryan, and Fairburn the CRTC project and Willard Kruger and Associates the Humanities–Lecture Hall. Architects Max Flatow and Jason Moore worked together on the design.

I had considered the idea of having a high-rise building in the academic area that could be a focal point for the campus since the library tower was not tall enough to make a strong statement. The designer of the Humanities Building, Robert Krueger of the W. C. Kruger firm, tried several schemes for a tall building but none of them seemed to be the answer and the idea was dropped. I did ask for a zaguan (an open passageway at ground level through a building) in the center of the Humanities Building to connect the plaza with the landscaped pedestrian way on the south side next to Woodward Hall (82). This provided a visual tie from that area to the main entrance to the library and solved a circulation problem.

The dean of the School of Medicine, Robert Stone, wanted the CRTC built adjacent to the hospital on the north side. Don Schlegel and I tried to convince him it would be better to build it to the west near the Basic Medical Sciences Building so it would not interfere with expansion of the hospital to the north. We lost the argument and since then the hospital has had difficulty finding space for additions and parking.

After the design for the CRTC had been completed and approved by the Campus Planning Committee, Moore and Flatow presented it to the Board of Regents at a meeting in Los Alamos on July 21, 1972. It has three floors with a basement that was fully excavated but only partially finished when the building was constructed. As money became available it was completed for laboratories and other uses. It connects to the tunnel system from the hospital and the Medical School. The building is designed, as are others on the Medical Campus, so more floors can be added in the future, an option not used so far.

Robert Torres, the architect for the Married Student Housing Project (317–329), presented the final design for that complex. It has clusters of one-, two-, and three-bedroom apartments built in two- and three-level configurations. The site is on the west side of Buena Vista Southeast north of Stadium (now Cesar Chavez)

Married student housing on Buena Vista Southeast. Architect: Robert Torres. Photograph by Jerry Goffe.

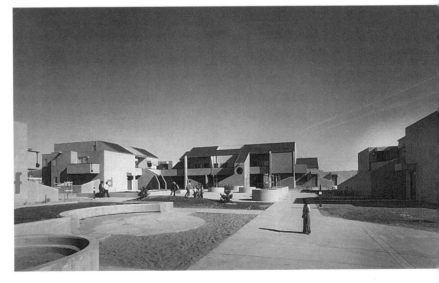

Logan Hall, the Psychology Building (34). Architect: Flatow, Moore, Bryan, and Fairburn. Photograph by Jerry Goffe.

Boulevard Southeast, a long rectangular ten-acre tract. The design was approved upon recommendation of the Campus Planning Committee. Torres said he hoped construction could be started by December and the units could be occupied by the start of the 1973 fall semester, but because of funding delays a construction contract was not signed until January 1974.

Another action taken by the regents resulted in the reduction to two of the remaining World War II barracks still in use on the campus. The board approved removing B-1 at the corner of Ash and Redondo and T-10 north of Zimmerman Library. They both housed Department of Psychology projects that had been moved into the new Psychology Building (34). The two remaining barracks housed Dental Programs.

The Campus Planning Committee met on November 2, 1972, and recommended architects Dean and Hunt to design a second major addition to the east side of Zimmerman Library. Programming for the addition had been done by McKinley Nance of the University Architect's Office working with library management and building consultants, Dean of Library Services Paul Vassallo, Assistant Dean Alice Clark, and the library staff. At the regents meeting on November 10 approval was given to the appointment of the architects. Also approved were the design and budget for the bookstore and the design of the New Mexico State Bar Association Building (230).

During the 1972 legislative session, Representative Carl Engwall of Chaves County had introduced House Memorial 7, which asked the BEF to study the colleges and universities, identify architectural barriers faced by the handicapped, and develop a plan for correcting or removing them to meet the standards set by the Uniform Building Code. The BEF study released in December 1972 said at least $3 million would be required to make all the campuses in the state barrier-free. Campus Planner Joe McKinney estimated it would take a million and a half to make the UNM Albuquerque campuses comply.

Bids for construction of two major projects were received in early January 1973 and Lembke Construction Company was low bidder for the construction of the Humanities–Lecture Hall complex. George A. Rutherford was the successful bidder for the Cancer Research and Treatment Center. The Board of Regents, with new members Dr. Albert G. Simms II and Frank Emmet Garcia, mayor of Gallup, sitting for the first time, approved awarding the bids.

The Campus Planning Committee approved the design of the Nursing-Pharmacy building at a meeting in early February 1973; the regents concurred on February 23. At that meeting Vice President Smith presented a funding request for the coming allocation of the 1973 state bonds. Projects included the addition to Zimmerman Library, the Humanities–Lecture Hall complex, an addition to the Computing Center (153), and several small nonacademic projects.

At the regents meeting on May 4, 1973, Sherman Smith and the dean of the Medical School, Leonard Napolitano, asked approval for the addition of three floors to a planned four-story addition to the Bernalillo County Medical Center. It would be primarily medical faculty office space, which was sorely needed. Approval was given to proceed with planning.

At the May meeting the Board of Regents awarded a contract to Lembke Construction Company for the construction of the Bookstore. The equipment designed by Ken White was bid later. The Bookstore site between Popejoy Hall and Johnson Gym was chosen in order to give better public access including parking. That site was later rejected because the administration and the regents thought it would put the Bookstore in competition with privately owned bookstores in the University neighborhood. The site finally chosen was south of Ortega Hall east of Yale Boulevard. The architects for the project were Holmes and Giannini. The Bookstore connected to the covered walkway constructed with the Humanities–Lecture Hall complex, so it was designed with access from the ground level and the second-floor walkway. The first floor was a full story below grade. Skylights on the upper deck brought daylight into the sales and display areas below. The book sales area was designed with a balcony for the administrative offices while the ceiling was two stories high. On the south side were two levels,

UNM Buildings Receive Awards for Good Design

In mid-May 1973 the New Mexico Society of Architects held its annual awards banquet and presented an award to Pacheco and Graham for the design of the Physics Laboratories and Lecture Hall (35). At the same meeting, the New Mexico Arts Commission presented an award for "significant contribution to the environment" to William W. Ellison and Associates, project architects, Ernest J. Kump and Associates, design consultants, and Eckbo, Dean, Austin and Williams, landscape architects, for the residence hall complex: La Posada, the dining hall, and De Vargas and Laguna dormitories. The event was passed over by the local daily press, but V. B. Price later wrote in the *Independent*:

> More than any other "non-performing" art form, architecture is a product of rapport. As most architects will tell you, their works are usually "only as good as" the goals and values of their clients. . . . Louis Sullivan said, "As you are, so are your buildings; and, as are your buildings, so are you. You and your Architecture are the same. Each is a faithful portrait of the other."
>
> For as long as I've lived here, the University of New Mexico has been Albuquerque's one consistent claim to modern Southwestern civilization. Under the inspiration of such men as Sherman Smith, UNM's vice president for Administration and Development, the University—like it or not—has aspired to architectural integrity and excellence befitting its character and function. As a client, the University has had a profound influence, I should think, on the lives and work of those architects fortunate enough to receive its commissions. . . .
>
> Architecturally, the campus is an example of what comes from diligently pursuing the realization of an institutional "self image" at once dedicated to the betterment of its surroundings and the enrichment of its self-respect.

one for office and school supplies and the other for gifts, clothing, and some foods. Service was at the northwest corner at street level. Delivery trucks could come up Yale until it was closed, then they had to wind through the parking lot west of Northrop Hall (24) and between it and Carlisle Gymnasium (4). There were only a few reserved parking spaces for customers in front of the gymnasium. The old bookstore was located in the original Student Union Building (11) when it was built in 1936–37 and moved to the basement of the New Mexico Union when it was completed in 1959. It had 11,100 net square feet there, which was increased to 26,557 in this new building.

Professor Emeritus of English T. M. Pearce lived on Sigma Chi Road just north of the campus and took frequent walks around it. He wrote a memorandum to Myron Fifield on June 24, 1973, reporting on a tour he made of the original campus around Hodgin Hall (103). He had heard that Hodgin Hall was on the demolition list required

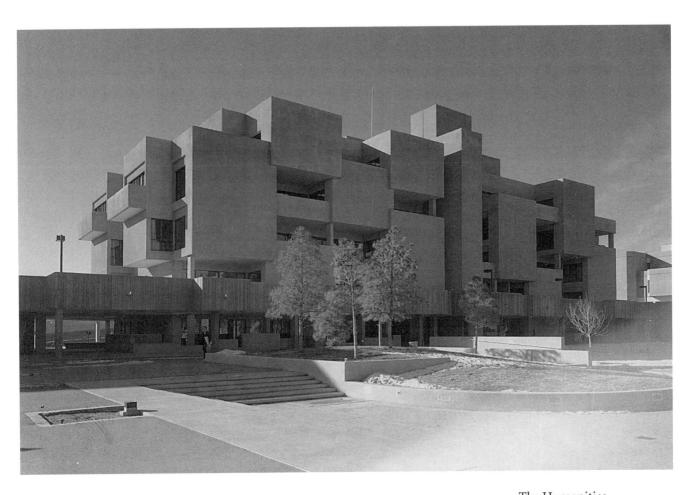

The Humanities Building (81). Architect: W. C. Kruger and Associates. Photograph by Jerry Goffe.

by the BEF and that an inspection by the State Fire Marshal's office had reported many problems. Pearce wrote that he would like to see Hodgin kept as an alumni hall and visitor center. He felt the massiveness of the building compared well with Farris Engineering Center (119) and the new Psychology Building (34), which were its close neighbors. Fifield arranged a to take Pearce through the building with Walter Lewis, the campus safety officer, to show him the poor condition of the interior.

Pearce was not moved by what he saw and wrote Fifield another letter on July 1, which was one of the first strong statements by anyone for keeping and restoring Hodgin Hall. He compared it to the Palace of the Governors in Santa Fe as a building of great historic significance, since its remodeling in 1907 by President Tight reestablished the Pueblo Style of architecture in the state. Pearce compared it to the old main building at his alma mater, the University of Montana, which was being preserved. He suggested the same uses for Hodgin as in his earlier memo and said the installation of a sprinkler system would help solve the fire code problems.

Hodgin Hall was placed on the National Register of Historic Places by the New Mexico Cultural Properties Review Committee. The Alumni Association's Hall of

Woodward Hall (82) and the Bookstore (83) were constructed at the same time. CSWR.

Fame and Preservation of Historic Items Committee, chaired by Association Vice President Tony Jackson, was working on plans to save the building and this action gave them needed impetus. In June 1975 the regents approved the appointment of Joseph D. Burwinkle Jr. to be the architect for the restoration of Hodgin Hall because of his long involvement with the Alumni Association's effort to preserve the building and the fact he had not done any previous University work.

The State Public Health Laboratory had been located in a building facing on Terrace Boulevard (12) since it was completed with PWA funds in 1936. The residential-scale building was completely inadequate for the expanding health laboratory services. Finally, in 1973, the legislature appropriated funds for a new facility, the State Scientific Laboratory Building, which would house the laboratory functions plus the Environmental Improvement Agency and the State Medical Examiner, the latter being operated by the University of New Mexico Medical School.

Interior of the Bookstore. Architect: Holmes and Giannini. Photograph by Jerry Goffe.

A site of about one acre was asked for on the North Campus. The Campus Planning Committee approved a site to the west of the Basic Medical Sciences Building (211) but far enough away to allow room for another building to be built between them. On May 20 the Board of Regents approved the site and a ninety-nine-year lease at one dollar per year. This was after discussion of the problems of non-University buildings located on campus.

The state-appointed architect, Richard Halford, prepared the preliminary drawings quickly. They were approved by the planning committee and presented to the regents in August. Ground-breaking for the State Scientific Laboratory Building was on April 1, 1974. The 1973 legislature appropriated funds for the project and the 1974 legislature added more. The project was administered by the Property Management Control Division of the State Department of Finance and Administration.

The preliminary design for the Art Building addition to the Fine Arts Center was presented to the board at the August meeting by architect Antoine Predock. It was attached to the west side of the Fine Arts Center by an overhead walkway allowing truck service beneath to the New Mexico Union. The building was set parallel to the north side of the City Reservoir located at Redondo and Yale. Even though the regents approved the design, it was some time before it could be put to bid because of funding problems. In the meantime, inflation was galloping along at 10 percent and more each year, so by the time it was bid, it had to be reduced in size.

Following Regent President Horn's idea of meeting in cities where there was a University presence, the Board of Regents met in Taos on August 28, 1973. They authorized the issuance of University bonds to pay UNM's part of a proposed $20 million building and renovation program. The balance would be sought from state bond funds and appropriations. The projects to be funded from this program included the Humanities–Lecture Hall, Nursing-Pharmacy, married student housing, and an addition to

Rendering of the proposed addition to Zimmerman Library. Architect: Dean and Hunt.

Bratton Hall. Renovation projects were the original part of Zimmerman Library, Scholes Hall, and the Computing Center. There would be some money for landscaping, roads, and campus lighting. In September the regents approved the award of a contract to Lembke Construction Company to build the addition to Zimmerman Library. George A. Rutherford was low bidder on the Nursing-Pharmacy Building (228). Regent Albert Simms asked for $100,000 for North Campus planning, which was approved.

Planning for new facilities continued in late 1973. Lavon McDonald had been appointed athletic director to succeed Pete McDavid who was retiring on January 1, 1974. McDonald wanted to proceed as soon as possible with expansion and improvements to both University Stadium (301) and the Basketball Arena (302). There had been talk of adding a balcony to the arena and I was convinced it could be done. I had an architect in my office do a cross-sectional study of the building, which proved there was enough ceiling height for a balcony completely around the arena and the sightlines would be very good. There were skeptics, including the architect for the original building. So Floyd Williams, assistant director of the Physical Plant Department, had his carpenters build a full-size section of the balcony in place with a ladder to reach it. We invited all interested parties, including President Heady, to come down and see for themselves.

The project, which added 2,370 balcony seats to the arena, was approved at the board meeting on April 23, 1974, and Joe Boehning, architect for the original arena, was appointed architect for the addition. The project also included widening the concourse, adding a wing containing space for the Lobo Club, a meeting room, expanded ticket sales space, visiting team dressing rooms, and storage for concession supplies.

Sherman Smith

"UNM Vice President Sherman Smith Dies" was the headline in the *Daily Lobo* on October 5, 1973. The article stated that Dr. Smith died on October 4 following complications from surgery. I was at the Gallup campus when I received a call telling me of his death. It was very hard for me to accept his death since I had worked very closely with Sherman for almost ten years. I had come to admire, respect, and appreciate his many fine qualities. He had become one of the best friends I ever had. It is difficult to write this more than twenty years later.

There were many articles and statements eulogizing him and his devoted work at UNM and his public service outside the University. President Heady said,

Vice President Sherman Smith *(right)* and the author confer about a landscape problem on the Central Campus. *Albuquerque Journal* photograph by Bill Anstett.

> The death of Sherman Smith is a tragic loss for the University. He was not only a man of many talents whose record of accomplishments for the University is unexcelled, but he also represented the highest type of faculty member and administrator.
>
> The list of his contributions to the University goes on and on. It is especially noteworthy in the areas of planning and development of the physical campus, representation before the legislature and other government bodies, and in the internal administration of the University.

Calvin Horn, president of the Board of Regents, said, "Few men or women have contributed as much to the University as Sherman Smith. We on the Board of Regents looked to him frequently for advice and counsel, and will sorely miss him in the future. Several of us have known him as a friend for many years."

An editorial in the *Albuquerque Journal* said, "He was a man of so many talents that they were outnumbered only by his wide range of interests: music, architecture, legislation, disadvantaged children and—most of all—people."

Sherman Smith came to UNM as chairman of the chemistry department, succeeding John Clark. In 1949, while still a faculty member, he was appointed director of student affairs and that same year he began representing the University before the legislature, which he continued to do until his death.

He became administrative vice president in 1965 and vice president for administration and development in 1970. In addition to his work with the legislature and the BEF, his principal responsibility was to steer the University's capital development program through a period of great expansion in the physical plant and enrollment. The central plaza was officially named Smith Plaza in honor of Vice President Sherman E. Smith.

I wrote a brief tribute to Dr. Smith in *New Mexico Architecture*: "The architects of New Mexico lost a good friend, because Sherman understood how architects work, their capabilities and limitations. He was interested in good design and planning, and insisted on the best from any firm that worked for the University. We will miss him."

McDonald also pushed hard for a new press box and VIP section to be added to the football stadium replacing the existing press box above the west side seat bank. It would be three levels above the concourse with the press box on top and a VIP lounge and seats in two levels below. For both projects McDonald's idea was to sell season tickets to the VIP area at a high enough price to pay for annual bond costs. It seemed to be a sound financial proposal and the Board of Regents agreed to it in 1974.

W. C. Kruger and Associates' final plans for the press box addition to University Stadium were approved by the regents on July 29, 1974, after clearing the Campus Planning Committee. It was planned for the construction to begin after the close of the 1974 football season and to be complete in time for the beginning of the 1975 season.

Preliminary plans for the arena remodeling were approved by the Campus Planning Committee and presented to the regents at their meeting on June 12. The plan was to bid the project as soon as the working drawings and specifications were ready, possibly bid the structural steel in advance, award the construction contract so work could begin as soon as the 1974–75 basketball season ended, and have it ready for use by the beginning of the 1975–76 season. It would take a concerted effort to make that schedule.

I was able to present the tabulation of bids for the arena project to the regents on February 1, 1975. The contract was awarded to George A. Rutherford. The final project cost, including all fees, equipment, the previously bid structural steel, and other expenses, was $2,801,337, more than the cost of the original building. Unfortunately we found out that work could not begin until the end of the Billy Graham Crusade, which had been booked into The Pit in March, leaving fewer than 200 working days for completion.

Other happenings at the end of 1973 included the dedication of Joaquin Ortega Hall (79) on December 8. Ortega came to UNM in 1941 and for seven years was director of the School of Inter-American Affairs as well as a professor. He retired in 1954. President Heady officiated at the ceremony, which included remarks by Professor Emeritus Robert M. Duncan and Professor and Chairman William Roberts, both from the Department of Modern and Classical Languages, colleagues of Joaquin Ortega.

The College of Business and Administrative Sciences was renamed the Robert O. Anderson Schools of Management, the first UNM academic division named for an individual. Anderson was board chairman of Atlantic Richfield, owned a ranch near Roswell, and headed the Lincoln County Livestock Company.

As 1973 ended six major buildings were under construction or just being completed: Woodward Lecture Hall, Humanities, the Bookstore, the Nursing-Pharmacy Building, the addition to Zimmerman Library, and the Cancer Research and Treatment Center. Together they totaled about 400,000 gross square feet, equal to the total square footage of all the buildings on the University of New Mexico campus in 1941.

Woodward Hall lecture hall. Architect: W. C. Kruger and Associates. Photograph by Jerry Goffe.

At the first meeting of the Board of Regents in 1974, January 17, the decision was made to proceed with the married student housing project on Buena Vista Southeast. Bradbury and Stamm had submitted a bid that was over the established budget but I stated that items could be cut from the project without hurting it. John Perovich said that federal red tape held up the project for one and a half years before bidding during an inflationary period.

Woodward Hall was occupied by the end of January by the Instructional Media Services (IMS) directed by Robert Kline, professor of secondary education. The main lecture hall seats 888 in front of a 10-by–24-foot screen, which, at the time, was one of the largest one-piece screens produced. On the north side are two 124-seat classrooms with rear-screen projection controlled by the lecturer and the capability of showing motion pictures, slides, and television. The material being shown in the main hall can be seen simultaneously in the small classrooms by closed-circuit television. IMS occupied the lower level where there were studios and laboratories for making films or video tapes for lectures.

For some time there had been discussions about the need for a library for the health sciences but finding the funds was a problem. One day I was talking with an architect from the National Institutes of Health and I asked him if there was any money for medical libraries available. He said there was some funding for libraries that were allied with biomedical communications and there was still time to apply. He said the funds would be divided among seven schools. I immediately called the dean of the Medical School, Leonard Napolitano, who set things in motion to prepare an application for a construction grant with space for biomedical communications included. The application was approved by the regents at their meeting on March 14, 1974.

Dean Napolitano appointed a building committee with Robert O. Kelley, professor of anatomy, as chairman to work with McKinley Nance from my office in programming the library. There were members representing the School of Medicine, the Colleges of Nursing and Pharmacy, Biomedical Communications, and the medical library. After the Campus Planning Committee interviewed several architectural firms, Harvey Hoshour Architects was recommended to the regents and they approved the appointment.

The University administration finally agreed with New Mexico Union Director Ted Martinez and the Student Union Board that the present facility was overtaxed to meet the demand of an increasing student body. A study would have to be made to determine the immediate needs and the long-range requirements since the union would have to be kept in operation during the remodeling. After interviewing several architectural firms, the Campus Planning Committee recommended Antoine Predock to be the architect. The regents confirmed the appointment at the June meeting. A program had been prepared by Patricia Richards working with Martinez and his staff.

Predock immediately began the process of "advocacy planning." With the help of some graduate students in architecture, the New Mexico Union management and board, the University administration, my office, and student organizations, Predock wrote to more than 150 offices and organizations on campus saying in effect, "Here's your chance to have some say-so about the new SUB." He had large boards erected covered with paper on which he asked for people to write or draw their ideas. More than 200 people showed up at the first general meeting held to discuss the project. Small groups were formed to consider various aspects of the program. Out of this planning came some very good ideas, but the tight budget limited how they could be implemented.

John R. Lavis Construction Co. was awarded the contract to remodel the College of Education Classroom Building (67), which included updating the classrooms and adding steel beams over the roof tied to the concrete slabs below to stabilize the roof structure and the second floor that was deflecting. At that same regents meeting in July, the architectural plans for the press box at University Stadium were approved.

The completion of the Humanities Building (81) in August precipitated a large relocation of departments and other functions. The Honors Program and the Graduate School occupied the first floor; the second floor housed the English Department; on the third floor were American Studies, the Council for the Humanities, and Vo-Tec Education; the Department of Mathematics and Statistics was on the fourth floor; and the Departments of Philosophy and Linguistics and the Navajo Reading Study were on the top floor. Other departments moved into the spaces vacated by those going into Humanities: student publications and art studios went into Marron Hall (9), and Bandelier East (8) received several small programs. The Air Force ROTC was moved to a remodeled residence at 1901 Las Lomas.

In September the regents named the new state bar building the Dale Bellamah Law Center and approved the award of a contract to Weaver Construction Company. At the same meeting they authorized the purchase of the Phi Gamma Delta house at 1700 Las Lomas and the Pi Kappa Alpha house at Roma and University.

The Campus Planning Committee and the Board of Regents approved the site on the northwest corner of Tucker Boulevard and Yale for the Children's Psychiatric Center. The center was planned to have fifty-three beds for emotionally disturbed children. It was to be operated jointly by UNM and the State Department of Hospitals and Institutions. The fiscal responsibility lay with the state. Barker-Bol was the architectural firm chosen by the state.

Cyrene (Mrs. Frank) Mapel left the Board of Regents on December 31, 1974, after serving twelve years. She was the regent representative on the Campus Planning Committee for almost that entire time and contributed much to the planning of the campus and the design of buildings. For example, she always insisted that no unsightly mechanical equipment should be placed on rooftops unless completely hidden.

Also on that day Myron F. (Fife) Fifield retired as director of the Physical Plant Department after having held the position for more than twenty-three years. He was succeeded by Floyd B. Williams who had been associate director since 1973. Edmund Pitt Ross was appointed manager of construction and maintenance.

Fifield's retirement coincided with the announcement of the death of Earl Bowdich, who was manager of Buildings and Grounds, now the Physical Plant Department, from 1933 to 1951. Bowdich served under three presidents—Zimmerman, Wernette, and Popejoy—and saw the University through the depression and the building boom of the PWA-WPA days, World War II, and the invasion of the barracks afterward. Bowdich carried on a running battle with John Gaw Meem and his firm over design details and choices of materials.

Not long after the Health Sciences Learning Resource Center (the Medical Center Library) was completed, a very upset Harvey Hoshour, architect for the library, appeared in my office with a copy of an architectural journal. In it was an article about a new library at an Ohio university that bore a striking resemblance to his library. It was about the same size, had a triangular plan, and even the elevation was similar. Harvey wanted me to know he had never heard of this building until now and it had had no influence on his design. I assured him I knew that was true and not to worry about it further.

The John Gaw Meem Archive of Southwestern Architecture

Dean of Library Services John Harvey had the great idea of collecting the papers of ten noted New Mexicans for the library. He asked me if I would see if John Gaw Meem would donate his material to UNM. I agreed and bided my time until I caught Meem in the right frame of mind. One day I had stopped by the office of William Buckley in the old Meem office building on Camino del Monte Sol in Santa Fe. As I was leaving, Meem came out and we started a conversation next to our cars. At the right moment I asked him what he was going to do with all of his drawings and papers. He said he didn't know, so I suggested he give them to the University library. He said he thought it was a great idea and would relieve him of worrying about the problem.

I took upon myself the task of getting the material properly packed and moved to Albuquerque. I had the Physical Plant Department make several shallow wooden crates large enough to hold the drawings that were hanging in the office vault. It took me four days to index the material, which included several file cabinets, office furniture, a library of several hundred books, the many diplomas and awards Meem had received, and miscellaneous things such as the beautiful old Indian pot that sat in the unused fireplace in Ruth Heflin's office. Unless you looked you would not know the whole back side of the pot had been smashed long ago. When everything was packed the Physical Plant sent up trucks to move the material to Zimmerman Library.

The gift was announced to the public in May 1975 and a dinner in John and Faith Meem's honor was sponsored by the Friends of the University Libraries. The Meem family gave a substantial endowment to the library for the maintenance of the collection.

The History Department elected not to be included in the Humanities Building, opting instead to stay in Mesa Vista Hall where the faculty offices were much larger, about 240 square feet. The history faculty argued that Mesa Vista had sufficient wall space for shelving their books, which would not be true in the Humanities Building.

CHAPTER TWELVE

Focus on the North Campus

On February 1, 1975, the Alumni Association presented a proposal to the Board of Regents to save Hodgin Hall and restore it to house the association, the Alumni and Development Offices, and a collection of memorabilia. The presentation was made by Dr. Jack Redman, Judge Ben C. Hernandez, and architect Joseph D. Burwinkle Jr., an alumnus, who had made drawings showing the restored building. I was asked what the project might cost and off the top of my head I estimated between $400,000 and $500,000. It turned out to be twice that. Dr. Redman said he believed the alumni would provide some money for the project, perhaps for furnishings and interior work.

The regents voted unanimously for the preservation of Hodgin Hall as a University historical landmark and for its renovation for University uses as money became available. The Office of the University Architect was instructed to develop detailed plans for the restoration and to establish a timetable for the work.

Many actions were taken at the regents meeting on March 18, 1975, including approval of the plans for renovating the New Mexico Union (60). Architect Antoine Predock's plan considered remodeling the entire building in phases, starting with the basement and the first floor.

The Basketball Arena remodeling project suffered a slight setback when a stubborn fire broke out in the truss space in the southwest corner around 3:25 on Friday afternoon, May 30, 1975. It was caused, as many University fires have been, by a spark from a welder's torch. Some insulation and other material burned, producing a great deal of smoke but not much damage. Most of the damage was done by the firemen who had to chop a hole in the steel wall panels to reach the fire. There was no delay in the work and the December completion date was met.

The remodeling of the second floor of Scholes Hall was completed in the spring of 1975. Included in the work was the creation of a new regents meeting room on the

John Keyser's sculpture *Static Motion* on the deck above the Physics Laboratories. Photograph by Terry Gugliotta, UNM Archive.

west side, which was named the Roberts Room in memory of Dr. Thomas R. Roberts, a Los Alamos physicist and president of the Board of Regents at the time of his death in 1968. He served on the board for seven years and was instrumental in founding the School of Medicine. He also guided the search committee that selected Ferrel Heady as UNM president in 1967 and at one time he was chairman of the regents' budget committee.

A large walnut table that would seat the regents, the University secretary, the president, student representatives, and people making presentations was donated by Dr. Roberts's widow, Ms. Carol Roberts Kinney. The table and a side table, which matched the room's walnut wall paneling, were made by Albuquerque craftsman Max Chavez, a UNM graduate.

The addition to the Law Library in Bratton Hall (218) had been previously approved, programming was complete, and funding was in sight. The Campus Planning Committee interviewed several architectural firms and recommended Stevens, Mallory, Pearl, and Campbell because of their experience in library design. The regents approved the appointment at their meeting on June 17, 1975, and said they wanted the preliminaries completed before the beginning of the 1976 legislative session. My instruction to the architects was to make the design of the addition conform exactly to that of the original building so that you could not tell where it connected.

The funding for the Art Building (84) was long in coming. More than half a million dollars had been appropriated from the 1971 state bond issue and with the 1975 bond funds the total reached almost $3.5 million. Because of the dramatic increase in inflation from 1971 to 1975, the original funds were mostly lost so there had to be cutbacks in the building program. Dean of Fine Arts Clinton Adams was happy to get the funds short though they were. He said, "Art departments are the last major departments to receive new buildings even though the character of the department calls for special facilities; this has been traditional on American campuses." Antoine Predock, architect for the project, was instructed to proceed with the final design, working drawings, and specifications for early bidding.

On August 8, 1975, the Cancer Research and Treatment Center (227) was dedicated. First Lady Clara Apodaca, the honorary state crusade chair for the American Cancer Society, represented the state. Introductions

The Physics Laboratories and Lecture Hall project included some money for art. Dean Clinton Adams and I decided a competition would be a good way to select a sculptor and a design for a piece to be placed on the deck. A committee was appointed of Adams and me and representatives from the Physics Department and the College of Engineering. John Keyser's *Static Motion*, a steel piece, was selected from several entries. Keyser built the sculpture in his graduate studio in the old boiler plant, later the Comedia Theater. The finished sculpture is painted red orange, which brings a nice bit of color to the plaza.

The Cancer Center
(227). Architect:
Flatow, Moore,
Bryan, and
Fairburn.
Photograph by the
author.

The Nursing-
Pharmacy Building
(228). Architect:
Flatow, Moore,
Bryan, and
Fairburn.
Photograph by
Jerry Goffe.

were made by Dr. Morton M. Kligerman, director of the center. The name of the facility was later changed to the University of New Mexico Cancer Center.

Other UNM buildings completed in the summer were the married student housing complex (317–329) on Buena Vista Southeast and the Dale Bellamah Law Center (230) adjacent to Bratton Hall on the North Campus. The VIP lounge and the press box at the football stadium were delayed because of problems in obtaining equipment. The regents met next on August 26, 1975, and took the Campus Planning Committee's recommendation of Dale Crawford to be the architect for the Family Practice Center (248). The committee had met on August 11 and 14 with Vice President John Perovich as chairman and Regent Henry Jaramillo in attendance to interview the many architects seeking the job.

At the regents meeting on September 27, 1975, authorization was given to begin planning the Dental Programs Building, which was high on the priority list. The

The southeast addition to the University Hospital. Architect: Flatow, Moore, Bryan, and Fairburn.

program was occupying the last two World War II barracks left on the campus and they were in terrible condition. Director Monica Novitski and her faculty and students were pushing hard for a new building. Holmes-Giannini was the firm appointed as architects for the Dental Programs Building (249) upon the recommendation of the Campus Planning Committee, which had met with representatives of the Dental Programs and the College of Pharmacy and interviewed prospective architects.

William E. "Bud" Davis became president of the University of New Mexico on October 1, 1975. Before accepting the appointment he was president of Idaho State University. Before he left Idaho, I visited him and his wife, Polly, to see what would have to be done to the president's house at UNM to accommodate them and their young twin daughters, Brooke and Bonnie. I produced designs showing how the existing garage could be made into a family room and a new garage added, but only the family room conversion was done. The early 1950s kitchen was completely done over to better meet the demands of entertaining large crowds. Davis was very interested in the University building and planning program and was a pleasure to work with.

The Nursing-Pharmacy Building (228) was dedicated on Saturday, October 18, 1975. Vice President for the Health Sciences Robert Kugel presided and speakers included President Davis, outgoing President Ferrel Heady, Dean of Nursing Louise Murray, and Dean of Pharmacy Carman A. Bliss. The UNM Brass Quintet, directed by Karl Hinterbichler, played on the Health Sciences Plaza. One of the features of the building that drew much attention was the greenhouse, which had a display of medicinal plants. At the meeting of the Board of Regents on December 1, 1975, I presented proposed site locations for the addition to Bratton Hall (218) and the Family Practice Center (248). The latter was to be located northwest of the Basic Medical Sciences Building. The library addition to the Law School was an extension of the present library to the west. Both sites were approved.

At that meeting Perovich presented the bids for construction of the medical library and explained that one-third of the project cost would come from UNM revenue bonds and the balance from federal funds. Regent Horn noted that this was a precedent-setting move since in the past the University had not used its general campus credit to guarantee payment of bonds for Health Sciences Center construction nor had the Medical School been included as a beneficiary of state general obligation bonds. Perovich pointed out that overhead from federal grants to the Medical School was included in the University's general revenue used to guarantee bond payments. In accepting the bid from Lembke Construction Company, the regents specified that the University revenue bonds needed to pay UNM's part would be repaid exclusively from Health Sciences income.

At a previous meeting Regent Albert Simms had requested more planning for the medical campus and my office had prepared a detailed plan. I felt a more experienced person in medical school planning should critique the plan and expand upon it so I asked for additional funds for this and they were approved.

The City of Albuquerque found it advisable to replace the steel roof on the Yale Reservoir at Yale and Central because of severe rusting. Stevens, Mallory, Pearl, and Campbell were employed to design the exterior of the reservoir including landscaping the west and south sides, which were mostly on city prop-

UNM received an untold amount of nationwide television exposure in 1975 when the manufacturers of Desenex, a powder for the relief of athlete's foot, made a commercial touting studies done in UNM's Medical School on the efficacy of the product. The ad was filmed with the Humanities Building in the background instead of one of the medical buildings.

The City Reservoir was an unsightly place until it was redesigned by architect George C. Pearl. Photograph by Jerry Goffe.

President Thomas Lafayette Popejoy

Former President Tom Popejoy died at the Bernalillo County Medical Center on Friday, October 24, 1975, at the age of seventy-two after having been in ill health for several years. He was born on a ranch in Colfax County east of Raton and went to school in Raton before entering UNM as a freshman in 1921. He was to stay for the next forty-seven years as a student, professor, administrator, and president. He did graduate work at the University of Illinois and the University of California before obtaining a master's degree in economics at UNM in 1929. In 1937 he was appointed comptroller, an office he held until he became president in 1948.

Popejoy brought UNM to its recognized status as the flagship institution of higher education in the state. He fought many battles for the University, including the annual struggle with the BEF and the legislature over funding, and with those in the state, including the American Legion, who sought to limit academic freedom. One of his strong arguing points with legislative committees was that, based on enrollment, UNM was not getting its fair share of the funding.

Until he became president, the state had contributed only about $100,000 toward the building of the campus, and he had to find other ways to finance buildings and the infrastructure that makes a campus. Student fees, income from University services such as housing, and research overhead funded buildings, by backing University bond issues.

Two accomplishments Popejoy prided himself on were the construction of the Concert Hall and the establishment of the Medical School, which he said was important to the state but also to the University community in rounding out a complex institution.

Popejoy tried to work with Mayor Tingley and the city to build a joint-use performing arts center, but after years of frustration he gave the city an ultimatum: either reach an agreement or the University will build its own, which it did with money from the sale of land in the northeast heights.

Tom Popejoy loved the game of golf. While he was comptroller, working with President Zimmerman, he found funds to build the

erty. The University agreed to landscape the north and east slopes. Because of conflicting surveys, it was impossible to locate the boundaries accurately so a compromise was reached acceptable to both parties. It was apparent the city was not going to give up the site anytime soon as we hoped they would.

The big event closing the year 1975 was the reopening of the Basketball Arena following a several-months-long renovation, which included adding a balcony with more than 2,000 theater-type seats. The lounge–meeting room was named the Pete McDavid Honor Lounge for the former athletic director. The official opening was on December 3 with a game against the California State University at Los Angeles Diablos. The game on December 9 with New Mexico State University drew the biggest crowd in our state's history, 18,008.

University Golf Course, which extended from Central and Girard into what is now the North Campus. A good part of the funding came from PWA-WPA grants. When the course was reduced by the pressure for building sites, he headed the effort to build the South Course.

Popejoy was keenly aware of the need for long-range campus planning, and he made shrewd decisions about expanding to the North and South Campuses and about buying and selling land.

No person ever contributed more to UNM than Tom Popejoy and I doubt if anyone ever will. The native son was totally dedicated to the school. He had opportunities in business and industry that would have paid him much more, but he stayed with UNM. He said late in life that he never regretted the decision.

The Popejoys lived in the house on the campus for about twenty years. They maintained a quiet family life without much entertaining and asked for only minimum renovations. While I was working in the office of Meem, Zehner, and Holien, I was given the task of helping plan a sunroom on the south side and renovating the

Thomas Lafayette Popejoy, president of the University from 1948 to 1968. Photograph by Clarence E. Redman.

kitchen. That was around 1954–55, and I do not think much else other than routine maintenance was ever done during his presidency. Tom and his wife, Bess, kept a small cornfield in the northeast corner of the property. Popejoy was a very unpretentious person; he was what he was.

It was my opinion the arena needed a sparkling new image on the interior so I selected Anita Corey, head of the Corey Design and Planning Group in New York City. Her organization had just done the interiors in the renovated Madison Square Garden, as well as many other major projects around the country. Although she was a member of the Osuna family in New Mexico, born in Albuquerque, the daughter of a former UNM professor, an alumna of UNM, and a woman who did very well in her profession as an interior designer and graphic artist, I received criticism for hiring an out-of-state person.

Corey did a graphics program for both the arena and the football stadium press box. On both buildings she designed some super-graphics of athletes in motion. In the arena they were located on the walls in the four quadrants of the concourse. Unfortunately they were painted over later at the direction of the Athletic Department.

(Right) A view of a game from the University Arena balcony. Architect: Joe Boehning. Photograph by Jerry Goffe.

(Below) The concourse in the basketball arena was widened with the addition of the balcony. Photograph by Jerry Goffe.

On January 23, 1976 the Board of Regents also approved the plans for the addition to Bratton Hall, the Law School, which were presented by Robert Campbell of the architectural firm of Stevens, Mallory, Pearl, and Campbell. Then the board renewed the motion, made and approved at the February 1, 1975, meeting, to request passage of a bill in the legislature to appropriate funds for the project.

I introduced Jess Holmes, architect for the Dental Programs Building (249), who presented the preliminary plans for it. Director Monica Novitski, who had represented the faculty in the programming and planning process, expressed strong approval of the design. The regents accepted the design and asked that the legislature be informed that this was the University's second priority project. The building was located on the North Campus west of the State Scientific Laboratory Building on the slope north of the AMAFCA flood control channel. There were offices, classrooms, laboratories, and a dental clinic.

I told the regents that design approval of the Family Practice Center (248) was needed no later than February 13 in order to get the project bid and meet deadlines. The board delegated authority to the Campus Planning Committee to approve the design if the regents were notified of the time and place of the meeting. When the

University Stadium press box. Architect: W. C. Kruger and
Associates. Photograph by Jerry Goffe.

meeting was held, Regents Henry Jaramillo and Austin Roberts attended. The design
was approved with the request that architect Dale Crawford make the entrance to the
emergency medicine area on the ground floor south side more prominent.

An effort had been made during the 1975 legislative session to obtain an appropriation for construction of the library addition to the Law School. The bill passed the
House at a lower level of funding than that asked for and was killed in a Senate committee. Dean Fred Hart, who headed up the appeal, had been told to come back in
1976 when he would probably get full funding. An appropriation bill was introduced
in the 1976 session and late one afternoon I got a call from William "Bill" Weeks, legislative liaison for UNM, to get Dean Hart and come to Santa Fe for a hearing that
night before Aubrey Dunn's Senate Finance Committee. We got there as soon as we
could and then sat around until about two o'clock the next morning before we were
able to put on our "dog and pony show" as Dunn called those presentations. The bill
was tabled to be considered after all requests had been heard.

Committee on University Planning

The Committee on University Planning (COUP) was formed by the regents on November 9, 1973, to study the total planning process, including physical and academic planning, funding, and other long-range needs. It consisted of representatives of all facets of University life: regents, administrators, faculty, students, alumni, and friends. Paul Silverman, vice president for research, was named chairman and led the group for the entire life of the study. Subcommittees were formed to examine certain aspects of University functions including facility planning and building. The work of COUP was to be finished by the end of the 1973–74 academic year but it was extended through the summer of 1974.

The section about campus planning and construction stressed that there was no correlation between academic planning and physical planning and no existing mechanism to achieve it. This was mainly because there was no firm academic plan, written or otherwise, and no real desire on the part of the administration to have one. The COUP report referred to "hip-pocket" and "spur-of-the-moment" decisions putting out one brushfire after another, which was typical of most institutions of higher learning. The report said, "It is to the credit of the central administration that the University has progressed as well as it has."

This reminded me of a meeting I attended at O'Hare Inn in Chicago in the 1960s. A group of university architects was called together by Louis Demonte, campus architect at the University of California at Berkeley, because he was frustrated in his campus planning effort by the lack of an academic plan. It turned out that of the sixteen schools represented only one, Tulane University, had a written plan. As I remember, Tulane had received a grant of $2 million from a foundation to accomplish it. There was no firm conclusion drawn about how a university architect can influence the institution to produce an academic plan if there is no real desire to have one. The general feeling was that the regents, trustees, presidents, chancellors, and other top administrators do not want to make written, long-range statements that would be taken by deans, faculty, and others to be firm commitments for program enhancements and building projects.

Among the other recommendations of COUP was to get a better inventory of space than required by the BEF. It should include, beyond just numbers of seats, actual numbers of students in classes and frequency of use, state of repair, and establishment of a life-cycle maintenance program. Funds should be sought for landscaping, sculpture, and quality in building materials and design. The report called attention to the rising number of new programs that needed space and the shortages of space in certain areas, and suggested establishment of a policy and a central office for assignment of faculty offices. The role of the Campus Planning Committee should be studied in relation to the need for centralized University-wide planning, which included resolving the relationship of North Campus planning with the rest of the University. One last recommendation was the improvement of visitor services, which at that time, were almost nonexistent.

An overnight retreat to study the report was held at the D. H. Lawrence Ranch in April 1975. I led a group that was interested in the portion of the report about physical planning. After the group meetings were concluded, everyone met in the auditorium and each part of the report was discussed. It seemed to me the report was well received by most of the attendees.

The COUP report did not make an immediate impact on the University, but many of the recommendations remained in the minds of the people involved and were considered in future planning.

Second priority for the Dental Programs Building did not sit well with the dental students who were still housed in two ramshackle barracks at University and Ash. On February 12, 1976, before the end of the legislative session, the students organized a march on Regent President Calvin Horn's office at the Horn Oil Company. He had advance warning of their coming and called me to come to his office to help explain the situation. We spoke with three of the leaders of the group in Horn's office while the demonstrators outside chanted, "We wanna new building. We wanna be number one."

Horn explained that the Law School project was the top priority because Dean Hart had gone before the legislature personally, with the regents' tacit consent, to ask for funds. Horn assured the students they would get their building since they would be top priority once the Law School addition was funded, as he presumed it would be. I told them the architect had been selected and the preliminary planning completed so work could proceed without delay once the funds were in place. Horn pointed out that a general obligation bond issue from which funding could come was on the November ballot and the voters had never turned one down. The demonstrators left and the regents soon approved President Davis's request to have final drawings and specifications completed so bids could be received, assuming the state bond issue passed in November.

At the end of the session, the bill for funding the Law School addition was passed and $2,978,100 was appropriated from the general fund, the first time a direct appropriation for construction of a University building was ever made. The low bid on the addition to the Law Building was within the available funds and Bradbury and Stamm were awarded the contract. The work consisted of a major addition to the Law Library, offices, classrooms, and modifications to the heating and air conditioning system in the original building.

When Myron Fifield died, the following tribute appeared in the Physical Plant Department publication *El Servicio Real,* which he had founded and edited for many years:

> Myron F. "Fife" Fifield, who directed physical plant operations at UNM for 23 years, died in early February 1976. He had retired from the University in December 1974.
>
> After becoming director of the Physical Plant Department in June 1951, he led a concerted effort to have maintenance personnel recognized for their value to the overall organization through UNM's affiliation with national and regional associations and the sponsoring of training programs and workshops. . . .
>
> Fifield was a tireless booster of UNM and wrote many articles for magazines about buildings and the history of the campus. He started a

Aerial view of the Children's Psychiatric Hospital. Courtesy of the architect Hildreth Barker.

newsletter in the department and wrote a column, "Dipping Into History," which told little-known facts about the campus and University people.

The design for the Children's Psychiatric Center, a state project, was presented to the regents at their meeting on May 16, 1976. The site was at the northwest corner of Tucker and Yale. I stated that the Campus Planning Committee had given its approval with the stipulation that within two years the State Department of Hospitals and Institutions must come up with a plan for stabilizing the steep south and west slopes of the site. The site location and the design were approved. The name of the facility was later changed to the University of New Mexico Children's Psychiatric Hospital.

The project was to handle fifty-three in-patients and out-patients in a family-like environment. Disturbed children between three and sixteen would be evaluated and treated in the facility, and medical students would use the unit in their fieldwork. Several houses were designed for patients and counselors, and recreational and administrative units were included.

Bids were received on July 15 for construction of the Art Building (84) and I presented a tabulation to the regents on July 20. Lembke Construction Company's bid was accepted and now construction could be started on the long-awaited project. Unfortunately, because of the limited budget, the building did not totally meet the needs of the department. The building was designed with three floors and only a small basement for the mechanical equipment. On the first floor there are classes that require large equipment and work space such as photography, printing, ceramics, sculpture, and lapidary work. The second floor holds the administrative offices, a teaching gallery, and classrooms. There is an atrium over the lobby with a skylight above. Many of the spaces are lit by high north windows and north-facing skylights. The third floor has faculty offices, classrooms for art history, the slide library, and drawing and painting studios. At the rear of the building, against the City Reservoir, are ceramic kilns and exterior work spaces. On the south side, opposite the main north entrance, is a patio for displaying sculpture and other art works. The overhead concourse was extended from the Bookstore through the Art Building at the second level and taken into the second level of the Fine Arts Center.

200. Model of proposed Art Building (84). Architect: Antoine Predock. Photograph by Jerry Goffe.

At this same meeting, I presented a five-year building need projection that had been put together by my office in consultation with President Davis and Vice President Perovich. The total estimated cost was $24.3 million and contained funds for seventeen new buildings and additions to buildings. The number one priority was the Dental Programs Building; the Mechanical Engineering Building was number two. Regent President Horn was hesitant to make such a commitment beyond one year, but Davis and Perovich said the list could be approved in its present form subject to reestablishing the priorities beyond the first year. With that understanding, it was approved.

In September, John Perovich sold $8.5 million worth of bonds he had held back for several months and saved $300,000 in lower interest rates. These bonds were used to pay for the Basketball Arena addition, the press box, the Student Union remodeling, and the University's part of the Family Practice Center and the Medical Center Library.

At a meeting on September 7, 1976, the regents approved the selection of Pacheco and Graham to be the architects for the proposed Mechanical Engineering Building (122) and allocated money for preliminary planning. Vice President Perovich explained that the building had not yet been funded but could be funded from a state bond issue or appropriated funds.

Family Practice Center (248). Architect: Dale Crawford. Photograph by the author.

Lou Hoffman, a representative of Public Service Company of New Mexico, and I explained that an early start on planning was desirable in order to make application for a $300,000 to $400,000 design grant from the Electrical Power Research Institute. The grant would allow the University to incorporate solar heating elements in the building for both operation and instruction.

Bids came in on August 25 for the Family Practice Center (248) and K. L. House Construction Company received the contract. This was a four-level building containing 58,230 gross square feet. It was built into the side of a south-facing slope, so at the lower grade level there are entrances to the Medical/Legal Bookstore on the east and to the Emergency Medicine section on the south. On the next level, entered on grade on the north, is the entrance lobby for the upper levels, the Family Practice Clinic examining rooms, laboratory, waiting rooms, and offices. The third level is offices for the faculty and the top floor is space for the Department of Psychiatry.

The request for a land lease on the South Campus by the UNM Tennis Foundation was approved in principle but final approval was withheld pending receipt of more information about the foundation's organizational and management plans. The foundation, headed by Fred Vogl, an Albuquerque banker, proposed to develop a nineteen-court tennis complex south of University Stadium. It would be funded by a membership of 600 and staffed by UNM tennis coaches. In return for a lease at a nominal price, the foundation would allow UNM tennis teams to use the facilities for practice, and the foundation would provide scholarships and other help to the team. Final approval of the contract was given in February 1977.

Bill Brannin, UNM Alumni Association president, announced in November a drive to raise $200,000 toward the restoration of Hodgin Hall. Brannin said, "All alumni will want to help restore and preserve Hodgin Hall," which he termed a symbol of the University and its heritage.

The temperature dropped to ten degrees over the Thanksgiving holidays, which caught the University unprepared and caused an estimated $800,000 to $1 million in damages. Most of the damage was caused by water from pipes that burst above ceilings and in chases. Thermostats had been set at fifty-eight degrees over the holidays to conserve energy and this contributed to the problem. Buildings affected included Zimmerman Library, University Stadium press box, Marron Hall, the Fine Arts Center, the Computing Center, Johnson Gymnasium, and the UNM Press offices.

The just-completed Duck Pond designed by landscape architect Garrett Eckbo.
Photograph by Jerry Goffe.

The Duck Pond

At the end of the 1974 fall semester, the parking lot between Scholes Hall and Zimmerman Library was closed, and the Physical Plant Department began to salvage material from Yatoka Hall (7), which was to be demolished to clear the site for the long-awaited landscape development. The Physical Plant Department began the actual demolition of Yatoka Hall and Y-1, a World War II wood-frame building, on January 6. Yatoka was built in 1928–29 as a men's dormitory. It was later made into offices for many different departments: the College of Business Administration, laboratories for the College of Nursing, a U.S. post office, art studios,

American Studies, and other functions at different times. On the ground floor south end was Mrs. Blum's coffee shop, where faculty and staff went for morning coffee and light lunches. Y-1 was remodeled into offices and at one time Sherman Smith had an office there along with others.

This landscape project required the closing and removal of Yale Boulevard from Roma on the north to the alley behind Mitchell Hall on the south. There was some complaining mostly about the loss of the parking lot on the east side of Scholes Hall. The lost spaces were not fully replaced by the lot on University Boulevard since there was reluctance on the part of some of the regents to tear down the Pi Kappa Alpha house.

When Garrett Eckbo developed his landscape plan for the area, he envisioned a large natural pond to the west of the library with mounds of earth surrounding it and an artificial waterfall carrying recirculated water into the pond. Eckbo designed a pedestrian bridge with a trellis covered with wisteria in the Japanese manner, which, unfortunately, we could not afford to do. The lake, early on named the "Duck Pond" by the students, was designed to have a maximum depth of four feet, but a member of the Campus Planning Committee insisted it be made much shallower so as not to be a hazard to small children. The depth of only two and a half feet caused an immediate problem with algae, which thrived in the warm shallow water.

Actual work began when John R. Lavis Construction Company was awarded a contract and started tree removal and excavation. The *Daily Lobo* referred to it as a concrete lake several times even though the real question on water containment was whether to use a plastic liner or bentonite, an expansive clay used to seal ponds and oil and water wells. The latter method was finally chosen because it was hoped it would give the pond a more natural look. It also gave the pond a soft bottom, which complicated maintenance.

The editors of the *Daily Lobo* had a field day criticizing the whole idea of the pond and the end result as they foresaw it. They called it the No-Name pond and said as each construction day went by it reached new heights of tackiness. One article said at least the parking lot it replaced was unobtrusive. The writer asked, "What could be more inappropriate for this campus than a pond?"

Professor Emeritus T. M. Pearce suggested it be named the "Pond of No Return" and the mound and waterfall be bulldozed so the whole area could be returned to its natural form with chamisa, desert willows, and other indigenous plants.

Water was pumped into the pond in February 1976 and work on the surrounding area was completed in the summer. Soon after completion trout and other native fish were introduced and people began to release ducks and goldfish into the water. The goldfish thrived and became large, colorful carp. There were so many ducks dumped at the pond that the flock has had to be thinned out occasionally by taking some to the water reservoirs on the South Campus golf course. The "wild" fish did not do so well, probably because the water was too warm.

Toward the end of 1976, when the turf had been installed, trees planted, and all construction debris removed, Vice President Chester Travelstead wrote, "I must insist that education at any level of study is greatly enhanced by beautiful surroundings. An aesthetically pleasing environment—whether in Ohio or New Mexico—is a great asset for any college or university. One need only observe the way UNM students are now enjoying the rolling grass slopes around the 'Duck Pond' to realize that classroom lectures and outside reading are strengthened by the opportunity to relax peacefully near water, trees and green grass."

The Duck Pond has been drained and cleaned and repaired on several occasions. Early in its life a walk was installed around the perimeter, the small island rebuilt, and the edges reinforced with large rocks. Small rocks did not stay long, perhaps because, as Travelstead remarked, each rock was labeled in script only small boys could read, "Pick me up and throw me in the water." When the pond was drained in 1992, the bentonite was removed and a plastic liner installed.

The Physical Plant Department wanted to fill in and pave over the pond, but it became an instant hit with the students who flocked to it when the 1975 fall semester opened. They soon found the area a great place for lounging, sunbathing, having lunch, and studying on the benches next to the water. It became a campus institution and a public attraction. Weddings are held on the peninsulas and the bridge is a choice place for pictures of wedding parties after ceremonies in the Alumni Chapel. Families picnic on the grassy slopes and children are brought by their teachers to see the ducks and fish. It is without question a high-maintenance area but, in my opinion, well worth it.

Aerial view of the campus, circa 1978.

While Van Deren Coke, director of the University Art Museum, was visiting the Los Angeles County Museum of Art in late 1977 or early 1978 he noticed the large water-activated mobile "Hello Girls" by Alexander Calder was sitting on a grassy knoll instead of in its reflecting pool. Because of water leaks in the pool the sculpture was removed and indications were that it would be sold. Coke thought it would be a great addition to the campus if it were placed in the Duck Pond and so did I. We set about trying to obtain donations to meet the suggested price of $75,000 and were reasonably successful until the museum decided it ". . . is too cherished a work to allow its departure from Los Angeles without excessive strain." Thus ended our quest for a Calder mobile for the campus.

Farewell to the Last Barracks

A final inspection of the remodeling work in the New Mexico Union, which had been done by K. L. House Construction Company, was made on Tuesday, February 15, 1977. Considering that work was done on all levels of the building while it was kept in use as much as possible, the construction work went smoothly. On the basement level, a new entrance to the theater was created on the south side and the lobby was remodeled. Wide stairs were built leading down to an entrance courtyard. On the northwest side the space formerly occupied by the bookstore was made into a three-level nightclub.

The bulk of the work was done on the first floor, which included remodeling the kitchen and serving and dining areas. An outdoor dining terrace was added on the east and southeast sides of the building. A lounge area was located on the south side. Extensive changes were made in the ballroom with new sound and lighting systems and decor. On the second floor were a cafeteria, dining room, and outdoor dining terrace. Casa del Sol, the tent-covered dining space, was enlarged and service from the kitchen below improved.

An article about the project titled "From the Ridiculous to the Sublime" appeared in the November 1978 edition of the now-defunct magazine *Progressive Architecture*. I thought it was an unfortunate title. There were many problems with the original design, but it was not "ridiculous." The New Mexico Union was originally planned and programmed in the middle 1950s for a projected enrollment of 10,000.

Everything considered, the remodeling created a good working facility within a very tight budget. It was to have been the first of a three-part project, but the last two phases have not been carried out, so the building does not function as well as it would if totally renovated.

Since there was going to be a lot of money from an increase in state revenue generated by the severance tax on minerals, which included oil, gas, and uranium, the

Remodeled Student Union dining area. Architect: Antoine Predock.

The addition to the south side of the Student Union. Photograph by the author.

University decided to go for a direct appropriation from the 1977 legislature to build the Mechanical Engineering Building (122). Representative Lenton Malry of Bernalillo County introduced a bill, and Dean of Engineering William Gross and I made a presentation to the House Appropriations Committee on February 28, 1977. The bill was tabled to be considered later when all requests were in. It passed and went to the Senate Finance Committee where the dean and I made our pitch to Aubrey Dunn and company. It was put in the $126.1 million "Christmas tree bill"—so named because legislators had hung some seventy-five other projects on it. Final approval really went down to the wire when, with ten minutes left, it squeaked by the House and the Senate immediately concurred.

Approval was given at the meeting of the regents on April 6 for my request to demolish the Pi Kappa Alpha house at University and Roma to allow for additional parking. I cited the extremely poor condition of the fraternity house and an estimate of $200,000 to bring it up to current code requirements.

I had obtained the appointment of Harland B. Thompson from the University of California at Los Angeles and Robert Crommelin and Associates, parking and traffic planning consultants, to update their previous plan for UNM. Their new plan was presented to the regents at the May 3 meeting. The consultants restated their previous recommendations that all who park on campus must pay and that the parking system must be self-supporting. Yale and Girard should be widened to four lanes and two-lane left-turn bays should be installed at main entrances. The plan included recommendations for building parking structures and improving surface lots. The regents authorized the Campus Planning Committee to implement the noncontroversial traffic-control recommendations and to hold public hearings, primarily about the parking fee proposals, after the beginning of the fall semester. As with most plans, some of the ideas were adopted but there was reluctance to make everyone pay a parking fee. Free parking was still provided on the North Campus and buses, paid for from parking fees, conveyed the users to the main campus.

In order to carry on the planning of the North Campus, I employed Howard Hakken, formerly the university architect for the University of Michigan at Ann Arbor. He had been involved for years in the planning and expansion of the medical center there and had gone into private practice doing planning for other medical schools. A parking-transportation plan for both campuses was being prepared. The planning would be coordinated by the Office of the University Architect.

At the May meeting of the board, I introduced Hakken, who presented his report titled "Guidelines for the Use and Development of Lands and Buildings on the North Campus." The report included the following recommendations: study the acquisition of adjacent land for expansion of the health-related facilities; study the relation of Bernalillo County Medical Center to the University; institute program planning for facilities for the health sciences and related units; develop preliminary studies of space

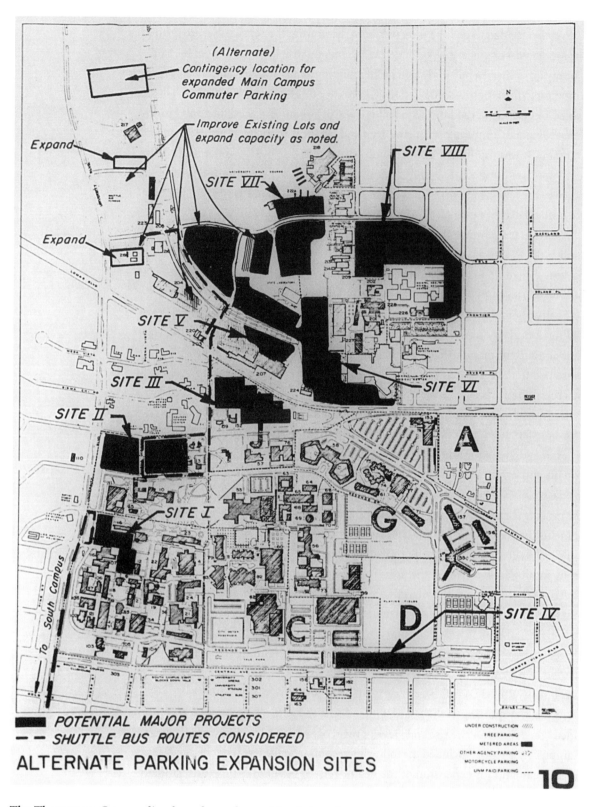

(Alternate)
Contingency location for
expanded Main Campus
Commuter Parking

Improve Existing Lots and
expand capacity as noted.

Expand

SITE VIII

SITE VII

Expand

SITE V

SITE VI

SITE III

SITE II

A

SITE I

G

D

SITE IV

To South Campus

C

█ **POTENTIAL MAJOR PROJECTS**
– – **SHUTTLE BUS ROUTES CONSIDERED**
ALTERNATE PARKING EXPANSION SITES

UNDER CONSTRUCTION /////
FREE PARKING
METERED AREAS ███
OTHER AGENCY PARKING
MOTORCYCLE PARKING
UNM PAID PARKING - - - -

10

The Thompson-Crommelin plan of 1977 for parking lots and structures.

needs and organization of space for the hospital; and study the possibility of erecting a new building for physics and astronomy and converting the existing building for the health sciences. Hakken divided the North Campus into zones separating health education and patient care from health-related functions, academic areas, a residential area, and other University activities. He emphasized continuous planning to keep abreast of the rapidly developing needs of the health center.

I stated that the Campus Planning Committee had reviewed the report and recommended its acceptance with certain minor revisions. Regent Phillip Martinez moved that the report be studied further by the regents with action deferred until a later date. The motion carried. The report was never formally approved but it did serve as a planning tool during later development.

The serious need for additional research space in the School of Medicine led to the appointment of a building committee to plan a biomedical research facility: Max Bennett, planning officer for the Medical School; Phillip W. Day, director of the animal research facility; Chairman of Pediatrics Robert Greenberg; Chairman of Anatomy John Ladman; Professor of Pathology Noel Warner; and me, plus two members chosen for their expertise and experience: George Voelz from Los Alamos National Laboratory and Richard Classen from Sandia National Laboratory.

The Dental Programs Building had to be reduced to bring it within the budget. Colton Construction Company was awarded the contract in May 1977 and work began immediately.

During this time, planning for the Mechanical Engineering Building (122) was proceeding. The programming had been done by Patricia Richards working with my office and people from the Department of Mechanical Engineering including Chairman William E. Baker and Professor Maurice Wilden. Richards told me later how impressed she was with their enthusiasm and desire to have a building that was state-of-the-art in solar energy and energy conservation design. Jesse Pacheco, of the

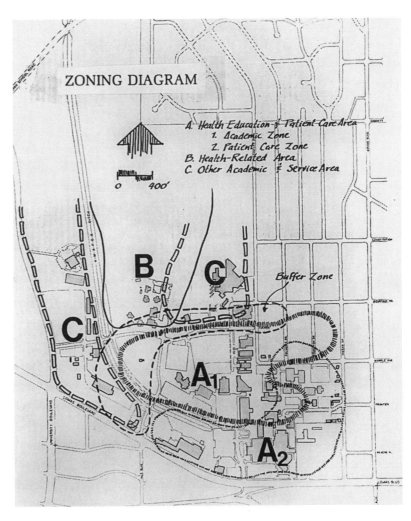

Howard Hakken's zone plan for the North Campus.

Novitski Hall (249), named for Dr. Monica Novitski, houses the Dental Programs for which she was the first director. Architect: Holmes and Gianinni. Photograph by Jerry Goffe.

The Medical Center Library (234). Architect: Harvey Hoshour Architects. Photograph by Michael Mouchette, UNM Photo Service.

firm Pacheco and Graham, headed up the design team. Because of the complexity of the program, the experimental nature of the building, and the incorporation of the solar elements, the preliminary design was not ready until April 1978.

Ground was broken in September for the 5.5-acre tennis complex on the South Campus. Ten courts were to be finished in 1977 and ten more later. There was a pro shop with locker rooms and a lounge included. Van Gilbert was the architect.

When the New Mexico Society of Architects held its annual award banquet in December 1977, UNM buildings received many honors. Harvey Hoshour received an honor award for the Medi-

The entrance to the Mechanical Engineering Building (122). Architect: Pacheco and Graham. Photograph by the author.

cal Center Library, and merit awards went to Holmes-Giannini for the bookstore and to W. C. Kruger and Associates for the Humanities Building. A special award was given Joe Boehning for the remodeling of the basketball arena.

Programming had proceeded on the Biomedical Research Building (253) planned for the area east of the Basic Medical Sciences Building (211) to the point that an architectural firm was needed to prepare preliminary drawings. When the Board of Regents met on January 24, 1978, they appointed W. C. Kruger and Associates. Robert Krueger was to be the project architect and chief designer.

Vice President John Perovich reminded the board that it had agreed to participate with the Alumni Association in the remodeling and restoration of Hodgin Hall. He said the association was beginning a fund-raising drive and it would be advantageous to have a preliminary design to show prospective donors. The regents approved funds for the design work and advertising.

At the regents meeting on April 21, 1978, I introduced Jesse Pacheco, of the firm of Pacheco and Graham, who presented the preliminary design of the Mechanical Engineering Building (122). The building was to be located at the corner of Redondo Drive (South) and Redondo Drive (West). The nearest neighbor is Hodgin Hall, and in respect for the old building the designers used fenestration recalling the size and square tops of the Hodgin windows. The round heads of some of them had been covered in the Tight remodeling.

The University set a world record during the summer of 1979 when an experimental solar pond developed by the Physics Department on the North Campus reached a temperature of 227 degrees Fahrenheit, breaking the old record of 217 degrees reached in a solar pond near the Dead Sea. The pond contained a high concentration of salt, which captured heat that could potentially be used to heat buildings.

Bainbridge Bunting Picks Albuquerque's Best and Worst Buildings

The editors of *Albuquerque Magazine* asked Professor Bainbridge Bunting, art and architecture historian at UNM, to write an article for the October 1977 issue spotlighting some of Albuquerque's best buildings, from an architectural standpoint, and to point his finger at one structure he thought to be most lacking in architectural merit.

Bunting wrote, "Although much of the architectural record of Albuquerque over the past thirty years has been dismal—including the loss of the Alvarado Hotel and Huning Castle and numerous Model Cities fiascos—two significant advances must be acknowledged: the development of the UNM campus and La Luz, a 150-unit condominium on five hundred acres on the west side of the Rio Grande."

He singled out UNM's Smith Plaza, designed by landscape architect Garrett Eckbo, saying it possessed both human scale and variety plus other qualities essential to a fine public space. He liked the variations in elevation, the plantings, and the different kinds of paving, which helped to reduce the apparent space.

Two libraries caught his eye: the Albuquerque Public Library downtown and the additions to Zimmerman Library on the UNM campus. He thought the city library was a modern building that had kept the feeling of New Mexico. As for the additions to Zimmerman, he said it was rare in American architecture to find architects showing such respect for an old building. "Zimmerman Library demonstrates what excellent results obtain when architects are humble enough to recognize value in a predecessor's work and try to design in harmony with it." Bunting was referring to George Pearl who designed the first addition and Dean and Hunt who did the addition in 1973.

When it came to choosing the ugliest building, Bunting got very diplomatic. He said almost any downtown skyscraper could qualify and no one shopping center is uglier than any other. So he said it would be best to pick on UNM since he had written nice things about it already. Bunting chose

This was to be the first solar-heated building on the UNM campus and a teaching and research laboratory for heat storage and recovery. Four large concrete tanks were built under the basement level to store solar-heated water for research purposes. In the basement, a half-level in the ground, there were laboratories that, because of the nature of the equipment used, had to be isolated from the structure of the building to avoid vibration. A wing to the north housed the engineering shops; it was covered with a walking deck of precast concrete pavers.

In the early planning, there was to be an open patio in the center surrounded by three stories of offices, laboratories, and classrooms. However, more roof space was needed for the solar collectors so the patio was roofed over, and sloping "saw-tooth" windows facing north were installed along with the collectors, which faced south. This created an extremely interesting interior space like none other on the campus. The

Johnson Gymnasium saying it was about the last building on campus where the architect tried to simulate the Spanish-Pueblo tradition—"that line of development which began so brilliantly with the Administration Building and Zimmerman Library in the 1930s." He faulted the symmetrical plan, which is contrary to the Pueblo Style irregularities, the enormity of the "cube," the ineffectiveness of the ornamentation designed to provide a Pueblo Style flavor, and the large amount of window area, which destroyed the compactness.

The last paragraph of the article gave a good insight:

The evolution of UNM architecture in the post–World War II years makes an instructive study. As economic conditions changed, it became increasingly difficult to include the hand-wrought features such as carved balconies or corbel brackets which added so much to Meem's designs in the 1930s. Wood was replaced with cast concrete; the double-hung sash with wooden divisions which imparted such good scale gave way to iron windows and these to aluminum. The result was a dreadful compromise. A different method of responding to the historic tradition of the region had to be found. Experimentation along this line began with the Education Complex in 1961 and has gone forward on several lines of development and with considerable success.

I agree with Bunting's analysis. Buildings that followed the College of Education such as the Law School, Humanities, Regener Hall, the Laguna-DeVargas-La Posada Complex, the Mechanical Engineering Building, and the Health Sciences Library moved campus architecture toward a compatible relationship with Pueblo Style buildings by using mass, color, and material. The architects did not try to twist the Pueblo Style, which they were not skilled in duplicating and which is inappropriate to our needs, into a design solution I could not have approved.

main entrance to the building faces northeast and is entered up a wide staircase. Upon entering the building you are immediately in the large atrium. On this level are the departmental offices, classrooms, a coffee shop, and the control offices for the operation and monitoring of the solar heating system. On the south side of the top level is an open deck used for outdoor experiments and equipment, which can be monitored in indoor laboratories.

Two buildings had to be demolished to make way for the Mechanical Engineering Building. One was the original campus heating plant. The first Pueblo Style building on the campus, it was used by the Department of Drama for many years and called the Comedia Theater; it was later used by the Department of Art for sculpture studios. The other was the National Youth Administration Building, which had been turned into a shop for the College of Engineering.

The south elevation of the Mechanical Engineering Building as seen through Tight Grove. Photograph by Jerry Goffe.

K. L. House Construction Company was awarded the contract for construction of the Mechanical Engineering Building. Redondo Drive was closed from Grand Avenue to the front of the Psychology Building and a fence erected, which was to stay up for about fifteen months. This complicated automobile and pedestrian traffic in that part of the campus. At the same time the area between Woodward Hall and the Fine Arts Center was blocked while it was being landscaped.

While the building was being constructed against the side of the Nuclear Engineering Laboratory (121), the excavation exposed a sagging exterior wall of a double wall system. The double wall held in place earth fill that acted as a radiation shield. Water had penetrated into the fill from a leak in the roof flashing, causing the wall to settle about two inches. There was concern on campus about possible radiation exposure, but we knew the wall was in trouble when the new building was designed so precautions were taken. The contractor installed steel cables around the building to hold the wall in place while caissons sixty feet deep were placed in the ground to support both walls.

Approval having been given for an addition to the Architecture Building (158), I let a committee from the school, chaired by Professor Edith Cherry, select an architectural firm for the project. Their choice was the Architects of Taos; the Campus Planning Committee approved the nomination. William Mingenbach of the firm was introduced to the regents who then approved the selection.

On August 2, 1978, in the middle of the afternoon, a fire broke out in a 600-ton cooling tower east of the Ford Utility Center. The fire destroyed the tower, which was estimated to cost about $200,000 to replace. The tower had not been used for some time and the redwood fins had dried out when an electrical short started the conflagration.

The American Society of Landscape Architects gave a special award to Garrett Eckbo, FASLA, for his work on the UNM campuses. Eckbo had been the consulting landscape architect for UNM since 1962. The University shared in the award as the owner and client. The ASLA Awards Committee made the presentation at a ceremony in the Mayflower Hotel in Washington, D.C., in late summer of 1978. I attended as the representative of the University. An article in *Landscape Architecture* said, "The general objective has been a pedestrian campus unified by a fine sequence of spaces enlivened by variable patterns of light and shade, and diversified by many intimate arrangements of a sculptural and furnishing nature."

The jury comment read: "Seems to respect and reinforce the original plan. The campus looks very good. Planting, spaces, surface textures and grade changes are all very pleasing. An asset is there is no clear demarcation between old and new. Good lighting fixtures. Kiosks are a nice touch. A soft/hard look. Trying to make it an oasis rather than maintain the arid quality of the desert."

At the September 1978 meeting of the regents, Vice President Perovich explained that the Board of Educational Finance and the State Department of Finance and Administration required a four-year capital outlay projection. I stated that it would have to be updated each year and then explained the priorities for state funding: (1) Biomedical Research Facility, (2) remodeling of Johnson Gymnasium, and (3) a thermal tank on the North Campus. Emphasis would be placed on the first building, and if state funds were received, the University would not pursue funds for the other two projects at the 1979 legislative session. Bonding would be an alternative method of funding. The four-year plan was approved.

Funds in the Bratton Hall budget were used to match a grant from the National Endowment for the Arts for a piece of sculpture between the two wings of the addition, which with the original building formed a three-sided patio open to the north. Lloyd Hamrol was selected to

Highground, the sculpture by Lloyd Hamrol on the north side of Bratton Hall, the Law School. Photograph by Michael Mouchette, UNM Photo Service.

do the piece, which he titled *Highground*. It consists of two sloping concrete walls, elliptical shaped, that enclose a sloping grassed area. Alana Wolfe, who did a survey of the art on the campus, wrote, "It is worth the hike to the North Campus to contemplate this weighted earthwork and the unstable, dynamic play between opposing forces vying for justice."

The year 1978 ended on a high note on December 29 when the last two remaining wooden barracks, relics of World War II, were bulldozed. A total of thirty-eight barracks had been brought to the campus in the years immediately after the war to take care of the influx of veterans enrolling under the GI Bill. The demolition was covered by city and campus news media as the significant event it was.

In February 1979 it was announced that Senator Aubrey Dunn, chairman of the powerful Senate Finance Committee, was in favor of funding the Biomedical Research Building. The project had already received the endorsement of Governor King when he approved planning money. The appropriations bill passed both houses but with the stipulation that the project cost should not exceed $8.8 million. The architects, W. C. Kruger and Associates, were told to proceed with the construction documents for bidding in early 1980.

Dean Napolitano was impressed with a portable laboratory equipment system developed by researchers at the Albuquerque Veterans Hospital. The only fixed items would be the fumehoods and the sinks. Each laboratory would have the same equipment and if something else was wanted it would have to be bought with research grant funds. There was to be a vestibule at each laboratory with a sink and space for equipment such as refrigerators and centrifuges. There was a central dishwashing facility and on each floor a laboratory for special experiments that required 100 percent air exhaust.

The preliminary design called for the building to be set forty-five feet west of the Basic Medical Sciences Building with open walkways connecting the two buildings at each floor except at the first level, which was enclosed and had an entrance located on the north side. The north wall of the Animal Resource Facility formed the south side of the open space. I was concerned about exhaust fumes from the new building being sucked into the ground-level air intakes of the Basic Medical Sciences Building. Wind tunnel tests showed that exhaust velocities of a certain speed had to be designed and the stacks had to be located as close to the east wall of the new building as possible and at a certain height.

Energy conservation was on everyone's mind in those days and many energy-saving features were designed into the Biomedical Research Building and the support systems. Bridgers and Paxton Consulting Engineers were asked to study the added heating and cooling requirements of the North Campus. They recommended installing a very efficient 1,000-ton electrically driven centrifugal heat pump in the North Campus Chilled Water Plant. The medical buildings required simultaneous heating and cooling year-round and the heat pump could recover otherwise wasted heat during the cooling process. For several reasons it did not work as efficiently as planned and was then used as a conventional electrically powered chiller.

Preliminary plans for the Biomedical Research Building were approved by the Campus Planning Committee and presented to the regents at the June l meeting. I explained that UNM had received a planning grant of half a million dollars and the legislature stipulated that the University must have bids in hand before the opening of the 1980 legislative session in order to receive the $8.8 million additional appropriation. The preliminary plans received approval and the architects were told to work toward a bid in early 1980.

The sculpture *Two Lines Oblique, Variation III* by George Rickey, which is located east of the Duck Pond, was damaged by a windstorm in December 1978. It was taken down by the Physical Plant Department, which contacted Rickey for instructions on how to repair the bent arm. Some time later, when the bearings on one of the rotating arms failed, a triangular stainless steel arm fell to the ground and was damaged. A grounds crew picked it up and took it to the city dump. The dump was searched but the arm could not be found; more than a year passed before a replacement could be constructed.

When the regents met on March 20, 1979, Campus Planner Joe McKinney and I presented a plan for the future use of the land north of Scholes Hall from Las Lomas on the north to University Boulevard on the west and Yale on the east. This was in response to a request by Regent Calvin Horn for a planning study of this area. McKinney explained the plan and said the first phase would be the construction of a two-story administrative office building, which the people in our office had called the "P" Building. It would house the offices of Personnel, Purchasing, Police and Parking Services, Photo Service, and Public Information and some other functions. We felt it should be named, of course, the Perovich Building. The former residences being used for offices would be removed as required to clear the site. Phase two would include another office building and a parking structure for about four hundred cars. The regents complimented the office for developing the "excellent" plan and asked for a more definite proposal soon.

During the summer, the landscaping between the Family Practice Center and the Health Sciences Learning Resources Center was completed by Lee Landscapes. An outstanding feature of the plaza is the beautiful brick fountain designed by landscape architects Guy Robert Johns and Campbell Okuma Perkins and Associates and built by Robert Majeskie of the landscape firm. The courtyard received an award from the New Mexico Society of Architects at their annual meeting in December 1979. It was also given an award by the Colorado Chapter of the American Society of Landscape Architects of which New Mexico was a part.

One day in March 1979 a student walking by the Duck Pond was chased by an angry goose, so he took off after the bird with a metal pole. The campus police were swamped with calls about the incident. They picked up the young man, but after questioning him decided it was a case of self-defense. Neither goose nor student was injured.

The Family Practice Plaza. The handsome brick fountain in the center was constructed by Robert Majeskie of Lee Landscapes. Landscape architect: Robert Johns and Campbell Okuma Perkins and Associates.

At this same meeting, the Physics Laboratories and Lecture Hall (35) was named Regener Hall in honor of Victor H. Regener, the just-retired chairman of the Department of Physics and Astronomy. Upon recommendation of the Memorial Committee, President Davis asked that the Department of English Library be named for Professor Leon Howard and the Humanities Theater be named for Professor Franklin Dickey.

The Board of Regents met on Thursday, July 12. After the meeting a two-day workshop was held in which the regents were briefed on many facets of the University operation, including a presentation by me and my staff on Friday morning. We spent about three hours explaining the operation of the office, the building and planning program, and a look at future development of the University.

On June 13, the New Mexico Building Branch of the Associated General Contractors honored O. G. Bradbury and Charles Lembke who were reaching their ninetieth birthdays. Both men had founded leading construction firms. The Lembke company had built Johnson Gymnasium, the Zimmerman Library addition, the Humanities Building, Woodward Hall, and the Basic Medical Sciences Building to name a few. Bradbury and Stamm's work on campus included Mesa Vista Hall, the Psychology

Building, Alumni Chapel, the Journalism Building, Northrop Hall (geology), and Bratton Hall II (the Law School).

When the regents met on August 28, 1979, I presented a report regarding the feasibility of constructing additional parking facilities for employees of BCMC. This study was done in response to a memorial passed in the House of Representatives during the first session of the Thirty-fourth Legislature. The document was prepared by Steve Morgan, chief of capital programming for the Department of Health and Environment; William H. Johnson, Jr., associate director of BCMC; Max Bennett, planning officer for the Medical Center; William Wegner, administrator of the Bernalillo County Mental Health–Mental Retardation Center; Joe McKinney, the campus planner; and a representative of Parking Services.

The report recommended building a parking structure for 336 cars over an existing parking lot northeast of BCMC at Frontier and Vassar, moving the Ambulatory Care Program, and reallocating professional and patient parking. President

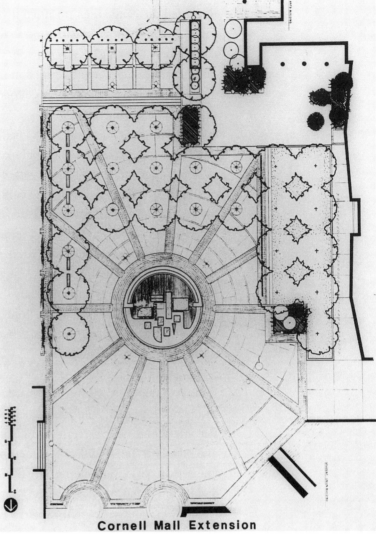

Cornell Mall Extension

Davis, in response to a question from Regent Ann Jourdan, said the proposal was in direct competition with all academic requests for capital outlay funds. The only action required was the acceptance of the study, which was given with a request for the administration to continue study of the entire parking problem.

The fountain in the plaza at the south end of the Cornell (or Union) mall was bid in August 1979 but was not completed until the summer of 1980. (One of the difficulties in describing exterior spaces on the campus is that except for Smith Plaza they have never been named. University Secretary Anne Brown, Development Director Robert Lalicker, and I tried to no avail to get the regents to place names on some of the major open spaces.) This space had not been paved and landscaped for years after the mall between the New Mexico Union and Mesa Vista Hall was finished. A major entrance to the campus from the parking lots along Central Avenue, it was rough

Plan of the landscaping between the New Mexico Union and the Fine Arts Center. Landscape architect: Robert Johns with Garrett Eckbo consulting.

ungraded dirt, and when it rained it was a quagmire. At a regents meeting, Ann Jourdan said she was embarrassed to watch Governor Bruce King in his polished cowboy boots picking his way between the mudholes to get to a meeting on campus. She demanded that something be done and it was. Funds were found for the project and the campus landscape architect Robert Johns was put to work. Garrett Eckbo was called in as a consultant.

I remembered a visit Eckbo and I paid to the yard of Rocky Mountain Stone Company on north I-25 some years before. In the yard were several long rectangular squared travertine marble pieces with fluted quarry marks, which had come from a quarry in the hills west of Belen. They reminded me of the pieces of marble columns on the Acropolis and I wondered at the time how they could be used on the campus. Johns designed the fountain using several of these stones.

Smith Plaza, named for Vice President Sherman E. Smith, was dedicated on October 5, 1979, during homecoming. Smith was honored for his untiring effort to beautify the whole campus and especially this core area. President Davis addressed the assembled people after the homecoming luncheon where slides of the campus development had been shown. Provost Chester Travelstead spoke about Smith's accomplishments on the campus.

Programming for the Student Services Building, to be located east of Mesa Vista Hall, was completed by Patricia Richards. She worked mostly with directors and deans including Director of Student Financial Aid Fred Chreist Jr., Dean of Admissions and Records Robert Weaver, Dean of Students Karen Glaser, and Registrar William Haid, and met with staff and faculty. Questionnaires were distributed to students. Programmed to go in the building were the Registration Center, the Office of Admissions and Records, Student Accounts, the Dean of Students, the Career Services Center, the College Enrichment Program, Student Financial Aid, Student Employment, the Veterans Counselor, and Special Services. The program included some remodeling in Mesa Vista Hall and a two-story corridor connecting the two buildings. A zaguan, a passageway, was cut through the first floor of Mesa Vista Hall to provide access from the Student Services Building to the landscaped mall and the buildings to the west.

A number of student organizations, including New Mexico Public Interest Research Group, Student Veterans Association, UNM Mountain Club, and the Child Care Co-Op, were told they would have to move out of the north wing of Mesa Vista Hall so it could be remodeled for College of Education computer laboratories and faculty offices. The groups protested but moved when required.

I reported to the regents on October 18 that I had sent letters to all registered resident architects in the state informing them of the upcoming selection of architects for the addition to Johnson Gymnasium and the new Student Services Building. I asked the architects to send information about their firms. I received replies from forty-eight firms. A subcommittee of the Campus Planning Committee reviewed the

The completed landscape between the Student Union and Fine Arts Center showing the marble fountain in the center. Photograph by Michael Mouchette, UNM Photo Service.

submittals and requested ten firms to make short presentations. After the presentations, three firms for each project, ranked in the order of preference, were recommended to the Campus Planning Committee. Finally, that committee recommended the Santa Fe firm of Dorman-Nelson for the gymnasium addition and John Reed for the Student Services Building. The regents approved the selections. This was the most difficult, time-consuming selection process I had handled since I had been at the University.

During 1979 the Hodgin Hall Restoration Committee, chaired by Bill Brannin, continued its effort to raise $200,000. Before any work could be done on Hodgin Hall, a report had to be prepared based on criteria furnished by the Historic Preservation Bureau, part of the State Planning Division. Edward B. T. Glass, the assistant to the University architect, was assigned the task of preparing the *Hodgin Hall Structure Report,* which was completed and published in 1979. Glass did an extremely thorough study of the history of the building. Photogrammetry was used to document the exterior. A copy of this report is available in Zimmerman Library.

The name of the Bernalillo County Medical Center was officially changed by the regents on November 20 to the University of New Mexico Hospital–Bernalillo County Medical Center. Dean Leonard Napolitano explained that the name change would recognize UNM's responsibility with respect to the operation of the hospital.

The Physical Plant Department was trying to save money against the escalating energy costs of the 1970s by hiring Lawrence J. Schuster, a mechanical engineer, as the energy conservation coordinator. Schuster initiated several money-saving ideas and worked with Mechanical Engineering Professor Thomas Feldman who had a National Science Foundation grant to study heat recovery systems. Feldman designed boiler economizer coils to fit on the exhaust stacks of the two 100,000-pound-per-hour boilers in the heating plant. The boilers expelled combustion gases at the rate of 30,000 cubic feet per minute, wasting usable energy up the stacks. The new coils, which are composed of hundreds of water-transporting, steel-finned pipes, capture much of this heat and feed it back into the boilers. The heat recovery coils almost recovered their cost in natural gas savings in the first year of operation. Schuster announced that teams were analyzing fifty University buildings that represented 75 percent of the annual energy consumption. One observation they made early on was that every secretary in every building wanted the thermostat set at a different temperature. They complimented the dormitory students for turning off unnecessary lights in corridors and bathrooms.

CHAPTER FOURTEEN

The Building Boom Begins to Slow Down

When the regents met on January 10, 1980, I reported that a bill was passed during the previous legislative session requiring the board to "establish a priority for arriving at solutions to the parking needs at the University." The 1977 Transportation and Parking Study was built around the premise that any physical improvements for parking would have to be paid for by parking fees and therefore the alternative of building parking structures was not seriously considered because of initial cost. My update pointed out that if the legislature was willing to assist the University in constructing parking structures and paving certain lots on the Central and North Campuses the parking problem could be solved for some time to come. The study recommended construction of two parking structures and three surface lots on the Central Campus and the expansion of one surface lot on the North Campus and one structure and two surface lots for the University of New Mexico Hospital–Bernalillo County Medical Center. The Board of Regents approved the study to be presented to the legislature.

I presented the bids for the construction of the Biomedical Research Facility at the meeting of the regents on January 29, 1980, and a contract with K. L. House Construction Company was authorized. Because of favorable bids, Medical School Dean Leonard Napolitano and I recommended the project budget be reduced to $8.55 million. The regents approved subject to receiving the appropriation from the current legislature. The unprecedented decrease in the funding request made points for UNM with the legislators.

I told the regents that my office and Leon Griffin, chairman of the Department of Health, Physical Education, and Recreation, Professor Armond Seidler, and other faculty members had been working for more than a year with the architectural firm of Dorman-Nelson on the preliminary plans for the remodeling of Johnson Gymnasium. The gymnasium was built in 1957 to accommodate an enrollment of 10,000 and had had only one addition to it, the Olympic-size swimming pool. I pointed out that

The additions to Johnson Gymnasium. Architect: Dorman-Nelson. Photograph by the author.

Student Services Building. Architect: John Reed. Photograph by the author.

in comparison with other institutions and national norms, the department was deficient in all spaces except for swimming. I introduced architect Douglas Nelson who explained the proposed plan in detail and answered questions from the regents. The addition would provide expanded office and classroom space, new racquetball and handball courts, additional gym space, expanded locker rooms for men and women, dance facilities, and a gymnastics gym. The board approved the preliminary plan and the proposed project budget of $7.4 million.

My office prepared a wish list for the forthcoming legislative session that was extremely optimistic but also a realistic statement of the needs of the growing campus. The top priority went to the renovation of Johnson Gymnasium; then the Student Services Building; followed by the Administrative Annex (or "P" Building, which was never built); a new engineering science and library building; a complex for the Anderson Schools of Management, Economics, and Social Sciences; a new telephone system; a parking structure; an addition to University Hospital, and many smaller projects.

Architect John Reed and I presented the preliminary plans for the Student Services Building already approved by the Campus Planning Committee to the regents on September 15. The project contained 89,000 square feet at an estimated cost of $5.7 million. Four tennis courts east of Mesa Vista Hall would be taken up, but six new ones would be added to the tennis complex at Girard and Central.

At the regents meeting on May 14, 1982, I reported that Brooks and Clay was the low bidder for the construction of the Student Services Building (85). The project included some remodeling in Mesa Vista Hall and a new roof and exterior repairs. The regents approved the award.

The new Mechanical Engineering Building (122) was dedicated on Saturday, October 11, 1980, following a symposium on energy-conservation design. To open the ceremonies, U.S. Senator Pete Domenici pushed the proper button on a computer keyboard and a robot armed with a pair of scissors whirled into motion and cut the ribbon. The robot then laid down the scissors, picked up a UNM banner, and waved it to and fro above the heads of the dignitaries on the podium who by this time were standing and applauding. In attendance were U.S. Senator Harrison Schmitt, Representative Manuel Lujan, Governor Bruce King, and Jerry Geist, president of the Public Service Company of New Mexico. They all made short statements and were followed by Senator Domenici who said he was disturbed by the drop in enrollment in science and engineering and emphasized the need for more federal funding for solar energy research.

John Meigs, artist, restoration expert, and executive director of the Lincoln County Heritage Trust, was hired by the Alumni Association to gather antique and reproduction furnishings for Hodgin Hall. Meigs furnished each floor in a style typical of one of the University's first three decades. The top floor was opened into one large meeting room named in memory of Irma Bobo, a long-time Albuquerque elementary school teacher. This was at the request of Caswell Silver of Denver, a 1940 UNM graduate who offered to underwrite the work on this room to honor his former landlady.

Arturo Sandoval, a reporter, interviewed me in early 1981 about the future of construction on the campus. I said the building boom of the past two decades

The Thompson Art Gallery in the lower level of the New Mexico Union opened on February 8, 1984. It was named for Esther Atkinson Thompson who managed the first campus Student Union from 1937 to 1959. Mayor Harry Kinney, who as a student worked part-time for Ms. Thompson, declared March 8 Esther Thompson Day. The formal dedication took place at that time.

would begin to taper off with the completion of the work on Johnson Gymnasium and the Student Services Center. And in fact there were never more than one or two major projects under construction at the same time for years to come. I predicted there would be more additions and remodelings of existing buildings and fewer new free-standing structures. Indications were that enrollment would begin to level off with a peak of 25,000, the ideal maximum number of students for this and most major university campuses. I told Sandoval we would concentrate on landscaping areas of the campus that had been passed over because of other priorities. Most of my predictions came to pass except for the limitation of enrollment, which as I write in 1998 has not been imposed by the Board of Regents. Enrollment has stayed below 25,000, for various reasons, but it will rise again as state population increases, straining utilities, parking, maintenance of outdoor space, student services, and the campus environment in general.

Some solutions to these problems have been explored, such as building an undergraduate campus on other University properties (possibly the South Campus), erecting more parking structures, improving shuttle bus service, and using more of the North Campus, including the golf course, for such things as a student union, dormitories, and married student housing. The University cannot continue to allow the Central Campus population to grow uncontrolled without destroying the pleasing campus environment developed over the first one hundred years.

In March 1981 the University received two beautification awards from the City of Albuquerque. One was for the Children's Psychiatric Center; the other was in recognition of "University Park," more commonly known as the Duck Pond. Mayor David Rusk presented the certificate to Robert Johns, Joe McKinney, and me, all from the Office of the University Architect.

Things began to get wild in the "Roundhouse" in Santa Fe as the 1981 legislative session came to a close. A capital projects bill was making its way through the legislature, and the members were adding more and more pet projects. John Mershon of Lincoln County, chairman of the House Appropriations and Finance Committee, said, "You are seeing a first-class example of what happens when you have a Christmas tree bill." The University was watching the happenings closely because funding was being sought for the Johnson Gymnasium work as well as other smaller projects. The Senate passed a bill authorizing a $37 million severance tax bond issue, which would fund seventeen construction projects, but when the House got done it had added $10.8 million and four more projects including the gymnasium remodeling. The next week, the House Taxation and Revenue Committee voted to kill ten bills, including the one for Johnson Gymnasium, saying they could not pick and choose among the projects. The whole process had become dominated by politics. The vote followed lines of opposition drawn between loyalist Democrats and the conservative coalition that had controlled the House for the past three years. Governor King called a special

session to resolve the impasse and out of that the University received only funds for equipment.

In September 1981 University Landscape Architect Robert Johns said the space between the Art Building on the south and Woodward Hall on the north would be landscaped in 1981 or 1982. Art Department Chairman Garo Antreasian had complained, along with several faculty members, that the Art Building was five years old and the Mechanical Engineering Building was only two but the area around it had already been landscaped. He said, "It's ironic that we in the business of beauty have the least desirable looking buildings."

Architecture students Daniel Boardman and Michael Hill responded to Antreasian's statement with an invitation to visit the School of Architecture and Planning Building (158). They wrote in the *Lobo*: "We doubt that there is a building in use on campus that can boast such functional inadequacy or can lay claim to a more dismal and emotionally oppressive atmosphere. The building, a leaky-roofed converted furniture warehouse, is in a sad state of disrepair and contains a number of possible building code violations."

William Wegner, deputy director of the Bernalillo County Mental Health–Mental Retardation Center, reported to the regents that construction of a thirty-bed adolescent-geriatric unit at the center would begin soon thanks to a county bond issue.

The landscaping on the south side of Woodward Hall was designed by Robert Johns. Photograph by the author.

West elevation of the Biomedical Research Building (253). Designed by Robert Krueger of the firm of W. C. Kruger and Associates. Photograph by Jerry Goffe.

The University administration was approached by a group of people who asked for land on which they could construct a Ronald McDonald House, a support residence for families from out of town who bring their children to the University facilities for treatment. I presented a preliminary drawing of the proposed building and explained that McDonald's had already donated $25,000 toward the estimated $250,000 project and promised two promotions to raise money. The Campus Planning Committee had approved a site north of the Children's Psychiatric Center. The regents approved the concept of the proposal and the site.

A proposal by the Air Force ROTC to install an F-80 decommissioned fighter plane at a campus entrance as a memorial to New Mexico's Vietnam War veterans had been approved by the Campus Planning Committee. However, the committee decided to restudy the proposal after it met with opposition from peace advocates and religious groups that said the plane was "an instrument of death" and not a fitting memorial. Vice President Marvin D. "Swede" Johnson opposed it, as did Mark Rutledge, director of United Campus Ministries, who pointed out that the F-80 was never used in Vietnam. In spite of arguments in favor of the F-80 by Lt. Col. Don Richard, commander of the Air Force ROTC program, the committee reversed its previous approval.

I was interviewed again by Arturo Sandoval who wrote that I parceled out my words like adobes. He said they were carefully shaped and neatly arranged and not one was wasted. I guess I got this habit of speech because I had been misquoted so many times and I wanted everything I said clearly understood. He and I took a stroll around the campus and discussed the buildings and the landscaping, present and future. I appreciated the paragraph of the article where he praised the results of our planning and wrote, "UNM has grown from an ugly-duckling appearance nearly two decades ago to a more graceful, swan-like beauty today." Perhaps his metaphor was inspired by the residents of the Duck Pond.

An announcement was made on March 13, 1982, that President Davis was resigning to take the position of chancellor of the Oregon State System of Higher Education on July 1. He said, "I am very proud of the University of New Mexico, and I feel there is a real vitality and spirit here and much is being accomplished."

The Biomedical Research Building (253) was dedicated on March 20 with Dean Napolitano presiding. Remarks were made by President Davis, Governor King, and Henry Jaramillo Jr., president of the Board of Regents. Mark Bitensky, leader of the Life Sciences Division at the Los Alamos National Laboratory, introduced the main speaker, Lewis Thomas, M.D., chancellor of Memorial Sloan-Kettering Cancer Center.

The Board of Regents met on April 1, 1982, and appointed John Perovich acting president until such time as a new president could be appointed. A search committee chaired by Provost Emeritus Chester Travelstead had been appointed previously. Perovich was quoted as saying, "I think any transition is going to be difficult, but with the support and cooperation of the staff and Regents we ought to be able to get through it. I am not a presidential candidate."

The Campus Planning Committee screened more than fifty architectural firms and recommended Dean and Hunt Associates for the Electrical and Computer Engineer-

Architect's sketch of patio between the Basic Sciences and Biomedical Research Buildings.

ing–Centennial Library Complex (46); Kruger, Lake, Hutchinson, and Brown for the Anderson Schools of Management, Economics, and Social Sciences Complex (57 and 87); and Boehning, Protz, Cook, and Associates for the Administrative Annex. The board authorized funds for preliminary drawings for each project, which were now required with submittals to the BEF for approval. John Perovich and I presented the annual update of the five-year plans for the University and the Medical School for submission on June 1 to the BEF. Projects for which UNM would request funding in 1983 were the Electrical and Computer Engineering–Centennial Library Complex, the Anderson Schools of Management, Economics, and Social Sciences Complex, a three-hundred-seat lecture hall, and $1 million for deferred maintenance. Projects for funding from University revenue bonds were Department of Health, Physical Education, and Recreation facilities, and land and property acquisition.

Bids were opened on June 1, 1982, for restuccoing and repairing the exterior of Scholes Hall and the original part of Zimmerman Library. In January a contract had been awarded to Bishop Construction Company to repair the exterior of Carlisle Gymnasium and do some minor interior renovations, and the company was low bidder on the Scholes and Zimmerman work. The stucco on Zimmerman Library had given trouble since it was applied originally and had been removed in the 1940s and replaced with uncolored cement stucco, which was then painted. There had been some spalling of the structural clay tile in the walls. The Drivit system instead of cement stucco was to be used for the repairs. Drivit is an epoxy product applied over a fiberglass mesh that makes a hard finish but is flexible enough to resist cracking. The final coat is integrally colored. Included in the work was the replacement of some window panes and some rotted wood. All three buildings were reroofed.

The Child Care Co-Op (now the Child Care Center) had been housed in Mesa Vista Hall since it was founded in 1970 but it had to move because of the remodeling of the building in conjunction with the construction of the Student Services Building. First it was relocated to Manzanita Center in the College of Education and later to the former home of Professor Robert Duncan at 1919 Las Lomas. A site on University Boulevard north of the KNME-TV studios was selected, and architectural plans for a new building were drawn by Christopher Larsen in the Office of the University Architect. Because time was so short, the idea was to use prefabricated buildings connected to form one unit. Bids were not taken until June 17 and Scotsman of Colorado was given the contract. The agreement stated that the buildings had to be ready for occupancy by September 3. Some changes had to be made in the plans to comply with state laws concerning child care facilities, so the completion was delayed creating all kinds of problems and frustrations. The center was allowed to stay in the Duncan house until the new quarters were completed. The grand opening and dedication of the Child Care Center (255) took place on Sunday afternoon, December 12, 1982. Guests of honor were the new president, John Perovich, and State Senator Tom Rutherford who had championed youth programs and the center.

Hodgin Hall interior. Photograph by Robert Reck.

On August 23, 1982, the regents named the Art Education Building (68) for Professor Alexander Masley. A dedication ceremony was held on September 12 along with the opening of a retrospective exhibition of his work in the new gallery.

The big item on the agenda at the September 29 regents meeting was my report that bids had been received on September 16, 1982, for the renovation of Hodgin Hall. Bill Stuckman Construction Company was the low bidder at $988,589; unfortunately that was over budget. The regents decided not to make any cuts, and the contract was signed for the bid amount. William Brannin, chairman of the Hodgin Hall Committee, said he believed his committee could raise the necessary funds from the private sector to cover the overrun once construction began. The final project cost was $1,355,000, which included $154,595 for furnishings. Change orders caused by the discovery of problems during the remodeling accounted for almost $100,000. The project was worth the cost because Hodgin has become a period showplace, a museum of University memorabilia, a home to the Alumni Association and the UNM Foundation, and a site for entertaining. It is always a stop for visitors touring the campus.

During construction a decision was made to add some authentic tin light fixtures to the building. I adapted some designs from John Meem's early buildings and took them to tinsmiths Emilio and Senaida Romero who made perfect fixtures on a table in their kitchen in Santa Fe.

Hodgin Hall was unveiled to the public on November 5, 1983, as part of the annual homecoming activities. It had taken five years of planning and construction to remodel, restore, and furnish UNM's original building.

A large enrollment increase in the fall semester 1982 strained the parking resources on the Central Campus. An area north of the Child Care Center off University Boulevard was graded and graveled for a free parking lot. The shuttle bus service was expanded and the purchase of more buses was considered.

The author checks
on progress of the
renovation of
Hodgin Hall by
contractor Bill
Stuckman.

A great opportunity to acquire improved lighting for University Stadium came about when the Turner Broadcasting System decided to televise the UNM-Hawaii game on November 20. After the commitment was made the lighting was found to be too dim for television coverage. The Western Athletic Conference (WAC) agreed to pay $135,000 for temporary lights. To Athletic Director John Bridgers, me, and others that seemed a waste of money that could be applied to upgrading the lighting on a permanent basis, estimated to cost $165,000. The WAC agreed to allow their contribution to be applied to a permanent system if UNM would pay the difference. Time was very short so I called Robert Uhl of Uhl and Lopez, electrical engineers, and got him to put together specifications for bidding. Musco Sport Lighting of Iowa was to furnish the fixtures and install them as subcontractors. Bids were taken on November 10, as short a bidding time as was legally possible, and Bradbury and Stamm were low at $195,000, over budget but still an inexpensive way to get a new lighting system. As soon as Musco finished manufacturing the fixtures, they were loaded on special trucks that rushed them to Albuquerque. Bradbury and Stamm had removed the old lighting system. The Musco crew worked nonstop and had all 216 metal-halide lights installed in time to be adjusted for the game on Saturday night.

The search for a new president hit a snag and the regents decided to make John Perovich the president. The search committee had recommended six finalists to the board but the regents could not agree on any of them. The announcement that Perovich would continue in the office was unfortunately made at halftime during the UNM-Hawaii football game. Most everyone approved the decision but deplored the way the announcement was made and the search handled.

At the meeting of the Board of Regents in January 1984, Calvin Horn resigned after serving two six-year terms. Governor Toney Anaya appointed Dr. John D. Paez to fill the vacant seat and reappointed Colleen Maloof.

A bus stop shelter and a piece of sculpture jointly funded by UNM and the City of Albuquerque were planned for the northwest corner of Girard and Central. The city's portion would come from the "One Percent for the Arts" included in a transportation bond issue. The sculptors, O. K. Harris and William Drexel, were selected in a city-sponsored competition. Howard Kaplan was the architect for the shelters. The sculpture *Solar Arc* was later removed by the city to a new location in the North Valley.

President Perovich, in a memorandum to all University employees in March, wrote, "In many ways the [1983 legislative] session was the best in recent years for UNM. In areas where money was available, such as the severance tax bond fund, UNM requests were supported at record levels." The legislature appropriated $9.9 million for the Electrical and Computer Engineering–Centennial Library Complex including the Engineering-Science Library, and $402,000 for planning the Anderson Schools of Management, Economics, and Social Sciences Complex.

Tapestries by Evelyn Anselevicius were hung in the atrium of the Mechanical Engineering Building. Photograph by the author.

Evelyn Anselevicius approached me about having a show of her tapestries on the campus. Her work has been described as "more of an architectural statement than a painterly one." Since many of the tapestries are quite large and need a high space to display them properly, I thought of the atrium of the Mechanical Engineering Building. The pieces were hung by Robert Johns, the University landscape architect. It was a wonderful display, but after they were taken down the department faculty said they wanted veto power over any artwork displayed, so I dropped plans for a similar show.

Work to get the Pit ready for the NCAA Final Four basketball tournament on April 2–4, 1983, proceeded smoothly until inspectors from the State Fire Marshal's Office found CBS trailers violating the fire code by blocking the west side fire lane. They conceded it was too late to move them and would rely on UNM and CBS to clear a fire lane west of the trailers. The show could go on. The exterior of the Pit had a fresh coat of paint, and signs welcomed the NCAA participants and guests. Additional fixtures were installed to increase the light level on the court by 40 percent; NCAA logos were painted on the floor; fourteen rows of seats were taken on the west side for the press; four TV camera mounts were built; and a new building on the south side was completed in time to provide interview and work space for the sportswriters and broadcasters. North Carolina State won the tournament. The new building was later used for gymnastics.

UNM requested $7.5 million for construction of the Anderson Schools of Management and Parish Library (87), Social Sciences (78), and the remodeling of former Bratton Hall (57) for Economics—all one project, but the BEF applied certain formulas for space allocation, which the University felt were unjustified, and recommended only $6.5 million. The main reduction was in library space, which was cut from 18,000

to 13,000 net square feet. It was proposed to the regents on July 6 that UNM resubmit the proposal and request $7.9 million, which would cover two years of inflation and restore the library space. Dean of Library Services Paul Vassallo explained the Parish Library needs and the board approved adding 3,000 square feet to the original request and the increased budget.

A plan for landscaping Yale Boulevard north from Redondo Drive to Mitchell Hall that had been designed by Robert Johns in consultation with Garrett Eckbo was approved by the board, but unfortunately it was not funded. It was several years before the area was landscaped using a modified version of the design.

A ground-breaking ceremony for the U-shaped critical care wing on UNM Hospital was held on April 30, 1983. The construction was planned to add 48,800 square feet of space to expand the hospital's trauma unit and to provide new quarters for surgical and medical intensive care and cardiac care, the burn unit, and the emergency department. Included in the addition is a new burn center of 10,410 square feet, which contains ten private rooms equipped with individual climate control. The Jaynes Corporation of Albuquerque submitted the low bid on the project designed by W. C. Kruger and Associates. The two-story wing was financed by a county bond issue approved in 1980. The bonds were sold in August 1981 and had earned enough interest by 1983 so that the hospital officials could negotiate a change order with Jaynes to add a third-floor pediatric facility of fifty-six beds. A heliport was placed on the roof above the emergency–critical care unit. The facility was dedicated on November 11, 1984, by county officials and UNM President John Perovich.

A drawing of the critical care addition to UNMH.

John Gaw Meem.

John Gaw Meem, Architect

John Gaw Meem IV, architect for many University buildings from 1934 until he retired in 1959, died in Santa Fe on August 4, 1983, at eighty-eight years of age. Meem was born to John Gaw Meem III and his wife, Elsie, Episcopal missionaries in Pelotas, Brazil, on November 17, 1894. At age fifteen he came to the United States to enter Virginia Military Institute where he received a bachelor of science in engineering degree.

Second Lieutenant Meem was called to active duty in World War I and afterward entered the banking business. He developed tuberculosis and came to the Sunmount Sanatorium in Santa Fe to recover. While a patient he became interested in studying architecture and, with his physician's blessing, Meem moved to Denver and enrolled in the Atelier, a branch of the Beaux Arts Institute of Design. Meem worked by day in the architectural offices of Fisher and Fisher and attended design classes at night. This proved too much for him and he was soon back in bed at Sunmount.

While recovering Meem became involved with the Committee for the Preservation and Restoration of New Mexico Mission Churches and later the Old Santa Fe Association. He established his office in 1924 and his practice prospered as his reputation for designing Pueblo Style buildings and restoring mission churches spread.

The story of John Meem's long association with UNM has been told in preceding chapters but nothing has been written here about who he was. A memorial service was held at Saint John's College in Santa Fe on November 6, 1983, and I gave a brief biography and concluded with these paragraphs:

I've told you briefly about his work, his accomplishments, but what about the man? He was rather small in stature, soft-spoken, very unassuming, kind and considerate, but a man who got things done both as an architect and as a leader in civic affairs. As Bainbridge Bunting said in his book *John Gaw Meem,* "His is a rare blend of characteristics—the sensitivity and perceptiveness of an artist, the practicality and discipline of the engineer, the decisiveness and acumen of a man of affairs."

His success as an architect was his ability to communicate with his clients. He always assumed responsibility for the mistakes of his office. He inspired loyalty from his employees and his associates. He was very generous to educational and religious causes, and to the profession of architecture.

He was my friend.

And I might add that he was, in every sense of the word, a gentleman.

Renovation of Johnson Gymnasium (59) was first proposed in 1981 at an estimated cost of $7.4 million but was rejected by the BEF. When it was resubmitted the following year at an increased cost the BEF dropped it to a lower category of need. The Student Services Center was then given first priority. President Perovich told the regents at their meeting on August 29, 1983, that the Johnson Gymnasium remodeling and expansion project had not received approval for state funding after six or seven years of planning and at the last legislative session the administration said it would determine a way for the University to fund all or part of the project. Perovich proposed that money from the University Building Renewal and Replacement Fund be used for phase one. The preliminary plans by the Dorman, Nelson, Breen firm were presented and approved, as was the method of funding. The plans showed the existing building being enveloped with additions that provided classrooms, office space, a large general-use gymnasium, handball and racquetball courts, and renovation and additions to locker rooms. A new entrance and lobby were shown on the west side.

The BEF, meeting on October 7, 1983, approved the Johnson Gymnasium project and the method of funding after a heated argument between a board member and University representatives over the use of funds generated by student fees, which he felt were too high and were hidden in discussions of the total cost of sending a son or daughter to UNM. The State Board of Finance gave its approval on October 27, which cleared the way for the project to proceed to construction. On April 3, 1984, the regents approved the award of the contract for the Johnson Gymnasium project, phase one, to Brooks and Clay, Albuquerque contractors who had just completed the Student Services Building.

Using the same argument that had cut space in the Parish Library, the BEF in early September recommended reducing space in the Electrical and Computer Engineering–Centennial Library from 61,000 to 42,000 square feet. Eliminated was space for government publications, maps, computer terminals, and growth for the existing collection. Dean Vassallo said the library could contend with less space by greater use of microforms and automated video disk access, but library users tend to prefer printed material. Perovich said he hoped the library could be built to its original size by use of supplementary funds beyond the $9.9 million allocated by the legislature.

The Albuquerque Conservation Association's highest award—the Bainbridge Bunting Award of Merit for historic preservation of a public building—went to UNM's Hodgin Hall. It was presented at the association's annual awards ceremony on July 26, 1984. The jurors wrote, "Its conservation has preserved for many more generations of students, alumni, and city residents one of our most treasured landmarks." UNM received an orchid for its excellence in landscaping at the first Orchids and Onions banquet. University Landscape Architect Robert Johns accepted the award. The Albuquerque Chapter of the American Institute of Architects and the Associated General Contractors cosponsored the program to promote community concern for

(Top) The below-grade construction of the Electrical and Computer Engineering–Centennial Library project. The total excavation was about forty feet. Courtesy of Dean and Krueger.

The completed Electrical and Computer Engineering–Centennial Library Complex (46). Photograph by the author.

quality of life, environmental amenities, and resource conservation. The judges said if UNM could solve its parking problem, it could be considered for an orchid for urban planning. Onions were given to the worst places around the city. About a year later the New Mexico Society of Architects gave an award to the Office of the University Architect for having established an equitable method for selecting architects. The state chapter of the American Society of Heating, Refrigeration, and Air Conditioning Engineers cited the Mechanical Engineering Building (122) for its energy-efficient design. After three years of occupation it was being operated at less than half the cost of similar buildings.

The preliminary design for the Electrical and Computer Engineering–Centennial Library (46) was presented to the regents on November 18 by Hal Dean of Dean, Hunt, and Associates. He had prepared a large model of the building that showed its relationship to all the surrounding structures. As proposed the 162,000-square-foot building was to be almost two-thirds underground to prevent it from dominating the area and to keep as much open space as possible. There were to be two levels of engineering and computer laboratories below grade topped by three stories of offices and classrooms above. The library was totally underground except for an entrance structure. Light wells were designed to bring illumination to the lowest level.

The Bernalillo County Mental Health–Mental Retardation Center dedicated a new $1.6-million wing for adolescent and geriatric patients on January 10, 1984. The existing spaces for these functions were slated to be remodeled.

At the regents meeting on January 31 I introduced James Brown of Hutchinson, Brown, and Partners, architects for the Anderson Schools of Management, Economics, and Social Sciences project. Brown described the design and said the buildings would be a transition between the Pueblo Style of nearby old Bratton Hall (57) and the modern buildings of the UNM School of Medicine. The Campus Planning Committee had been very complimentary of the design when it had approved it. Regent John

Paez questioned whether the angular shape of the buildings would make old Bratton Hall "stand out like a sore thumb." Regent Phillip Martinez amended a motion to approve the design to have the architects restudy the exterior, break up the long bands of windows, and soften the corners. They were to bring the revised design to the board at the next meeting.

The altar screen in the Alumni Chapel, built by Art Professor John Tatschl and two graduate art students with donated material, had been left without paintings for lack of funds. In late 1983 private funds permitted the employment of a santero, John M. Gonzales, to paint images of saints who had some relation to New Mexico. A committee, chaired by Robert Stamm, appointed to oversee this project was careful to exclude any image that might be offensive to any religion, but there were objections and the panels have to be covered with a roll-down screen during certain ceremonies.

The altar screen in the Alumni Memorial Chapel (25) with the painted panels by santero John M. Gonzales was funded by the UNM Alumni Association. Photograph by Dale C. Montgomery.

The 1984 legislature wrapped up its $200 million capital outlay package in the early morning hours of March 22. Included were two items for UNM to be funded by general obligation bonds that would be voted on in November: the Anderson Schools of Management, Economics, and Social Sciences Complex and a Central Campus parking structure.

During the winter about forty ducks were taken to the South Campus Golf Course ponds while the Duck Pond was cleaned. By the time the pond was refilled the ducks had become too wild and could not be captured, so people were asked to donate a dozen or so. A blue algae retardant was added to the Duck Pond water giving it an unnatural appearance, like Tidy Bowl the *Lobo* said.

For some time Athletic Director John Bridgers and Track Coach Del Hessel had been calling attention to the need for a new running track. Hessel had not been able to hold a meet at UNM for three years because of the poor condition of the track around the perimeter of the football field. Their idea was to construct the track on the east side of the football stadium and use the seat-bank slope for 2,500 to 3,000 spectator seats.

On November 18, 1984, a ten-room addition for the Ronald McDonald House was announced. Plans for the 5,700-square-foot addition included a new family room and an enlarged kitchen. Zoltan John Nagy of the architectural firm of Stevens, Mallory, Pearl, and Campbell was in charge of the project.

Bridgers said the existing track would be removed with the renovation of University Stadium for which the legislature had appropriated funds for planning. He said he had collected half a million dollars in pledges for the track from businesses and individuals, and he asked the University to match it. Max Flatow of the firm of Flatow, Moore, Bryan, and Associates was selected to be the architect. The design called for a conventional eight-lane oval track with facilities for field events inside the oval. The regents approved the design and the budget at the meeting on May 11, 1984. The John Baker Memorial Warm-Up Lounge was added to the project in memory of the outstanding young runner from Albuquerque who died of cancer.

Bradley Construction Company was awarded the contract to construct the running track starting on October 15 with completion set for March 15. John Bridgers next turned his attention to getting the football stadium renovated and the seating increased. It seemed to me that a development plan was needed for the athletic facilities area of the South Campus that would address traffic and pedestrian circulation and the increased demand for parking during football games. I convinced the administration to fund a study by Flatow, Moore, Bryan, and Associates that was completed around the end of 1984. Robert McCabe was the project manager.

At the June 19 regents meeting Joe McKinney, campus planner, requested regent approval to remove former residences on Roma and Las Lomas to increase parking space. University policy for years had been to buy the houses in that area as they became available. The proposal met with strong opposition from student and ethnic organizations housed in the residences that would be relocated to remodeled Mesa Vista Hall. After listening to the arguments, the regents agreed to table the discussion until more information was available on the proposed Mesa Vista relocation. The regents later agreed that the houses could be removed as needed once the occupying units had been relocated. The regents approved several architectural appointments at that meeting: Westwork Architects for the Center for Non-Invasive Diagnosis (260); Stevens, Mallory, Pearl, and Campbell with the Walker Company to design the Lomas Boulevard parking structure (172); and Flatow, Moore, Bryan, and Associates for the University Stadium expansion.

The UNM campus was chosen as the location for a motion picture, *Animal Behavior,* to be filmed by Robert Redford's Sundance Institute of Utah in the spring of 1985. One of the stars was "Banjo," a very smart chimpanzee, who bit one of the costars. The movie was later shown on television.

Nicholas A. Matwiyoff from the Los Alamos National Laboratory was appointed director of the newly created Center for Non-Invasive Diagnosis (CNID). The diagnostic equipment can produce images of the interior of the body using magnetic forces to provide information about disease processes not available with X-ray or CAT scan. Money had been appropriated to start the center in 1983 and more funds were anticipated. Programming began on the project and interviews were held with manufacturers. General Electric was given the contract to furnish the equipment. Two units were to be installed, one for human diagnosis with a bore large enough for a body to be placed inside, and another with a smaller bore for chemical analysis.

Site selection was very important at that time because the units had to be shielded from all electrical interference or moving metal objects such as automobiles. A remote site on the west side of Yale Boulevard north of the Children's Psychiatric Hospital was finally accepted. No ferrous metal could be used in the construction, so it looked like adobe brick would be the logical building material.

On Friday night February 24, 1984, an eight-inch city water main in Terrace Boulevard near Clark Hall broke, sending water rushing down the utility tunnel into Ford Utility Center. It shorted out three electrical feeders on the way and filled the center with six feet of water, shutting down telephones, power, and steam generation systems. More than thirty buildings were without power. Physical Plant crews had most of the outages corrected by Monday. This was a warning about the deterioration of the campus infrastructure.

When the regents met on November 20, 1984, they approved the design of the CNID, also called the Magnetic Resonance Imaging Center. When bids for the center were received in April 1985, the low bidder, R. M. Swain and Son, was over the budget so the proposal to use adobe construction was dropped in favor of wood-frame with aluminum nails.

When I heard the Masonic Temple at 1634 University Boulevard was for sale, I contacted Rupert Trujillo, dean of Continuing Education and Community Services. After a visit to the building we decided that with little remodeling it could be used for the growing noncredit programs. Approval for the purchase and financing were obtained through the effort of Vice President Alex Sanchez, and the property was bought for about $1.8 million. Included with the building were several acres of land with a large paved parking lot.

The University completed the purchase in August of the old body shop of Galles Motor Company at the southwest corner of Copper Avenue and Ash Street for the Art Department's ceramic and sculpture studios. It was a large open warehouse-type structure that was later remodeled with new lighting and electrical service, mechanical work, roofing, and other minor construction work. The building was later named the Mattox Sculpture Center (123) in honor of Charles Mattox, professor emeritus of art.

Approval was given at the regents meeting on September 4 to award the contract for the construction of the Electrical and Computer Engineering–Centennial Library project to Page and Wirtz Construction Company for $10,915,523. This was the most expensive educational facility constructed in the state up to that time. A ground-breaking ceremony was held on October 13 with Dean of Engineering Gerald May presiding. Other action at that meeting included the approval of a 1.5-acre site on the North Campus for the CNID facility and design approval of an addition to the State Scientific Laboratory facility, now called the Tri-Services Building, by architects Burns and Peters.

The board was briefed on capital outlay projects based on projected needs through 1989. I explained that only the 1985 projects were prioritized and could be changed. The first on the list was a learning technology center that was to house all the communication branches of UNM including speech communication, journalism, student publications, and part of Instructional Media Services. This project was eventually dropped. Second on the list was phase two of the Johnson Gymnasium remodeling to allow more

John Perovich

John Perovich graduated from Raton High School in 1941 and entered UNM that fall to study business administration but the war came along and it was not until 1948 that he completed his degree requirements. He then started working part-time in the UNM business office at about the time Tom Popejoy, also from Colfax County, left the position of comptroller to become president.

Perovich served on almost all of the committees related to campus planning and development including chairing the Campus Planning Committee. As comptroller both the Physical Plant Department and the Office of the University Architect were directly responsible to him. However, his main contribution to campus building and planning was management of the finances. He proposed and oversaw issuance of University bonds and controlled the expenditures of state bonds and legislative appropriations. His wise investment of these funds until needed saved the University millions.

Perovich's title was changed to vice president for business and finance but his responsibilities remained much the same. In 1982 he was named interim president by the Board of Regents, and later confirmed as the University's twelfth president. John Perovich retired in 1985 after serving the University for almost forty years.

John Perovich

classrooms, offices, and handball and racquetball courts. Other projects were the expansion of the football stadium, a utility expansion package, a North Campus student services–union facility, and a South Campus technology building to house functions now on the Central Campus such as Contract Archaeology, the Technology Application Center, and the National Park Service Chaco Canyon project. Later most of these proposed buildings were either dropped or the space needs were taken care of otherwise.

The State Land Office proposed a land swap that would provide the State Fair with a new site on the Mesa del Sol land and allow UNM to expand to the fairgrounds at Central and San Pedro. President Perovich said he was amenable to the swap idea but wanted more study. He said, "We are fortunate that the University has done a good job of land planning. But we seem to be consuming land faster." There was a legal question as to whether the Land Office could give the land to UNM, as Land Commissioner Jim Baca wanted to do, or would have to sell it at fair market value. Governor Toney Anaya approved the idea and there were talks between the parties but the proposal was eventually abandoned.

On November 6, 1984, the voters approved a $64 million education bond issue by almost three to one. From this issue the University received financing for the Lomas Boulevard parking structure and the Anderson Schools of Management, Economics, and Social Sciences Complex.

(Opposite) "A Master Plan for the U.N.M. South Campus Sports Complex" was developed by Robert McCabe of the firm Flatow, Moore, Bryan Architects.

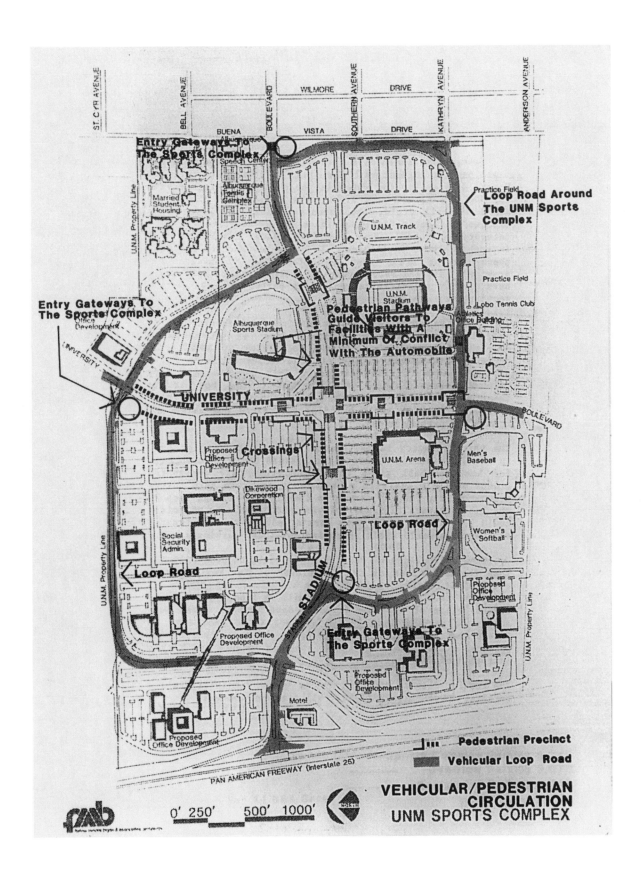

Entry Gateways To The Sports Complex

Loop Road Around The UNM Sports Complex

Entry Gateways To The Sports Complex

Pedestrian Pathways Guide Visitors To Facilities With A Minimum Of Conflict With The Automobile

Crossings

Loop Road

Loop Road

Entry Gateways To The Sports Complex

ST. C FR AVENUE
BELL AVENUE
BOULEVARD
WILMORE
SOUTHERN AVENUE
DRIVE
KATHRYN AVENUE
ANDERSON AVENUE

BUENA
VISTA
DRIVE

U.N.M. Property Line
Married Student Housing
Speech Center
Albuquerque Tennis Complex
U.N.M. Track
Practice Field
Practice Field
Lobo Tennis Club

Office Development
UNIVERSITY
Albuquerque Sports Stadium
U.N.M. Stadium
Athletics Office Building

UNIVERSITY
BOULEVARD

Proposed Office Development
U.N.M. Arena
Men's Baseball

Dikewood Corporation
Women's Softball

Social Security Admin.
Proposed Office Development

UNM Property Line
UNM Property Line

STADIUM
Proposed Office Development
Entry Gateways To The Sports Complex

Proposed Office Development
Motel
Proposed Office Development

PAN AMERICAN FREEWAY (Interstate 25)

┊┈┊ **Pedestrian Precinct**
▬▬ **Vehicular Loop Road**

0' 250'   500' 1000'

NORTH

VEHICULAR/PEDESTRIAN CIRCULATION UNM SPORTS COMPLEX

Controversial Public Art

Two major pieces of sculpture were proposed for the UNM campus in early 1984: *Abstract Stadium* by Bruce Nauman and *Dreams and Nightmares: Journey on a Broken Weave* by Dennis Oppenheim. A grant for the Nauman sculpture had been obtained from the National Endowment for the Arts' Art in Public Places program with matching funds from the UNM Foundation and the Friends of Art. The National Endowment for the Arts had appointed a committee to select a sculptor for the piece funded from the endowment. Since 1979, Nauman, who had become world renowned for his work, had lived near Pecos, New Mexico, keeping an arms-length relationship with the art world. Nauman designed *Abstract Stadium* to interact with the space in Smith Plaza. It was to be an inverted V sixty feet long, thirty feet wide, and fifteen feet high, with the interior lighted by sodium-vapor lamps. The artist said, "The idea is a kind of echo of the Mexican pyramids."

The input on Nauman's piece was so negative that the Campus Planning Committee refused to approve it. Nauman declined to consider doing another design for the plaza but after some time he agreed to design a sculpture for the site on Yale Boulevard between Mitchell Hall and Ortega Hall. It is named *Center of the Universe* and proved to be almost as controversial as his first design. It was completed early in 1988, and there were many articles and reviews in the newspapers. Nauman was quoted as saying: "I didn't think of the title until I started working on it. Nobody knows where the center of the universe is anyway. This piece takes you out of this place and puts you where the

Center of the Universe by sculptor Bruce Nauman. Photograph by the author.

center might be. It puts you into the huge scale of the universe, which is, after all, an interior space—you can only imagine it." The piece was criticized by many people and praised by others, particularly those in the art world. The comments went on in the news media all summer and graffiti appeared and some vandalism was attempted but it is still there. An *Albuquerque Journal* editorial raised the unanswerable question, But is it art? "No one knows how history will judge . . . this sculpture. But if controversial films, art, literature, ideas can't be expressed at a university, where can they be? Professors and students, lobby the legislature. Write the regents. Picket the administration. But don't pick on a work of art."

The Oppenheim piece was commissioned by the Albuquerque Arts Board with funds coming from the "One Percent for the Arts" portion of a transportation bond issue. He had been a visiting artist at UNM and hoped students could build the piece from his drawings, but it did not prove practical, so a local contractor was employed.

Dreams and Nightmares: Journey on a Broken Weave received committee approval even though some said they did not understand the artist's intent. I proposed it be located on a triangle of land at the intersection of Las Lomas and Lomas Boulevard across from the University Hospital. At the May meeting the regents raised questions about safety and postponed a decision approving the site and the design. It was approved at the June meeting with Regent Colleen Maloof dissenting.

Dreams and Nightmares: Journey on a Broken Weave by sculptor Dennis Oppenheim is located opposite UNMH on Lomas Boulevard. Photograph by the author.

On November 20, 1984, the Board of Regents approved the purchase of five vacant residential lots within a subdivision that adjoins University land south of The Pit. The acquisition is part of a plan to acquire all the land in the area for future use.

A very comprehensive study examined the existing football facility and compared it to those of other Western Athletic Conference schools as to cost and visual impact. UNM scored low on the latter as well as having the lowest seating capacity. The planners studied the traffic and parking during times of highest impact, including the proposed increase of stadium seating to 45,000. Recommendations included:

> Turn the stadium into a bowl by further lowering the field and building seats around both ends. Under the seats build the support facilities: locker rooms, ticket offices, concession stands, and maintenance space (as was proposed in W. C. Kruger's original design).

> Install artificial turf to allow greater use of the field and reduce maintenance costs.

> Pave all parking lots.

> Increase parking capacity to 11,500 spaces.

> Build loop roads from Stadium Boulevard around the north and south ends of the athletic complex. This would allow University and Stadium Boulevards to be closed during athletic events without seriously interrupting through traffic.

The plan was completed and ready to be implemented if the University Stadium expansion was approved.

CHAPTER FIFTEEN

Building for the Twenty-First Century and Beyond

The middle and late 1980s were a period of belt-tightening at the state level that started in fiscal year 1982–83 when general fund expenditures exceeded income. Two factors were falling oil and gas prices and reduced federal spending. Each year a list of proposed capital projects was submitted to the Board of Educational Finance only to be drastically cut or eliminated entirely before they were referred to the legislative committees. In the early part of the 1985 legislative session, Senator Joe Carraro said mineral-based severance taxes would continue to fall for several years and the state must find other revenue sources. Senator Manny Aragon was quoted as saying, "There will be no capital projects this year. That means there won't be any equipment for the Medical School as well as no new buildings."

Newly appointed President Thomas J. Farer appeared at the Board of Regents meeting on January 16, 1985, after having spent only two weeks on campus. Former Governor Jerry Apodaca and businessman Robert Lee Sanchez were appointed to the board by Governor Toney Anaya to replace Regents Phillip Martinez and Henry Jaramillo.

The board met next on February 5, 1985, and approved the purchase of the building at 1128 University Northeast that had been vacant for some time until leased to Carrie Tingley Hospital for an out-patient clinic. The 19,350-square-foot building sits on a 1.93-acre site. The agreement was for the University to buy it when the Carrie Tingley Hospital lease expired in December 31, 1985, and use it for the UNM Hospital (UNMH) business functions. Carrie Tingley was now located in the former University Heights Hospital on the west side of University Boulevard.

In the legislature Senator Les Houston introduced a bill to finance the renovation and expansion of University Stadium even though it had not been approved by the BEF. The bill died in committee and the legislature adjourned with no appropriation of capital outlay funds for UNM.

SUB West was completed during the summer of 1985 on the deck of Regener Hall to provide food service to the southwest part of the campus. Union Director Cliff Holt called it a "take-out shop." It was designed by Allen Taylor of the Office of the University Architect.

Aerial view of the campus, circa 1985.

Campus Planner Joe McKinney met with representatives from the city and the neighborhoods surrounding UNM to discuss plans for developing Yale Park. He outlined several options including rerouting Redondo Drive to the south side from Yale Boulevard to Redondo East thus bringing the park into the campus. A planting strip would be left between the drive and Central Avenue. A site would be created for a proposed art museum just south of Popejoy Hall. Another plan called for converting the park into a "soft" parking lot with grass turf between recessed concrete blocks with the loss of only two trees. McKinney also proposed to create a pedestrian mall in the Cornell Drive alignment east of the Fine Arts Center and to carry a bridge over Central Avenue to meet the mall. Unfortunately none of these plans came to fruition.

Water from a broken pipe to a water fountain flooded the basement of the Anthropology Building (11) where material from the Maxwell Museum was stored. Thousands of dollars of damage occurred but most of the artifacts were stored on shelves and in cabinets the four-inch-deep floodwaters did not reach. All the water pipes in the basement had been sheathed and placed outside storage rooms to prevent this type of flooding but the water broke through the storage room walls.

At the regents meeting at the Los Alamos Campus on March 5, I introduced representatives of the Stevens, Mallory, Pearl, and Campbell firm who presented the design for a multilevel parking structure to be located on Lomas Boulevard across from the University Hospital. It was designed to have 898 parking spaces about half of which would be for the hospital. A pedestrian bridge would connect to the hospital across Lomas Boulevard. Against the better judgment of the designer George Pearl, I had him incise "University of New Mexico" in large letters in the stucco on the railing of the bridge.

The Jaynes Corporation was low bidder on the Lomas Boulevard Parking Structure (172) and well below the estimate. With the surplus funds it was possible to add another full bay on the east side that brought the total spaces to 997. The regents approved the contract award and the additional bay at their meeting on June 11. They also approved the purchase of the building at 1829 Sigma Chi Road (171) for use by Latin American programs.

President Farer received approval from the regents at the board meeting on April 2, 1985, to proceed with plans to develop the South Campus research park. Dean of Library Services Paul Vassallo received approval to develop an archives policy for the University. Budget Director James Wiegmann asked the regents again for approval to remove all the University-owned buildings in the 1700 and 1800 blocks of Roma Avenue and Las Lomas Road. He said the land was needed for parking to replace what was lost to the construction of the Anderson Schools of Management, Economics, and Social Sciences project. Approval was given subject to agreement by the BEF and the State Board of Finance.

There were objections to the removal of the former residences that housed, among other functions, Native American Studies, Afro-American Studies, Chicano Student Services, and the Women's Center. When the plan was taken to the next BEF meet-

The first unit of the Lomas Boulevard Parking Structure was designed by George C. Pearl of Stevens, Mallory, Pearl, and Campbell. Photograph by the author.

A view of the Anderson Schools of Management, Economics, and Social Sciences Complex. Architect: Hutchinson Brown and Partners. Photograph by the author.

ing, concerns were stated about the aesthetic effect of replacing the buildings with a parking lot. Wiegmann cited the Warnecke Plan, which showed this as an expansion area and said the buildings were too expensive to maintain and were in need of extensive remodeling. The demolition was to be done in three phases depending on when the occupants could be relocated to Mesa Vista Hall. The board tabled the plan. During the summer a proposal to renovate nine of the buildings and create an "ethnic mall" was submitted to President Farer primarily by Ted Jojola, director of Native American Studies. A feature of the plan was a lecture hall at the west end of the mall. Farer said he was impressed with the plan but did not feel he could take a position without more information.

William H. Johnson, chief administrator for UNMH, presented a proposal to enlarge and remodel the 1968 surgical suite to accommodate surgical techniques that required larger support facilities. Dean, Hunt, Krueger, and Associates were to be the architects. The project was approved.

I asked for half a million dollars for equipment to be added to the project budget of the Anderson Schools of Management, Economics, and Social Sciences Complex, which was approved after the board requested a detailed list of the items. I also presented the administration's five-year capital outlay plan with only the 1986 projects listed by priority. They were equipment for the Electrical and Computer Engineering–Centennial Library Complex; a communications instructional center; a building for materials technology; a South Campus technology building; a building for the University Press, printing plant, and post office; a North Campus multipurpose building; utilities; University Stadium expansion; and general campus improvements. The list was approved but the chances of obtaining funding were poor to nil.

At the next regents meeting on October 1, Wiegmann presented the bids for the Anderson Schools of Management, Economics, and Social Sciences Complex that had been received on September 17. Page and Wirtz were low and Wiegmann asked for approval of the contract and a revised project budget of $8.6 million, which were granted.

Athletic Director John Bridgers was again calling attention to the proposed renovation of University Stadium when *Albuquerque Journal* sports editor Dennis Latta quoted President Farer on November 5 as saying, "I think we need a new football stadium, but it's a matter of what you need most." Farer said he would not stand in the way if Bridgers wanted to do some politicking. A *Journal* editorial the next day said, "If the legislators can find the money to fund stadium renovation—after funding the items ahead of it on Farer's list of priorities—that is good. But if not, Farer has set a course of capital outlay projects that is best, overall, for UNM." Bridgers continued his effort to the end of the year even though some legislators were saying there was to be little money for capital outlay projects in the coming session.

A five-foot-high bronze sculpture, the head of a Lobo, patterned after the piece by John Tatschl at Johnson Gymnasium, was dedicated on October 26, 1985. It was placed in front of Hodgin Hall. The sculptor was Tommy Hicks, and the work was cast by Shidoni Foundry in Tesuque. It was financed by Dr. Randolph Seligman, his wife, Eleanor, and their three daughters.

The UNM Lettermen's Association proposed to add a sports museum to the southeast corner of Hodgin Hall and that brought immediate protests from some architects, historians, and planners. Thomas Merlan, state historic preservation officer, warned that an addition could threaten Hodgin Hall's landmark status. A compromise plan was finally reached, which cut the proposal in half and placed the entrance within the recessed wall of the existing staircase.

The restoration of the first University library, the Art Annex (105), was completed for use by graduate art students. Art Professor Nick Abdalla noted the students had been in eleven different buildings in sixteen years and now they had both this building and the Mattox Sculpture Center (123) at Copper and Ash.

At the urging of several UNM alumni members, the Kiwanis Club of Albuquerque raised money and obtained donations of labor and material to construct a replica of the round pool that was once in the old part of the campus. It was said that engineering students were tossed into the pool upon graduation and on other occasions. The new pool is centered on the north entrance to the Art Annex (105) and the

The Social Sciences Building (57). Architects: Hutchinson Brown and Partners. Photograph by the author.

east entrance to Hodgin Hall. Unfortunately nothing has been done with the pool since it was built so it sits empty and the fountain in the middle is seldom turned on.

At about this time Gwinn "Bub" Henry, director of Hodgin Hall and the Alumni Chapel, began talks with the local Mexican consul, Doña Galindo Saroz, about a gazebo on the campus honoring the friendship between Mexico and New Mexico. The result was the attractive structure on the east side of Hodgin Hall that was dedicated in 1991. The Mexican government employed the architect, Nahim Dagdug Califé, and furnished materials and labor. Theo R. B. Crevenna of the UNM Latin American Institute served as the interpreter during the negotiations.

Several projects were under construction early in 1986, including the Electrical and Computer Engineering–Centennial Library Complex (46), the Center for Non-Invasive Diagnosis (260), the Lomas Boulevard Parking Structure (172), and the Anderson Schools of Management, Economics, and Social Sciences Complex. But there was not much in the pipeline since new construction funds had to come from the University's own resources.

The gallery on the north side of the Art Museum was named for Van Deren Coke, former director of the museum and well-known authority on the history of photography. The building at the corner of Copper and Ash was renamed the Sculptural Research–Charles Mattox Center. Fine Arts Dean Donald McRae presented the recommendations to the regents. When the regents met on February 4, 1986, they approved the purchase of a house at 1005 Columbia Northeast and money to remodel it for Medical School programs.

The 5,000-square-foot two-story building on the northwest corner of Lomas and Yale (originally a one-story structure built by architect A. W. Boehning Sr. for his office) had been remodeled and a floor added for Continuing Education in 1968. It was remodeled again in 1986 for the Office of the University Architect (203). Allen Taylor, an architect on the University architect's staff, planned the remodeling.

While the Cold War was raging following the end of World War II, fallout shelters and evacuation centers were created on campus mostly in basements of concrete frame buildings. In 1985 Joe McKinney, the campus planner, reported that the upkeep of the shelters had ceased in the 1960s, and the rations and supplies kept in them had deteriorated or been stolen. "The crackers were rancid several years ago," he said; "the alcohol kept in metal tins has evaporated. The water has been sitting there since 1962, and the batteries for the Geiger counters have exceeded their shelf life." Most of the spaces were remodeled or returned to storage use.

The legislature changed the name of the BEF to the New Mexico Commission on Higher Education (CHE) and created a Higher Education Reform Committee. Governor Toney Anaya appointed the Governor's Task Force on Higher Education Reform. Reports from the committee and the task force were due around the end of the year.

At the regents meeting on February 4, 1986, Bridgers was rebuffed again when approval of the football stadium expansion was denied. One reason was the $799,000 Athletic Department deficit in the last fiscal year. Bridgers said, "I'm going to take a few days off. My enthusiasm died a little today, but I'll be back."

Some students and faculty objected to President Farer's remodeling of his office suite, part of a project that included new floor covering and ceilings in the first floor of Scholes Hall. Departmental budgets had been cut; faculty travel was restricted; classroom supplies were sometimes bought by faculty; and students were facing a large tuition increase. Farer wanted to remove the heavy wooden furniture designed for President Davis and install a smaller-scale desk and seating. New carpeting and paint were part of the redecoration planned by Black Tie Design. The total cost for the president's office was $7,624 out of a total project budget of around $60,000. Nothing but plaster patching and occasional painting had been done to the corridors since the building was built in 1936.

Alan Prickett, the University real estate director, and Joseph V. Scaletti, acting vice president for research, presented a report in early 1986 on the selection of a developer for the South Campus Research Park beginning with a brief history of recent efforts to revive interest in the park. A research park planning committee had been appointed by President Farer composed of Wiegmann, Carroll Lee (associate vice president for business and comptroller), Joe McKinney, Prickett, Scaletti, and me. The University had committed to a study of the park's potential by a consortium of local planners headed by the architectural firm of Barker-Bol. This study indicated enough possibilities for a successful development for UNM to advertise nationwide for a development firm. Seven letters of interest were received by November 1, 1985, and requests for proposals were sent to four of those. Of these two were selected to visit the campus and make presentations in April. Prickett then received approval to negotiate with either Continental Development Company–Kroh Brothers Construction Company or Glenborough Development Company–Frank Morrow and Associates.

In June the Board of Regents agreed not to extend President Farer's contract and appointed Dean of Engineering Gerald W. May president.

A list of capital outlay projects for 1987 presented to the regents in August was pretty much the same as the previous year with the exception of the Health Sciences and Services Building (previously called the North Campus Multipurpose Building), which had become top priority, with a computing and support facility second. The former was proposed to house a number of Allied Health Sciences programs, including Medical Technology, Occupational Therapy, Physical Therapy, Respiratory Therapy, Radiological Sciences, and Maternity and Infant Care. The building rose from fifth place in the priorities because it was the only project that contained classrooms and laboratories and that was what the CHE was supporting. The third floor was built as a shell and completed later. A basement storage area was created for the Health Sciences Library and connected to it with a tunnel. A chilled water plant was built on the northeast corner to increase the cooling capacity in the north part of the North Campus. Architects for the project were Holmes, Sabatini, Smith, and Eeds.

During the early planning of the Health Sciences and Services Building, I was determined the location should follow the plan for the area developed by Harvey Hoshour and the building should not obstruct the view of the mountains from the library. When a proposed footprint of the building was completed by architect William Sabatini, anchored helium-filled balloons were flown to the height of the parapets at the building corners and some of us stood in the library and observed the results. The view is unobstructed.

Bids for the construction of the Health Sciences and Services Center (266) were received on May 10, 1988, and the contract was awarded to Davis and Associates of Santa Fe; the building was completed on June 6, 1989.

At the August 12, 1986, Board of Regents meeting Regent Jerry Apodaca introduced a "Policy for Approval of UNM Construction Projects." Any project over $100,000 but less than $300,000 had to go to the regents' Finance and Audit Committee for review and comment; projects over $300,000 had to go to the full board by way of the president and the committee. The plan was approved and immediately put into effect.

John Bridgers's project to expand the football stadium was disapproved by the regents' Finance and Audit Committee when it met on August 6. This ended the drive to expand the stadium

The University-owned telephone system that went into operation in early 1984 quickly used up all the 9,500 lines on the NEAX 2200 switch. A 3,000-line NEAX 2400 switch was added in 1987 at a cost of $1,165,063, which also included upgrading the existing switch and the accounting system. It was predicted to meet the University's telephone requirements for only three to five years.

at least for the time being. The sixty-four-year-old Bridgers announced his retirement a few months later to be effective on June 30, 1987.

The regents meeting on November 4, 1986, changed the priorities for capital outlay funds for 1987 to reflect the likelihood of little or no funds from the legislature. The revised list gave priority to renovating classrooms: the lecture halls in Clark, Castetter, and Tapy Halls, the major classrooms in the College of Education, and all the classrooms in Mitchell Hall at $3 million. Other wish list items were planning for a materials technology center, $150,000; $2 million to turn Yale and Terrace streets into pedestrian malls; and a $2.4 million cogeneration plant.

Dedications were held during October 1987 for the Center for Non-Invasive Diagnosis, with U.S. Senator Pete Domenici as the main speaker, and the Electrical and Computer Engineering Building. Chairman of Electrical Engineering Peter Dorato used a laser beam to cut the ribbon opening the facility.

The largest donation of architectural material to the John Gaw Meem Archive of Southwestern Architecture came in 1986 with the drawings, papers, and photographs from W. C. Kruger and Associates. Kruger had died in 1984 and the firm was being dissolved. The firm, founded in 1937, had designed hospitals, schools, state buildings, and military installations throughout New Mexico. For many years it was the largest architectural firm in the state.

A 2,000-square-foot building, the Crystal Growth Facility (331), was sited on University Boulevard Southeast north of the city baseball stadium because it needed to

The Health Sciences and Services Building (266) was designed by William Sabatini of Holmes and Sabatini to form the southeast wing of a future main entrance to the Medical School focused on the Medical Library. Photograph by the author.

be isolated from other facilities since on occasion fumes were emitted by the manufacturing process that might be sucked into nearby air conditioning systems. It was designed by Westwork Architects. The contract was awarded to Britton and Rich Contractors. It was a very small building but it received much attention because of its fine design.

When the regents met on December 8, 1986, Ann Jourdan of Hobbs left the board after serving twelve years. President May declared it to be "Ann Jourdan Day—in honor of her trust and belief in the University of New Mexico and in higher education as the key to a better world." Regent Jourdan, the wife of a building contractor, served on the Campus Planning Committee and was always interested in campus planning and development.

In 1977 the University had leased some South Campus land southwest of the Athletic Department Building (308) to the UNM Tennis Club Foundation and granted a mortgage to build a tennis complex. The money was from the University endowment fund. The club would pay off the mortgage with dues from an expected 600 members. At that time tennis was increasing in popularity in Albuquerque and people were waiting in line to play on the few courts available around the city. University tennis teams would share the courts and any profits would go to scholarships and to pay part of the coaches' salaries.

Then-regent Calvin Horn said, "As I recall, the regents' feelings were, 'Well, if it works like the private foundation feels it will work, that'll be great. If it doesn't, we'll have a nice facility.'" It did not work. An audit showed the club in arrears on interest and the mortgage that had been increased by two additional loans. Membership had reached only about 200. The appraised value of the complex was $450,000, so the regents approved foreclosing on the property so it could be used by the tennis teams and the public.

As 1987 began, incoming Governor Garrey Carruthers appointed three new members to the newly enlarged seven-member Board of Regents: Ken Johns, an Albuquerque automobile dealer; Frank Borman, a former astronaut and Las Cruces businessman; and Siegfried Hecker, director of Los Alamos National Laboratory and a nationally recognized scientist. Carruthers admonished them, "Be a board member. Don't be an administrator." At the organization meeting in February Ken Johns was elected president, succeeding Jerry Apodaca.

The CHE announced it would not approve any new construction in 1987, so the University submitted the previously approved list concentrating on remodeling and landscaping. The CHE then cut the list in half with only $50,000 for the planning of the materials technology center. The legislature ended with a total capital outlay package of $37.9 million of which UNM received only the materials technology planning money and $150,000 for campus improvements.

There was little money for building and planning in the foreseeable future, and as I was nearing age sixty-six I thought it time to turn the job over to younger hands. I had been very fortunate to have been the University architect for almost twenty-five years—one-fourth of UNM's existence. I wrote a letter to President May saying my retirement would be effective June 30, 1987.

At the April 23 meeting the regents approved a $2.4 million cogeneration plant to be located in an addition to the Lomas Boulevard Parking Structure. The estimated payout time from energy saved was only ten years. The plan was that waste heat from the gas-driven power generator would also be used to generate chilled water and heat for nearby buildings. The generator would provide a stable power source for the Computer and Information Resources and Technology Building (153), with Public Service Company of New Mexico as a backup. The cogeneration plant (part of 172) was financed with a tax-exempt commercial banknote, a method of financing not used since the early days of the University when the regents borrowed money for construction. Sunwest Bank offered the best proposal of four submitted at $3,185,000 on a ten-year note with semiannual payments.

In December 1986 the regents had approved the concept of a house on the North Campus, named Casa Esperanza, for use by cancer patients from out of town receiving treatment at UNMH and the Cancer Center. The site selected was next to the Ronald McDonald House on the west side of the Golf Course. This was in the area designated on the North Campus plan for health-related facilities. The fourteen-bed

The interior of the cogeneration plant, which is part of the Lomas Boulevard Parking Structure (172). Courtesy of Larry Schuster.

unit was sponsored by the New Mexico and Albuquerque Boards of Realtors and endorsed by the Cancer Center's board of advisers. W. C. Kruger and Associates had donated the plans for the building. But when it was presented to the Campus Planning Committee, a delegation of neighborhood residents and their organization, Friends of the North Golf Course, objected. The planning committee, by a one-vote margin, voted to postpone approval, and proponents of the project said they would appeal the decision to the Board of Regents.

The regents met on May 14 before an overflow crowd of people angrily protesting the location of Casa Esperanza. Their main complaint was that the neighborhood had not been consulted about the location. They feared the golf course was going to be developed and the ambience of the area destroyed. The board approved the project, and President Ken Johns said in the future neighborhood groups would be brought into campus planning considerations. He said the land was valuable and irreplaceable and should be preserved as long as possible. When all the neighborhood representatives were added, the Campus Planning Committee became more of a forum than a committee. My feeling was that UNM should be a good neighbor but this was state property bought by taxpayers from all over New Mexico for future University expansion, and planning decisions should not be held hostage to localized concerns.

UNM graduates employed at Bohannon-Huston coordinated a project to landscape the area between Tapy Hall and the new Electrical and Computer Engineering–Centennial Library Complex. They raised funds for sidewalks, an irrigation system, shrubs, and trees. Karl G. "Gil" Berry, campus landscape architect, worked with the group in developing the plan.

In June the State Board of Finance approved the University research park to be located on about ninety acres on the South Campus. (This came twenty years after a start was made by President Tom Popejoy and the Albuquerque Industrial Development Corporation to establish the park. At that time objections were raised by realtors that the University had no business getting into real estate development, and the regents and later administrations made no effort to move the park forward after the first two buildings were erected.) The proposal by Glenborough New Mexico and Frank Morrow and Associates was for 1.5 million square feet of research, business, and commercial facilities. They hoped to attract high-tech tenants interested in physical and intellectual proximity to UNM and Sandia National Laboratories. There would be no manufacturing, except for prototypes, in the park. UNM would receive a share of rental and lease income. It was estimated to take twelve to eighteen months to acquire all city approvals and build the infrastructure.

My retirement was announced to the regents at the meeting on May 14, 1987, and some comments were made that I appreciated. Regent John Paez said, "Mr. Hooker has fought long and hard to maintain the integrity of the campus's southwestern architecture through dealings with numerous personalities and various Boards of Regents." President May said, "The University owes a debt of gratitude to Mr. Hooker

for the aesthetics of our campus. Through his devotion to quality he has helped set the tone of our beautiful campus." Berry was appointed interim director of the office, and the name was changed to the Department of Facilities Planning.

Regent Robert Sanchez reported for the Finance and Audit Committee on the selection of architects for the UNMH Ambulatory Care Facility (269). A list of five architectural firms was approved in order of preference and the hospital administration was to negotiate with them. Dean-Krueger and Associates was chosen.

A system revenue refunding bond issue of $25.2 million was approved by the regents in August. President May presented a list of capital projects to go to the legislature in 1988 including classroom remodeling, an opto-electronic materials center, Central Campus improvements and security, laboratory renovations, a communication and printing building, UNMH equipment, and educational equipment for the Central Campus. North Campus projects were the Ambulatory Care Facility and campus improvements.

After the list was reviewed by the CHE the University was recommended to receive funding for classroom improvements, planning money for the opto-electronic materials facility, and funds for improving campus security and UNMH equipment.

When the board met in October it approved the purchase of the Dane Smith residence at 1809 Roma with the agreement that ninety-year-old Mrs. Smith could live in the house during her lifetime.

Honors came to UNM in October 1987 when the New Mexico Society of Architects presented an award to Westwork Architects for the design of the Center for Non-Invasive Diagnosis (260). The building was cited for its integrated massing, definition and clarity, and use of concrete to set off "more predictable" stucco. The annual Orchids and Onions program, sponsored by the Associated General Contractors and

The ambulatory care addition to UNMH was designed by Dean-Krueger and Associates. Photograph by the author.

The Centennial Celebration

Planning for the University's centennial was well under way by 1988. At the request of the Alumni Association and others, a budget was approved and a small temporary staff was hired. Centennial Director Rose Mary "Redd" Eakin was soliciting proposals from the entire campus community, and many of them involved paying tribute to or expanding upon the University's architecture and artwork. The list included:

Designation of September 23, 1989, as UNM Architecture Day, highlighted by the opening of an exhibit titled *Shaping the University: the UNM Campus Since 1960* in the Art Museum with a gallery talk by V. B. Price.

Two photography exhibits about architecture prepared by Wolfgang Preiser, professor of architecture. One, titled *Pueblo Style and Regional Architecture*, was displayed in the concourse of Bratton Hall, and sixty photographs of UNM buildings, titled *UNM Architecture—Centennial Photography Exhibit*, was mounted in the School of Architecture and Planning and later in the main corridor of Scholes Hall.

A centennial logo, featuring the tower of Mesa Vista Hall, which became the University logo.

The official poster, representing Darlene Wellborn's acrylic painting of Scholes Hall.

A self-guiding tour of Central Campus architecture, sculpture, and landscaping.

Plans for entry markers at Central and Yale, Central and University, and Girard and Campus similar to the one on Lomas Boulevard across from UNMH.

A fresco by Frederico Vigil of Santa Fe in the History Department Commons Room in Mesa Vista Hall depicting New Mexico history from the domestication of corn to the development of nuclear power.

Naming of the new engineering-science library the Centennial Library.

The centennial logo. UNMA.

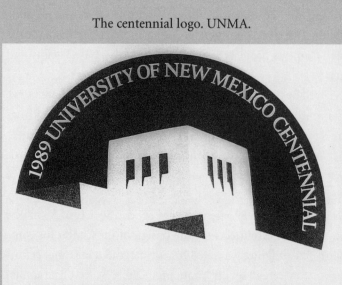

the American Institute of Architects, included an orchid for the landscaping of the north entry to the Central Campus on Lomas opposite the hospital.

At the Board of Regents meeting on February 9 approval was given to purchase the property on the southwest corner of Yale and Lomas. The building on the site, then occupied by a restaurant with a twelve-month lease, was designed by architect Max Flatow for his firm's office sometime in the 1950s.

The General Honors Center was named for its founder, Professor Emeritus Dudley Wynn, at a ceremony on April 21, 1988. He started the Honors Program in 1961 while dean of the College of Arts and Sciences. Wynn spent thirty-one very productive years at UNM.

A 3,500-square-foot mural in the curving stairway on the south end of the SUB was painted by art major Esther Lowe depicting buildings and fountains on the Central and North Campuses and the Valencia Campus.

UNM 2000, the report of a sixteen-member committee that had worked for six months, was presented in May 1988. The authors said it focused on change: "Our aim is to present a vision of the future and to suggest the changes which must be embarked upon to make the vision a reality." The report touched on many aspects of the University's future but almost nothing was said about campus planning and development, the University's best-known asset. I understand that a statement was prepared for the committee that pointed out the values of the campus environment but it was rejected.

When the regents met on June 14 they approved the purchase of the property at 1200 University Boulevard Northeast for half a million dollars. It is a 56,556-square-foot lot zoned C-3 with a 6,350-square-foot office building on it. The building now houses some KNME-TV functions. The board also approved the University Hospital's purchase of the office and warehouse building at 1209 University. The 20,000-square-foot building sits on 2.17 acres and would be used to house the hospital's business and personnel offices.

In August 1988 several landscape projects were under way: the courtyard on the east side of Mesa Vista Hall; the College of Education; the Anderson Schools of Management, Economics, and Social Sciences Complex; and Novitski Hall on the North Campus. A parking lot with seventy-five spaces was being constructed at Coronado Dormitory. (I had voted against this project in the Campus Planning Committee because I hated to see a nicely landscaped area destroyed for a parking lot.) The dirt lot east of University Stadium was being paved through an arrangement with the State Highway Department at a cost of half a million dollars. As for buildings, Sara Raynolds Hall was being converted to three classrooms; the Family Studies (Home Economics) Building (66) in the College of Education was being remodeled; a new liner was being placed in the Olympic Pool; and twenty campus elevators were being retrofitted for handicap use.

The Center for Non-Invasive Diagnosis (260) by Westwork Architects received design awards and made the front cover of *Architecture,* the magazine of the American Institute of Architects. Photograph by the author.

The capital outlay proposals for 1989 were presented to the regents in August and included a science and technology complex, more classroom and laboratory renovations, improved handicap accessibility, an addition to the Lomas parking structure, educational equipment, roofing, street paving, hospital equipment, and North Campus site improvements.

Vice President for Business and Finance David L. Mc Kinney received approval to issue bonds to finance the following projects: the ambulatory care addition to the University Hospital, an 800-space addition to the Lomas parking structure, the purchase of 1200 University Northeast, and debt service and expenses. He explained that there would be no student fees involved, because revenue generated by the projects would pay for the bonds.

The University expressed interest in providing a site for a proposed performing arts center for the city east of I-25 south of the Big-I across from Albuquerque High School. The UNM Art Museum would be incorporated into the proposed center. The regents approved the proposal, but nothing ever came of it.

A ceremony was held in the rotunda of the state capitol in Santa Fe on February 28, 1989, commemorating the one hundredth anniversary of the creation of the University of New Mexico by the Territorial Legislature. Many descendants of Governor Edmund Ross, who signed the bill into law, attended the ceremony. President May made a short address to the crowd composed of many legislators and friends of the University from around the state.

Thus ended the first one hundred years of building a special place, a task that will never end as long as there is a University of New Mexico.

What about the future? The following excerpt from the *Development Plan Report* prepared in 1958 for the University of Birmingham (England) points out the difficulties of planning the physical growth of an ever-expanding university.

It is a truism that a university is a society founded for advancement of learning and the dissemination of knowledge. This means that it is constantly changing, always on its way, its work never completed. Departments expand, contract, quadruple in size, or virtually disappear within a few years, often in defiance of the most knowledgeable and expert forecasts. Every building and each layout, so optimistically and thoroughly designed, seems to become within a decade not only out of date but physically hampering to the future. Any attempt therefore to constrict its movement artificially, either academically or physically, seems doomed, and rightly doomed, to failure.

Pueblo on the Mesa, the fiftieth anniversary history of UNM by Dorothy Hughes, was reprinted by the University for the centennial. She was feted with a reception in Zimmerman Library on March 1, 1989. When she wrote the book in 1939 she ended with a chapter titled "Another Fifty Years" in which she prophesied what UNM would be like in 1989. Since I cannot possibly predict what UNM will be like a hundred years from now, I can think of no better way to end this book than quoting her last paragraph:

The University of New Mexico, being a part of the unusual country in which it stands, is unique in 1989 because it is old and new, in an era inclined to forget the old in the stress of the new. Moving on into the new world, recognizing its obligations to present and to future, never forgetful of the past, it still has the aim expressed by a former president, to give "the highest type of service and leadership in all those phases of living which contribute to the material and spiritual progress of this state," and beyond this to the people of the new world. And after another fifty years, and another and another, it will continue to be that University as it stands, a pueblo on the mesa.

Appendix 1

Awards Made to the University of New Mexico
and Its Architects and Landscape Architects for
Building Design, Landscaping, and Administration

American Society of Landscape Architects

Special Award—Central Campus
 Garrett Eckbo, FASLA; Eckbo, Dean, Austin,
 and Williams; and the University of
 New Mexico, 1978

American Society of Landscape Architects—Colorado Chapter

Merit Award—Family Practice Courtyard
 Office of the University Architect; Robert Johns
 and Campbell Okuma Perkins Associates,
 1979

American Society of Landscape Architects—New Mexico Chapter

Honor Award—For Continued Support of
Landscape Architecture
 Van Dorn Hooker, University Architect, 1982

American Institute of Architects, Western Mountain Region

Award of Merit—Golf Course Club House
 John Reed, Architect, 1968

Commendation—Physics Laboratories and
Lecture Hall
 Pacheco and Graham, Architects, 1972

Citation—University Arena Expansion
 Joe Boehning, Architect, 1976

Silver Medal—Development of the University of
New Mexico Campus
 Van Dorn Hooker, University Architect, 1980

New Mexico Society of Architects

Honor Award—Addition to the Biology Building
 Flatow, Moore, Bryan, and Fairburn, Architects,
 1970

Honor Award—Physics Laboratories and
Lecture Hall
 Pacheco and Graham, Architects, 1973

Honor Award—For Service as President
of the Society
 Van Dorn Hooker, University Architect, 1973

Honor (Posthumous) Award—For Work in the
Development of the University of New Mexico
Campus
 Sherman E. Smith, Vice President for
 Administration, 1974

Merit Award—UNM Bookstore
 Holmes-Giannini, Architects, 1977

Merit Award—Humanities Building
 W. C. Kruger and Associates, Architects, 1977

Honor Award—Medical Center Library
 Harvey Hoshour, Architect, 1977

Special Award—University Arena Expansion
 Boehning, Protz, and Cook, Architects, 1977

Honor Award—Environmental Planning,
Family Practice Courtyard
> Office of the University Architect; Robert Johns
> and Campbell Okuma Perkins Associates,
> 1979

Merit Award—Equitable Way of Selecting
Architects
> Van Dorn Hooker, University Architect, 1984

Honor Award—Valencia Campus
> Royston, Hanamoto, Alley, and Abey,
> Landscape Architects, 1986

Award of Excellence—Center for Non-Invasive
Diagnosis
> Westwork Architects, 1987

Albuquerque Chapter AIA

Honor Award—College of Education
> Flatow, Moore, Bryan, and Fairburn, Architects,
> 1965

Honor Award—Golf Course Club House
> John Reed, Architect, 1967

Honor Award—University Arena
> Joe Boehning—Architect, 1967

Award of Merit—Chemistry Building Addition
> Ferguson, Stevens, Mallory, and Pearl,
> Architects, 1969

Award of Merit—College of Business
Administration
> John Reed, Architect, 1969

New Mexico Arts Commission

Excellence in New Construction—Dormitory
Complex
> William Ellison and Associates, Architects
> Ernest J. Kump and Associates, Design
> Architects
> Eckbo, Dean, Austin, and Williams, Landscape
> Architects, 1973

City of Albuquerque

Certificate of Appreciation—Civic Beautification:
Duck Pond and Children's Psychiatric Center
> Office of the University Architect, 1981

College and University Business

Design Excellence Award—College of Education
> Flatow, Moore, Bryan, and Fairburn, Architects,
> 1967

Industrial Design

Design Excellence Award—Graphics and Signage,
University Arena Expansion
> Corey Planning and Design Group, 1976

Associated General Contractors

Orchid Award for UNM Campus Landscaping, 1983

Orchid Award for UNM John Baker Memorial
> Track, 1985

Orchid Award for UNM Campus Landscaping, 1987

The Albuquerque Conservation Association (TACA)

Landscape Award—For Contributing to the
Quality of Our Nation's Environment
> Office of the University Architect, 1983

Bainbridge Bunting Award of Merit—Hodgin Hall
Restoration
> UNM Alumni Association, 1984

Award of Merit—Center for Non-Invasive
Diagnosis
> Westwork Architects; Office of the University
> Architect, 1986

Award of Merit—Landscaping around *Dreams and
Nightmares: Journey on a Broken Weave,* Sculpture
by Dennis Oppenheim
> University of New Mexico, 1987

In 1979 the City of Albuquerque received an award
from TACA for the redesign of the Yale Reservoir.
George Pearl was the design architect with the firm
of Stevens, Mallory, Pearl, and Campbell.

The University of New Mexico Board of Regents

Regents' Recognition Medal to Van Dorn Hooker
> For protecting and preserving the unique
> campus, 1985

Appendix 2
University Buildings on the
National Register of Historic Places

Art Annex, formerly the University Library
   (105)
Carlisle Gymnasium (4)
The Estufa
Harwood Foundation, Taos
Hodgin Hall (103) and Tight Grove
President's Residence, University House (51)
Sara Raynolds Hall (104)
Scholes Hall (10)

All the above buildings are also on the New
Mexico State Register of Cultural Properties. The old
Chemistry Building (2) is on the state register but not
the national.

Appendix 3

Building Statistics

The buildings on the Albuquerque campuses that were considered "major" when built are included in this list. The Chemistry Building (2), constructed in 1916–17, cost some $32,000 and would be a minor project today when much larger buildings are costing many millions, but it was a sizable addition to the campus of 1917. I have also included some "minor" buildings in terms of cost and square footage that were well designed and contributed to the fabric of the campuses.

You will see there are several categories of costs: contract amount, bid price, construction cost, and project cost. The total cost of early buildings is difficult to determine from existing records, so in some cases the contractor's bid price or the contract amount is all that is available. The cost data kept by architect John Gaw Meem's office do not agree with the University's. After the Office of the University Architect was established we kept what we considered accurate accounts, which included all costs pertaining to planning, constructing, and equipping the building. But I have found differences with those figures and the comptroller's accounts, where items were sometimes added for equipment and other costs of which we had no record. If data are missing from an entry, it is because the information is not available.

I used minutes of the Board of Regents meetings for much of the information on early buildings since the board was involved in approving all expenditures be they ever so minute. Accounts from the Comptroller's Office and later the Budget Office have been referred to. When the five-year plans were first required in the early 1980s, an effort was made to establish the cost of existing buildings and buildings that had been removed from the campuses. What we have here is cost information that is, to the best of my knowledge, fairly accurate and gives a picture of the relative cost of each building.

Construction cost includes the contract with the general contractor, change orders to the contract, fixed (built-in) equipment, and site and utility work. It is not the same as the bid amount.

Project cost includes the construction cost plus professional fees, resident inspection, surveys and testing, movable furnishings, and any other costs attributed to the project.

After 1963 project numbers were assigned by the Office of the University Architect for administrative purposes. Having the project number will be of help to a researcher in locating files in the architectural archives in the UNM Center for Southwest Research.

The bid date is the day the bids were opened. The bid price is not necessarily the same as the contract price since bids were often negotiated downward and bid alternates were accepted or rejected.

The completion date is either the date of occupancy or the date of "substantial completion," which is the date when the contractor can receive final payment. Often small items held up the completion date but did not preclude use of the building. I have not differentiated between the two but have used the occupancy date where possible.

The *Engineering News Record* cost index at the time of construction compared to the current cost index figure was used by the Department of Facilities Planning to establish the value, or replacement cost, of each building. The project cost of each building is used if it is available. It factors in all the remodeling and renovation projects as well as additions. The 1998 estimated total value of the campus buildings totaled more than $900 million, which did not include landscaping, streets, and the utility distribution systems. If you add those in, the value of the campus buildings and infrastructure would easily reach $1.25 billion in 1998 dollars. Quite a growth in one century for a university that started with twenty acres and $25,000 to build and furnish its first building!

BUILDING 2
Building names: Chemistry; Crafts Annex; Classroom Annex; Engineering Computer Center
Architect: Francis Barry Byrne; J. S. LaDriere, local architect
General contractor: Campbell Brothers
Bid date: 7/10/16
Contract amount: $20,384
Separate bids were taken on plumbing, heating, electrical, fixtures, laboratory equipment, other furnishings, etc.
Construction cost: $32,424
Completion date: 1917
Gross square feet: 7,437
1998 value: $1,308,339

BUILDING 4
Building name: Carlisle Gymnasium
Architect: Gaastra, Gladding, and Johnson
General contractor: Alfred Wikstrom
Bids received: 9/6/27
Contract amount: $77,825
Construction cost: $84,965
Completion date: 1928
Gross square feet: 34,929
1998 value: $2,342,462

BUILDING 7
Building name: Yatoka Hall
Architect: Gaastra, Gladding, and Johnson
General contractor: Edward Lembke and Co.
Bid date: 9/6/27
Bid price: $25,475
Plumbing, heating, and electrical work bid separately
Project cost: $33,422
Completion date: 1928
Building demolished in 1974 to make way for the Duck Pond

BUILDING 8
Building names: Dining Hall; Bandelier East

Architect: George Williamson and Co.
General contractor: Edward Lembke and Co.
Bids received: 9/14/29
Construction cost: $40,574
Project cost: $46,780 est.
Completion date: 1930
Gross square feet: 9,573
1998 value: $1,157,970

BUILDING 9
Building name: Marron Hall (an addition to the Women's Dormitory Complex that included Hokona Hall and two other additions)
Architect: John Gaw Meem–Hugo Zehner and Associates
Contract date: 9/16/40
Construction cost: $91,427
Completion date: 1941
Gross square feet: 19,982
1998 value: $1,213,417

BUILDING 10
Building Names: Administration; Classroom-Laboratory; Scholes Hall
Architect: John Gaw Meem
General contractor: Thomas Bate
Bid date: 11/22/34
Contract amount: $173,487
Construction cost: $262,420
Completion date: January 1936
Gross square feet: 49,210
1998 value: $8,355,878

BUILDING 11
Building names: Student Union; Anthropology (including Maxwell Museum)
Architect: John Gaw Meem
General contractor: Kilbourne House
Construction start: September 1936
Construction cost: $127,553
Dedicated: 9/25/37
Gross square feet: 27,880

Project 648
Maxwell Museum Addition
Architect: McHugh and Kidder
General contractor: Bradbury and Stamm
Bid date: 7/1/71
Construction cost: $971,399
Project cost: $1,099,539
Completion date: 6/30/73
Gross square feet: 28,435
1998 value: $6,559,396

BUILDING 12
Building names: State Health Laboratory: Anthropology Annex
Architect: John Gaw Meem
General contractor: Kilbourne House
Bid accepted: 3/21/36
Contract amount: $40,547
Construction cost: $51,627
Completion date: 1937
Gross square feet: 9,823

Project 365
Remodeling for Anthropology– Contract Archaeology, 1982
Architect: Patrick McClernon
General contractor: Will F. Cole
Construction cost: $382,970
Project cost: $478,173
Completion date: 11/8/82
1998 value: $1,513,761

BUILDING 16
Building names: Men's Dormitory; Bandelier Hall; Bandelier West
Architect: John Gaw Meem–Hugo Zehner and Associates
General contractor: Buildings and Grounds Department
Construction cost: $92,124
Completion date: 1941
Gross square feet: 15,073
1998 value: $1,918,531

BUILDING 19
Building names: Pharmacy; Biology Annex

Architect: John Gaw Meem–Hugo
Zehner
General contractor: K. L. House
Construction Co.
Contract date: 2/2/48
Contract amount: $68,095
The bid was $115,848 which was
over budget. It was negotiated
to the contract amount and
some of the work was done by
UNM forces. Built-in
equipment was bid separately.
Construction cost: $105,606
Completion date: 12/4/48
Gross square feet: 7,894
1998 value: $1,661,477

BUILDING 21
Building names: Biology; Castetter
Hall
Architect: Meem, Zehner, and
Holien
General contractor: O. G.
Bradbury
Contract date: 8/21/51
Construction cost: $509,219
Completion date: 1952

Project 616
Addition of Loren Potter Wing
Architect; Flatow, Moore, Bryan,
and Fairburn
General contractor: George A.
Rutherford, Inc.
Bid date: 7/2/66
Construction cost: $1,963,367
Project cost: $2,563,238
Completion date: 9/15/67
Gross square feet of original
building and addition: 126,871
Total 1998 value: $17,526,134

BUILDING 22
Building names: Chemistry; Clark
Hall
Architect: Meem, Zehner, and
Holien
General contractor: K. L. House
Construction Co.
Bid accepted: 8/21/51
Contract price: $465,791

Project cost: $505,709
Completion date: 1952
Gross square feet: 34,992

Project 628
Riebsomer Wing Addition
Architect: Ferguson, Stevens,
Mallory, and Pearl
General contractor: Bradbury and
Stamm
Bid accepted: 10/19/68
Construction cost: $1,559,137
Project cost: $1,843,465
Completion date: 12/31/69
Total square feet of original
building and addition: 81,696
Total 1998 value: $18,010,275

BUILDING 23
Building names: Classroom
Building; Mitchell Hall
Architect: Meem, Zehner, Holien,
and Associates
General contractor: K. L. House
Construction Co.
Bid date: 6/12/50
Bid amount: $500,672
Construction start: 6/19/50
Construction cost: $539,851
Project cost: $750,000 est.
Completion date: 6/27/52
Gross square feet: 46,965
1998 value: $8,054,920

BUILDING 24
Building names: Geology
Building; Northrop Hall
Architect: Meem, Zehner, Holien,
and Associates
General contractor: Lembke,
Clough, and King
Contract date: 1/11/52
Construction cost: $911,636
Completion date: 6/2/53

Project 649
Third Floor Addition to Northrop
Hall, 1972
Architect: William R. Buckley
General contractor: Bill Stuckman
Construction cost: $551,796

Project cost: $618,934
Total square feet of original
building and addition: 75,745
Total 1998 value: $11,682,950

BUILDING 25
Building name: Alumni Memorial
Chapel
Architect: Holien and Buckley
General contractor: Bradbury and
Stamm
Bid date: 2/2/60
Construction cost: $100,063
Completion date: February 1962
Gross square feet: 4,261
1998 value: $693,325

BUILDING 34
Project 622
Building names: Psychology
Building; Logan Hall
Architect: Flatow, Moore, Bryan,
and Fairburn
General contractor: Bradbury and
Stamm
Bid date: 6/15/71
Construction cost: $1,832,141
Project cost: $2,077,131
Completion date: 1972
Gross square feet: 56,762
1998 value: $7,024,554

BUILDING 35
Project 050
Building names: Physics
Laboratories and Lecture Hall;
Regener Hall
Architect: Pacheco and Graham
General contractor: Bradbury and
Stamm
Bid date: 6/15/71
Construction cost: $813,921
Project cost: $923,238
Completion date: 1972
Gross square feet: 22,177
1998 value: $3,206,839

BUILDING 46
Project 250
Building name: Electrical and
Computer Engineering–
Centennial Library

Architect: Dean, Hunt, and
Associates
General contractor: Page and
Wirtz
Bid accepted: 9/4/84
Construction cost: $11,563,446
Project cost: $17,165,926
Completion date: 9/19/86
Gross square feet: 170,227
1998 value: $24,258,114

BUILDING 51
Building names: President's
Residence; University House
Architect: George Williamson and
Co.; Miles Brittelle, designer
General contractor: Joseph Gagner
Bid date: 2/4/30
Bid price: $21,750
Completion date: 5/15/30
Gross square feet: 5,522
1998 value: $1,029,795

BUILDING 52
Building name: Stadium Building
Architect: Brittelle and Wilson
Contract for structural steel in
place: 7/31
Contract for interior completion
awarded to Mead and Mount
after bid in June 1934 for
$24,850
Construction cost: $129,000 est.
Project cost: The building was bid
in stages over a long period of
time. The project cost is not
available.
Completion date: 1934
Building removed to make way for
Ortega Hall (79)

BUILDING 53
Building names: Main Library;
Zimmerman Library
Architect: John Gaw Meem
General contractor: Platte Rogers,
Inc.
Bid date: 10/31/36
Construction cost: $341,424
Project cost: $460,080 est.

Completion date: March 1938
Gross square feet: 61,578

Project 614
Addition 1, Zimmerman Library
Architect: Ferguson, Stevens,
Mallory, and Pearl
General contractor: Lembke
Construction Co.
Bid date: December 1964
Bid price: $1,769,684
Project cost: $2,593,430
Completion date: 1/19/67

Project 290
Addition 2, Zimmerman Library
Architect: Dean, Hunt, and
Associates
General contractor: Lembke
Construction Co.
Bid date: 9/25/73
Bid price: $1,679,634
Construction cost, including
$251,862 to remodel existing
building: $1,780,339
Project cost: $2,412,000
Completion date: 2/10/76

Project 7–05430
Addition 3, Zimmerman Library
Architect: Van Gilbert, with
Shepley, Bulfinch, Richardson,
and Abbott
General contractor: Jaynes
Corporation
Bid date: 12/18/91
Construction cost: $5,717,355
Project cost: $6,992,147
Completion date: 7/3/93
Total gross square feet in
Zimmerman Library: 264,212
Total 1998 value: $37,917,767

BUILDING 56
Project 250
Building names: 400-Man
Dormitory; Mesa Vista Hall
Architect: John Gaw Meem–Hugo
Zehner and Associates
General contractor: O. G.
Bradbury

Contract date: 8/18/48
Construction cost: $1,431,098
Completion date: 7/6/50
Gross square feet: 111,870
1998 value: $17,755,491

BUILDING 57
Building names: Law School;
Bratton Hall I; 1915 Roma;
Economics
Architect: Meem, Zehner, Holien,
and Associates
General contractor: O. G.
Bradbury
Bid date: 7/31/51
Contract price: $254.365
Construction cost: $287,993
Completion date: 1952
Gross square feet: 21,786
Remodeled in 1971 and 1987
1998 value: $3,479,653

BUILDING 58
Building names: Women's
Dormitory; Hokona Hall II
Architect: Meem, Zehner, Holien,
and Associates
General contractor: Robert E.
McKee General Contractor,
Inc.
Contract date, phase 1: 3/26/55
Construction cost: $1,478,435
Contract date, phase 2: 4/21/55
Construction cost: $975,762.20
Project cost: $2,666,077
Completion date: September 1956
Gross square feet: 187,187
1998 value: $22,966,404

BUILDING 59
Building names: Johnson
Gymnasium; Johnson Center
Architect: Meem, Zehner, Holien,
and Associates
General contractor: Lembke,
Clough, and King
Bid date: 11/16/55
Bid price: $1,964,591
Project cost: $2,169,889
Completion date: 1957
Gross square feet: 179,102

Project 619
Olympic Swimming Pool
    Addition to Johnson
    Gymnasium
Architect: Buckley, Luna, and
    Merker, a joint venture
General contractor: K. L. House
    Construction Co.
Bid date: 7/22/71
Construction cost: $1,247,091
Project cost: $1,469,293
Completion date: 1972
Gross square feet: 34,394

Project 470
Additions to Johnson Gymnasium
    Phase 1
Architect: Dorman-Nelson
General contractor: Brooks and
    Clay
Bid date: 3/27/84
Construction cost: $5,597,401
Project cost: $6,580,678
Completion date: 8/10/87
Gross square feet of added space:
    66,409

Project 396
Additions to Johnson Center
    Phase 2
Architect: Dorman-Nelson-Breen
General contractor: Silver
    Construction Inc.
Bid date: 7/15/86
Project cost: $1,683,459
Completion date: 1988
Total gross square feet in Johnson
    Center: 303,961
Total 1998 value of Johnson
    Center: $35,876,980

BUILDING 60
Building names: New Mexico
    Union; Student Union Building
    (SUB)
Architect: Meem, Holien, and
    Buckley
General contractor: Farnsworth
    and Chambers

Bid date: 4/1/58
Contract amount: $2,256,298
Project cost: $2,807,112
Completion date: 1959

Project 124
General Alterations, New Mexico
    Union
Architect: Antoine Predock
General contractor: K. L. House
    Construction Co.
Bid date: 1/15/76
Construction cost: $1,295,079
Project cost: $1,547,811
Completion date: 1977
Total gross square feet: 150,042
Total 1998 value: $22,726,331

BUILDING 61
Building name: Santa Clara Hall
    (Dormitory)
Architect: William W. Ellison
General contractor: Lembke
    Construction Co.
Bid date: 9/26/62; bid in
    combination with Oñate Hall
    (Building 156)
Project cost: $778,595 est.
Completion date: 10/16/63
Gross square feet: 39,751
1998 value: $4,488,286

BUILDING 62
Building name: Fine Arts Center,
    includes library, museum,
    Music Department, 1970
    classroom addition, and Rodey
    Theater wing (Popejoy Hall
    [Building 72] and the Art
    Building [Building 84] are
    listed separately)
Architect: Holien and Buckley
General contractor: Lembke
    Construction Co.
Bid date: 1/3/62
Contract amount: $2,340,000
Project cost: $2,733,449
Completion date: 1964
Gross square feet: 122,424

Project 612–3
Drama Addition to Fine Arts
    Center
Architect: William R. Buckley
Theater consultant: George C.
    Izenour
Acoustical consultant: Purcell and
    Knoppe
General contractor: George A.
    Rutherford, Inc.
Bid date: 4/19/72
Construction cost: $2,051,746
Project cost: $2,358,089
Completion date: 10/3/73
Gross square feet: 52,569
Total gross square feet in Fine Arts
    Center: 174,993
Total 1998 value of Fine Arts
    Center: $27,385,304

BUILDINGS 63–70
Building name: College of
    Education Complex, includes
    63-Education Offices; 64-
    Industrial Arts; 65-
    Administration; 66-Home
    Economics, now Family
    Studies; 67-Classrooms; 68-Art
    Education, now Masley Hall;
    69-Kiva; 70-Manzanita Center
    (Educational Laboratory). All
    the buildings were bid together.
Architect: Flatow, Moore, Bryan,
    and Fairburn
General contractor: Underwood
    and Testman
Bid date: 1/3/62
Contract amount: $2,030,000
Project cost: $2,179,208
Completion date: 3/30/63
Gross square feet: 123,505
1998 value: $15,752,428

BUILDING 71
Building name: Santa Ana Hall
Architect: William W. Ellison
General contractor: K. L. House
    Construction Co.
Bid accepted: 10/8/64; bid with
    Alvarado Hall (Building 157)

Construction cost for both
  buildings:$1,512,714
Project cost of Santa Ana:
  $742,833 est.
Completion date: 10/1/65
Gross square feet: 41,615
1998 value: $4,056,757

BUILDING 72
Project 612–2
Building names: Concert Hall;
  Popejoy Hall
Architect: Holien and Buckley
Theater consultant: George C.
  Izenour
Acoustical consultant: Bolt,
  Beranek, and Newman (Jack
  Purcell)
General contractor: Lembke
  Construction Co.
Bid accepted: 1/13/65
Construction cost: $2,373,521
Project cost: $2,671,200
Dedicated: 10/1/66

Project 7–05830
Lobby Renovations to Popejoy
  Hall
Architect: Van Gilbert
General contractor: Silver
  Construction Co. of New
  Mexico
Bid date: 4/25/95
Construction cost: $8,770,506
Project cost: $10,873,180
Completion date: 3/1/96
Total gross square feet: 71,558
1998 value: $22,390,509

BUILDING 73
Project 617
Building name: Student Health
  Center and University College
Architect: Holien and Buckley
General contractor: George A.
  Rutherford, Inc.
Bid accepted: 3/24/67
Construction cost: $1,214,348
Project cost: $1,415,744
Completion date: 6/20/68

Gross square feet: 42,853
1998 value: $6,813,451

BUILDING 74, BUILDING 75, BUILDING 77
Building names: Laguna Hall (74);
  DeVargas Hall (75); La Posada
  Dining Hall (77)
Design Architect: Ernest J. Kump
  and Associates
Project Architect: William W.
  Ellison
General contractor: Lembke
  Construction Co.
Bid accepted: 5/25/68
Construction cost: $3,165,338
Project cost: $3,727,959
Completion date: 9/8/69
Gross square feet: Laguna 43,901;
  DeVargas 43,973; La Posada
  40,354
1998 value; $16,979,522

BUILDING 76
Project 624
Building names: College of
  Business Administration;
  Anderson Schools of
  Management
Architect: John Reed
General contractor: Lembke
  Construction Co.
Bid accepted: 8/4/67
Construction cost: $906,419
Project cost: $1,115,524
Completion date: 9/5/68
Gross square feet: 46,405
1998 value: $5,317,978

BUILDING 77 (see Building 74)

BUILDING 78, BUILDING 87
Project 440
Building names: Social Sciences
  (78); Parish Library (87)
Architect: Hutchinson, Brown,
  and Partners
General contractor: Page and
  Wirtz
Bid date: 9/17/85

Construction cost: $7,298,131
Project cost: $8,872,000
Completion date: 1987
Total gross square feet: 86,425
Total 1998 value: $9,599,783

BUILDING 79
Project 640
Building names: Faculty Office–
  Classroom Building; Ortega
  Hall (2)
Architect: Ferguson, Stevens,
  Mallory, and Pearl
General contractor: K. L. House
  Construction Co.
Bid date: 5/20/70
Construction cost: $1,453,524
Project cost: $1,757,994
Completion date: 6/30/71
Gross square feet: 53,873
1998 value: $6,349,863

BUILDING 81
Project 175
Building name: Humanities
  Building
Architect: W. C. Kruger and
  Associates
General contractor: Lembke
  Construction Co.
Bid date: 12/12/72
Construction cost: $2,447,645
Project cost: $2,837,570
Completion date: May 1974
Gross square feet: 70,859
1998 value: $8,474,346

BUILDING 82
Project 170
Building names: Lecture Hall;
  Woodward Hall
Architect: W. C. Kruger and
  Associates
General contractor: Lembke
  Construction Co.
Bid date: 12/12/72
Construction cost: $1,768,407
Project cost: $2,036,648
Completion date: January 1974
Gross square feet: 39,622
1998 value: $6,329,179

BUILDING 83
Project 641
Building name: UNM Bookstore
Architect: Holmes and Gianinni
General contractor: Lembke
    Construction Co.
Bid date: 4/18/73
Construction cost: $955,783
Project cost: $1,233,432
Completion date: 7/7/74
Gross square feet: 42,443
1998 value: $3,506,418

BUILDING 84
Project 251
Building name: Art Building
Architect: Antoine Predock
General contractor: Lembke
    Construction Co.
Bid date: 7/15/76
Construction cost: $2,564,569
Project cost: $3,334,000
Completion date: 10/11/77
Gross square feet: 76,875
1998 value: $8,466,447

BUILDING 87 (see Building 78)

BUILDING 89 (85)
Project 490
Building name: Student Services
    Center
Architect: John Reed
General contractor: Brooks and
    Clay
Bid date: 5/6/82
Construction cost: $5,357,213
Project cost: $6,450,000
Completion date: 1983
Gross square feet: 79,770
1998 value: $9,159,745

BUILDING 103
Building names: Main Building;
    Administration Building;
    Hodgin Hall
Architect: Jesse M. Wheelock
General contractor: Digneo and
    Palladino
Bid date: 9/15/1890

Contract amount: $26,196
Completion date: 1892

Project 227
1983 Hodgin Hall Renovation
Architect: Joseph Burwinkle
General contractor: Bill Stuckman
Bid date: 9/16/82
Construction cost: $1,031,643
Project cost: $1,355,000
Open house and dedication: 11/5/83
Completion date: 1984
Gross square feet: 19,475
1998 value: $3,369,896

BUILDING 104
Building name: Sara Raynolds
    Hall
Designer: Arno K. Leupold
Project architect: E. B. Cristy
General contractor: E. J. Marchant
Bid date: 6/28/20
Construction cost: $16,032
Completion date: 1921
Gross square feet: 3,316
1998 value: $508,420

BUILDING 105
Building names: Library; Art
    Building; Art Annex
Architect: Elson H. Norris
General contractor: E. J. Marchant
Bid date: 9/15/24
Construction cost: $42,351
Completion date: 1925
Gross square feet: 15,000
1998 value: $1,518,671

BUILDING 106
Building names: Practical
    Mechanics Building;
    Mechanical Arts; Engineering
    Building; Hadley Hall II; now
    part of Civil Engineering
    Research Laboratory
Designer: Arno K. Leupold
General contractor: Campbell
    Brothers
Bid date: 6/11/19
Construction cost: $35,000 est.

Completion date: 1919
Partially destroyed by explosion in
    1949

BUILDING 107
Building names: Heating Plant;
    Mechanical Engineering;
    Engineering Annex
Architect: John Gaw Meem
contractor: Thomas Bate and Sons
Bid date: 3/21/36
Contract amount: $146,402
Construction cost: $158,413
Completion date: 1937
Gross square feet: 17,324
1998 value: $2,421,229

BUILDING 111
Building name: Chemical
    Engineering
Architect: John Gaw Meem–Hugo
    Zehner and Associates
contractor: K. L. House
    Construction Co.
Construction start: 10/8/46
Construction cost: $52,239.09
Completion date: 9/3/47
Gross square feet: 4.400
1998 value: $750,931

BUILDING 115
Building names: Journalism;
    Printing Plant (housed
    Printing Plant, post office, and
    UNM Press)
Architect: John Gaw Meem–Hugo
    Zehner and Associates
Contractor: O. G. Bradbury
Contract date: 11/12/48
Construction cost: $147,398
Project cost: $166,470
Completion date: 8/3/49
Gross square feet: 17,205

1963 Addition
Architect: Meem, Zehner, Holien,
    and Associates
General contractor: Weaver
    Construction Co.
Construction cost: $161,898
Total gross square feet: 31,127

Total 1998 value, including 1991
renovation: $3,172,164

BUILDING 116
Building names: Ford Utility
Center; Boiler Plant; Heating
Plant
Architect: John Gaw Meem–Hugo
Zehner and Associates
General contractor: L. M. Mauldin
Construction Co.
Contract date: 11/12/48
Contract Amount: $67,256
Completion date: December 1949
There have been several additions
to the building including
enclosed cooling towers and
expanded plant and office
space, which added 5,593 square
feet in 1969 and 2,700 square
feet in 1975. Much new
equipment has been added
through the years.
Gross square feet of original
building: 9,155
Total gross square feet: 22,361
Total 1998 value: $11,938,927

BUILDING 117
Building names: Civil
Engineering; Wagner Hall
Architect: John Gaw Meem–Hugo
Zehner and Associates
General contractor: Lembke,
Clough, and King Construction
Co.
Construction start: 6/6/49
Construction cost: $126,766
Project cost: $142,617
Completion date: 12/8/49
Gross square feet: 12,898
1998 value: $1,302,253

BUILDING 118
Building names: Electrical
Engineering; Tapy Hall
Architect: Meem, Zehner, Holien,
and Associates
General contractor: George A.
Rutherford, Inc.

Contract date: 10/23/53
Contract price: $283,085
Project cost: $304,255
Completion date: 11/24/54
Gross square feet: 21,632
1998 value: $2,663,145

**BUILDING 119 AND BUILDING
121 BID TOGETHER**
Project 621
Building names: Farris
Engineering Center (119) and
Nuclear Engineering (121)
Architect: Flatow, Moore, Bryan,
and Fairburn
General contractor: K. L. House
Construction Co.
Bid accepted: 5/27/67
Construction cost: $2,149,873
Project cost: $2,628,350
Completion date: 11/15/68
Gross square feet: Building 119:
68,339; 121: 5,599
1998 value: $11,607,856

BUILDING 121 (see Building 119)

BUILDING 122
Project 320
Building name: Mechanical
Engineering
Architect: Pacheco and Graham
General contractor: K. L. House
Construction Co.
Bid date: 12/21/78
Construction cost: $4,597,016
Project cost: $5,072,806
Completion date: 1980
Gross square feet: 72,362
1998 value: $9,244,732

BUILDING 151
Building names: Men's
Cooperative Dormitory; Mesa
Vista Hall I; Student Infirmary;
NROTC Building; Naval
Sciences
Architect: John Gaw Meem
General contractor: None. The
adobe building was constructed

by Buildings and Grounds
personnel directed by Earl
Bowdich.
Construction cost: $66,142 est.
Completion date: 1941
Gross square feet: 12,040
1998 value $1,096,623

BUILDING 152
Building name: Jonson Gallery
Architect: John Gaw Meem–Hugo
Zehner and Associates
General contractor: K. L. House
Construction Co.
Contract date: 3/10/49
Construction cost: $46,739
Completion date: November 1949
Gross square feet: 6,241
1998 value: $628,212

BUILDING 153
Building names: State Highway
Testing Laboratory; Research
Center; Computing Center;
Computer and Information
Resources and Technology
(CIRT)
Architect: John Gaw Meem–Hugo
Zehner and Associates
General contractor: S. V. Patrick
Bid date: 2/20/50
Bid price: $105,215
Project cost: $134,279
Completion date: 1950
Gross square feet: 14,608

Project 643
Addition for Mathematics
Architect: William R. Buckley
General contractor: R. M. Swain
and Son
Bid date: 9/5/68
Construction cost: 204,842
Project cost: $357,518
Completion date: 5/14/69
Gross square feet: 7,200

Project 150
Addition for Data Processing
Architect: William R. Buckley
Project cost: $428,893

Completion date: 1970
Gross square feet: 16,031

Project 151
1977 Expansion of Data Processing
Architect: William R. Buckley
General contractor: Springer
    Construction Co.
Bid date: 11/20/75
Construction cost: $414,965
Project cost: $483,000
Completion date: March 1977
Gross square feet: 6,953
Total gross square feet in complex:
    44,774
Total 1998 value, including all
    additions: $6,472,114

BUILDING 155
Building names: Men's
    Dormitory; Coronado Hall
Architect: Shaefer, Merrell and
    Associates
General contractor: Lembke
    Construction Co.
Bid accepted: 3/1/58
Contract amount: $1,350,168
Project cost: $1,507,603
Completion date: 1959
Gross square feet: 93,880
1998 value: $10,916,359

BUILDING 156
Building name: Oñate Hall
Architect: William W. Ellison
General contractor: Lembke
    Construction Co.
Bid date: 9/26/62; bid in
    combination with Santa Clara
    Hall (Building 61)
Project cost: $735,135 est.
Completion date: 10/16/63
Gross square feet: 41,416
1998 value: $4,113,116

BUILDING 157
Project 615
Building name: Alvarado Hall
Architect: William E. Ellison
General contractor: K. L. House
    Construction Co.

Bid accepted: 9/26/64; bid in
    combination with Santa Ana
    Hall (Building 71)
Project cost for Alvarado: $742,881
    est.
Completion date: 10/1/65
Gross square feet: 40,896
1998 value: $4,057,019

BUILDING 172
Project 226
Building name: Lomas Parking
    Structure
Architect: Stevens, Mallory, Pearl,
    and Campbell
General contractor: Jaynes
    Corporation
Bid date: 5/29/85
Construction cost: $3,868,933
Project cost: $4,317,800
Completion date: 1986
Parking spaces: 997
Gross square feet: 233,409

1990 Phase 2 Addition
Architect: Stevens, Mallory, Pearl,
    and Campbell
General contractor: Jaynes
    Corporation
Bid date: 11/9/89
Project cost: $3,659,295
Completion date: 1/25/91
Parking spaces: 782
Gross square feet: 260,350
Total gross square feet: 493,759
Total 1998 value: $10,726,649

BUILDING 176
Project 7–04860
Building name: Cogeneration
    Plant
Architect: Stevens, Mallory, Pearl,
    and Campbell
Engineer: Bridgers and Paxton
General contractor: Brooks and
    Clay
Bid date: 3/23/88
Construction cost: $1,225,753
Project cost: $3,185,000
Completion date: 3/31/89
Gross square feet: 4,664
1998 value: $4,197,837

BUILDING 207
Building names: Physics and
    Meteoritics; Physics and
    Astronomy
Architect: Meem, Zehner, and
    Holien
General contractor: John T.
    Testman
Contract date: 8/31/51
Construction cost: $169,282
Project cost: $183,261
Completion date: 1/28/53
Gross square feet: 22,673

Project 613
1966 Addition to Physics and
    Astronomy
Architect: Ferguson, Stevens,
    Mallory, and Pearl
General contractor: George A.
    Rutherford, Inc.
Bid accepted: 11/27/64
Construction cost: $829,863
Project cost: $1,066,510
Completion date: September 1966
Gross square feet: 36,080
Total 1998 value: $6,822,825

BUILDING 211
Project 600
Building names: Basic Sciences
    Building; Basic Medical
    Sciences; Medical Building
    Number 1
Architect: W. C. Kruger and
    Associates
General contractor: Lembke
    Construction Co.
Bid accepted: 10/9/65
Construction cost: $4,980,378
Project cost: $6,448,612
Completion date: 11/30/67
Gross square feet: 170,318
1998 value: $35,155,424

BUILDING 218
Project 636
Building names: Bratton Hall II;
    Law School
Architect: George Wright

General contractor: Bradbury and
    Stamm
Bid date: 9/30/69
Construction cost: $1,734,842
Project cost: $2,040,721
Completion date: 2/1/71
Gross square feet: 64,496

Project 218
Addition to Bratton Hall
Architect: Stevens, Mallory, Pearl,
    and Campbell
General contractor: Bradbury and
    Stamm
Bid date: 12/8/76
Construction cost: $2,238,623
Project cost: $3,146,133
Completion date: 1978
Gross square feet: 52,437
Total 1998 value: $19,115,418

BUILDING 227
Project 360
Building names: University of
    New Mexico Cancer Center;
    Cancer Research and Treatment
    Center (CRTC)
Architect: Flatow, Moore, Bryan,
    and Fairburn
General contractor: George A.
    Rutherford, Inc.
Bid date: 12/21/72
Construction cost: $4,306,423
Project cost: $4,980,985
Completion date: 6/28/74
Gross square feet: 110,327
1998 value: $17,136,153

BUILDING 228
Project 060
Building name: Nursing-
    Pharmacy
Architect: Flatow, Moore, Bryan,
    and Fairburn
General contractor: George A.
    Rutherford, Inc.
Bid date: 8/8/73
Construction cost: $3,501,436
Project cost: $4,249,806
Completion date: 3/30/75

Gross square feet: 93,645
1998 value: $11,882,639

BUILDING 229
Project 7–05800
Building name: Cancer Research
    and Treatment Center (see
    Building 227)
Architect: Dekker-Perich and
    Associates, PC
General contractor: Bradbury and
    Stamm
Bid date: 3/19/96
Construction cost: $11,316,344
Project cost: $13,831,900
Completion date: 2/6/98
Gross square feet: 81,137
1998 value: $15,147,461

BUILDING 230
Project 215
Building names: New Mexico Bar
    Association Building; Dale
    Bellamah Law Center; New
    Mexico Law Center
Architect: Robert Walters
Bid date: 8/20/74
Construction cost: $390,638
Project cost: $467,000
Completion date: May 1975
Total gross square feet: 12,047
1998 value: $1,592,277

BUILDING 234
Project 162
Building names: Medical Center
    Library; Health Sciences
    Learning Resource Center
    (HSLRC)
Architect: Harvey Hoshour
    Architect, Ltd.
General contractor: Lembke
    Construction Co.
Bid date: 11/26/75
Construction cost: $2,678,332
Project cost: $3,241,111
Completion date: 1977
Gross square feet: 65,804
1998 value: $7,890,325

BUILDING 235
Building names: Bernalillo
    County–Indian Hospital (BC-
    I); Bernalillo County Medical
    Center (BCMC); University of
    New Mexico Medical Center;
    University of New Mexico
    Hospital (UNMH)
The hospital is owned by
    Bernalillo County and operated
    by the University of New
    Mexico. Construction has been
    done by the county.
Architect for BC-I first building:
    Ferguson and Stevens
Opened to the public: 10/15/54

1974 Addition
Architect: Flatow, Moore, Bryan,
    and Fairburn
General contractor: George A.
    Rutherford, Inc.
Bid date: 4/11/74
Bid amount: $5,520,833

Emergency–Critical Care Addition
Architect: W. C. Kruger and
    Associates
General contractor: Jaynes
    Corporation
Bid date: 4/7/83
Bid and contract amount:
    $5,078,571
Construction cost: $7,791,500
A $2.6 million change order
    adding a third floor was
    negotiated in December 1983.
Completion date: 1984

Ambulatory Care Addition
Architect: Dean–Krueger and
    Associates
General contractor: Jaynes
    Corporation
Construction cost: $16,686,160
Project cost: $19,630,777
Gross square feet of addition:
    187,000
Completion date: 1991

BUILDING 248
Project 065
Building name: Family Practice
    Center

Architect: Dale Crawford and
  Associates
General contractor: K. L. House
  Construction Co.
Bid date: 8/25/76
Construction cost: $2,426,803
Project cost: $3,035,890
Completion date: 1977
Gross square feet: 58,230
1998 value: $6,728,416

BUILDING 249
Project 166
Building names: Dental Programs;
  Novitski Hall
Architect: Holmes and Gianinni
General contractor: Colton
  Construction Co.
Bid date: 3/15/77 Rebid: 5/18/77
Construction cost: $1,377,127
Project cost: $1,887,784
Completion date: 1978
Gross square feet: 27,976
1998 value: $3,861,466

BUILDING 253
Project 330
Building name: Biomedical
  Research Facility
Architect: W. C. Kruger and
  Associates
General contractor: K. L. House
  Construction Co.
Bid date: 1/15/80
Construction cost: $7,446,103
Project cost: $8,977,253
Completion date: 1981
Gross square feet: 105,190
1998 value: $13,759,911

COMPLEX 254
Names: Children's Psychiatric
  Center; Children's Psychiatric
  Hospital
Architect: Barker-Bol and
  Associates
General contractor: K. L. House
  Construction Co.
Construction cost: $2,500,000
Completion date: 1978

Built by the State of New Mexico;
  operated by the University of
  New Mexico

BUILDING 260
Project 432
Building names: Center for Non-
  Invasive Diagnosis (CNID);
  Magnetic Resonance Imaging
  Facility; Clinical and Magnetic
  Resonance Research Center
Architect: Westwork Architects
General contractor: R. M. Swain
  and Son, Inc.
Bid date: 4/25/85
Construction cost: $1,571,668
Project cost: $1,753,000 est.
Completion date: 1986
Gross square feet: 9,000
1998 value: $2,096,431

BUILDING 266
Project 392
Building names: Health Sciences
  and Services Building; Health
  Sciences Center
Architect: Holmes, Sabatini,
  Smith, and Eeds
General contractor: Davis and
  Associates
Bid date: 5/10/88
Construction cost: $4,829,172
Project cost: $5,400,000
Completion date: 6/6/89
Gross square feet: 51,534

BUILDING 301
Names: Football Stadium;
  University Stadium
Architect: W. C. Kruger and
  Associates
General contractor: George A.
  Rutherford, Inc.
Separate bids were taken for
  various phases of the work and
  the Physical Plant Department
  did some work.
Project cost: $815,050 est.
Completion date: 9/17/60

Project 284
Press Box Addition to University
  Stadium
Architect: W. C. Kruger and
  Associates
General contractor: George A.
  Rutherford, Inc.
Bid date: 12/19/74
Construction cost: $1,854,276
Project cost: $2,043,526
Completion date: July 1976
Gross square feet of addition:
  27,401
Total 1998 value of addition:
  $10,462,823

BUILDING 302
Project 626–100/200/300
Building names: Basketball Arena;
  University Arena; The Pit
Architect: Joe Boehning
General contractor: K. L. House
  Construction Co.
Bid date: 12/16/65
Construction cost: $1,620,654
Project cost: $1,737,496
Completion date: 1/12/67
Gross square feet: 105,380

Project 282
Balcony Addition to University
  Arena
Architect: Joe Boehning
General contractor: George A.
  Rutherford, Inc.
Bid date: 1/21/75
Construction cost: $2,558,244
Project cost: $2,801,337
Completion date: 12/3/75
Gross square feet of addition:
  51,272
Total gross square feet: 156,652
Total 1998 value: $22,002,961

BUILDING 303
Project 618
Building name: South Campus
  Golf Course Clubhouse
Architect: John Reed

General contractor: Weaver
    Construction Co.
Bid accepted: 3/19/66
Construction cost: $325,212
Project cost: $358,717
Completion date: 12/17/66
Gross square feet: 19,050
1998 value: $2,093,115

BUILDING 307
    Project 626
Building names: Athletic
    Administration; Athletics
    Building
Architect: Joe Boehning
General contractor: Nation-Payne
Bid date: 1/13/70
Construction cost: $667,369
Project cost: $871,180

Completion date: 12/14/70
Gross square feet: 26,805
1998 value: $5,319,006

BUILDINGS 317–29
    Project 280
Names of complex: Married
    Student Housing; Student
    Family Housing
Architect: Robert Torres
General contractor: Bradbury and
    Stamm
Bid date: 1/8/74
Construction cost: $3,710,155
Project cost: $4,111,711
Completion date: 1975
Gross square feet: 240,457
1998 value: $10,780,396

Selected Bibliography

Collections

Museum of Albuquerque Photographic Archives

University of New Mexico Center for Southwest Research
Board of Regents. Minutes.
Board of Regents Executive Committee. Minutes. Executive committees functioned from about 1912 to the middle 1920s.
Board of Regents Policy Manual. Section 2.10. September 12, 1996.

John Gaw Meem Archive of Southwestern Architecture
Drawings and papers of Meem and many other New Mexico architects.

University of New Mexico Archives
Alumni News and its other names.
Barker-Bol and Associates. *University Land Development: A Report*, 1984.
Boyd, David Ross. Papers.
Bryan, G. W. D. Papers.
Campus Improvement Committee. Minutes.
Campus News.
Campus Planning Committee. Minutes.

Clark, John D. Papers.
Committee on University Planning. A Report, 1975.
Committee to Implement the Master Plan. Minutes.
Daily Lobo and its other names.
Department of Facility Planning. *Five-Year Facilities Master Plan, 1989–1993*, August 1988.
El Servicio Real. Edited by Myron Fifield. UNM Physical Plant Department.
Fergusson, Erna. Scrapbooks, 1919–1942. Mostly newspaper articles concerning University activities.
Hodgin, Charles. Papers.
Hooker, Van Dorn. Collection. Acquisition 023. Photographs, letters, and miscellaneous files.
Master Plan Committee. Minutes.
McColeman, Susan. "A History of the Buildings of the University of New Mexico, 1890–1934." Manuscript.
Mirage.
Office of the University Architect. Building brochures.
———. *Building Project Status Reports.*
———. Collection. Acquisition 028. Project files, drawings and specifications, and photographs of University building and planning projects.

———. *Five-Year Facilities Master Plan, 1981–1986,* August 1981.

———. *Five-Year Facilities Master Plan, 1982–1987,* June 1982.

———. Scrapbooks. 10 vols., 1889–1990. Articles from newspapers, magazines, books; drawings, photographs, letters, and other documents pertaining to building and planning the University.

Presidents' Annual Reports.

Reeve, Frank D. *History of the University of New Mexico.* Master's thesis, 1928.

Travelstead, Chester C. "I Was There." Manuscript, 1990.

UNM Bulletin, 1919–1921.

UNM Catalogs. Albuquerque and Gallup Campuses.

UNM Faculty-Staff Directory and its other titles.

UNM Weekly.

Periodicals

Albach, Carl P. "UNM's Fine Arts Center." *New Mexico Professional Engineer* 19 (January 1974).

Benson, Harold. "It's Fun to Shop at Winrock." *New Mexico Architecture* 3 (May–June 1961): 8–12.

Boehning, Joe. "Arena Design and Construction Capitalize on Site and System." *Building Construction* (October 1966).

———. "The UNM Arena Expands." *New Mexico Architecture* 18 (November–December 1976): 10–14.

Brooks, H. Allen, Jr. "The Old Chemistry Building at the University of New Mexico, Its Antecedents and Traditions." *New Mexico Architecture* 2 (July–August 1960): 16–22.

Bunting, Bainbridge. "Albuquerque's Best . . . and Worst." *Albuquerque* (October 1977): 77–86.

Chaney, S., and M. Candler. "Santos." *Parnassus* 7 (1935).

Conron, John P. "A Conversation with Allen Temko." *New Mexico Architecture* 6, nos. 11 and 12 (1960): 9–15.

Crosbie, Michael J. "Calming Setting for High-Tech Medicine." *Architecture* 76 (January 1987): 43–47.

DeVolder, Arthur L. "John Gaw Meem, F.A.I.A.: An Appreciation." *New Mexico Historical Review* 54 (July 1979): 209–25.

Dober, Richard P. "Pueblo Style and Campus Image: Some Observations on the University of New Mexico Albuquerque Campus." July 11, 1988, draft of an "Appreciation."

Fifield, Myron F. "Arena Design and Construction—Capitalize on Site and Systems." *Building Construction* (October 1966).

———. "How We Built a Stadium in Twelve Months." *College and University Business* (March 1961).

———. "My Personal Association with President Thomas Lafayette Popejoy." *New Mexico Professional Engineer* 20, no. 9 (1968): 3–18.

———. "A Unique University Arena." *New Mexico Professional Engineer* 19, no. 1 (January 1967).

Hillerman, Tony. "Birthday for a College." *New Mexico* (February 1964): 2–7.

———. "UNM's New Education Building Complex." *New Mexico School Review* (October 1963).

Hooker, Van Dorn. "The Bond Issue—And the Growth of New Mexico Universities." *New Mexico Architecture* 16, nos. 1 and 2 (1974): 11–25.

———. "The University of New Mexico: Its History and Expansion." *New Mexico Architecture* 10 (July–August 1968): 11–22.

Howard, Melissa. "Hodgin Hall." *UNM Alumnus* 52, no. 8 (May 1980).

———. "How Does Hooker Do It?" *UNM Alumnus* 55, no. 2 (September 1982): 6–9.

Hunt, Amy Passmore. "Milestone in Architecture." *New Mexico* (March 1964): 6–9.

Johnson, E. Dana. "A University Pueblo." *World's Work* 14, no. 6 (October 1907): 9468–72.

Juardo, Ramon. "Prehistoric Home for New University." *Technical World* (June 1909): 367–75.

Meem, John Gaw. "A Contemporary Regional Style Based on Traditional." *New Mexico Architecture* 14, nos. 3 and 4 (March–April 1972): 8–9.

———. "Old Forms for New Buildings," *Mass: Journal of the School of Architecture and Planning, University of New Mexico,* spring 1983.

Nason, Thelma, and Katherine Simons. "John Gaw Meem's Library." *Century* (July 6, 1983).

Papademetriou, Peter C. "From the Ridiculous to the Sublime." *Progressive Architecture* (September 1978).

Pearl, George Clayton. "Buildings of Context: Van Dorn Hooker at UNM." *Century* (October 1, 1980): 14–18.

Price, Jess. "Totem Pole." *IMPACT/Albuquerque Journal Magazine* (October 16, 1984).

Price, V. B. "Campus Architecture: Unity, Diversity, and 'A Sense of Place.'" *New Mexico Alumnus* (December 1977): 4–17.

———. "Flexible Zoning Is the Key to a Policy Which Respects Old and New." *Independent* 82, no. 45 (July 14, 1978).

———. "The Pueblo University." *New Mexico* (September 1978): 17–24.

———. "The University's Architect." *Century* (September 15, 1982): 10–11.

———. "We'll Miss Sherman Smith." *Independent* 77, no. 51 (October 10, 1973).

Schlegel, Don P., "Long Range Campus Planning: The University of New Mexico's North Campus." *New Mexico Architecture* 9, nos. 3 and 4 (1967): 17–21.

Smith, Sherman E. "Pattern for Growth." *UNM Alumnus* (May 1972): 4–10.

Udy, John M. "A Plan for UNM—A Critical Appraisal." *New Mexico Architecture* 4, nos. 1 and 2 (January–February 1962): 16–19.

Yguado, Jose Luis. "A Plan for UNM—A Critical Appraisal." *New Mexico Architecture* 4, nos. 3 and 4 (March–April 1962): 21–23.

Publications

Barney, Robert K. *Roy W. Johnson.* Albuquerque: N.p., 1963.

Biebel, Charles D. *Making the Most of It.* Albuquerque: Albuquerque Museum History Monograph, 1981.

Birrell, James. *Walter Burley Griffin.* Melbourne: University of Queensland Press, 1964.

Brooks, H. Allen, ed. *Prairie School of Architecture.* New York: Van Nostrand Reinhold, 1988.

Bunting, Bainbridge. *John Gaw Meem.* Albuquerque: University of New Mexico Press, 1983.

Chauvenet, Beatrice. *John Gaw Meem.* Santa Fe: Museum of New Mexico Press, 1985.

Dober, Richard P. *Campus Planning.* New York: Reinhold Publishing, 1963.

Flatow, Moore, Bryan, and Associates. *A Master Plan for the U.N.M. South Campus Complex.* N.p.: n.d.

Glass, Edward B. T. *Hodgin Hall Structure Report.* Albuquerque: Office of the University Architect, 1979.

Hakken, Howard. *Guidelines for Use and Development of Lands and Buildings, North Campus.* February 1977.

Harris, Cyril M. *Dictionary of Architecture and Construction.* New York: McGraw-Hill, 1975.

Heady, Ferrel. *One Time Around.* Albuquerque: Cooper Press, 1999.

Hinton, Betty Huning. *Lena Clauve.* Albuquerque: Guynes Publishing, 1989.

———. *Elizabeth P. Simpson.* Albuquerque: Guynes Publishing Company, 1989.

Horn, Calvin. *The University in Turmoil and Transition.* Albuquerque: Rocky Mountain Publishing, 1981.

Hughes, Dorothy. *Pueblo on the Mesa.* Albuquerque: University of New Mexico Press, 1938.

Ingle, Marjorie. *The Mayan Revival Style.* Salt Lake City: Gibbs M. Smith, 1984.

Izenour, George. *Theater Design.* New York: McGraw-Hill, 1977.

Kessell, John L. *The Missions of New Mexico Since 1776.* Albuquerque: UNM Press, 1980.

Kropp, Simon F. *That All May Learn.* Las Cruces: New Mexico State University, 1972.

Kubler, George. *Religious Architecture of New Mexico.* Chicago: Rio Grande Press, 1962.

LaFarge, Oliver. *Santa Fe.* Norman: University of Oklahoma Press, 1959.

Markovich, Nicholas C., Wolfgang F. E. Preiser, Fred Sturm, eds. *Pueblo Style and Regional Architecture.* New York: Van Nostrand Reinhold, 1990.

Nash, Gerald D., and Gunther Rothenberg. *Expanding Horizons: A Pictorial History of the University of New Mexico.* Albuquerque: UNM Alumni Association, 1964.

New Mexico Office of the Secretary of State. *New Mexico Blue Book, 1995–1996.* Santa Fe: Sunstone Press, 1995.

Ortiz, Alfonso, ed. *Handbook of North American Indians.* Vol. 9. Washington, D.C.: Smithsonian Institution, 1979.

Remembrance Wakes. Albuquerque: University of New Mexico Press, 1939.

Rybczynski, Witod. *Looking Around—A Journey through Architecture.* New York: Penguin Books, 1992.

Simmons, Marc. *Albuquerque.* Albuquerque: University of New Mexico Press, 1982.

———. *New Mexico: A History.* New York: W. W. Norton, 1977.

Spidel, Jake W., Jr. *Doctors of Medicine in New Mexico—History of Health and Medical Practice, 1886–1986.* Albuquerque: University of New Mexico Press, 1986.

Warnecke, John Carl, and Associates. *A Preliminary Analysis of Projected Growth and Non-residential Building Needs of the University of New Mexico.* San Francisco: John Carl Warnecke and Associates, 1959.

———. *General Development Plan.* San Francisco: John Carl Warnecke and Associates, 1960.

Index